APPROACH TO AESTHETICS

Approach to Aesthetics

Collected Papers on Philosophical Aesthetics

Frank Sibley

Edited by
John Benson, Betty Redfern,
and Jeremy Roxbee Cox

CLARENDON PRESS · OXFORD
2001

OXFORD

UNIVERSITY PRESS

Great Clarendon Street, Oxford OX2 6DP

Oxford University Press is a department of the University of Oxford.
It furthers the University's objective of excellence in research, scholarship,
and education by publishing worldwide in

Oxford New York

Athens Auckland Bangkok Bogotá Buenos Aires Calcutta
Cape Town Chennai Dar es Salaam Delhi Florence Hong Kong Istanbul
Karachi Kolkata Kuala Lumpur Madrid Melbourne Mexico City Mumbai
Nairobi Paris São Paulo Shanghai Singapore Taipei Tokyo Toronto Warsaw

with associated companies in Berlin Ibadan

Oxford is a registered trade mark of Oxford University Press
in the UK and in certain other countries

Published in the United States
by Oxford University Press Inc., New York

British Library Cataloguing in Publication Data

Data available

Library of Congress Cataloging in Publication Data
Sibley, Frank, 1923–1996.
Approach to aesthetics: collected papers on philosophical aesthetics/Frank Sibley;
edited by John Benson, Betty Redfern, and Jeremy Roxbee Cox.
p. cm.
Includes bibliographical references.
1. Aesthetics. I. Benson, John. II. Redfern, H.B. (Hildred Betty). III. Roxbee Cox,
Jeremy. IV. Title.
BH39.S5258 2001   111'.85—dc21   2001016295

ISBN 0–19–823899–1

1 3 5 7 9 10 8 6 4 2

Typeset in Minion by
Cambrian Typesetters, Frimley, Surrey

Printed in Great Britain
on acid-free paper by
Biddles Ltd
Guildford & Kings Lynn

Cliffs of fall . . . no man fathomed

Merely idle chatter of a transcendental kind

CONTENTS

Editors' Introduction   ix

1. Aesthetic Concepts   1
2. Aesthetics and the Looks of Things   24
3. Aesthetic and Non-aesthetic   33
4. About Taste   52
5. Colours   54
6. Objectivity and Aesthetics   71
7. Particularity, Art, and Evaluation   88
8. General Criteria and Reasons in Aesthetics   104
9. Originality and Value   119
10. Arts or the Aesthetic—Which Comes First?   135
11. Making Music Our Own   142
12. Adjectives, Predicative and Attributive   154
13. Aesthetic Judgements: Pebbles, Faces, and Fields of Litter   176
14. Some Notes on Ugliness   190
15. Tastes, Smells, and Aesthetics   207
16. Why the *Mona Lisa* May Not be a Painting   256

Bibliography of the Publications of Frank Sibley   273

EDITORS' INTRODUCTION

For some years before his death in January 1996 Frank Sibley had been considering gathering together his papers in aesthetics and publishing them as a book. Such a collection he regarded as a substitute for the book he had long planned to write that would present his views in aesthetics in a single unified treatise. Even when he realised that he would not live long enough to complete such a major task, he did not set about the less arduous, but still laborious, task of preparing his papers for publication, because he had work in progress, and all his remaining energy went into the attempt to complete it. At his request, shortly before his death, we undertook to edit the collected papers, as a service to the philosophical public and as our personal tribute to a friend and colleague of many years.

As a guide to our work we had a list of the published papers that he would have wanted to include 'if I had to be content with a book of collected papers'. All the papers he listed, including ones against which he placed a query, are included here, in the order in which he listed them (an order which the reader will readily see to be non-accidental). In addition, we had a second list, of papers all of which were unpublished, and some unfinished: of these he would have wanted to include as many as he had been able to complete. Eight pieces are listed, of which five were left in complete versions. These have needed varying degrees of editorial attention, but no imaginative reconstruction, to produce texts that can be presented as Sibley's own. They are the last five items in the collection.

'Adjectives, Predicative and Attributive' is one of two papers in the volume—the other is 'Colours'—which are not explicitly concerned with aesthetics. Its topic is one to which Sibley was led because of its relevance to the nature of certain aesthetic terms, but he devoted a lot of hard work to sorting out the basis of the distinction as one that applied to adjectives in general. This paper was left in a version that needed very little to bring it to a publishable state.

'Aesthetic Judgements: Pebbles, Faces, and Fields of Litter' appears to be the latest version of a paper that went through various versions, with various titles. It is one of a pair of papers, the other being 'Some Notes on Ugliness', which apply to aesthetic terms the results of the theoretical enquiry into adjectives, in this case 'beauty' and related terms. Sibley prepared it for oral presentation, and it began with several pages summarizing the argument of 'Adjectives, Predicative and Attributive', for the benefit of an audience necessarily unacquainted with that paper. 'Notes on Ugliness', for the same reason, was provided with a résumé of that paper. Strictly speaking these résumés could be dispensed with in this volume, but in the end we decided not to excise them. 'Adjectives' is a long and complex paper which many readers would need several readings to digest fully; it is useful to have a clear outline of what Sibley takes himself to have shown. Besides, the original reason for their inclusion still holds good for those readers who want to get to the aesthetic applications without the lengthy prolegomenon: the papers on the beautiful and the ugly can be read as relatively independent treatments of their respective topics.

'Tastes, Smells, and Aesthetics' was a paper that occupied Sibley over a number of years. Other than marking omissions so as to reduce it to a piece that could be presented orally, he did not revise it. He notes that it needed some rearrangement and some cutting ('it got a bit extravagant in the examples'), and, 'I think I'd want to reconsider (but not much) the later parts on valuing'. We have not attempted to guess what rearrangements he might have decided on, nor of course in what way he might have revised his remarks on valuing; nor have we had the heart to take the editorial shears to the proliferating examples.

'Why the *Mona Lisa* May Not be a Painting' had a Postscript 1995 which Sibley noted he would need to look over. As it stood it seemed to us to be inconclusive, so it is not included here.

The four papers following 'Adjectives' have required rather more editorial interference. Apart from supplying references for quotations, and sorting out occasional syntactical muddles, we have had to exercise judgement in three types of case. First, the typescripts of these papers are thickly annotated with alternative words or phrases, often with no indication of whether one of the alternative readings would have been finally preferred. Secondly, there are many deletions indicated, some most probably made only for the purpose of oral presentation. Thirdly, a few passages seemed obscure, usually as a result of incomplete reworking. We have done our best to make these decisions as scrupulously as he would have done; whether we have got them *right* is an unanswerable question.

The remaining three papers, unhappily, do not exist even in draft form; to complete them on the basis of surviving notes would be impossible. It may be of interest to give the titles or topics of these three embryonic papers. One was to be a sequel to 'Making Music Our Own'; Sibley notes 'I've all the material and argument but in scraps and notes. I'll need to work to put it together as I want'. Another, 'Aesthetic Concepts Revisited' was to be a reply to critics and restatement of his position, setting it in the context of his earlier and later work, published and unpublished. Sibley mentions that there are 'a lot of written sections, done at different times' which would presumably have been worked up for this piece, but there is no indication of which they are or how they would have been used. He adds a note that gives some clue to what he had in mind: 'The paper on Beardsley ["General Criteria and Reasons in

Aesthetics", Ch. 8, this vol.] states a bit of the general context for critical reasoning into which "Aesthetic Concepts" fits as a level at which general reasons don't occur'. Finally there was to be a paper—'if I could pull several existing scraps together'—'On the Origins and Nature of the Aesthetic'. On this we must be content with 'Arts or the Aesthetic—Which Comes First?', Chapter 10 of this volume, and the extensive remarks in 'Tastes, Smells, and Aesthetics', Chapter 15 of this volume.

This volume includes all of Sibley's published work in aesthetics that he wished to appear in the full dress of a book, and all the unpublished work that could be presented in a form that might have satisfied his exacting standards. It does not include his work outside aesthetics except for the two papers already mentioned, which illustrate the way in which he saw work in aesthetics as requiring and itself illuminating investigations in other parts of philosophy. Of the unpublished work in aesthetics which we have not been able to include, there are papers, portions of papers, and notes which ought to be preserved; these are deposited in the Library of Lancaster University.

The title of the collection, 'Approach to Aesthetics', was Sibley's own choice either for the projected book or for a collection of his papers—it is not clear which he meant—and he described it as 'deliberately ambiguous'. The two epigraphs, likewise, were his choice. They felicitously hint that in his approach to aesthetics he took his subject seriously, but himself, not too seriously.

JB
BR
JRC

ACKNOWLEDGEMENTS

We thank the following people for assistance of various kinds in the preparation of this volume: Emily Brady of the Philosophy Department of Lancaster University, Terry Diffey of Sussex University, and Ronald Hepburn of Edinburgh University. We also thank Helen Clish, Assistant Librarian of the Lancaster University Library, who has arranged for Frank Sibley's papers to be kept in the Library.

1

Aesthetic Concepts

The remarks we make about works of art are of many kinds. For the purpose of this paper I wish to indicate two broad groups. I shall do this by examples. We say that a novel has a great number of characters and deals with life in a manufacturing town; that a painting uses pale colours, predominantly blues and greens, and has kneeling figures in the foreground; that the theme in a fugue is inverted at such a point and that there is a stretto at the close; that the action of a play takes place in the span of one day and that there is a reconciliation scene in the fifth act. Such remarks may be made by, and such features pointed out to, anyone with normal eyes, ears, and intelligence. On the other hand, we also say that a poem is tightly-knit or deeply moving; that a picture lacks balance, or has a certain serenity and repose, or that the grouping of the figures sets up an exciting tension; that the characters in a novel never really come to life, or that a certain episode strikes a false note. It would be natural enough to say that the making of such judgements as these requires the exercise of taste, perceptiveness, or sensitivity, of aesthetic discrimination or appreciation; one would not say this of my first group. Accordingly, when a word or expression is such that taste or perceptiveness is required in order to apply it, I shall call it an *aesthetic* term or expression, and I shall, correspondingly, speak of *aesthetic* concepts or *taste* concepts.[1]

Aesthetic terms span a great range of types and could be grouped into various kinds and sub-species. But it is not my present purpose to attempt any such grouping; I am interested in what they all have in common. Their almost endless variety is adequately displayed in the following list: *unified, balanced, integrated, lifeless, serene, sombre, dynamic, powerful, vivid, delicate, moving, trite, sentimental, tragic.* The list of course is not limited to adjectives; expressions in artistic contexts like *telling contrast, sets up a tension, conveys a sense of,* or *holds it*

[Reprinted from J. Margolis (ed.), *Philosophy Looks at the Arts*, New York: Scribners, 1962; a reprint with minor revisions of the original publication in *The Philosophical Review*, 68 (1959).]

[1] I shall speak loosely of an 'aesthetic term', even when, because the word sometimes has other uses, it would be more correct to speak of its *use* as an aesthetic term. I shall also speak of 'non-aesthetic' words, concepts, features, and so on. None of the terms other writers use, 'natural', 'observable', 'perceptual', 'physical', 'objective' (qualities), 'neutral', 'descriptive' (language), when they approach the distinction I am making, is really apt for my purpose.

together are equally good illustrations. It includes terms used by both layman and critic alike, as well as some which are mainly the property of professional critics and specialists.

I have gone for my examples of aesthetic expressions in the first place to critical and evaluative discourse about works of art because it is there particularly that they abound. But now I wish to widen the topic; we employ terms the use of which requires an exercise of taste not only when discussing the arts but quite liberally throughout discourse in everyday life. The examples given above are expressions which, appearing in critical contexts, most usually, if not invariably, have an aesthetic use; outside critical discourse the majority of them more frequently have some other use unconnected with taste. But many expressions do double duty even in everyday discourse, sometimes being used as aesthetic expressions and sometimes not. Other words again, whether in artistic or daily discourse, function only or predominantly as aesthetic terms; of this kind are *graceful, delicate, dainty, handsome, comely, elegant, garish.* Finally, to make the contrast with all the preceding examples, there are many words which are seldom used as aesthetic terms at all: *red, noisy, brackish, clammy, square, docile, curved, evanescent, intelligent, faithful, derelict, tardy, freakish.*

Clearly, when we employ words as aesthetic terms we are often making and using metaphors, pressing into service words which do not primarily function in this manner. Certainly also, many words *have come* to be aesthetic terms by some kind of metaphorical transference. This is so with those like 'dynamic', 'melancholy', 'balanced', 'tightly-knit' which, except in artistic and critical writings, are not normally aesthetic terms. But the aesthetic vocabulary must not be thought wholly metaphorical. Many words, including the most common (*lovely, pretty, beautiful, dainty, graceful, elegant*), are certainly not being used metaphorically when employed as aesthetic terms, the very good reason being that this is their primary or only use, some of them having no current non-aesthetic use. And though expressions like 'dynamic', 'balanced', and so forth *have come* by a metaphorical shift to be aesthetic terms, their employment in criticism can scarcely be said to be more than quasi-metaphorical. Having entered the language of art description and criticism as metaphors they are now standard vocabulary in that language.[2]

The expressions I am calling aesthetic terms form no small segment of our discourse. Often, it is true, people with normal intelligence and good eyesight and hearing lack, at least in some measure, the sensitivity required to apply

[2] A contrast will reinforce this. If a critic were to describe a passage of music as chattering, carbonated, or gritty, a painter's coloring as vitreous, farinaceous, or effervescent, or a writer's style as glutinous, or abrasive, he *would* be using live metaphors rather than drawing on the more normal language of criticism. Words like 'athletic', 'vertiginous', 'silken' may fall somewhere between.

them; a man need not be stupid or have poor eyesight to fail to see that something is graceful. Thus taste or sensitivity is somewhat more rare than certain other human capacities; people who exhibit a sensitivity both wide-ranging and refined are a minority. It is over the application of aesthetic terms too that, notoriously, disputes and differences sometimes go helplessly unsettled. But almost everybody is able to exercise taste to some degree and in some matters. It is surprising therefore that aesthetic terms have been so largely neglected. They have received glancing treatment in the course of other aesthetic discussions; but as a broad category they have not received the direct attention they merit.

The foregoing has marked out the area I wish to discuss. One warning should perhaps be given. When I speak of taste in this paper, I shall not be dealing with questions which centre upon expressions like 'a matter of taste' (meaning, roughly, a matter of personal preference or liking). It is with an ability to notice or see or tell that things have certain qualities that I am concerned.

I

In order to support our application of an aesthetic terms, we often refer to features the mention of which involves other aesthetic terms: 'it has an extraordinary vitality because of its free and vigorous style of drawing', 'graceful in the smooth flow of its lines', 'dainty because of the delicacy and harmony of its colouring'. It is as normal to do this as it is to justify one mental epithet by other epithets of the same general type, *intelligent* by *ingenious*, *inventive*, *acute*, and so on. But often when we apply aesthetic terms, we explain why by referring to features which do *not* depend for their recognition upon an exercise of taste: 'delicate because of its pastel shades and curving lines', or 'it lacks balance because one group of figures is so far off to the left and is so brightly illuminated'. When no explanation of this latter kind is offered, it is legitimate to ask or search for one. Finding a satisfactory answer may sometimes be difficult, but one cannot ordinarily reject the question. When we cannot ourselves quite say what non-aesthetic features make something delicate or unbalanced or powerful or moving, the good critic often puts his finger on something which strikes us as the right explanation. In short, aesthetic terms always ultimately apply because of, and aesthetic qualities always ultimately depend upon, the presence of features which, like curving or angular lines, colour contrasts, placing of masses, or speed of movement, are visible, audible, or otherwise discernible without any exercise of taste or sensibility. Whatever kind of dependence this is, and there are various relationships between aesthetic qualities and non-aesthetic features, what I want to make clear in this paper is that there are no non-aesthetic features which serve in *any* circumstances as logically *sufficient conditions* for applying aesthetic terms. Aesthetic or taste concepts are not in *this* respect condition-governed at all.

There is little temptation to suppose that aesthetic terms resemble words which, like 'square', are applied in accordance with a set of necessary and sufficient conditions. For whereas each square is square in virtue of the *same* set of conditions, four equal sides and four right angles, aesthetic terms apply to widely varied objects; one thing is graceful because of these features, another because of those, and so on almost endlessly. In recent times philosophers have broken the spell of the strict necessary-and-sufficient model by showing that many everyday concepts are not of that type. Instead, they have described various other types of concepts which are governed only in a much looser way by conditions. However, since these newer models provide satisfactory accounts of many familiar concepts, it might plausibly be thought that aesthetic concepts are of some such kind and that they similarly are governed in some looser way by conditions. I want to argue that aesthetic concepts differ radically from any of these other concepts.

Amongst these concepts to which attention has recently been paid are those for which no *necessary-and-sufficient* conditions can be provided, but for which there are a number of relevant features, A, B, C, D, E, such that the presence of some groups or combinations of these features is *sufficient* for the application of the concept. The list of relevant features may be an open one; that is, given A, B, C, D, E, we may not wish to close off the possible relevance of other unlisted features beyond E. Examples of such concepts might be 'dilatory', 'discourteous', 'possessive', 'capricious', 'prosperous', 'intelligent' (but see below p. 8). If we begin a list of features relevant to 'intelligent' with, for example, ability to grasp and follow various kinds of instructions, ability to master facts and marshall evidence, ability to solve mathematical or chess problems, we might go on adding to this list almost indefinitely.

However, with concepts of this sort, although decisions may have to be made and judgement exercised, it is always possible to extract and state, from cases which have *already* clearly been decided, the sets of features or conditions which were regarded as sufficient in those cases. These relevant features which I am calling conditions are, it should be noted, features which, though not sufficient *alone* and needing to be combined with other similar features, nevertheless carry some weight and can count only in one direction. Being a good chess player can count only *towards* and not *against* intelligence. Whereas mention of it may enter sensibly along with other remarks in expressions like 'I say he is intelligent because . . .' or 'the reason I call him intelligent is that . . .'; it cannot be used to complete such negative expressions as 'I say he is unintelligent because . . . '. But what I want particularly to emphasize about features which function as conditions for a term is that *some* group or set of them *is* sufficient fully to ensure or warrant the application of that term. An individual characterized by some of these features may not yet qualify to be called lazy or intelligent, and so on, beyond all question, but all that is needed is to add some further (indefinite) number of such characterizations and a point is reached where we have enough. There are individuals possessing a number of such features of whom one cannot deny, cannot but admit, that they are intelligent. We have left necessary-and-sufficient conditions behind, but we are still in the realm of sufficient conditions.

But aesthetic concepts are not condition-governed even in this way. There are no sufficient conditions, no non-aesthetic features such that the presence of some set or numbers of them will beyond question logically justify or warrant the application of an aesthetic term. It is impossible (barring certain limited exceptions, see below pp. 10–12) to make any statements corresponding to those we can make for condition-governed words. We are able to say 'If it is true he can do this, and that, and the other, then one just cannot deny that he is intelligent', or 'if he does A, B, and C, I don't see how it can be denied that he is lazy', but we cannot make *any* general statement of the form 'If the vase is pale pink, somewhat curving, lightly mottled, and so forth, it will be delicate, cannot but be delicate'. Nor again can one say *any* such things here as 'Being tall and thin is not enough *alone* to ensure that a vase is delicate, but if it is, for example, slightly curving and pale coloured (and so forth) as well, it cannot be denied that it is'. Things may be described to us in non-aesthetic terms as fully as we please but we are not thereby put in the position of having to admit (or being unable to deny) that they are delicate or graceful or garish or exquisitely balanced.[3]

No doubt there are some respects in which aesthetic terms *are* governed by conditions or rules. For instance, it may be impossible that a thing should be garish if all its colours are pale pastels, or flamboyant if all its lines are straight. There may be, that is, descriptions using only non-aesthetic terms which are incompatible with descriptions employing certain aesthetic terms. If I am told that a painting in the next room consists solely of one or two bars of very pale blue and very pale grey set at right angles on a pale fawn ground, I can be sure that it cannot be fiery or garish or gaudy or flamboyant. A description of this sort may make certain aesthetic terms *in*applicable or *in*appropriate; and if from this description I inferred that the picture was, or even might be, fiery or gaudy or flamboyant, this might be taken as showing a failure to understand

---

[3] In a paper reprinted in *Aesthetics and Language*, ed. by W. Elton, Oxford: Blackwell, 1954, 131–146, Arnold Isenberg discusses certain problems about aesthetic concepts and qualities. Like others who approach these problems, he does not isolate them, as I do, from questions about verdicts on the *merits* of works of art, or from questions about *likings* and *preferences*. He says something parallel to my remarks above: 'There is not in all the world's criticism a single purely descriptive statement concerning which one is prepared to say beforehand, "if it is true, I shall *like* that work so much the better" ' (p. 139, my italics). I should think *this* is highly questionable.

these words. I do not wish to deny therefore that taste concepts may be governed *negatively* by conditions.[4] What I am emphasizing is that they quite lack governing conditions of a sort many other concepts possess. Though on *seeing* the picture we might say, and rightly, that it is delicate or serene or restful or sickly or insipid, no *description* in non-aesthetic terms permits us to claim that these or any other aesthetic terms must undeniably apply to it.

I have said that if an object is characterized *solely* by certain sorts of features this may count decisively against the possibility of applying to it certain aesthetic terms. But of course the presence of *some* such features need not count decisively; other features may be enough to outweigh those which, on their own, would render the aesthetic term inapplicable. A painting might be garish even though much of its colour is pale. These facts call attention to a further feature of taste concepts. One *can* find general features or descriptions which in some sense count in one direction only, only *for* or only *against* the application of certain aesthetic terms. Angularity, fatness, brightness, or intensity of colour are typically *not* associated with delicacy or grace. Slimness, lightness, gentle curves, lack of intensity of colour are associated with delicacy, but not with flamboyance, majesty, grandeur, splendour or garishness. This is shown by the naturalness of saying, for example, that someone is graceful *because* she's so light, but *in spite of* being quite angular or heavily built; and by the corresponding oddity of saying that something is *graceful* because it is so heavy or angular, or delicate *because* of its bright and intense colouring. This may therefore sound quite similar to what I have said already about conditions in discussing terms like 'intelligent'. There are nevertheless very significant differences. Although there is this sense in which slimness, lightness, lack of intensity of colour, and so on, count only towards, not against, delicacy, these features, I shall say, at best count only *typically* or *characteristically* towards delicacy; they do not count towards in the same sense as condition-features count towards laziness or intelligence; that is, no group of them is ever logically sufficient.

One way of reinforcing this is to notice how features which are characteristically associated with one aesthetic term may also be similarly associated with other and rather different aesthetic terms. 'Graceful' and 'delicate' may be on the one hand sharply contrasted with terms like 'violent', 'grand', 'fiery', 'garish', or 'massive' which have characteristic non-aesthetic features quite unlike those for 'delicate' and 'graceful'. But on the other hand 'graceful' and 'delicate' may also be contrasted with aesthetic terms which stand much closer

---

[4] Isenberg (in Elton, *Aesthetics and Language*, 132) makes a somewhat similar but mistaken point: 'If we had been told that the colors of a certain painting are garish, it would be *astonishing* to find that they are *all* very pale and unsaturated' (my italics). But if we say 'all' rather than 'predominantly', then 'astonishing' is the wrong word. The word that goes with 'all' is 'impossible'; 'astonishing' might go with 'predominantly'.

to them, like 'flaccid', 'weakly', 'washed out', 'lanky', 'anaemic', 'wan', 'insipid'; and the range of features characteristic of *these* qualities, pale colour, slimness, lightness, lack of angularity and sharp contrast, is virtually identical with the range for 'delicate' and 'graceful'. Similarly many of the features typically associated with 'joyous', 'fiery', 'robust', or 'dynamic' are identical with those associated with 'garish', 'strident', 'turbulent', 'gaudy', or 'chaotic'. Thus an object which is described very fully, but exclusively in terms of qualities characteristic of delicacy, may turn out on inspection to be not delicate at all, but anaemic or insipid. The failures of novices and the artistically inept prove that quite close similarity in point of line, colour, or technique gives no assurance of gracefulness or delicacy. A failure and a success in the manner of Degas may be generally more alike, so far as their non-aesthetic features go, than either is like a successful Fragonard. But it is not necessary to go even this far to make my main point. A painting which has only the kind of features one would associate with vigour and energy but which even so fails to be vigorous and energetic *need* not have some other character, need not be instead, say, strident or chaotic. It may fail to have any particular character whatever. It may employ bright colours, and the like, without being particularly lively and vigorous at all; but one may feel unable to describe it as chaotic or strident or garish either. It is, rather, simply lacking in character (though of course this too is an aesthetic judgement; taste is exercised also in seeing that the painting has no character).

There are of course many features which do not in these ways characteristically count for (or against) particular aesthetic qualities. One poem has strength and power because of the regularity of its metre and rhyme; another is monotonous and lacks drive and strength because of its regular metre and rhyme. We do not feel the need to switch from 'because of' to 'in spite of'. However, I have concentrated upon features which are characteristically associated with aesthetic qualities because, if a case could be made for the view that taste concepts are in any way governed by sufficient conditions, these would seem to be the most promising candidates for governing conditions. But to say that features are associated only *characteristically* with an aesthetic term *is* to say that they can never amount to sufficient conditions; no description however full, even in terms characteristic of gracefulness, puts it beyond question that something is graceful in the way a description may put it beyond question that someone is lazy or intelligent.

It is important to observe, however, that in this paper I am not merely claiming that no sufficient conditions can be stated for taste concepts. For if this were all, taste concepts might not be after all really different from one kind of concept recently discussed. They could be accommodated perhaps with those concepts which Professor H. L. A. Hart has called 'defeasible'; it is a characteristic of defeasible concepts that we cannot state sufficient conditions for them because, for any sets we offer, there is always an (open) list of defeating conditions any of which might rule out the application of the concept. The most we can say schematically for a defeasible concept is that, for example, A, B, and C together are sufficient for the concept to apply *unless* some feature is present which overrides or voids them. But, I want to emphasize, the very fact that we *can* say this sort of thing shows that we are still to that extent in the realm of conditions.[5] The features governing defeasible concepts can ordinarily count only one way, *either* for *or* against. To take Hart's example, 'offer' and 'acceptance' can count only towards the existence of a valid contract, and fraudulent misrepresentation, duress, and lunacy can count only against. And even with defeasible concepts, if we are told that there are no voiding features present, we can know that some set of conditions or features, A, B, C, . . ., is enough, in this absence of voiding features, to ensure, for example, that there is a contract. The very notion of a defeasible concept seems to require that some group of features *would* be sufficient in *certain circumstances*, that is, in the absence of overriding or voiding features. In a certain way defeasible concepts lack sufficient conditions then, but they are still, in the sense described, condition-governed. My claim about taste concepts is stronger; that they are not, except negatively, governed by conditions at all. We could not conclude even in certain circumstances, e.g., if we were told of the absence of all 'voiding' or uncharacteristic features (no angularities, and the like), that an object *must* certainly be graceful, no matter how fully it was described to us as possessing features characteristic of gracefulness.

My arguments and illustrations so far have been rather simply schematic. Many concepts, including most of the examples I have used (*intelligent*, and so on, p. 4), are much more thoroughly open and complex than my illustrations suggest. Not only may there be an open list of relevant conditions; it may be impossible to give precise rules telling how many features from the list are needed for a sufficient set or in which combinations; impossible similarly to give precise rules covering the extent or degree to which such features need to be present in those combinations. Indeed, we may have to abandon as futile any attempt to describe or formulate anything like a complete set of precise conditions or rules, and content ourselves with giving only some general account of the concept, making reference to samples or cases or precedents. We cannot fully master or employ these concepts therefore *simply* by being equipped with lists of conditions, readily applicable procedures or sets of rules, however complex. For to exhibit a mastery of one of these concepts we must be able to go ahead and apply the word correctly to new individual cases, at least to central ones; and each new case may be a uniquely different object, just as each intelligent child or student may differ from others in relevant

---

[5] H. L. A. Hart, 'The Ascription of Responsibility and Rights' in *Logic and Language*, First series, ed. by A. G. N. Flew, Oxford: Blackwell, 1951. Hart indeed speaks of 'conditions' throughout, see p. 148.

features and exhibit a unique combination of kinds and degrees of achievement and ability. In dealing with these new cases mechanical rules and procedures would be useless; we have to exercise our judgement, guided by a complex set of examples and precedents. Here then there is a marked *superficial* similarity to aesthetic concepts. For in using aesthetic terms too we learn from samples and examples, not rules, and we have to apply them, likewise, without guidance by rules or readily applicable procedures, to new and unique instances. Neither kind of concept admits of a simply 'mechanical' employment.

But this is *only* a superficial similarity. It is at least noteworthy that in applying words like 'lazy' or 'intelligent' to new and unique instances we say that we are required to exercise *judgement*; it would be indeed odd to say that we are exercising *taste*. In exercising judgement we are called upon to weigh the pros and cons against each other, and perhaps sometimes to decide whether a quite new feature is to be counted as weighing on one side or on the other. But this goes to show that, although we may learn from and rely upon samples and precedents rather than a set of stated conditions, we are not out of the realm of general conditions and guiding principles. These precedents necessarily embody, and are used by us to illustrate, a complex web of governing and relevant conditions which it is impossible to formulate completely. To profit by precedents we have to understand them; and we must argue consistently from case to case. This is the very function of precedents. Thus it is possible, even with these very loosely condition-governed concepts, to take clear or paradigm cases of *x* and to say 'this is *x* because . . .', and follow it up with an account of features which logically clinch the matter.

Nothing like this is possible with aesthetic terms. Examples undoubtedly play a crucial role in giving us a grasp of these concepts; but we do not and cannot derive from these examples conditions and principles, however complex, which will enable us, if we are consistent, to apply the terms even to some new cases. When, with a clear case of something which is in fact graceful or balanced or tightly-knit, someone tells me why it is, what features make it so, it is always possible for me to wonder whether, in spite of these features, it really is graceful, balanced, and so on. No such features logically clinch the matter.

The point I have argued may be reinforced in the following way. A man who failed to realize the nature of aesthetic concepts, or someone who, knowing he lacked sensitivity in aesthetic matters, did not want to reveal this lack might by assiduous application and shrewd observation provide himself with some rules and generalizations; and by inductive procedures and intelligent guessing, he might frequently say the right things. But he could have no great confidence or certainty; a slight change in an object might at any time unpredictably ruin his calculations, and he might as easily have been wrong as right. No matter how careful he has been about working out a set of consistent principles and conditions, he is only in a position to think that the object is very possibly delicate. With concepts like *lazy, intelligent,* or *contract,* someone who intelligently formulated rules that led him aright appreciably often *would* thereby show the beginning of a grasp of those concepts; but the person we are considering is not even beginning to show an awareness of what delicacy is. Though he sometimes says the right thing, he has not seen but guessed, that the object is delicate. However intelligent he might be, we could easily tell him wrongly that something was delicate and 'explain' why without his being able to detect the deception. (I am ignoring complications now about negative conditions.) But if we did the same with, say, 'intelligent' he could at least often uncover some incompatibility or other which would need explaining. In a world of beings like himself he would have no use for concepts like delicacy. As it is, these concepts would play a quite different role in his life. He would, for himself, have no more reason to choose tasteful objects, pictures and so on, than a deaf man would to avoid noisy places. He could not be praised for exercising taste; at best his ingenuity and intelligence might come in for mention. In 'appraising' pictures, statuettes, poems, he would be doing something quite different from what other people do when they exercise taste.

At this point I want to notice in passing that there are times when it may look as if an aesthetic word could be applied according to a rule. These cases vary in type; I shall mention only one. One might say, in using 'delicate' of glassware perhaps, that the thinner the glass, other things being equal, the more delicate it is. Similarly, with fabrics, furniture, and so on, there are perhaps times when the thinner or more smoothly finished or more highly polished something is, the more certainly some aesthetic term or other applies. On such occasions someone might formulate a rule and follow it in applying the word to a given range of articles. Now it may be that sometimes when this is so, the word being used is not really an aesthetic term at all; 'delicate' applied to glass in this way may at times really mean no more than 'thin' or 'fragile'. But this is certainly not always the case; people often *are* exercising taste even when they say that glass is very delicate because it is so thin, and know that it would be less so if thicker and more so if thinner. These instances where there appear to be rules are peripheral cases of the use of aesthetic terms. If someone did merely follow a rule we should not say he was exercising taste, and we should hesitate to admit that he had any real notion of delicacy until he satisfied us that he could discern it in other instances where no rule was available. In any event, these occasions when aesthetic words can be applied by rule are exceptional, not central or typical, and there is still no reason to think we are dealing with a logical entailment.[6]

---

[6] I cannot in the compass of this paper discuss the other types of apparent exceptions to my thesis. Cases where a man *lacking* in sensitivity might learn and follow a rule, as above, ought to be distinguished from cases where someone who *possesses* sensitivity might know, from a non-aesthetic description, that an aesthetic term applies. I have stated my

It must not be thought that the impossibility of stating any conditions (other than negative) for the application of aesthetic terms results from an accidental poverty or lack of precision in language, or that it is simply a question of extreme complexity. It is true that words like 'pink', 'bluish', 'curving', 'mottled' do not permit of anything like a specific naming of each and every varied shade, curve, mottling, and blending. But if we were to give special names much more liberally than either we or even the specialists do (and no doubt there are limits beyond which we could not go), or even if, instead of names, we were to use vast numbers of specimens and samples of particular shades, shapes, mottlings, lines, and configurations, it would still be impossible, and for the same reasons, to supply any conditions.

We do indeed, in talking about a work of art, concern ourselves with its individual and specific features. We say that it is delicate not simply because it is in pale colours but because of *those* pale colours, that it is graceful not because its outline curves slightly but because of *that* particular curve. We use expressions like 'because of *its* pale colouring', 'because of *the* flecks of bright blue', 'because of *the* way the lines converge' where it is clear we are referring not to the presence of general features but to very specific and particular ones. But it is obvious that even with the help of precise names, or even samples and illustrations, of particular shades of colour, contours and lines, any attempt to state conditions would be futile. After all, the very same feature, say a colour or shape or line of a particular sort, which helps make one work may quite spoil another. 'It would be quite delicate if it were not for that pale colour there' may be said about the very colour which is singled out in another picture as being largely responsible for its delicate quality. No doubt one way of putting this is to say that the features which make something delicate or graceful, and so on, are combined in a peculiar and unique way; that the aesthetic quality depends upon exactly this individual or unique combination

thesis as though this latter kind of case never occurs because I have had my eye on the logical features of *typical* aesthetic judgements and have preferred to over- rather than understate my view. But with certain aesthetic terms, especially negative ones, there may perhaps be some rare genuine exceptions when a description enables us to visualize very fully, and when what is described belongs to certain restricted classes of things, say human faces or animal forms. Perhaps a description like 'One eye red and rheumy, the other missing, a wart-covered nose, a twisted mouth, a greenish pallor' may justify in a strong sense ('must be', 'cannot but be',) the judgments 'ugly' or 'hideous'. If so, such cases are marginal, form a very small minority, and are uncharacteristic or atypical of aesthetic judgements in general. Usually when, on hearing a description, we say 'it *must* be very beautiful (graceful, or the like)', we mean no more than 'it surely must be, it's only remotely possible that it isn't'. Different again are situations, and these are very numerous, where we can move quite simply from 'bright colours' to 'gay', or from 'reds and yellows' to 'warm', but where we are as yet only on the borderline of anything that could be called an expression of taste or aesthetic sensibility. I have stressed the importance of this transitional and border area between non-aesthetic and obviously aesthetic judgements below (p. 21).

of just these specific colours and shapes so that even a slight change might make all the difference. Nothing is to be achieved by trying to single out or separate features and generalizing about them.

I have now argued that in certain ways aesthetic concepts are not and cannot be condition- or rule-governed.[7] Not to be so governed is one of their essential characteristics. In arguing this I first claimed in a general way that no non-aesthetic features are possible candidates for conditions, and then considered more particularly both the 'characteristic' *general* features associated with aesthetic terms and the individual or *specific* features found in particular objects. I have not attempted to examine what relationship these specific features of a work do bear to its aesthetic qualities. An examination of the locutions we use when we refer to them in the course of explaining or supporting our application of an aesthetic term reinforces with linguistic evidence the fact that we are certainly not offering them as explanatory or justifying *conditions*. When we are asked why we say a certain person is lazy or intelligent or courageous, we are being asked in virtue of what do we *call* him this; we reply with 'because of the way he regularly leaves his work unfinished', or 'because of the ease with which he handles such and such problems', and so on. But when we are asked to say why, in our opinion, a picture lacks balance or is sombre in tone, or why a poem is moving or tightly organized, we are doing a different kind of thing. We may use similar locutions: 'his verse has strength and variety *because of the way* he handles the metre and employs the caesura', or 'it is nobly austere *because* of the lack of detail and the restricted palette'. But we can also express what we want to by using quite other expressions: 'it is the handling of metre and caesura which is *responsible for* its strength and variety', 'its nobly austere quality is *due* to the lack of detail and the use of a restricted palette', 'its lack of balance *results from* the high-lighting of the figures on the left', 'those minor chords *make it* extremely moving', 'those converging lines *give it* an extraordinary unity'. These are locutions we cannot switch to with 'lazy' or 'intelligent'; to say what *makes* him lazy, what is *responsible* for his laziness, what it is *due to*, is to broach another question entirely.

---

[7] Helen Knight says (Elton, *Aesthetics and Language*, 152) that 'piquant' (one of my 'aesthetic' terms) 'depends on' various features (a *retroussé* nose, a pointed chin, and the like), and that these features are *criteria* for it; this is what I am denying. She also maintains that 'good', when applied to works of art, depends on *criteria* like balance, solidity, depth, profundity (my aesthetic terms again; I should place piquancy in this list). I would deny this too, though I regard it as a different question and do not consider it in this paper. The two questions need separating: the relation of non-aesthetic features (*retroussé*, pointed) to aesthetic qualities, and the relation of aesthetic qualities to 'aesthetically good' (verdicts). Most writings which touch on the nature of aesthetic concepts have this other (verdict) question mainly in mind. Mrs Knight blurs this difference when she says, for example, ' "piquant" is the same kind of word as "good".'

One after another, in recent discussions, writers have insisted that aesthetic judgements are not 'mechanical': 'Critics do not formulate general standards and apply these mechanically to all, or to classes of, works of art'. 'Technical points can be settled rapidly, by the application of rules', but aesthetic questions 'cannot be settled by any mechanical method'. Instead, these writers on aesthetics have emphasized that there is no 'substitute for individual judgment' with its 'spontaneity and speculation' and that 'The final standard . . . [is] the judgment of personal taste'.[8] What is surprising is that, though such things have been repeated again and again, no one seems to have said what is meant by 'taste' or by the word 'mechanical'. There are many judgements besides those requiring taste which demand 'spontaneity' and 'individual judgement' and are not 'mechanical'. Without a detailed comparison we cannot see in what particular way *aesthetic* judgements are not 'mechanical', or how they differ from those other judgements, nor can we begin to specify what taste is. This I have attempted. It is a characteristic and essential feature of judgements which employ an aesthetic term that they cannot be made by appealing, in the sense explained, to non-aesthetic conditions.[9] This, I believe, is a logical feature of aesthetic or taste judgements in general, though I have argued it here only as regards the more restricted range of judgements which employ aesthetic terms. It is part of what 'taste' means.

II

A great deal of work remains to be done on aesthetic concepts. In the remainder of this paper I shall offer some further suggestions which may help towards an understanding of them.

The realization that aesthetic concepts are governed only negatively by conditions is likely to give rise to puzzlement over how we manage to apply the words in our aesthetic vocabulary. If we are not following rules and there are no conditions to appeal to, how are we to know when they are applicable? One very natural way to counter this question is to point out that some other sorts of concepts also are not condition-governed. We do not apply simple colour words by following rules or in accordance with principles. We see that the book is red by looking, just as we tell that the tea is sweet by tasting it. So

[8] See articles by Margaret Macdonald and J. A. Passmore in Elton, *Aesthetics and Language*, 118, 41, 40, 119.

[9] As I indicated, p. 3 above, I have dealt only with the relation of *non-aesthetic* to aesthetic features. Perhaps a description in *aesthetic* terms may occasionally suffice for applying another aesthetic term. Johnson's *Dictionary* gives 'handsome' as 'beautiful with dignity'; Shorter *OED* gives 'pretty' as 'beautiful in a slight, dainty, or diminutive way'.

too, it might be said, we just see (or fail to see) that things are delicate, balanced, and the like. This kind of comparison between the exercise of taste and the use of the five senses is indeed familiar; our use of the word 'taste' itself shows that the comparison is age-old and very natural. Yet whatever the similarities, there are great dissimilarities too. A careful comparison cannot be attempted here though it would be valuable; but certain differences stand out, and writers who have emphasized that aesthetic judgments are not 'mechanical' have sometimes dwelt on and been puzzled by them.

In the first place, while our ability to discern aesthetic features is dependent upon our possession of good eyesight, hearing, and so on, people normally endowed with senses and understanding may nevertheless fail to discern them. 'Those who listen to a concert, walk round a gallery, read a poem may have roughly similar sense perceptions, but some get a great deal more than others', Miss Macdonald says; but she adds that she is 'puzzled by this feature "in the object" which can be seen only by a specially qualified observer' and asks, 'What is this "something more"?'[10]

It is this difference between aesthetic and perceptual qualities which in part leads to the view that 'works of art are esoteric objects . . . not simple objects of sense perception'.[11] But there is no good reason for calling an object esoteric simply because we discern aesthetic qualities in it. The *objects* to which we apply aesthetic words are of the most diverse kinds and by no means esoteric: people and buildings, flowers and gardens, vases and furniture, as well as poems and music. Nor does there seem any good reason for calling the *qualities* themselves esoteric. It is true that someone with perfect eyes or ears might miss them, but we do after all say we *observe* or *notice* them ('Did you notice how very graceful she was?', 'Did you observe the exquisite balance in all his pictures?'). In fact, they are very familiar indeed. We learn while quite young to use many aesthetic words, though they are, as one might expect from their dependence upon our ability to see, hear, distinguish colours, and the like, not the earliest words we learn; and our mastery and sophistication in using them develop along with the rest of our vocabulary. They are not rarities; some ranges of them are in regular use in everyday discourse.

The second notable difference between the exercise of taste and the use of the five senses lies in the way we support those judgements in which aesthetic concepts are employed. Although we use these concepts without rules or conditions, we do defend or support our judgements, and convince others of their rightness, by talking; 'disputation about art is not futile', as Miss Macdonald says, for critics do 'attempt a certain kind of explanation of works

---

[10] Macdonald in Elton, *Aesthetics and Language*, 114, 119. See also 120, 122.
[11] Macdonald, *ibid.* 114, 120–123. She speaks of non-aesthetic properties here as 'physical' or 'observable' qualities, and distinguishes between 'physical object' and 'work of art'.

of art with the object of establishing correct judgments'.[12] Thus even though this disputation does not consist in 'deductive or inductive inference' or 'reasoning', its occurrence is enough to show how very different these judgements are from those of a simple perceptual sort.

Now the critic's talk, it is clear, frequently consists in mentioning or pointing out the features, including easily discernible non-aesthetic ones, upon which the aesthetic qualities depend. But the puzzling question remains how, by mentioning these features, the critic is thereby justifying or supporting his judgements. To this question a number of recent writers have given an answer. Stuart Hampshire, for example, says that 'One engages in aesthetic discussion for the sake of what one might see on the way . . . if one has been brought to see what there is to be seen in the object, the purpose of discussion is achieved . . . The point is to bring people to see these features'.[13] The critic's talk, that is, often serves to support his judgements in a special way; it helps us to *see* what he has seen, namely, the aesthetic qualities of the object. But even when it is agreed that this is one of the main things that critics do, puzzlement tends to break out again over *how* they do it. How is it that by talking about features of the work (largely non-aesthetic ones) we can manage to bring others to see what they had not seen? 'What sort of endowment is this which *talking* can modify? . . . Discussion does not improve eyesight and hearing' (my italics).[14]

Yet of course we do succeed in applying aesthetic terms, and we frequently do succeed by talking (and pointing and gesturing in certain ways) in bringing others to see what we see. One begins to suspect that puzzlement over how we can possibly do this, and puzzlement over the 'esoteric' character of aesthetic qualities too, arises from bearing in mind inappropriate philosophical models. When someone is unable to see that the book on the table is brown, we cannot get him to see that it is by talking; consequently it seems puzzling that we might get someone to see that the vase is graceful by talking. If we are to dispel this puzzlement and recognize aesthetic concepts and qualities for what they are, we must abandon unsuitable models and investigate how we actually employ these concepts. With so much interest in and agreement about *what* the critic does, one might expect descriptions of *how* he does it to have been given. But little has been said about this, and what has been said is unsatisfactory.

---

[12] ibid. 115–16; cf. also John Holloway, *Proceedings of the Aristotelian Society*, Supplementary Vol. 23 (1949), 175–6.

[13] Stuart Hampshire in Elton, *Aesthetics and Language*, 165. Cf. also remarks in Elton by Isenberg (pp. 142, 145), Passmore (p. 38), in *Philosophy and Psycho-analysis* by John Wisdom, Oxford: Blackwell, 1953, 223–224, and in Holloway, *Proceedings*, 175.

[14] Macdonald in Elton, *Aesthetics and Language*, 119–20.

Aesthetic Concepts

Miss Macdonald,[15] for example, subscribes to this view of the critic's task as presenting 'what is not obvious to casual or uninstructed inspection', and she does ask the question 'What sort of considerations are involved, *and how*, to justify a critical verdict?' (my italics). But she does not in fact go on to answer it. She addresses herself instead to the different, though related, question of the interpretation of art works. In complex works different critics claim, often justifiably, to discern different features; hence Miss Macdonald suggests that in critical discourse the critic is bringing us to see what he sees by offering new interpretations. But if the question is 'what (the critic) does and how he does it', he cannot be represented either wholly or even mainly as providing new interpretations. His task quite as often is simply to help us appreciate qualities which other critics have regularly found in the works he discusses. To put the stress upon *new* interpretation is to leave untouched the question how, by talking, he can help us to see *either* the newly appreciated aesthetic qualities or the old. In any case, besides complex poems or plays which may bear many interpretations, there are also relatively simple ones. There are also vases, buildings, and furniture, not to mention faces, sunsets, and scenery, about which no questions of 'interpretation' arise but about which we talk in similar ways and make similar judgements. So the 'puzzling' questions remain: how do we support these judgements and how do we bring others to see what we see?

Hampshire,[16] who likewise believes that the critic brings us 'to see what there is to be seen in the object', does give some account of how the critic does this. 'The greatest service of the critic' is to point out, isolate, and place in a frame of attention the 'particular features of the particular object which *make it ugly or beautiful*'; for it is 'difficult to see and hear all that there is to see and hear', and simply a prejudice to suppose that while 'things really do have colors and shapes ... there do not exist literally and objectively, concordances of colors and perceived rhythms and balances of shapes'. However, these 'extra-ordinary qualities' which the critic 'may have seen (in the wider sense of "see")' are 'qualities which are of no direct practical interest'. Consequently, to bring us to see them the critic employs 'an unnatural use of words in description'; 'the common vocabulary, being created for practical purposes, obstructs any disinterested perception of things'; and so these qualities 'are normally described metaphorically by some transference of terms from the common vocabulary'.

Much of what Hampshire says is right. But there is also something quite wrong in the view that the 'common' vocabulary 'obstructs' our aesthetic purposes, that it is 'unnatural' to take it over and use it metaphorically, and

[15] ibid. see pp. 127, 122, 125, 115. Other writers also place the stress on interpretation, cf. Holloway, *Proceedings*, 173 ff.

[16] In Elton, *Aesthetics and Language*, 165–8.

that the critic 'is under the necessity of building . . . a vocabulary *in opposition to the main tendency of his language*' (my italics). First, while we do often coin new metaphors in order to describe aesthetic qualities, we are by no means always under the necessity of wresting the 'common vocabulary' from its 'natural' uses to serve our purposes. There does exist, as I observed earlier, a large and accepted vocabulary of aesthetic terms some of which, whatever their metaphorical origins, are now not metaphors, at all, others of which are at most quasi-metaphorical. Second, this view that our use of metaphor and quasi-metaphor for aesthetic purposes is unnatural or a makeshift into which we are forced by a language designed for other purposes misrepresents fundamentally the character of aesthetic qualities and aesthetic language. There is nothing unnatural about using words like 'forceful', 'dynamic', or 'tightly-knit' in criticism; they do their work perfectly and are exactly the words needed for the purposes they serve. We do not want or need to replace them by words which lack the metaphorical element. In using them to describe works of art, the very point is that we are noticing aesthetic qualities related to their literal or common meanings. If we possessed a quite different word from 'dynamic', one we could use to point out an aesthetic quality unrelated to the common meaning of 'dynamic', it could not be used to describe that quality which 'dynamic' does serve to point out. Hampshire pictures 'a colony of aesthetes, disengaged from practical needs and manipulations' and says that 'descriptions of aesthetic qualities, which for us are metaphorical, might seem to them to have an altogether literal and familiar sense'; they might use 'a more directly descriptive vocabulary'. But if they had a new and 'directly descriptive' vocabulary lacking the links with non-aesthetic properties and interests which our vocabulary possesses, they would have to remain silent about many of the aesthetic qualities we can describe; further, if they were more completely 'disengaged from practical needs' and other non-aesthetic awarenesses and interests, they would perforce be blind to many aesthetic qualities we can appreciate. The links between aesthetic qualities and non-aesthetic ones are both obvious and vital. Aesthetic concepts, all of them, carry with them attachments and in one way or another are tethered to or parasitic upon non-aesthetic features. The fact that many aesthetic terms are metaphorical or quasi-metaphorical in no way means that common language is an ill-adapted tool with which we have to struggle. When someone writes as Hampshire does, one suspects again that critical language is being judged against other models. To use language which is frequently metaphorical might be strange for some *other* purpose or from the standpoint of doing something else, but for the purpose and from the standpoint of making aesthetic observations it is not. To say it is an unnatural use of language for doing *this* is to imply there is or could be for this purpose some other and 'natural' use. But these *are* natural ways of talking about aesthetic matters.

To help understand what the critic does, then, how he supports his judgements and gets his audience to see what he sees, I shall attempt a brief description of the methods we use as critics.[17]

1. We may simply mention or point out non-aesthetic features: 'Notice these flecks of colour, that dark mass there, those lines'. By merely drawing attention to those easily discernible features which make the painting luminous or warm or dynamic, we often succeed in bringing someone to see these aesthetic qualities. We get him to see B by mentioning something different, A. Sometimes in doing this we are drawing attention to features which may have gone unnoticed by an untrained or insufficiently attentive eye or ear: 'Just listen for the repeated figure in the left hand', 'Did you notice the figure of Icarus in the Breughel? It is very small.' Sometimes they are features which have been seen or heard but of which the significance or purpose has been missed in any of a variety of ways: 'Notice how much darker he has made the central figure, how much brighter these colours are than the adjacent ones', 'Of course, you've observed the ploughman in the foreground; but had you considered how he, like everyone else in the picture, is going about his business without noticing the fall of Icarus?' In mentioning features which may be discerned by anyone with normal eyes, ears, and intelligence, we are singling out what may serve as a kind of key to grasping or seeing something else (and the key may not be the same for each person).

2. On the other hand we often simply mention the very qualities we want people to see. We point to a painting and say, 'Notice how nervous and delicate the drawing is', or 'See what energy and vitality it has'. The use of the aesthetic term itself may do the trick; we say what the quality or character is, and people who had not seen it before see it.

3. Most often, there is a linking of remarks about aesthetic and non-aesthetic features: 'Have you noticed this line and that, and the points of bright colour here and there . . . don't they give it vitality, energy?'

4. We do, in addition, often make extensive and helpful use of similes and genuine metaphors: 'It's as if there were small points of light burning', 'as though he had thrown on the paint violently and in anger', 'the light shimmers, the lines dance, everything is air, lightness and gaiety', 'his canvasses are fires, they crackle, burn, and blaze, even at their most subdued always restlessly flickering, but often bursting into flame, great pyrotechnic displays', and so on.

5. We make use of contrasts, comparisons, and reminiscences: 'Suppose he had made that a lighter yellow, moved it to the right, how flat it would have been', 'Don't you think it has something of the quality of a Rembrandt?' 'Hasn't it the same serenity, peace, and quality of light of those summer evenings in Norfolk?' We use what keys we have to the known sensitivity, susceptibilities, and experience of our audience.

---

[17] Holloway, *Proceedings*, 173–4, lists some of these very briefly.

Critics and commentators may range, in their methods, from one extreme to the other, from painstaking concentration on points of detail, line and colour, vowels and rhymes, to more or less flowery and luxuriant metaphor. Even the enthusiastic biographical sketch decorated with suitable epithet and metaphor may serve. What is best depends on both the audience and the work under discussion. But this would not be a complete sketch unless certain other notes were added.

6. Repetition and reiteration often play an important role. When we are in front of a canvas we may come back time and again to the same points, drawing attention to the same lines and shapes, repeating the same words, 'swirling', 'balance', 'luminosity', or the same similes and metaphors, as if time and familiarity, looking harder, listening more carefully, paying closer attention may help. So again with variation; it often helps to talk round what we have said, to build up, supplement with more talk *of the same kind*. When someone misses the swirling quality, when one epithet or one metaphor does not work, we throw in related ones; we speak of its wild movement, how it twists and turns, writhes and whirls, as though, failing to score a direct hit, we may succeed with a barrage of near-synonyms.

7. Finally, besides our verbal performances, the rest of our behaviour is important. We accompany our talk with appropriate tones of voice, expression, nods, looks, and gestures. A critic may sometimes do more with a sweep of the arm than by talking. An appropriate gesture may make us see the violence in a painting or the character of a melodic line.

These ways of acting and talking are not significantly different whether we are dealing with a particular work, paragraph, or line, or speaking of an artist's work as a whole, or even drawing attention to a sunset or scenery. But even with the speaker doing all this, we may fail to see what he sees. There may be a point, though there need be no limit except that imposed by time and patience, at which he gives up and sets us (or himself) down as lacking in some way, defective in sensitivity. He may tell us to look or read again, or to read or look at other things and then come back again to this; he may suspect there are experiences in life we have missed. But these are the things he does. This is what succeeds if anything does; indeed it is all that can be done.

By realizing clearly that, whether we are dealing with art or scenery or people or natural objects, this is how we operate with aesthetic concepts, we may recognize this sphere of human activity for what it is. We operate with different kinds of concepts in different ways. If we want someone to agree that a colour is red we may take it into a good light and ask him to look; if it is viridian we may fetch a colour chart and make him compare; if we want him to agree that a figure is fourteen-sided we get him to count; and to bring him to agree that something is dilapidated or that someone is intelligent or lazy we may do other things, citing figures, reasoning and arguing about them, weighing and balancing.

These are the methods appropriate to these various concepts. But the ways we get someone to see aesthetic qualities are different; they are of the kind I have described. With each kind of concept we can describe what we do and how we do it. But the methods suited to these other concepts will not do for aesthetic ones, or vice versa. We cannot prove by argument or by assembling a sufficiency of conditions that something is graceful; but this is no more puzzling than our inability to prove, by using the methods, metaphors, and gestures of the art critic, that it will be mate in ten moves. The questions raised admit of no answer beyond the sort of description I have given. To go on to ask, with puzzlement, how it is that *when* we do these things people come to see, is like asking how is it that, when we take the book into a good light, our companion agrees with us that it is red. There is no place for this kind of question or puzzlement. Aesthetic concepts are as natural, as little esoteric, as any others. It is against the background of different and philosophically more familiar models that they seem queer or puzzling.

I have described how people justify aesthetic judgements and bring others to see aesthetic qualities in things. I shall end by showing that the methods I have outlined are the ones natural for and characteristic of taste concepts from the start. When someone tries to make me see that painting is delicate or balanced, I have some understanding of these terms already and know in a sense what I am looking for. But if there is puzzlement over how, by talking, he can bring me to see these qualities in this picture, there should be a corresponding puzzlement over how I learned to use aesthetic terms and discern aesthetic qualities in the first place. We may ask, therefore, how we learn to do these things; and this is to inquire (1) what natural potentialities and tendencies people have and (2) how we develop and take advantage of these capacities in training and teaching. Now for the second of these, there is no doubt that our ability to notice and respond to aesthetic qualities is cultivated and developed by our contacts with parents and teachers from quite an early age. What is interesting for my present purpose is that, while we are being taught in the presence of examples what grace, delicacy, and so on are, the methods used, the language and behaviour, are of a piece with those of the critic as I have already described them.

To pursue these two questions, consider first those words like 'dynamic', 'melancholy', 'balanced', 'taut', or 'gay' the aesthetic use of which is quasi-metaphorical. It has already been emphasized that we could not use them thus without some experience of situations where they are used literally. The present inquiry is how we shift from literal to aesthetic uses of them. For this it is required that there be certain abilities and tendencies to link experiences, to regard certain things as similar, and to see, explore, and be interested in these similarities. It is a feature of human intelligence and sensitivity that we do spontaneously do these things and that the tendency can be encouraged and developed. It is no more baffling that we should employ aesthetic terms of this sort than that we should make metaphors at all. Easy and smooth transitions by which we shift to the use of these aesthetic terms are not hard to find. We suggest to children that simple pieces of music are hurrying or running or skipping or dawdling, from there we move to lively, gay, jolly, happy, smiling, or sad, and, as their experiences and vocabulary broaden, to solemn, dynamic, or melancholy. But the child also discovers for himself many of these parallels and takes interest or delight in them. He is likely on his own to skip, march, clap, or laugh with the music, and without this natural tendency our training would get nowhere. In so far, however, as we do take advantage of this tendency and help him by training, *we do just what the critic does*. We may merely need to persuade the child to pay attention, to look or listen; or we may simply *call* the music jolly. But we are also likely to use, as the critic does, reiteration, synonyms, parallels, contrasts, similes, metaphors, gestures, and other expressive behaviour.

Of course the recognition of similarities and simple metaphorical extensions are not the only transitions to the aesthetic use of language. Others are made in different ways; for instance, by the kind of peripheral cases I mentioned earlier. When our admiration is for something as simple as the thinness of a glass or the smoothness of a fabric, it is not difficult to call attention to such things, evoke a similar delight, and introduce suitable aesthetic terms. These transitions are only the beginnings; it may often be questionable whether a term is yet being used aesthetically or not. Many of the terms I have mentioned may be used in ways which are not straightforwardly literal but of which we should hesitate to say that they demanded much yet by way of aesthetic sensitivity. We speak of warm and cool colours, and we may say of a brightly coloured picture that at least it is gay and lively. When we have brought someone to make this sort of metaphorical extension of terms, he has made one of the transitional steps from which he may move on to uses which more obviously deserve to be called aesthetic and demand more aesthetic appreciation. When I said at the outset that aesthetic sensitivity was rarer than some other natural endowments, I was not denying that it varies in degree from the rudimentary to the refined. Most people learn easily to make the kinds of remarks I am now considering. But when someone can call bright canvasses gay and lively without being able to spot the one which is really vibrant, or can recognize the obvious outward vigour and energy of a student composition played *con fuoco* while failing to see that it lacks inner fire and drive, we do not regard his aesthetic sensitivity in these areas as particularly developed. However, once these transitions from common to aesthetic uses are begun in the more obvious cases, the domain of aesthetic concepts may broaden out, and they may become more subtle and even partly autonomous. The initial steps, however varied the metaphorical shifts and however varied the experiences upon which they are parasitic, are natural and easy.

Much the same is true when we turn to those words which have no standard non-aesthetic use, 'lovely', 'pretty', 'dainty', 'graceful', 'elegant'. We cannot
say that these are learned by a metaphorical shift. But they still are linked to
non-aesthetic features in many ways and the learning of them also is made
possible by certain kinds of natural response, reaction, and ability. We learn
them not so much by noticing similarities, but by our attention being caught
and focused in other ways. Certain phenomena which are outstanding or
remarkable or unusual catch the eye or ear, seize our attention and interest,
and move us to surprise, admiration, delight, fear, or distaste. Children begin
by reacting in these ways to spectacular sunsets, woods in autumn, roses,
dandelions, and other striking and colourful objects, and it is in these circumstances that we find ourselves introducing general aesthetic words to them,
like 'lovely', 'pretty', and 'ugly'. It is not an accident that the first lessons in
aesthetic appreciation consist in drawing the child's attention to roses rather
than to grass; nor is it surprising that we remark to him on the autumn
colours rather than on the subdued tints of winter. We all of us, not only children, pay aesthetic attention more readily and easily to such outstanding and
easily noticeable things. We notice with pleasure early spring grass or the first
snow, hills of notably marked and varied contours, scenery flecked with a
great variety of colour or dappled variously with sun and shadow. We are
struck and impressed by great size or mass, as with mountains or cathedrals.
We are similarly responsive to unusual precision or minuteness or remarkable
feats of skill, as with complex and elaborate filigree, or intricate wood carving
and fan-vaulting. It is at these times, taking advantage of these natural interests and admirations, that we first teach the simpler aesthetic words. People of
moderate aesthetic sensitivity and sophistication continue to exhibit aesthetic
interest mainly on such occasions and to use only the more general words
('pretty', 'lovely', and the like). But these situations may serve as a beginning
from which we extend our aesthetic interests to wider and less obvious fields,
mastering as we go the more subtle and specific vocabulary of taste. The principles do not change; the basis for learning more specific terms like 'graceful',
'delicate', and 'elegant' is also our interest in and admiration for various non-
aesthetic natural properties ('She seems to move *effortlessly*, as if floating', 'So
very *thin* and *fragile*, as if a breeze might destroy it', 'So *small* and yet so *intricate*', 'So *economical* and *perfectly adapted*').[18] And even with these aesthetic

---

[18] It is worth noticing that most of the words which in current usage are primarily or
exclusively aesthetic terms had earlier non-aesthetic uses and gained their present use by
some kind of metaphorical shift. Without reposing too great weight on these etymologi-
cal facts, it can be seen that their history reflects connections with the responses, interests,
and natural features I have mentioned as underlying the learning and use of aesthetic
terms. These transitions suggest both the dependence of aesthetic upon other interests,
and what some of these interests are. Connected with liking, delight, affection, regard,
estimation, or choice—*beautiful, graceful, delicate, lovely, exquisite, elegant, dainty*; with

terms which are not metaphorical themselves ('graceful', 'delicate', 'elegant'), we rely in the same way upon the critic's methods, including comparison, illustration, and metaphor, to teach or make clear what they mean.

I have wished to emphasize in the latter part of this paper the natural basis of responses of various kinds without which aesthetic terms could not be learned. I have also outlined what some of the features are to which we naturally respond: similarities of various sorts, notable colours, shapes, scents, size, intricacy, and much else besides. Even the non-metaphorical aesthetic terms have significant links with all kinds of natural features by which our interest, wonder, admiration, delight, or distaste is aroused. But in particular I have wanted to urge that it should not strike us as puzzling that the critic supports his judgements and brings us to see aesthetic qualities by pointing out key features and talking about them in the way he does. It is by the vary same methods that people helped us develop our aesthetic sense and master its vocabulary from the beginning. If we responded to those methods then, it is not surprising that we respond to the critic's discourse now. It would be surprising if, by using this language and behaviour, people could *not* sometimes bring us to see the aesthetic qualities of things; for this would prove us lacking in one characteristically human kind of awareness and activity.

---

fear or repulsion—*ugly*; with what notably catches the eye or attention—*garish, splendid, gaudy*; with what attracts by notable rarity, precision, skill, ingenuity, elaboration—*dainty, nice, pretty, exquisite*; with adaptation to function, suitability to ease of handling—*handsome*.

2

Aesthetics and the Looks of Things

Many questions of aesthetics are concerned with the looks of things or with appearances. 'In at least the simpler cases,' says J. O. Urmson,[1] we are interested in 'the way the object . . . looks, the way it sounds, smells, tastes or feels'. Sometimes it is claimed that an aesthetic approach to things is *always* concerned with looks or appearances; more strongly still, that *only* appearances are relevant. Vincent Tomas, discussing the special case of aesthetic *vision*,[2] says that when we see things with 'ordinary vision' we notice the things, but do not notice how they appear or look; but 'When we see things aesthetically, our attention is directed toward appearances and we do not particularly notice the thing that presents the appearance, nor do we care what, if anything, it is that appears . . . the question of reality does not arise'. This he believes 'formulates a necessary, though not a sufficient, condition of aesthetic vision'. He adds that 'the distinction between "*appearing* so-and-so" and "*being* so-and-so" ', which for the practical man and 'the common way' of perceiving 'is of first importance', is 'of no importance' for the aesthetic perceiver. These are interesting claims; but Appearance and Reality are a shifty couple, liable to multiply senses on the sly. I want first, therefore, to elucidate some senses in which a claim like Tomas's about appearances and aesthetic *vision* may and may not be taken. Later, broadening the discussion to include not only how an object looks but how it feels, etc., I shall suggest that only certain looks, feels, etc. can be ultimate grounds of aesthetic admiration.

Even at the outset, one way of taking Tomas's words which would render his claim false springs to mind. We try hard, rightly, to see what paintings and statues are *really* like, what their characteristics really are, not what they might appear to a casual or careless observer to be. Of course, Tomas tries to make clear how his remarks quoted are to be taken, and, up to a point at least, I believe the broad bearing of his thesis is correct. But some of his examples and

[From *The Journal of Philosophy*, 66 (1959). Presented in the symposium on 'Aesthetics' at the 56th annual meeting of the American Philosophical Association, Eastern Division.]
[1] 'What Makes a Situation Aesthetic?' *Proceedings of the Aristotelian Society*, Supplementary Vol. 31 (1957).
[2] 'Aesthetic Vision', *Philosophical Review*, 68 (1959).

formulations tend to suggest much less plausible interpretations of the thesis; I think, therefore, that if we are to assess the claim that attention to appearances is a necessary condition of aesthetic vision, we must examine the senses that 'appearances' can and cannot bear. In any case, since the subject is liable to confusion and is of interest in its own right, I want to make independently and in greater detail a number of distinctions.

I begin with some of the examples Tomas uses to illustrate looks or appearances; in each case he suggests that by 'the common way' of seeing we fail to notice these appearances. The implication is therefore that, for the aesthetic way of seeing, we are required to notice them. In reading a newspaper one commonly does not notice 'how the letters look', that is, (1) 'whether, in *The Times*, a "t" appears short . . . or long', or (2*a*) 'whether an "o" has a fat and jolly look or a lean and hungry look'. I wish to distinguish (1) from (2*a*), though Tomas does not explicitly do so. (3) The ordinary perceiver does not notice that a dark cloud may be 'very like a whale'. (4) A penny from one angle 'will appear, or look, round', from another, elliptical; a white dress in sunlight looks white, at another time, blue-grey. We ordinarily do not notice these apparent variations of sensible qualities. (5) 'The appearance of a man and the appearance of a portrait of a man could be identical'; one might look just like the other, the same description of features and colouring might apply to each. (6) I shall add a further distinction, not discussed by Tomas, but suggested by, and perhaps the most normal understanding of, the pair of phrases he mentions, 'appearing so-and-so' and 'being so-and-so'. This is the distinction between the penny which *merely looks* elliptical but is round, or the dress which *merely looks* bluish but is white. Other senses of 'looks' and 'appearances' are relevant to aesthetics; but this is enough to begin.

The forgoing senses vary greatly. If aesthetic vision requires attention to appearances in one sense, it may not require it in another. For instance, we can dispose of sense (3), the 'very like a whale' example, at once. To notice that a cloud has the appearance of a whale is to note a (fanciful) resemblance. But noticing resemblances is certainly not necessary for aesthetic vision. We may comment appreciatively on a building or statue by mentioning its mass, solidity, or grandeur; these are primary aesthetic observations. We might perhaps (though we rarely do) say 'it's like a whale (or a mountain)'; but such remarks are of a secondary kind, neither necessary nor self-explanatory. If someone uses them we ask 'Why?' or "How do you mean?', and the reply is, 'Well, it has an extraordinary solidity and grandeur'. *These* are the important features, and we note them independently of seeing resemblances to whales, etc.

Consider next example (1). Truly we often do not notice how the letters in a newspaper look. But if asked to describe how they look, we are being asked whether they are long or short, round or oval, straight or slanting. Failing to notice their appearance is failing to notice what their features, colours, shapes *are*. Appearance in sense (1) simply consists of the visible features (features that *appear* or *show*) which a thing actually has. It is the sense (or part of it, see below) in which we praise, or the police issue a description of, a person's appearance. We exclude from such a description the features (e.g., 'a greyish face') that someone or something might merely appear to have under unusual lighting or from odd angles. Similarly, it would be foolish if, asked suddenly to describe how the letter 't' in the newspaper looked, we held it at an angle and replied 'very short and dumpy'. 'Appearance' here then concerns the *reality*, is what we usually contrast with 'mere appearance', and falls, for a familiar use of those expressions, on the side of '*being* so-and-so', not of '*appearing* so-and-so'. This is surely the most obvious sense suggested by the newspaper letters example. It contrasts sharply with sense (6) which I introduced: the penny is round and merely *looks* elliptical, the grass is green and merely *looks* blue-grey under the trees. 'Appearance' in (6), or 'the look it has', includes only visual characteristics the object does *not* really possess.

I have isolated these possible meanings of 'appearances' in order to make clearer in what senses the dictum 'aesthetic vision requires attention to appearances' might be taken. But though one normal interpretation of the newspaper example might suggest that the dictum is concerned with sense (1), and though the emphasis on 'appearing so-and-so' as against 'being so-and-so' might suggest on the contrary that it concerns sense (6), Tomas's claim is not really concerned with just one or other of these senses. For instance, the example of (4), which include *both* circular *and* elliptical appearances of the penny, obviously involve a broader sense which embraces *both* the real visual qualities of (1) *and* the apparent qualities of (6). Sense (4) then, despite other possible interpretations of examples, is obviously nearer the sense of 'appearances' Tomas intended.

There are several other kinds of 'looks'. One is illustrated by (2*a*) above, 'the "o" looks fat and jolly'; another (2*b*) by 'the building has a top-heavy (solid) look', 'the car looks fast'; another again (2*c*) by 'the picture has a warm look'. In these new examples, the contrast between 'looks' and 'is' is not a contrast between the thing's appearance in unusual conditions and its appearance in normal conditions. If a thing *is* red, that is still part of its appearance; and when something *is* fast or top-heavy, this is not part of its appearance (cf. 'intelligent' and 'intelligent-looking'). *Being* white and *merely looking* white are both appearances in the broad sense (4), but it is only *looking* top-heavy that is an appearances at all. However, these new examples also differ among themselves. A building might really *be* top-heavy or a car fast. A picture or a colour might even really *be* warm (e.g., if standing in the sun) as well as having a warm look; nevertheless this is very different, because 'fast look' connects closely with appearances or expectations of speed whereas warm colours are not usually or expected to be literally warm. But a 't' could not literally be hungry or an 'o' jolly. Notice also that all these looks grouped under (2) can themselves be veridical or non-veridical, real or apparent; the contrast of (1) and (6) applies to them. A building that does not *really* look top-heavy might look this way in a mist or from an unusual angle.

When the looks just discussed are veridical, they form part, along with (1), of the appearance of a thing in the 'police description' sense, and when non-veridical, they may be grouped with (6). Moreover, together with (4), which was the totality of real and non-veridical *sensible* qualities (red, elliptical, etc.), they help to make up the still wider class (5). Indeed, (5) includes much else besides; e.g., having 'a mustache and small beard' is an appearance of both men and portraits which Tomas mentions. Thus, (5) is the broadest sense we have listed, consisting of real and non-veridical looks of all kinds.

We can now ask whether the thesis that aesthetic vision *requires* attention to appearances is acceptable, and with these distinctions behind us we can understand it more clearly by seeing in which senses it is not true. Will anything narrower than (5) suffice? Clearly sense (6) will not do; aesthetic vision does not require attention simply to *mere* appearances. With works of art we must attend to *real* looks or appearance. We look at pictures and stat-ues in good light and judge them on their 'intrinsic' qualities, not for qualities lent them accidentally by tricks of lighting. This might lead us to conclude that aesthetic vision requires attention to appearances only in sense (1). But our everyday aesthetic experiences prove this conclusion false; the appear-ances we find beautiful are usually heavily dependent on sun and shadow, etc. It is not the uniform green of the field but the apparent variation of colour that matters. If one wanted to give sense to sayings like 'beauty is in the object' and 'beauty lies in mere appearances, in the eyes of the observer', the case of art tends to favour the former, that of nature the latter. But even with art there are exceptions; eye-shadows in the uniformly white marble of a statue are important, so are shadows and foreshortening of figures high on a building or column, the colours of an alter piece may be adapted to the dim light of the church, and the pigment a painter uses may be dictated by how it looks when surrounded by the other colours on the canvas.

Of the multiple senses of 'looks' and 'appearances' mentioned, then, only the widest is suitable for the dictum under discussion. Anything less renders it false. But even interpreted thus, is it true? For it implies that *all* cases of aesthetic vision require attention to appearances. If we hold tightly to *vision*, I think it is true, indeed analytic. To take a *visual* aesthetic interest in anything, we must certainly be concerned with what appears, can be seen. (Parallel argu-ments hold for aesthetic listening, touch, or smell.) The interest of the claim, in part, lies in making clear, as I have tried to do, what exactly 'appearances' must mean. Otherwise it might be taken to imply that we are never interested in what really is; but I have shown that this is false. Taken in one obvious way, 'we do not particularly notice the thing that presents the appearance' is unten-able. Notice too, in passing, that if we replace 'aesthetic *vision*' by 'aesthetic *interest*', the dictum does not hold. In literature we are not mainly concerned with appearances in the sense outlined; elsewhere too. The comment that two people are perfectly suited, each setting off the other, might be an aesthetic one; but it concerns their characters, temperaments, or interest, not appearances.

I want also to comment briefly on the further claim that for aesthetic vision 'the question of reality never arises' and that we are not concerned with something '*being* so-and-so'. I have given one sense in which this is false. In another sense it is doubtless true: with looks of the restricted types falling under (2), the question whether something *is* warm, fast, or top-heavy never arises. But the view Tomas intends seems different again. The question of reality which he holds never arises for aesthetic vision is, I think, the question 'What is it?' or 'Is it really a . . . ?', a question of classification or identification. But such questions do seem to arise often. We might distinguish three cases. (i) Tomas's example, 'Is it a penny or a subway token?'; we might add 'Is it a tie or a girl's sash?', 'Is it a man or a bearded lady?' (ii) Speaking of a painting, 'Is it a bunch of flowers, a rocky landscape, or purely non-representational?' (iii) 'Is it a man or a portrait?', 'Is it a painting or a view through a window?' The third is Tomas's main concern. I shall comment on this only. Some features we may remark on aesthetically, independently of the question whether the object is a painting or the real thing; e.g., 'the colours are rich and varied', 'the face is serene (ecstatic, sad)'. But there are also appreciative comments we can make on the one but not on the other. Comments (in tones of admiration) like 'it really lives', 'it has the very air of life about it', 'so powerful as to be more than real' (and these do *not* mean merely 'lifelike') are not infrequently made about statues and portraits. 'You can almost see the clouds and spray flying, almost taste the salt air' and 'it has such depth' can be said about seascapes and landscapes but not about seaside and country. If some aesthetic comments on the looks of things can be made only when we know we are dealing with works of art, the question of reality in the sense indicated does arise. Perhaps Tomas did not mean to deny this. Perhaps he meant that *after* such questions are answered, no further concern with whether it is a real man or a portrait arises. From then on we care only about how it looks. But this, I have said, is analytic for aesthetic *vision*; it seems misleading to express it by saying that the question of reality never arises.

I have given a partial elucidation of the claim that attention to appearances is a necessary condition of aesthetic vision. I want now to take up the further question, which of the many appearances and qualities of things (not necessarily visual only) *can* one admire (or disapprove) aesthetically?

Tomas says that attention to appearances is not a sufficient condition of aesthetic vision, and this is, broadly speaking, true. Noticing the appearance of a white dress in shadow or a penny at an angle does not entail that one has looked with an aesthetic eye. But it is not always true. There are some qualities, typically aesthetic ones, the very noticing of which does betoken an aesthetic eye. If one notices how graceful, delicate, or elegant something is or appears, this is sufficient to prove *ipso facto* that one's vision has been in some degree aesthetic. And there are many other typically aesthetic qualities and appearances. Many (but not all) are noted by using certain expressions in a metaphorical or quasi-metaphorical way. If someone describes a letter as 'jolly' or a painting as 'warm', 'placid', or 'violent', speaks of the 'dull glow' of a velvet, or of 'rich' or 'vehement' colours (as opposed to saying simply 'it's red', 'it's angular', 'it has a matt surface'), his way of talking and the features he has noticed again indicate some degree of aesthetic sensitivity. If we are to discern and comment on certain qualities at all, some degree of aesthetic sensitivity is required. With perfect eyesight and intelligence but without this sensitivity, people do not see these qualities or make these comments. I cannot discuss these aesthetic qualities further here.[3] It is to the qualities and appearances that remain, aside from these 'typically aesthetic' ones, that I wish to confine my attention from now on. For there are many appearances that we do not need an aesthetic eye to notice. Anyone might be brought to see that things are smooth, white, square, transparent, or regular, that white looks bluish-grey in shadow, or that things look elliptical or trapezoid from certain angles. Yet though the noticing of these qualities does not itself require aesthetic sensitivity, many of them nevertheless can be admired aesthetically. Here we are noticing not 'typically aesthetic' features, but ordinary features in a certain way, with admiration, delight, or distaste. It seems not so much *what* as *how* we notice that makes our attention aesthetic. This often shows in the way we remark on these qualities. 'It is very smooth', said in a scientific or matter-of-fact tone, does not indicate aesthetic interest. 'It's *so* smooth (so wonderfully smooth, etc.)', said with admiration, usually has an aesthetic ring.

Now the point I want to make about these qualities the noticing of which does *not* require aesthetic sensitivity is that, out of their great variety, only certain ones *can* be admired aesthetically for themselves. Urmson says, rightly, that the 'really basic' grounds for aesthetic admiration or evaluation often consist in the looks, feel, etc., of things; 'Things may have sensible qualities which affect us favourably or unfavourably with no ulterior grounds'. But there are limits to the qualities which can sensibly serve as ultimate grounds for aesthetic judgements, in much the same way as a man's height cannot be of moral interest. Aestheticians sometimes speak as though, by simply changing to an aesthetic approach or 'contemplation', we can value or admire for itself any quality or appearance; but this is not so. There are, first, those looks and qualities we can admire in things for themselves, smoothness, high gloss, simplicity, translucence, and so on; no further explanation or justification is needed. We can express admiration by 'it's so smooth (highly polished, bright, pale, soft, pure, regular, transparent, clear, simple, intricate, vivid)'. We can

[3] I have said something on this topic in 'Aesthetic Concepts' [Ch. 1, this vol.].

qualify these remarks by suitable adverbs: 'beautifully', 'wonderfully'. (We can do this too with some colours: 'It's so blue (green, white)'; but see below.) Secondly, there are qualities that cannot stand alone as basic grounds; 'it's so (wonderfully) angular' seems to call for explanation in a way 'so smooth' and 'so brilliant' do not. But an explanation can often be supplied by a linkage with qualities that *can* stand alone aesthetically: 'Well, its angularity makes it so forbidding, violent, grotesque'. We can admire smoothness just for itself, but we cannot admire angularity *tout court*. And there may, thirdly, be some qualities where no linkage can be provided and which we cannot admire aesthetically at all. There is something logically very odd about saying 'It's so (wonderfully, beautifully) elliptical, equilateral, serrated, etc.'.

As an aside here it is interesting to ask where colours stand in this regard. They seem frequently to be the object of aesthetic admiration. Yet I believe we do not admire colours for themselves as we do brilliance, smoothness, or softness. In admiring colours we make use of two forms of words: 'it is *so* (beautifully) blue', and 'it is *such a* beautiful blue'. These expressions have different uses. I believe that when we use the former there has to be some special context; we can say 'the sky (lake, sea) is so wonderfully blue' but not 'her dress is so wonderfully blue'. 'So blue' (said admiringly) seems to be used of objects that are supposed at their best or most typically to be blue. 'So wonderfully brown (red, pink)' 'as expressions of admiration sound somewhat strange; they call up a context less readily. But, if we supply one, all is well: 'Those apples, so wonderfully red', 'The flesh, so pink'. I wonder, therefore, whether the possibility of admiring colours by using expressions like 'so blue' always depends on some connection and fitting-ness to subject-matter. It does not otherwise seem comprehensible to praise something just for its blueness or greenness. We praise fields for being so green, but not vases or pictures for being so green, or blue, or red. But we *can* praise things for being pure, soft, smooth, colourful, and bright, independently of special subject-matter. The second expression, however, '*such a* beautiful colour', '*a* beautiful blue', is not necessarily related to the typical or expected colours of things. We don't say 'Her dress is so beautifully blue', but we may say 'It is such a beautiful blue'. Here, then, we might seem to admire a colour, *simpliciter*, after all. But I believe this is still not so. 'It's such a wonderful blue' calls for 'In what way?' or 'How?' (just as 'a wonderful texture' calls for 'so smooth' or 'so soft'). We reply, 'Well, it's such a delicate (cool, pure, bright) blue' or 'such a rich (brilliant, vivid, flaming, cheerful) red'. We admire a colour for its character, the qualities it has, qualities which *are* capable of admiration *tout court*; it is not blueness we admire. But praise for smoothness, softness, purity, brilliance, or variety is not like this; such words do not require, but answer, questions like 'In what way is it beautiful?' Colours, then, despite appearances, seem not to be praised for themselves in the way some qualities are; we do not admire things simply for being blue or green. Rather we praise colours either for 'suitability' to subject, or for their qualities of warmth, purity, brilliance, glow, etc.

I have suggested a threefold division of the qualities and appearances I am discussing: we can take a favourable (or unfavourable) aesthetic interest in some for themselves, in others only with a suitable explanation, in others, again, perhaps not at all. Is it possible to say why this is so, or find principles that mark off the first class from the other two? Urmson suggests some such principle for the restricted class of looks I called (2*b*) above, e.g., 'it looks fast'; he says, 'it is looking to possess some quality which is non-aesthetically desirable that matters'. Whether this principle is too broad or too narrow I shall not stop to inquire. Certainly it seems that things might look to possess *some* non-aesthetically desirable qualities and yet not thereby be capable of being aesthetically admired, e.g., 'it looks hygienic (sanitary, arable, fertile)'. But it is not this class (2*b*) I am mainly considering, but rather appearances like red, square, elliptical, smooth, soft, translucent, and brilliant.

About them I shall merely make a suggestion of a quite vague and tentative kind. Is it, perhaps, that the qualities and appearances that can be admired aesthetically for themselves must be ones which somehow, putting aesthetic questions aside, are vitally involved in human experience? Awareness of and concern with warmth, light, brilliance, clarity, purity, regularity, cleanness, richness, softness, smoothness, and simplicity go deep into human life and interests. There is nothing artificial or accidental or superficial about them. They are as basic as the passions, fear, anger, hope, pity, longing, ecstasy, and despair, with which other aspects of art are concerned. By contrast, many of the qualities which, it seems, could not in themselves be ultimate grounds of aesthetic favour are abstract or specialized or artificial. 'Equilateral', 'elliptical', and 'square' are of this sort; if we come across such qualities in nature they are of no special concern to us for themselves, any more than mere curiosities like a hexagonal stone or a rock that looks like a face. But we cannot survive without warmth, peace, energy; we cannot avoid anger, violence, fear; and we concern ourselves deeply over purity, clarity, and simplicity. These are qualities we may value for themselves. Again, qualities like serrated, or hygienic, or sanitary are more specialized or peripheral, of interest less for themselves than for their instrumental value (contrast with them 'sharp' and 'biting', 'pure' and 'clean'). When we do praise something for being, e.g., fast-looking, we notice that 'fast' is not confined, like 'hygienic', to its instrumental value; it suggests dash, bravado, a way of life valued for itself. As for colours, while qualities like brilliance, light, and variety startle and attract us, and while warmth and purity mean much to us, redness as such means nothing to us. If it impresses us, it is by its vividness or brilliance or warmth, or else by what it indicates, suggests, or stands for, ripeness, richness, violence.

This is, I know, vague and speculative. It is not an explanation of why we can value some qualities aesthetically and not others, but rather a comment on those qualities. It suggests that qualities that can be objects of aesthetic interest reflect our vital concerns and the sort of creatures we are. As we saw, to make a quality like angularity aesthetically acceptable, we link it with some of these deeper concerns, with what touches home; we say it is violent or energetic or menacing. More artificial, specialized, or abstract notions, or purely instrumental ones, can be linked up in this way only with greater difficulty, if at all.

I do not know if these last vague comments throw any light upon the division between qualities that can and qualities that cannot be ultimate aesthetic grounds. In any case, the suggestion might be worth exploring further and my hints replaced by something more precise and adequate. But that there is such a division I am sure. Some qualities may be admired aesthetically without further explanation, but not others. It is sometimes said that what is aesthetically admired is wholly relative to a particular culture, and that other cultures might admire quite other things than we do. In its broadest sense I believe this is not so. If someone professed aesthetic admiration for equiangular or elliptical appearances as such, this would not mark an unusual, seldom met with sensitivity on his part; we should not understand him. Similarly, we should be puzzled if we were told of a people who admired ellipses or redness as such; we should ask what significance these qualities had for them. We do not ask this of people who admire smoothness, fine finish, brilliance, simplicity, or softness. If we were asked to imagine creatures who really do admire ellipticality or redness purely for themselves, it is not at all obvious that we could call their admiration aesthetic. For it to be so, these qualities, if my hints are correct, would have to be involved in their vital interests in a way they are not in human life; that being so, it is not clear what kind of creatures we are being asked to imagine.

I began by trying to elucidate the sense in which aesthetic vision requires attention to *appearances*. I then noted that there are appearances and qualities that require, as well as those that do not require, aesthetic sensitivity on our part if we are to notice them. Of the latter I said that only some can be admired for themselves or serve as ultimate grounds for aesthetic admiration. And I offered a very tentative suggestion on why this is so.

3

Aesthetic and Non-aesthetic

Many judgements about the shape, colour, sound, wording, subject-matter, or composition of things, including works of art, are such that it would be ludicrous to suggest that aesthetic sensitivity, perceptiveness, or taste had been exhibited in making them. Similarly, it would be ridiculous to suggest that aesthetic sensitivity was required to *see* or *notice* or otherwise *perceive* that something is, say, large, circular, green, slow, or monosyllabic. Accordingly, I speak of non-aesthetic judgements, qualities, descriptions, and concepts. By contrast, there are other judgements the making of which could clearly be said to exhibit an exercise of aesthetic sensitivity or perceptiveness. Similarly, it would be natural to say that aesthetic sensitivity was required to see, notice, or otherwise perceive, for instance, that something is graceful, dainty, or garish, or that a work of art is balanced, moving, or powerful. Accordingly, I speak of aesthetic judgements, qualities, descriptions, and concepts.[1]

I make this broad distinction by means of *examples* of judgements, qualities, and expressions. There is, it seems to me, no need to defend the distinction. Once examples have been given to illustrate it, I believe almost anyone could continue to place further examples—barring of course the expected debatable, ambiguous, or borderline cases—in one category or the other. To deny such a distinction is to be precluded from discussing most questions of aesthetics at all, just as one could hardly begin ethics without the prior recognition that some judgements and notions do, while others do not, concern morality. One must be able to recognize examples of one's subject-matter. Those who in their theoretical moments deny any such distinction usually show in their practice that they can make it quite adequately.

Some aesthetic judgements employ a characteristically aesthetic term ('graceful', 'balanced', 'gaudy') while others do not ('it's not pale enough', 'there are too many characters'); I am concerned with both sorts. About a third and much-discussed class of judgements, however, I have nothing to say in this paper. These are the purely evaluative judgements: whether things are aesthetically good or

[From *The Philosophical Review*, 74 (1965).]
[1] I have illustrated this distinction more fully by examples in 'Aesthetic Concepts' [Ch. 1, this vol.].

bad, excellent or mediocre, superior to others or inferior, and so on. Such judgements I shall call *verdicts*. Nor shall I raise any other questions about evaluation: about how verdicts are made or supported, or whether the judgements I am dealing with carry evaluative implications.

These judgements that I mean to discuss are the most common and perhaps the most important of aesthetic judgements. Making, supporting, and explaining them occupies much of a critic's time. We make them constantly, moreover, in realms where verdicts of good and bad, better and worse are rarely made at all—about scenery and sunsets, animals, faces, and people. Since aesthetics is largely occupied about the nature of aesthetic judgements, these (constituting as they do a central part of aesthetic discourse), together with the ways they may be supported, deserve examination. Yet it has more often been verdicts and their justification that have attracted attention, these other judgements being treated only in passing. Consequently, the many questions about them that do not parallel questions about verdicts have seldom been adequately raised. We need therefore to investigate how we make such judgements and how we justify and explain them; we need also to examine further the aesthetic qualities and concepts I began by illustrating. To do this, various relationship must be disentangled; for although it is obvious that there are close connections between the aesthetic and non-aesthetic properties of things, and relationships between some aesthetic and non-aesthetic judgements, these connections and relationships have even so not received due attention.

I Aesthetic Perception

In order to avoid various confusions I shall at once separate questions about relationships between aesthetic and non-aesthetic properties, concepts, and judgements from questions about aesthetic perception and judgement itself.

It is of importance to note first that, broadly speaking, aesthetics deals with a kind of perception. People have to *see* the grace or unity of a work, *hear* the plaintiveness or frenzy in the music, *notice* the gaudiness of colour scheme, *feel* the power of a novel, its mood, or its uncertainty of tone. They may be struck by these qualities at once, or they may come to perceive them only after repeated viewings, hearings, or readings, and with the help of critics. But unless they do perceive them for themselves, aesthetic enjoyment, appreciation, and judgement are beyond them. Merely to learn from others, on good authority, that the music is serene, the play moving, or the picture unbalanced is of little aesthetic value; the crucial thing is to see, hear, or feel. To suppose indeed that one can make aesthetic judgements without aesthetic perception, say, by following rules of some kind, is to misunderstand aesthetic judgement.

This therefore is how I shall use 'aesthetic judgement' throughout. Where there is no question of aesthetic perception, I shall use some other expression like 'attribution of aesthetic quality' or 'aesthetic statement'. Thus, rather as a colour-blind man may infer that something is green without seeing that it is, and rather as a man, without seeing a joke himself, may say that something is funny because others laugh, so someone may attribute balance or gaudiness to a painting, or say that it is too pale, without himself having judged it so.

II Some Relationships of Dependence

I turn now to statements of the relationships between aesthetic and non-aesthetic properties. These are of several sorts. The first two that follow are purely general, that is, they state relationships between *types* of qualities; I do no more than mention them. Thereafter I discuss statements of those relationships that interest me more particularly, namely, those holding between *specific* qualities. In (iii) and (iv) below I consider two sorts of relationships which may hold between specific qualities in *individual instances*. Later (Sects. VII and VIII) I shall consider various sorts of *general* relationships which hold between specific qualities.

(i) Aesthetic qualities are dependent upon non-aesthetic ones for their existence. They could no more occur in isolation than there could be facial resemblances without features, or grins without faces; the converse is not true.

(ii) The non-aesthetic qualities of a thing determine its aesthetic qualities. Any aesthetic character a thing has depends upon the character of the non-aesthetic qualities it has or appears to have, and changes in its aesthetic character result from changes in its non-aesthetic qualities. Aesthetic qualities are 'emergent'. Like (i) above, which it entails, (ii) concerns the nature of aesthetic properties in general.

(iii) In addition to being able to state the general truth that aesthetic qualities depend on and result from non-aesthetic characteristics, we can state particular truths about individual objects—for example, that these particular non-aesthetic qualities of this object (described as fully as one wishes) give it *some* aesthetic property rather than none, and that what they give it is, say, *grace* or *balance*. There are, however, two different relationships here that must be distinguished.

First, the particular aesthetic character of something may be said to result from the *totality* of its relevant non-aesthetic characteristics. It is always conceivable that, by some relatively small change in line or colour in a picture, a note in music, or a word in a poem, the aesthetic character may be lost or quite transformed (though possible also that by some considerable changes it may not be significantly altered). A somewhat different totality might result in an aesthetic difference. Features one would hardly think of singling out as notably contributing to its aesthetic character—say, background colours, hardly noticed brush strokes, and so on—nevertheless do contribute because, being as they are, they at least allow it to have the character it has, a character it conceivably might not have if they were altered. One might say that it is because everything about the work is exactly as it is—this colour here, that line there, and so on indefinitely—that it is graceful or moving or unbalanced. (Doubtless this possibility is one thing that leads people to speak of the uniqueness of works of art.) This third relationship might therefore appropriately be called the relation of *total specific dependence.*

(iv) The other relationship, the fourth, remains to be considered. A critic frequently tries, as one of his central occupations, to say why a picture is unbalanced, or what gives a complex work its grace, unity, or serenity. In doing so, he is not setting out to assert the merely general truth that its non-aesthetic features make it so; but neither is he ordinarily trying to state the kind of relationship just mentioned, that it is *all* these lines together with *all* those colours (describing the totality of features of the work as fully as he can) that make it so. He is usually interested in much more pointed explanations: he tries to select certain peculiarly important or salient features or details. He may mention a concentration of blues and greys as responsible for the unity of tone, certain wavy lines as giving a restless quality, a change in key as giving a sombre or indecisive character; more broadly, he may point out that the aesthetic character results from organization rather than from colouring, from changes of tempo rather than harmonic devices. In short, what the critic is doing is selecting from a work those features which are *notably* or *especially* responsible for its character. For often in a work there are some features that strike us as making the most outstanding contribution, usually those in which a small alteration would work a remarkable aesthetic change. This fourth relationship might therefore be called that of *notable specific dependence*; statements of such relationships bulk large in criticism.

Often, then, one can say without any conflict both that *all* the features of a thing are jointly responsible for its aesthetic character and that *one particular* feature is responsible. Usually in criticism it is remarks of the latter kind that interest us; even so, it must not be thought that remarks of the other kind are always trivial or pointless. When we have singled out certain features in a work that strike us as notably responsible, it may sometimes still be worthwhile for someone else to point out in turn that these particularly noticeable features achieve their effect only because other elements in the complex, elements that do not force themselves on our attention, are exactly as they are. Such comments may be especially worth making at times, since some works, unlike others, are so constructed that the slightest change, even in seemingly unimportant details, would altogether destroy their effect. A critic's comment that in this work it is everything together, ordered just as it is, that is responsible for its character may bring home to us that here is a work of that sort. Everything that could possibly be relevant seems on examination so exactly calculated that it plays a vital part in the work.

I have entitled this section 'Relationships of Dependence' to stress that aesthetic qualities, which, as I said above, are broadly speaking perceptual, are emergent or dependent. So too are many other qualities, Gestalt, physiognomic, and other. They thus contrast sharply with those perceptual qualities like red and green which do not depend for their character upon other perceptual qualities of things.

III Two Critical Activities

(i) The relationships that I have just described hold between qualities independently of a person's realizing in particular cases that they do. Whether or not one sees that a picture lacks balance, and lacks it notably because of the placing of a certain figure, in no way bears on the fact that the placing of the figure *is* what unbalances the picture. In describing the third and fourth relationships, however, we could not avoid mention of one of the central activities of critics: *explanation*. This consists largely in showing how aesthetic effects are achieved in a work by isolating and pointing out what is (notably, mainly, in part) responsible. Even when we have remarked the grace, unity, or ungainliness of something, we may yet be unable to say why it has these qualities. But a good critic should be able to point out what makes it so. Such explanations satisfy an interest and curiosity we often have about the aesthetic qualities of things (especially when the artist has achieved new effects or achieved something in an unusual way). But they may do more than this. When we see in detail how and why the work has its character, we may find our initial judgement strengthened and trust it more confidently. Moreover, as we come to realize how boldly or subtly, with what skill, economy, and exactness, the effect is achieved, how each detail is judged to a nicety and all work together with a fine precision, our appreciation is deepened and enriched and becomes more intelligent in being articulate.

Explanations of this sort frequently consist, as I said in discussing relationships (iii) and (iv), in mention of *non-aesthetic* features of things (colours, lines, composition). Frequently also, of course, they consist in reference to responsible *aesthetic* qualities ('The firmness and grace of line give the work both stability and elegance'). But in either case we have been led back from the discussion of independent relationships to activities involving aesthetic sensitivity and judgement. For it requires such sensitivity, both in the critic who gives and in those who follow his explanations, to see that these shapes and colours unbalance the picture, or that exactly this word order makes the poem moving, no less than to see initially that the works have these aesthetic qualities. So too, although aesthetic sensitivity is not involved in seeing that a figure is on the far left of a picture, it *is* involved in seeing that it is *too* far left for the composition to balance, or that it is *so* far to the left as to dissipate dramatic intensity. Explaining why a work has an aesthetic character, even where the reasons involve mentioning only non-aesthetic features, requires aesthetic discrimination.

(ii) The second activity I have in mind is less limited and more important than that of providing explanations for the aesthetic qualities one has already seen; it consists instead in helping people to see and judge for themselves that things have those qualities. Since, as I emphasized at the start, aesthetic perception is what is really vital, a major occupation of critics is the task of bringing people to see things for what, aesthetically, they are, as well as why they are. (This does exclude other activities like *re*interpretation, bringing people to see new and different features.) Contemporary philosophers have rightly emphasized this activity. The critic is successful if his audience began by not seeing, and ends by seeing for itself, the aesthetic character of the object. Sometimes when a critic helps us to see aesthetic qualities, we have missed them by simply overlooking some important and responsible non-aesthetic features, or by not seeing these in relation, in a certain light, or in the light of the title; one cannot expect to see a dancer's grace without in some degree noticing the features that make her graceful. But sometimes, although these *were* seen, the resultant aesthetic quality was still missed. Somewhat analogously one might, even after scrutiny, miss an aspect of a puzzle picture, see a face and not notice its tired look, or see two faces and be unable to see their resemblance.

How a critic manages by what he says and does to bring people to see aesthetic qualities they have missed has frequently puzzled writers. But there is no real reason for mystification. One might puzzle equally over how *on my own* I come to perceive, after ten minutes in front of a picture or several replayings of a sonata, what I had not previously perceived. What mainly is required is a detailed description of the sorts of things critics in fact do and say, for this is what succeeds if anything does. Prominent, of course, among these things is drawing attention to the features that are notably responsible for the effect the critic wants his audience to see ('Notice how the language used here echoes the previous stanza and sets a unity of tone'). But this is far from being the only thing that may bring success; the critic may make similes and comparisons, describe the work in appropriate metaphors, gesticulate aptly, and so on. Almost anything he may do, verbal or non-verbal, can on occasion prove successful. To go on to ask how these methods can possibly succeed is to begin to ask how people can ever be brought to see aesthetic (and Gestalt and other similar) properties at all. That they can is neither more nor less puzzling than that human beings can, by various means, be brought to do other things, such as distinguishing shades of colour, seeing facial resemblances or jokes, and so on. We do these things; and what critics say and do are the sorts of things that help us to do the one under discussion.[2]

A second question about this activity is whether it is a way of *supporting* or *justifying* aesthetic judgements. Some aestheticians have held that this—showing the work, getting people to see—is the only way of supporting an aesthetic judgement, even perhaps the only point of critical activity. This is to overlook a great deal; but I see no reason why it should not be called *a* way of supporting or justifying, even of proving, an aesthetic judgement. If I say the apples are sour and someone doubts my claim, I may ask him to taste them. With more complex or subtle things I may have to help him in appropriate ways. If I say that a figure can be seen as either a staircase or a cornice, that a cloud looks like a giraffe, that two people look somewhat alike, or that the brandy is soft and velvety, and he questions what I say, it may not be enough merely to invite him to look or taste. I may need to draw attention to this and that, suggest he look at the figure thus, or taste the brandy in a certain way. So too it may not do simply to play the music again or set the picture in a good light; I may give instructions, tell him to stand further off, to concentrate on certain features, to try to take in the whole at once; I may compare it with other works, describe it in metaphors, and so on indefinitely. If he then finds himself agreeing with me, I have vindicated my claim in the best possible way, by getting him to see for himself. There is no reason not to say, if one wishes, that I have supported, justified, or even proved my original judgement. One might refer to this activity therefore, as *perceptual proof*. (There is no excuse for confusing this with the activity of explanation already discussed. Both may proceed, it is true, by drawing attention to features responsible for aesthetic effects. But they have different aims; and much that may be said and done— by simile, repetition, comparison, gestures, almost any means—to open someone's eyes to the aesthetic qualities of an object could not count as explaining why it has those qualities.)

Nevertheless, if we do choose to call this *support* of an aesthetic judgement, we must be clear what kind it is and what kind it is not. The critic cannot be said to have *reasoned* in support of it. Where someone tries to bring another to agree with him by reasoning, or by offering rational support for a judgement, he offers statements which, if true, render it certain, likely, or reasonable to suppose, that his judgement was correct. The person to whom the reasons are offered may, after reviewing them, conclude or infer or decide that the

---

[2] For a fuller discussion, including a more detailed description of what things a critic usefully may do, see 'Aesthetic Concepts' [Ch. 1, this vol., 18f]. Cf. also John Holloway, 'What Are the Distinctive Features of Arguments Used in Criticism of the Arts?' *Proceedings of the Aristotelian Society*, Supplementary Vol. 23 (1949), 173–4; and Robert Hoffman, 'Aesthetic Argument', *Philosophical Quarterly*, 11 (1961), 309–12.

judgement is indeed correct or justified. He has been offered reasons for *thinking* something, and so may end accepting the judgement originally offered. But it was neither the aim nor the outcome of the critic's activity I described to provide reasons from which his audience might reasonably conclude that his judgement was true. He might have achieved that even in the absence of the work by telling, say, how many reliable and distinguished critics had independently made the same judgement. His aim was to bring his audience to agree with him because they perceived for themselves what he perceived; and this is what, if successful, he achieved. But an activity the successful outcome of which is seeing or hearing cannot, I think, be called *reasoning*. I may have reasons for thinking something is graceful, but not reasons for seeing it is. Yet aesthetic perception, I have said, is essential to aesthetic judgement; one could not therefore be brought to make an aesthetic judgement simply as the outcome of considering reasons, however good. It is a confusion of disparate activities to suppose that in this sense one could have a 'rational justification' for making an aesthetic judgement. Thus the aesthetic judgements I am concerned with can neither *have* nor *lack* a rational basis in this sense, namely, that they can either be or fail to be the outcome of good or bad reasoning. Perception is 'supported' in the manner described or not at all.

IV Reasons

Even if 'perceptual proof' is not a matter of giving reasons, and even if the notion of an aesthetic judgement being the outcome solely of considering reasons is an impossible hybrid, the question must nevertheless be raised whether the aesthetic judgements I am discussing may be justified or supported by reasons in some other way. Many writers insist that some sort of rational support must be possible. 'If criticism is a respectable enterprise at all', says one recent writer, and 'if it is correct to say that the critic gives reasons for his judgments, then it must be possible for us to see the reasons *as* reasons. . . . An adequate account of criticism should provide a way of seeing that the remarks offered in support can count as support.'[3]

Consider the following question. Suppose someone makes the aesthetic judgement that something is graceful. Regardless of whether he attempts to get *me* to see that it is, even indeed if I never see the object, is it possible for him, by presenting reasons, to support the *truth* of his claim and so, in this sense, to provide reasonable support for his judgement?

Now obviously, to meet as broad a request as this, he might offer all kinds

---

[3] H. R. G. Schwyzer, 'Sibley's "Aesthetic Concepts" ', *Philosophical Review*, 72 (1963), 74.

of supporting reasons—for example, 'It's likely my judgement is right because I'm usually reliable on such things', 'Many notable critics have also independently thought so', and so on. The question I intend to raise, however, is much narrower: whether any statements about the *non-aesthetic* qualities of a thing, judgements requiring no aesthetic sensitivity, could be made such that, even if one has not seen the work and *a fortiori* has not appreciated its qualities, one would have to admit that, if these statements are true, the work must be or probably is as the critic claims it to be. Could any statements about a thing's non-aesthetic properties alone serve as reasons for agreeing or concluding that it has a certain aesthetic property? If so, one would not, of course, have been brought by such arguments to *see* the grace of the work; nor therefore, as a result of them, would one have made an aesthetic *judgement* about it. It would simply be that, with justification, one could attribute to it certain aesthetic properties. It might be suggested that such a justification or support, even if possible, would be practically pointless and aesthetically worthless. For reasons it would take time to develop I do not altogether believe this. But in any case, the investigation into whether it is possible is a legitimate inquiry for aesthetics.

This inquiry will occupy the last sections of this paper (Sect. VII ff.). But I will postpone it a little longer. For after all, even if such a kind of support for aesthetic judgements were possible, it would still not account for the widespread inclination to say that the critic should have reasons for his judgements. Those who insist on this certainly mean that, in some sense, a critic will have made a responsible and trustworthy judgements only if there were reasons for making that judgement rather than some other, that he should have made it *because* he had those reasons, and that he should be able to cite those reasons. This therefore concerns reasons upon which, in some sense, a critic's judgement is based. But the supposed activity outlined in the previous paragraph would be quite different: it would be at best the auxiliary activity of providing reasonable *opinions* and of perhaps confirming by argument the judgements that the critic, confronting the work, had already independently made. How or in what sense then can a judgement be based on reasons given that, in one sense already explained (p. 40), judgements *cannot* be the outcome of reasons? Perhaps it is a matter of distinguishing two ways of using 'reason'.

V

In discussing the four relationships earlier, we saw that there must be some (ultimately non-aesthetic) features responsible for any aesthetic quality. Another way of putting this is that there always is, and must be, some *reason* why a thing has that quality. We also saw that critics largely occupy themselves in discovering the reasons why a work is, say, graceful or unbalanced; that someone who has seen that it is graceful must in some degree have noticed these responsible features; and that a good critic should be able to point out these reasons. But these are reasons why the *work* is graceful, and to be distinguished from reasons—good or bad, a critic's or anyone else's—for concluding or inferring that the work is graceful.

If a work is graceful there will be reasons why it is, and this will be so whether anyone ever knows, or thinks, or has any reasons for thinking it so or not. The reason one unnoticed pebble on a beach does not fit snugly against another may be that one is flat and the other slightly convex. The statement of such a reason is a statement why things are as they are. A person might notice that something is graceful, or that two pebbles do not fit closely, without yet knowing or being able to specify exactly the reason why. As 'reason' is used here, a man may judge something to be graceful and not be able to give the reason, though he may have tried hard to find it. But 'reason' is also used to mean roughly, a true statement or a fact such that, on the basis of knowing *it*, it would be reasonable, right, or plausible to infer, suppose, or believe that something is so.

I have already argued that it is absurd to ask that an aesthetic *judgement* (involving, as it does, perception) be based upon reasons in this latter way. The sense in which a responsible critical judgement should be based on reasons and in which a critic should be able to give reasons for his judgement depends on the other use of the word. To have reasons for his judgement he must have attended carefully enough, while seeing, hearing, or reading the work, to have noticed in some measure the features of the work that make it moving or unbalanced or ungraceful, and his judgement must have resulted from that. Moreover, he should be able to cite these features and, if challenged ('Why don't you think this line is graceful?'), reply with some mention of actual detail ('Well, it breaks and wobbles just in the middle'). In general, then, my suggestion is that two things are often confused: people insist that these aesthetic judgements should be based on, in the sense of rationally derived or derivable from, supporting reasons; but all they can sensibly insist is that the critic, having realized that the thing is or is not graceful, should be able to say what, in his opinion, makes it so.

The distinction is one that ought not to cause confusion. Consider some other cases. 'The reason the pack of cards is incomplete is that the ace of clubs is missing'. 'The reason he is sulking is that you refused his request'. 'The reason he looks so funny is that he screws up his eyes in an odd way'. 'The reason it sounds so solemn is that there are several long vowels in the line'. Each gives a reason why something is so. In each case someone might notice or know that this something is so first—that the pack is incomplete, that he is sulking, that his face looks funny—without yet knowing the reason or being able to say why. On the other hand one might notice or know the other fact first and independently—that the ace of clubs is missing, that you refused his request. Then, on the basis of *these* facts or reasons, one might infer that the pack is incomplete, that he is probably sulking, and so on. One would suppose it difficult to confuse these two activities; yet I believe they are sometimes confused, perhaps because quite often the very same words (for example 'because the ace is missing') may express either the reason why things are as they are, or an adequate or conclusive reason for thinking or concluding that they are. Thus if the reason the pack is incomplete is that it contains only three aces, it is also true that if one knew it contained only three aces one would have a conclusive reason for asserting that it was incomplete. Similarly, if the reason he is sulking is that you refused his request, it may also be true that if I know you refused his request I may have a good, though this time not conclusive, reason for thinking he is sulking.

But although one and the same clause may sometimes express either the reason why something is so or a good reason for believing it is, this is not always the case. The reason the music is sad at a certain point may truly be that just there it slows and drops into a minor key. The reason a man's face looks funny may be that he screws up his eyes in an odd way. But knowledge that a piece of music slows and drops into a minor key at a certain point or that a man screws up his eyes in an odd way would be very poor reasons for believing or inferring that the music must be, or even probably is, sad, or that the face looks funny. The music might instead be solemn or peaceful, sentimental, or even characterless; the face might look pained or angry or demonic. It is, then, a quite unwarranted assumption that, if a critic has noticed or discovered the reasons why something has a certain aesthetic quality and in *that* sense can cite reasons which support his judgement, he thereby has reasons the citing of which provide rational support for his judgement or show it to be reasonable. *A* may in fact *be* the reason why something is *B*, and yet the knowledge that that thing has *A* may provide *no* reason or justification for supposing that it has *B*.

If this is so, the supposition that, because critics do indeed give reasons for their judgements, it must be possible for them to give 'good, or cogent, reasons' needs further examination.[4] Monroe Beardsley, for instance, holds, as against the 'critical skeptic', that the critic 'armed with reasons' is a 'reasoner', and he attempts 'to make sense of what the critic does when he gives reasons, and back him up with a philosophical account of how those reasons really work'. Beardsley, however, like most writers, is concerned here especially with the support of *verdicts* or 'appraisals', a realm where the issues may not be the

---

[4] For this and following quotations, see Monroe C. Beardsley, 'On the Generality of Critical Reasons', *Journal of Philosophy*, 59 (1962), 477–80.

same and what he says may be correct. Since my present focus of attention is different, I do not here discuss his views. What is of interest is his account of what it is for a critic to give reasons for a judgement, since he says nothing about restricting this to reasons for verdicts. A reason, he says, is a proposition which cites some property of the work; and 'if one proposition is a reason for another, in the sense of actually supporting it, then there must be a logical connection of some sort between them. And, being a logical connection, it must relate general concepts in an abstract way.' Moreover, he adds, '*generality* . . . appears to be essential to reasons in the logical sense' and 'some form of generality is essential to reason-giving'. He therefore attacks those critical sceptics who 'hold that we can still talk of giving reasons in particular cases . . . without committing ourselves to any general principles at all'. Here then is a view about what giving reasons for aesthetic judgements consists in, and it can be asked whether it is applicable to the judgements I am discussing.

I have argued above that a critic may, in giving reasons for one of these judgements, offer considerations which do not allow generalization and do not support the judgement by permitting inference to its truth. I believe therefore that, in so far as critics give reasons for these judgements (and not merely auxiliary support for their truth) by citing non-aesthetic features, they are not giving reasons in Beardsley's sense of propositions having 'a logical connection' with the judgement they support, nor are they relating 'general concepts in an abstract way'. Consequently, when critics give such reasons, they are exemplifying an activity wherein we *can* in certain respects 'still talk of giving reasons in particular cases . . . without committing ourselves to any general principles'. There is a familiar and important form of reason-giving, at least for the aesthetic judgements under discussion, which does not consist in citing properties of the work in propositions which *logically* support—that is, make certain or likely—the truth of the critic's judgement. We must not therefore be misled by the fact that we frequently use the same words to ask for the reason on which someone's *inference* is based and for the reason *why something* has a certain quality. The question 'Why do you think these stones won't fit together?' may in both cases take the answer 'I think they won't because one is slightly convex'. But this may be asking and answering the question 'Why do you *infer* that they won't?' or the question 'What's *your* explanation of why they don't?' It is ordinarily in this latter sense that we ask the critic why he thinks something is graceful, and the reason he gives, even when he is correct, need not be deductively or inductively capable of justifying the claim that such is the case. In this latter sense, it is a mistake to say that the critic's claim ought to be rationally supported by his reasons, although this again is not to deny that some of a critic's reasons might be irrelevant, inappropriate, or absurd.

VI

I have now differentiated the following often confused topics (1) explanation of aesthetic effects, (2) support of a judgement by a 'perceptual proof', (3) the impossibility of making aesthetic judgements by deriving them from reasons, (4) the sense in which a critic may and should be able to give reasons why the work has the aesthetic character he claims, (5) the question (raised and postponed in Sect. IV) whether, given statements solely about non-aesthetic properties, one could be justified in making or accepting attributions of aesthetic qualities. This question, to which I turn now, commits us to an examination of certain other relationships.

The reasons for investigating this question are several. Aesthetic qualities are intimately connected with, and in various ways dependent on, non-aesthetic ones. It would seem therefore that statements truly attributing aesthetic qualities—and aesthetic judgements generally—are true because, and would not be true unless, certain statements attributing non-aesthetic qualities were true. If there are such relationships, does it follow that the truth of certain statements of the second sort supports, guarantees, makes likely, or excludes the truth of some aesthetic claims?

If this were so, although a critic would not ordinarily arrive at or support his aesthetic claims in this way, certain other things might be possible. Someone lacking aesthetic discrimination who could himself perceive the non-aesthetic qualities of an object might reason or conclude justifiably, and so find out or prove, that it was, say, graceful, citing possibly conclusive reasons for his opinion. Given the requisite information, he might even reach true and justified opinions about objects he had not seen. Someone who judged a statue graceful or a poem moving but felt unsure of his judgement might ascertain, independently of his own impression, or have additional reason for thinking, that they were so. There might thus sometimes be a way of verifying aesthetic judgements and an alternative way of correctly applying aesthetic terms. It is a matter of some importance to show whether or how far such things can be done. Certain answers to these questions would bear upon the truth of various traditional and contemporary theories; they should clarify some further relationships between the non-aesthetic and the aesthetic and so illuminate further the nature and logic of aesthetic terms and judgements.

VII Some Further Relationships: Conceptual

That there are certain *general* relationships or associations between various aesthetic and non-aesthetic features is fairly clear. Although attention has not usually been focused on the distinction between aesthetic and non-aesthetic, but rather on some broader one (basic properties and dependent, emergent, or Gestalt properties), the existence of relationships and the possibility of stating them generally has been widely assumed, especially by those who have attempted certain experimental researches.

In music and verse, quietness and slowness have some close connection with sadness and solemnity, and speed with gaiety and excitement; bright colours are somehow related to garishness and gaudiness, curving lines to gracefulness, and so on. I shall say that they are *typically* or *characteristically* associated. Similarly there are typical antitheses or oppositions: pale and gaudy, angular and graceful, fast-moving and solemn. Exactly what these general relationships are often remains clouded; certainly a common assumption, sometimes explicit, is that they are empirical and contingent.[5] That there may be certain conceptual relationships has been less noticed; in aesthetics, as elsewhere, logical or conceptual associations have commonly been taken to be contingent. In this section I discuss some kinds of conceptual relationships.

(i) First, let me consider certain relationships which do *not* hold. Although a thing's aesthetic character is dependent on and results from its non-aesthetic features, in general there are no sets of non-aesthetic features that are logically sufficient for it to have a certain aesthetic quality. In saying this I mean to exclude several possibilities. There is no *one* set, no *group* of sets of logically sufficient conditions, no 'defeasible' sets, and no wholly non-aesthetic descriptions which logically entail a certain aesthetic character or in virtue of which to deny such a character would be a linguistic error. Some qualities of a thing may be sufficient to make it graceful, but it will not be a case of *logical* sufficiency. No non-aesthetic conditions or descriptions logically require the application, though some may require the rejection, of an aesthetic term.[6]

Throughout the forgoing I have restricted myself entirely to the relation of non-aesthetic terms and judgements to aesthetic ones. It may be that some descriptions in aesthetic terms are logically sufficient for the application of another aesthetic term, but if there are such relationships I am not concerned with them.[7] Again, it is sometimes flatly said that the terms I call aesthetic are indefinable.[8] This is most probably false although, if I am correct, they cannot be defined in a certain way solely by *non-aesthetic* terms. But to make this

[5] See Monroe C. Beardsley, *Aesthetics: Problems in the Philosophy of Criticism*, New York: Harcourt Brace, 1958, 87, 331, and *passim*.

[6] I discuss this more fully in 'Aesthetic Concepts', [Ch. 1, this vol.]. Cf. a series of similar points made for other purposes by H. P. Grice, 'Some Remarks about the Senses', in R. J. Butler, *Analytical Philosophy*, Oxford: Blackwell, 1962, 142–3.

[7] See 'Aesthetic Concepts', n. 9 [Ch. 1, this vol., 13].

[8] See Beardsley, *Aesthetics*, 86, 192, 194; cf. also E. F. Carritt, *An Introduction to Aesthetics*, London: Hutchinson, 1947, 20–1.

point requires first admitting my initial distinction of two types, a distinction not explicitly made by many who allege the indefinability of these terms. Further, there are no doubt other concepts that lack sufficient or positive conditions (of some specified sort); hence I am not claiming that aesthetic concepts differ from all others in this respect. It should be noticed also that to discuss the relationships between my two sorts of concepts, the two sorts must be identified independently of such relationships. One could not distinguish aesthetic concepts from others by the fact that they lack a certain relationship to those others. I have taken the two types to be adequately indicated by my original examples and by what was said briefly about sensitivity or taste. I have not examined or analysed the distinction further, and since the arguments of this paper take it as given, they cannot be regarded as helping to explain the difference or to say what aesthetic sensitivity consists in.

Nevertheless, if it is, as I believe, an essential feature of aesthetic judgements in general (whether they contain aesthetic terms or not) that their truth is never logically assured by the truth of any number of non-aesthetic judgements, there are certain clear consequences. It will be impossible for a person to verify or infer, by appealing in the sense explained only to non-aesthetic properties, that a thing must of necessity have a certain aesthetic quality.

(ii) In making this negative claim I have not said that aesthetic concepts are governed by no logical conditions at all. Indeed it is apparent on very little reflection that they are.[9] First, certain non-aesthetic qualities seem to be *logically necessary* for some aesthetic qualities. Consider *gaudy* and *garish*. It seems clear that with only pale pastels and no instances of bright (or apparently bright) colours in existence, there could be no examples of gaudy or garish colouring, and it would be dubious whether anyone could have learned, or whether there would be, any such concepts. Similarly, if there were only bright and intense colours, there could be none describable aesthetically as delicate. If all lines and movements were either straight or sharply angular, never being or giving the impression of being curving of flowing, there might be no use for the term 'graceful'. Were such relationships merely contingent, it would be conceivable that we might find occasional exceptions, a graceful straight line or some garish pastels.

Secondly, some non-aesthetic qualities might be appropriately spoken of as *logically presupposed* by certain aesthetic qualities. It seems impossible to say of a dot, a flash, or a uniformly coloured surface either that it is or that it is not deeply moving, either that it has or that it lacks grace, unity, or balance. Roughly, only something with line, stance, or movement, or the appearance of such can be graceful or lack grace, and only something consisting of parts in relation can have or lack unity or balance.

---

[9] In 'Aesthetic Concepts' I had logical relationships in mind throughout in speaking both of 'negative conditions' and of 'characteristically associated features' [Ch. 1, this vol., 5–7].

Thirdly, however, there may be a characteristic association or relationship which, though still not merely contingent, is much less stringent than logical necessity of presupposition. Consider 'sad' as applied to music. Characteristics that typically come to mind are slow tempo, quietness, low pitch, pauses, falling intervals, minor key, and so on. Gaiety and sprightliness connect similarly with speed, rapid sequences of short notes, and so on. Now although some of these connections—that between sadness and minor key, for instance—may not be either obviously conceptual or obviously contingent, others are fairly obviously conceptual. Yet they are no more logically necessary than they are logically suffi-cient: sometimes despite its fast tempo a piece of music has a sad quality, and sometimes despite a certain angularity in a dancer's movements she is never-theless graceful. One can conceive of sad music which is not slow or soft, as one cannot conceive of a graceful line which is simply straight.

Among the features logically associated with any particular term in this looser way, some may be closer than others to being necessary without actu-ally being so; one might find a continuum of cases. The same is true of the same terms used in non-aesthetic contexts: an inclination to move slowly and without bustle seems more essential to sadness in people than a down-turned mouth or drooping shoulders. While its presence is not vital in any one case, its absence may be quite exceptional, whereas a downturned mouth is charac-teristic but less important. At the end of Section V, I said a critic's reasons might be inappropriate or absurd; the reason lies in the logical affinities and oppositions I have just discussed. To say a line is graceful because it is so straight or that a piece of music is cheerful because it is so slow is to say some-thing absurd or logically odd.

In Section VII (i) I denied that aesthetic concepts are governed by sufficient conditions; I have now sketched some ways in which they may be logically related to other concepts. Thus, if a thing has the aesthetic property A, it may be very likely to have, or may even necessarily have, certain non-aesthetic properties $N_1, N_2, N_3 \ldots$, the latter being properties with some conceptual relationship to A. But having the properties $N_1, N_2, N_3 \ldots$ is no guarantee of A; as far as logical connections go, all one can say is that it may well have A.

VIII Some Further Relationships: Contingent

I turn finally to general relationships of a contingent sort between the two sorts of qualities and the possibility, correspondingly, of making various sorts of empirical generalizations. It is important to see what plausible generaliza-tions can and cannot be made for several reasons, not least so as to avoid confusing them with statements of the empirical and logical relationships already discussed in Sections II and VII.

To do this I consider briefly what Beardsley says in discussing empirical generalizations. He does not explicitly discuss the relationship between aesthetic and non-aesthetic qualities, for he makes no such distinction; instead he speaks of relationships between 'regional qualities' (which are 'emergent') and their 'perceptual conditions'. His discussion therefore has a wider range, since some non-aesthetic qualities, like squarish and grinning, are examples of regional qualities, as well as aesthetic qualities like graceful and gaudy. But this does not matter, because my aesthetic qualities are, roughly, a subclass of his regional qualities.

I shall take just one of Beardsley's many examples, the connection between slowness and sadness in music, as a typical illustration of his views. The kind of empirical generalization he offers is expressed in several ways: when things have certain qualities they will tend as a result to have another (dependent or emergent) quality; for example, 'music having such and such features (slow tempo, and so on) . . . tends to be sad'; certain qualities 'tend to make' music sad; these are 'sad-making' qualities, and so on.[10]

Now various interpretations, resulting from the shiftiness of the verb 'tend,' might be put on these remarks. They might mean that slow music *will* be sad provided that other features present (say, a major key) do not bring an incompatible character that overwhelms the effect of the slow tempo. Slow tempo in itself *is* sad-making; the force of 'tends' is simply that the effect of the tempo may be swamped out. This, as I read him, is Beardsley's meaning,[11] and presumably, since he mentions no other, the pattern he would adopt for other examples, like *bright* and *gaudy*. Now it is true that he disavows any truth claim for the particular generalizations he uses as examples;[12] yet he does seem to suppose that many generalizations of this kind might be true and that his own probably are. But these and many similar generalizations seem in fact to be fairly obviously false: slow tempo is just as closely associated with *other* characters, like solemnity, majesty, pensiveness, and serenity, as with sadness. Even if one interprets these tendency statements in other ways that come to mind—for instance, that slow music is *usually* sad, or that it is *always somewhat* sad—they still seem false: much slow music is pensive, majestic, solemn, or serene, not sad, and there must have been thousands of slow compositions with no particular character at all.

There are many empirical generalizations one might make connecting aesthetic and non-aesthetic qualities. But many of those that seem true are not of Beardsley's type and are relatively weak—for example, that slow music is *sometimes* sad and, when it is, is often sad notably because of its tempo. Other statements, like 'sad music is usually slow' may be true too. But others again,

[10] Beardsley *Aesthetics*, 330–1. Cf. also 194 and 198.
[11] ibid. 331.
[12] ibid. 195.

like 'slow tempo tends to make music sad *rather than gay*' or 'slow tempo is the sort of feature that *may* make music sad', seem to me not obviously empirical.

I do not mean to deny that with care we might produce much more powerful generalizations telling in detail that works with various features always or usually have a certain aesthetic quality. All I have argued is that some tempting generalizations that have been proposed are questionable. I suggest that in part they may be offered because various relationships are not clearly differentiated or investigated. It is seen that some intimate connection of a general sort holds between, say, slow tempo and sadness; slowness is, if one wishes, a 'sad-making quality' (but only in the sense that it is the sort of quality that, unlike swiftness, *may* make something sad). The conceptual character of this relationship is overlooked, however, because specific claims that the slow tempo of this or that work is what in fact makes it sad are clearly contingent; and since these specific claims are often true, it is supposed that a fairly strong generalization can be made from them—namely, that slowness is a 'sad-making quality' in the sense that slowness in music 'tends to make it sad'.

IX 'Justification'

Having examined some of the relationships, logical, quasi-logical, and contingent, between the aesthetic and non-aesthetic realms, I return to the question whether it could ever legitimately be argued, solely from statements about the non-aesthetic properties of things, that certain aesthetic judgements must be, or even probably are, true.

I have already suggested in general (Sect. VII) that no statements about non-aesthetic qualities could by themselves logically ensure the truth, though some may logically ensure the falsity, of an aesthetic judgement. In this respect aesthetic judgements are not capable of rational or reasoned support. The question remaining is whether some non-aesthetic statements could by themselves provide, say, a reasonable measure of inductive support for the truth of an aesthetic judgement. Some writers seem to have held that in some such way aesthetic judgements might be adequately and rationally supported, indeed that criticism might in such a way be 'set on a rational basis'.

The procedure would presumably go thus. If someone wished to provide reasons supporting the truth of an aesthetic judgement, or reasons on the basis of which an aesthetic quality might be attributed to something, he would point out that the work has non-aesthetic properties of a kind which always or generally make a work sad or graceful or unified, and that therefore the claim that *this* work is so is a reasonable one. Now although the generalizations I examined in Section VIII seemed either false or too weak to function thus, with more careful research, it might be argued, we could perhaps provide reliable generalizations that would be at once strong and detailed enough. Given the complexity of most aesthetic objects and the fact that small differences are often of great significance, it seems most doubtful. But if we could, then it is at least conceivable that in the future people might with justified assurance attribute aesthetic properties solely by inference from non-aesthetic features. They might also employ such inferences to add confirmation to genuine and independently made aesthetic judgements, and in doing this their judgements might be said to have received a kind of rational support.

But this is of limited interest. In so far as people have sought, by empirical research, to provide rational justification *generally* for aesthetic judgements, claiming that without such justification criticism is unacceptable, the hope is forlorn. The programme of a general 'underpinning' is misconceived. For clearly, at least some of the aesthetic judgements from which the investigator began when he set out to establish his generalizations were necessarily without benefit of such justification, and yet had to be accepted as bona fide data. Without them, no investigation of 'perceptual conditions' could have got under way. This kind of 'justification' of aesthetic judgements by means of generalizations could not therefore be supplied for *all* such judgements.

X Footnote

I stress again that I have dealt only with certain kinds of aesthetic judgements. In considering how they may be supported by reasons, I have also restricted myself to reasons which cite the non-aesthetic properties of things. It is often said that works of art are unique and that each must be judged by its own standards; also that aesthetic judgements cannot be made mechanically or by following rules. These sayings are not unconnected. Moreover, given the diversity of issues they hint at, they can hardly to be rejected. I have not argued that aesthetic judgements (the kind I deal with) cannot be made mechanically, or by rules, or—as I take it this may mean—without aesthetic perception. I have treated this as analytic. But if what I have said about deductive and inductive support is correct, it is also the case for this class of judgements as a whole that their truth cannot be verified, confirmed, or supported 'mechanically' or by appeal to rules. I do not think this should prove surprising; but I have tried to show some of what lies behind it.

4

About Taste

Some traditional discussions of taste and the variability of taste have centred primarily on such questions as fashionable preferences, or personal likes and dislikes. These are of relatively low philosophic interest. Unfortunately they are constantly introduced into discussions about taste in rather different senses. Among the latter two are of fundamental philosophical importance: taste as an ability to discern the aesthetic qualities of things and taste as an ability to recognize aesthetic merit and make judgements of aesthetic worth. With these two questions—but not with those about likes and dislikes—issues concerning the extent and possibility of truth and error, discernment, and failures of discernment arise. It is in this context that traditional disputes over the reality, immutability, or variability of standards of taste may most profitably be discussed.

Once discussions of taste are focused in this way it becomes imperative to consider (1) whether, questions of evaluation aside, the view that things have aesthetic *properties* about which correct and mistaken claims can be made can be defended; and (2) whether it is possible to defend, as beyond question, various general principles of *evaluation*, for example that if something is graceful it has, *pro tanto* and barring special explanation, some aesthetic merit. Though these questions have constantly claimed some attention from aestheticians, they have never received the full and painstaking investigation they deserve. In ethics for instance philosophers have given some attention to matters that parallel the second question; but we still need to probe into why some qualities of things could, and others could not, answer to an interest or appreciation that could conceivably be called aesthetic.

As to the first question: the supposition that there are aesthetic properties of things to which we may be sensitive or blind and about which we can make correct or mistaken claims is often thought to bring with it insuperable difficulties. It supposedly introduces an aesthetic sense or perceptive faculty; it is alleged to lead to circularity—we can establish that people have this sense only by their success in correctly attributing aesthetic properties to objects, and we can establish the correctness of such attributions only by reference to whether they have the sense in question; and it is held to be a difficulty that in general

[From *British Journal of Aesthetics*, 6 (1966).]

we cannot prove, in cases of dispute, that an object really has such and such a property. But to allege such difficulties is to make apparent that we are far from understanding clearly the notion of a property. There are many matters which strike us as more or less objective—ranging from whether something is interesting or funny or moving, to whether it is graceful or balanced, to whether it resembles something else, whether it is magenta, whether it is red, and so on. But it seems as though in all these cases we run equally into abilities to discern which are in varying degrees analogous to the senses and into partially similar and not necessarily harmful circularities. As for the insistence upon proofs: it is not clear that we would know in detail any better how to give proofs, or what would be involved in giving a proof, that something is funny, or that two faces resemble each other, or even that something is red, than we do with aesthetic judgements. In short, the aesthetician's familiar demand for proofs is one we seldom encounter or know fully how to meet even in non-aesthetic matters of a relatively objective sort. The need no doubt is to abandon tendencies to think in black and white of properties and non-properties and to examine the many concepts, aesthetic and non-aesthetic, that range from the more to the less typically objective. But this is to examine, if not abandon, the inadequately investigated notion of a property both inside and outside aesthetics.

The programme that aestheticians must face is thus a large one, the charting of huge areas neglected by other philosophers working within their customary bounds. Indeed, far from its being true that aesthetics is peripheral to philosophy, aestheticians encounter ranges of concepts wider than and inevitably inclusive of those studied by most other branches of philosophy. A multitude of terms and concepts—too varied to fit into a few categories of properties or non-properties, but quite as important as the epistemologist's favourites for our characterization, comprehension, and organization of the world and our experience of it—remain unexplored, and it is largely left to aestheticians to explore them. The question is whether we can persuade ourselves to do the job systematically, for there is no doubt that it will be nasty, tedious, and long.

5

Colours

I

Most things we deal with are coloured. Things also have properties more fundamental than colours: we might still manage successfully if things were, in a chromatic sense, uncoloured, or if we were as completely colour-blind as most other mammals. I want to ask about what is involved in our being able to say that things have colours.

Matters to which the notions of truth and falsity, correctness and error, have application are sometimes spoken of as 'objective'. This is so with attributions of colour, and is one reason why the colours of things are often called 'properties'. The possibility of true and false attribution is certainly necessary to the notion of a property. I do not say it is sufficient: cases have been made for distinguishing colours from, say, shapes, and for withholding the term 'property' from colours. But these questions about a more or less restricted use of the term do not concern me here. Colours may in any event be truly or falsely attributed to things.

It is often said that where true or false attributions are possible (and *a fortiori* with properties), there must be conditions which would establish conclusively that a speaker is right, the statement true, and the thing in fact, say, green: a logically tight decision procedure or possibility of proof. So if I ask what it is for something to be green, I may substitute questions about what is involved in statements like 'X is green' being true. A stricter inquiry (perhaps too strict) would ask what logically guarantees that a thing is green, or the truth of 'X is green'.

I raise these queries about *colour* statements because the conditions, if any, which entail that an object is green are not that it possesses *other* properties, in the way that having three straight sides entails being triangular. What, if anything, entails that a thing is green must be facts of another sort; not facts about its other (non-colour) properties. What then must be true to make the statement that something is green unchallengeable?

For this inquiry I disallow certain answers. To say that a thing is green if it

[From *Proceedings of the Aristotelian Society*, 68 (1967–8).]

looks green to a normal person in normal conditions only postpones questions about what it is for something to look green, what normal vision consists in, and what establishes that someone has it. To say, as some do when replying to sceptics by appealing to paradigm-cases, that a thing is green if it is, or is the same colour as, a standard sample (labelled green, say, on a colour chart) omits consideration of what is involved in its being the *same* colour, and in the sample being in fact green.

What is often behind all this, sometimes explicitly, is a supposed logical guarantee that a thing is green if it is (or is the same colour as) a 'paradigm or teaching sample' where *this* means the sort of thing 'green' was invented to apply to. That is, certain arguments often look back implicitly to a ceremony of original naming, a kind of original agreement on conventions for using and applying colour words. But since any colour sample I am offered certainly is not a, or the, sample for which 'green' was introduced, the question remains, what ensures that it is the same colour as those things for which 'green' *was* introduced. It is not nonsensical to ask what guarantees that the sample now used for teaching, or offered to the sceptic, is in fact green, even if it is a natural substance, say, emerald.

Since it is often referred to implicitly and seldom discussed in detail, it is worth examining this quasi-fictional original introduction of colour language to see whether it does illustrate, by 'as-if' methods, what is involved in present linguistic practice, and throws light on the questions I have raised. We need to know (not assume), and in detail, that (and why) certain sceptical questions may be answered this way. For appeals to paradigms may be successful only if the sample offered can reasonably be shown to meet conditions the sceptic is *not* questioning and which themselves guarantee its colour.

II

I give, then, a skeletal account of how colour terms might have been introduced. I pretend that the language used was English; this merely allows me to simplify the argument. After all, colour vision might have developed late enough in history for English to have been a language then in use.

I depict the beginning of colour language thus. People hitherto used to distinguishing objects, but with black-grey-white or achromatic vision, gradually or suddenly develop colour vision. They find there is a new way in which they are making similar discriminations. They group things as alike and unlike, each person tending to group together the *same* objects as others do. They cannot make these new discriminations except by using their eyes; they can make them at a distance, when there is light, and when heads and eyes are turned in certain ways. Where objects of similar shape, size, and texture were previously indistinguishable by eye, being equally light or dark, they can now distinguish them. Since they already have (in black and white, so, to speak) the terminology of 'looking the same or different', they find it natural to say that these things now look different, though in a new respect. They not only distinguish some objects from others, but also mistake some for others, in similar ways; they still fail to pick out by eye the edge of some overlapping things, but can now tell by sight where the boundaries of others, hitherto indistinguishable, occur; they range things by eye in a continuum of likeness, and so on.

In this account of the introduction of colour language, the new activities must be describable without colour language (though since I have supposed that people already distinguish things as lighter and darker, and as sometimes *looking*, but not really *being*, lighter or darker, they already have important elements of the language of vision. I said that colours were among the less fundamental properties). Consequently, since the account must make clear that they are now dealing with *colour*, other things may need to be added. It must make sense to speak of the spatial boundaries of the new phenomena they see, and these boundaries may be straight, curved, etc. The boundaries often coincide with boundaries discoverable by touch, and by sight and touch combined, so that it becomes natural to speak often of the new phenomena as being on the surface of things. We may suppose also that they assimilate and distinguish just the things we do, grouping emeralds with grass, blood with rubies, etc.

This account may not yet suffice to tie their new awareness down to colours; but I see no obstacle to it being made sufficient. (It might be asked whether, when it has tied the matter down, among properties we *now* know about, to colours, i.e. excluding properties we discern by touch, hearing, or taste, some people might be distinguishing *another* set of visual properties that share the features already mentioned with colours but are of a type unknown to those of us who see colours. But this is a sophisticated version of the query whether your colour vision might differ systematically from mine, and can be handled, with appropriate changes, by what I say later about the latter. It is irrelevant to questions about the colours of *things*. For if Group A's 'non-colour visual experience' exactly corresponds to Group B's colour experience merely contingently, but *continues* to, the things they both learn to call green *are* green;[1] and if Group A's discriminations diverge later from those that Group B make, we can accept those who still judge emeralds, etc, to be unchanged as the group that see colours.)

There are tremendous complexities I must ignore. During a settling down period, initial agreements are systematically upset: people find that things look different as conditions change. But they discover regularities in this, begin to distinguish real from apparent colours, employ certain conditions

---

[1] But see note 2.

(e.g. daylight) as optimal, and so establish rules for distinguishing the colour a thing is from the colour it merely looks. We might imagine this period, from the first partial agreements to the eventual establishment of a complex language and behaviour like ours, telescoped into a short while. The outcome is that, in similar roughly specifiable conditions, everyone makes similar visual distinctions. I call this the *initial* discrimination-agreement, for this is a necessary condition for introducing a language to talk of colours as public phenomena, including words to name colours and to make attributions of colour to things. For things they group as alike, grass, emeralds, etc., they introduce 'green', and so on. I call this whole occasion 'naming time', and the people, 'the original namers'.

The initial similarity in discrimination, though necessary for a language of colour attribution, need not on its own yield such a language. For this the community, including newcomers, must continue to exhibit similar discrimination; and *also*, if forms like '*x* is green' are to operate as they do with us, people must apply the same word at any given time to the same things as those making the *maximum* discrimination on pain otherwise of being wrong. A language of attribution demands this. Where people do not agree, divergences are attributable either to differences of angle, lighting, temporary physical condition (dazzles), etc., and should prove removable by appropriate changes, or to inadequate mastery of language, or, ultimately to some defect, e.g. colour-blindness. The requirement that people must apply the same term to the same objects introduces the possibility of true or false colour attributions; that is, it introduces, as well as notions of colour-vision and vision testing, the notions of things *being* this or that colour, of being mistaken, and of explaining why someone is not just different, but wrong.

I have simplified drastically by picturing people with either full colour vision or totally achromatic vision. (There is, incidentally, no mention of majorities or minorities.) So we should also imagine some groups making fewer distinctions than others. The fully colour-sighted are those exhibiting *the maximum or most detailed discrimination-agreement.*[2] That is, the 'is' of

---

[2] I say that, what people who make maximum discriminations in selected conditions (e.g. daylight) learn to call green *is* green. But it is conceivable that things called the same colour might not be the same. If people had always been red-green colour-blind, it would be correct for them to say that emeralds, rubies, etc. were the same colour; but they are not. But to say this makes reference to the possibility, contrary to fact, that some beings might make an agreed regular visual distinction; such a community might come to exist later. Alternatively, without a new community, it could happen, with discovery of wavelengths, that people should accept *either* that a given colour (that of rubies and emeralds) is produced by wavelengths of two kinds, *or* that there are colour differences they cannot discern, the matter being settled by appeal to science, *or* that scientific and layman notions of colour diverge.

colour attribution, in our language, is linked to *this* group,[3] and they are selected by *performance* in agreeing and disagreeing, not by other (e.g. physiological) tests. Thus, no circularity occurs in saying that colours of things are settled by those with full colour-vision and that this in turn is settled by ability to see the colours of things.

The necessary conditions for introducing a language of colour attribution that I have mentioned are: initial agreement, the requirement that people must apply the same colour words to the same objects, and the adoption of a reference-group to whom the 'is' of attribution is linked. These conditions will not suffice for colour words to refer to *properties*, if, for different reasons, this label is withheld from colours. But for people with an already existing language of the sort I pictured (and all that implies), these conditions may suffice for attributions of colours to be true or false.

I considered the notion of naming time in order to throw light primarily on the conditions that, if met, settle the colours of things; but the notion is often implicitly supposed also to settle certain sceptical questions. Does the account given achieve these purposes? (A similar supposition is often relied on implicitly to exclude the possibility of people's *colour-vision* differing systematically. I comment on this question later. For the present I concentrate on the colours of *things*.) I divide the question into two parts—about naming time and about subsequent times (e.g. the present).

First, it does seem that we can dispose immediately of the suggestion that things are not coloured at all. The sketch of naming time excludes the supposition that colour words were introduced meaninglessly or without a standard and accepted manner of use and application to things (though if it is shown, for some sense of the technical term 'property', that, even when it is *true* that a thing is red, its redness is not a *property* of it, this may appear in the words 'it is not *really* red').

Secondly, could generally agreed judgements at naming time be wrong? Since I pictured naming time as a period when changes are going on (e.g. as people discover the effects of odd lighting), 'errors' in colour judgements *were* possible, and were constantly being corrected. But these were 'errors' the removal of which helped settle standard conditions for attribution and other conventions of the language. So, in a sense, they were not straightforward errors; naming time ends when and because these sorts of errors have been cleared up. The question is whether, if we imagine naming time telescoped into a brief period, the originators of colour language, at the *end* of naming time, could be mistaken about the colours of things, despite total agreement amongst themselves. It might, of course, be urged that naming time never ends, that things are never settled, and that this kind of 'error' could continue

[3] Though this is no accident, it is conceivable that a language of attribution might be linked to some other group. I comment on this in Sect. IV below.

as long as new decisions about how terms shall henceforth be applied are possible. These 'errors' are connected with *provisional* linguistic rules, and ours may be provisional. But it seems not unreasonable to assume that naming time is over: a fairly settled colour language has operated for a very long time, and it is this we can talk about.

At the end of naming time, then, i.e., at the beginning of our present use of colour language, what errors were, and were not, possible? Since we imagined people attributing colours to things at those times and in those conditions (e.g. close at hand, in daylight) when together they were making maximum agreed discriminations, the colours attributed to *many* common things do seem to be beyond question. For there already has been, *ex hypothesi*, the settling down period during which many things *have* been seen in those circumstances by many people. Since those making maximum distinctions with common and widely seen things have eliminated 'errors' in the course of selecting standard conditions, it is safe to say, limiting the claim to these familiar objects, that their colour attributions could not be mistaken. But if these conditions conclusively settle the colours of some things at naming time, what of subsequent times? Barring certain arguments discussed in Section III below, it seems that we can state decisive conditions. If with the same widely seen nearby objects, in daylight, people continue to make maximum (i.e. an equal range of) discriminations, if they all agree now in saying X is green, if they agree in saying that X has not changed colour (they might have continued to watch it), and if previously (at naming time) they (or those, also with maximum discrimination, who taught them) said X was green (records could show this), then X *is* green.[4]

Ordinary errors are, of course, possible at naming time or after, just as now, if a person attributes a colour when he is making less distinctions than others (say, while dazzled), or when conditions are not those in which attributions were originally made (e.g. at dusk, in shadow, or far off). But though erroneous judgements might persist about certain things that had never been seen by people at moments of maximum discrimination or in optimum conditions, this will not be so for many common things, flesh, blood, grass, etc. With such things the possibilities of error are exhausted as the possible explanations and sources of error are exhausted. Equally, the colour of *little-seen* things is settled (in principle, whether or not it is in fact) by whether they would look in daylight to all who are still making maximum discriminations the same colour as grass, say, or emeralds, given they all still agree on the colour of *these*. If the sceptic raises doubts about the common and much seen objects I have mentioned, it remains for him to suggest how the conditions have *not* been met by them. When someone offers a colour patch or a pillar

[4] This condition is stronger than it need be, since it is stated in terms of things that remain the same colour. This can be avoided at the cost of greater complexity.

box as an assured sample of red, he is usually justified, and right, in supposing it would meet the conditions; but it is red if and because it would.

I have argued against the possibility of certain widespread errors with
common objects at naming time, and also indicated the conditions, involving
overlapping agreement which links past to present, that, barring certain speculations yet to be considered, suffice to settle the truth of colour judgements
at subsequent times. That there has been this overlapping agreement at each
stage in the past is something we know. (Chaucer calls lips red, milk white,
grass green. We can regard naming time as any past time to which relevant
records extend.) To debate this is to take on a different sceptic, who questions
memories, records, etc. People now using colour language learned from their
forebears; for this there must have been continuously overlapping agreement
between teachers and learners, in such a way that familiar things we would
now agree are green would have been called green, unless people had *noted* a
change, at any previous time. If initial agreement permitted the establishment
of colour language, continuing agreement permits it to continue in existence.
Unless there are arguments from other sources, the sceptic, who, at the present
time, admits that something looks red to him, admits that anyone else would
agree in daylight that it is red, yet nevertheless questions its colour, seems
legitimately refuted.

III

I now turn to other arguments that might seek to show that present widely
shared agreement by people whose judgements are thus consistently linked
at each stage with widely agreed judgements in the past is not sufficient to
ensure the truth of present colour judgements. For convenience I now
distinguish two sorts of agreement. (1) People agree which things are alike
and unlike in colour, *and* also *what* colours they are: I call this 'name-agreement'. (2) People agree which things are alike and unlike in colour, but not
what their colours are (as if some had systematically mislearned colour
words). I now reserve 'discrimination-agreement' for this. To investigate
whether, despite overlapping agreement over the ages, we could today be
mistaken in our commonest colour judgements, or whether things that we
and our predecessors have agreed in calling the same colour might no longer
be the colour they were, we must consider certain fantastic hypotheses. We
must imagine the colours of all things *systematically* changed (to retain
discrimination-agreement), *and* a systematic reciprocal change in something else (to retain name-agreement also): there must be a *double* reversal.
As one sample of double change (others raise parallel considerations) I shall
discuss changes in the colours of *things* along with reciprocal changes in

people's *colour-vision*. I assume all else, memories, records, etc., remaining unchanged and unchallenged. To approach this, I comment first on hypothetical single reversals where discrimination-agreement remains maximum and constant, but there are systematic name-disagreements, some saying 'red' where others say 'yellow', 'yellow' where others say 'blue', and so on in a total shift of colour judgements.[5]

I realize that the internal coherence of these hypothetical cases may be questioned. I comment on this later. But it is not superficially obvious that everything (rather than just a few things, like litmus or leaves) could not, slowly or instantaneously, piecemeal or all together, change colour; nor that colour-vision, one person's or everyone's, could not change, slowly or suddenly, so that everything looked systematically different. It seems conceivable that with either change we might, however astonished, be able to carry on our lives. For the moment, therefore, I allow myself these suppositions. (A proof of their incoherence would simply disarm the sceptic at an earlier stage.)

1. People find one morning with astonishment that they no longer agree on the colours of things. Some, or many of them declare that normally yellow things look red, green things look orange, and so on systematically; the rest find no change. There is still discrimination-agreement; they agree entirely on differences and similarities among things. (Mr D. M. Taylor recently imagined a similar case:[6] 'Suppose that one morning someone we know, call him Fred, wakes up, looks round him and says, "Good grief, the sky is yellow, the grass is red, pillar boxes are green and lemons blue" '. Taylor goes on 'We shall soon point out to him that this is not so, and Fred will have to change to "The sky looks yellow etc." '. No doubt Taylor is right, and Fred's colour judgements are wrong. But Fred might ask, with reason, what justifies Taylor's confidence, and why he *must* be wrong.)

If this strange event can be coherently imagined, what, if anything, would conclusively settle whether emeralds, etc. were still green, or, as some now say, orange? First, we would surely seek an explanation, probably physiological. If we found systematic changes in the eye or optic nerve, we might say, (1a), that Fred's vision had changed, especially if physiologists found they could reverse and manipulate such changes thereafter. If we found no such changes, we would doubtless suppose some explanation to be discoverable, and, for simplicity, suppose *some* change in Fred. (Taylor, extraordinarily, by saying

---

[5] Since writing this I see that Mr. Bernard Harrison ('On Describing Colours', *Inquiry*, 10, (1967)) argues that, were there systematic colour-transpositions in people's vision, they must be 'on all fours with colour-blindness'. This implies that discrimination-agreement would not remain constant. If true, this might render certain of my arguments unnecessary; if not, my arguments offer a second line of defence against the sceptic.

[6] 'The Incommunicability of Content', *Mind*, 73 (1966).

nothing about such discovered or sought for explanation seems to suppose either that there were no correlatable (e.g. physiological) changes, or that they would be regarded as irrelevant. But if discoverable explanations are thus excluded, why should we attribute the change to Fred's *vision* rather than to brain damage, memory changes, or indeed to anything? We should perhaps just describe the change in Fred and his group as we already have, *viz.*, they say such and such, exhibit surprise, etc.)

2. *Everyone* wakes up agreeing how things now look. But they find themselves, with astonishment, disagreeing systematically with their remembered and recorded past colour judgements about those same things. If this is coherently imaginable (and why not, if (1) is?), I again assume an explanation would be sought. (If there were no correlatable changes, or they were considered irrelevant, there would be no reason, except convenience, to decide, this time, whether something had happened to us or to things.) Moreover, considerations seem conceivable that might incline us to either of the extraordinary explanations (2a) that everyone's *vision*, or (2b) that the *colours of things*, had systematically changed. The wavelengths of reflected light might tally with similar measurements in the past, while systematic changes were found in the eye or optic nerve (plus perhaps hosts of less recondite facts, e.g. insects that visit only blue flowers continuing to visit the same flowers, etc., throughout the animal world). Alternatively, systematic alterations might be found in measurements of reflected light, but no physiological changes in us (and insects 'bewildered', seeking other flowers, etc.). But if conceivable physical, physiological, or zoological facts could make us consider (2a) and (2b), should we not reconsider (1)? Could not considerations arise there to lead us to explanation (1b): that everything had changed colour while, simultaneously, an opposite systematic change had occurred in some or many people's vision? If so, still postponing difficulties that might be alleged, why not sketch the following situation?

3. Everyone wakes up apparently as usual, agreeing on the colours of things; *and* their present judgements of things accord fully with past judgements, their own and others. If (1b) is not incoherent, might not our present situation, in (3), be the result, not of (3a), that the colours of things we *say* are unchanged *and* our vision have both remained unchanged, but of (3b), that the colours of things and everyone's vision have at some time *both* changed reciprocally and simultaneously. If so, even with complete agreement from past to present and no change apparent to the layman, the sceptic might have a case, whether or not it is what he thought; if not, it will have been shown that (and why) these speculations call for no modification of the principles offered in Section II as sufficient for setting the colours of things. I turn therefore, though sketchily because of space, to the problematic aspect of these suppositions.

Questions about Science

(i) Does a hypothetical *double* change, in wavelengths and physiology, create special difficulties? I see no reason to suppose it more absurd or incoherent than the single changes considered separately (though no doubt there would be difficulties about accepting the independence of the two changes). So I turn to the single changes. (ii) Scientists would say, I believe, that the supposed systematic change of measurable light wavelengths would, given existing knowledge and theories of far-reaching scope, imply several independent changes of vast significance. And, as a scientific colleague put it, human beings would freeze or burn instantly. Not being competent to comment on this I turn to the main point. (iii) If somehow we did survive, apparently as before, but with all things transmitting light of systematically changed wavelengths, the question arises whether, with so many scientific findings changed and so many connected theories modified or abandoned, there would be an internal incoherence in *relying on* wavelength as an indication of colours any longer. But since the questions I mainly want to raise are linguistic, I note, but do not pursue, this possible incoherence with regard to scientific theory. Perhaps there is a way round it, or need be no real incoherence (as seems the case with the imagined *physiological* changes).

Questions about language

The crucial question is whether, even if the double scientific change *could* occur without incoherence, a change of *colours* and *vision* would have occurred. How would we describe what had happened, and would our descriptions constitute departures from our present language? There are various views about language to consider. For each there is a different answer to the sceptic we are considering. (A) It might be said that a *decision* would be required: either to adopt the rule that wavelengths and physiology, whatever happens, are irrelevant; or to say that they are relevant, and that overall agreement, past and present, does not guarantee the colours of things. (Some might say that what we would decide is yet unknown; others that the first decision would be the more natural and less radical departure from the original and present meaning of colour statements. This seems to me not *obviously* so, for, I have stressed, it seems conceivable that scientific considerations, animal behaviour, etc., might together carry much weight. But speculation on these alternatives is otiose, since, on the present assumption, scientific changes of this unsettling magnitude are not envisaged or legislated for, even implicitly, in our present linguistic rules or practice, and whatever we did would constitute a not-yet-taken decision about future rules and meaning.) If this is so, it might be held either (A1) that *until* we adopt another rule to fit (scientific) circumstances that have not yet arisen, overall agreement, in present usage, settles colours and could not be mistaken, or (A2) that, because our present language does not pronounce on the scientific change possibility, on *present* usage, overall agreement alone does not settle colours; but, equally, it does not allow the sceptic to say we could be mistaken or that things could be some other colour. In this case, though he can say agreement is consistent with colours being undetermined, he can claim that they *are* undetermined only by alleging that a double change *has* occurred. (B) Despite novel scientific circumstances, it might be said, no *decision* about language would be required, but only an explicit affirming of what is already implicit; and it is already an implicit rule of our colour language to disallow the relevance of scientific considerations.[7] If so, a double change would be irrelevant to colour judgements and, unless there are arguments from other sources, the colours of things cannot be other than we agree them to be. (C) It might be held that, since it has long been our practice to accept scientific facts as relevant when they come to light, the double scientific changes would indicate, in our *existing* language, that colours and vision had changed. The language already incorporates reference of wavelengths; *not* to allow scientific considerations to prevail would be a decision *away* from the spirit of existing practice. If (C) is true, overall agreement past and present would not suffice to make judgements true, for instance, if the scientific double change occurred. If no such change has occurred, our *agreed* judgements would be *in fact*, not necessarily, true. (C) is, therefore, the only assumption, of those considered, on which the sceptic might maintain that, with overall agreement as now, emeralds could conceivably be other than green. That is, we might interpret his point as being about the logic of colour language: that overall agreement about colours is compatible with error. But if we take his 'Perhaps rubies are green' as a factual suggestion about the present, he must suppose that a double scientific change has already occurred, undetected. This we can reject, at least about the recent (scientifically sophisticated) past, and have no reason to believe about earlier times.

I have argued that, if full overlapping agreement is not sufficient to guarantee the truth of colour judgements of common objects, some form of double (scientific) change must be a coherent possibility. Moreover, since the question is about our present, not some future or different colour language, something like (A2) or (C) would have to be the correct interpretation of the rules, explicit or implicit, of our language. The sceptic has not attempted to establish (nor I to refute) these dubious views. Indeed, I am not sure what

---

[7] Cf. here Grice's remark, made in another context, 'I ignore the possibility that the real colour might be made to depend on the wave-length of the light transmitted, which would involve depriving colour of its status as a purely sensibly determinable property', in R. J. Butler (ed.), *Analytical Philosophy*, Oxford: Blackwell, 149.

would conclusively establish which view about language (A, B, or C) is correct (though I am inclined to opt for A1 and reject B). Perhaps what we think of the current rules is shown only by how we choose to deal with the sceptic. Meanwhile, if my account in Section II is acceptable, it seems reasonable, until it is shown that a double scientific change is coherent *and* that (A2) or (C) is true, to accept overall agreement as sufficient.[8]

It remains to mention the counterpart to the view I attributed to Taylor earlier: that with *nothing* else changed (e.g., no scientific changes), colours and vision might both have changed. This spares us asking what rules are implicit in our usage for dealing with hypothetical changes. But now, if agreement settled colours originally, overall agreement between us and our predecessors settles them now, since nothing else, *ex hypothesi*, is envisaged as relevant. There might perhaps have been a rule or convention, with full agreement and nothing else changed, to say that colours and vision both changed (say, every midnight); but besides the questions it would raise about the meanings then of 'change', 'different' and 'same', that has never been a rule of our language.

The main purpose of these outlandish speculations has been to show why and in what circumstances common colour judgements about things cannot be questioned. I return now briefly to the topic of *vision*. Is it absurd or self-contradictory to suggest that some people's vision might be systematically different from others'? Again, I set out several answers rather than one; the conflicting answers often given may have resulted from different tacit assumptions.

As in (1), someone tomorrow makes systematically different colour judgements. As in (1*a*), physiological examination reveals that his eyes have changed, and differ from those of others examined whose reports have not changed. We then find that we can reverse people's reports by bringing about these physiological changes clinically; and that *other* people, whose reports have *not* recently changed, may have either physiological condition. Does this evidence of two systematically differing physiological groups open the possibility that, unknown, vision differed systematically all along? Did even naming time hide a systematic difference? Assuming systematic physiological change or difference to be less open to charges of theoretical incoherence than wavelength changes, the answer still rests on the nature of our present language. If (A) is true, that these discoveries require a *decision* whether to allow physiology to bear on what one's vision is like (the linguistic change appearing when we come to use 'they see differently' where now we say 'they see alike'), then, if (A1) is accepted, our vision now, before any decision, is and must be alike; if (A2) is accepted, our vision is alike, unless there are unknown systematic physiological differences, in which case the question is at present undetermined. If

[8] I cannot comment here on the sceptical supposition that gradual and imperceptible systematic changes in colours (or vision) might have occurred.

(B) is accepted, our vision must again be alike; if (C), your vision might, even now, differ from mine unknown to us, though this would be potentially discoverable. Again, I am inclined to accept (A1) and reject (B); but (A2) and (C) are not *obviously* non-starters. My main point is that even the attempt to make the matter empirical nevertheless raises linguistic questions.

I said earlier that since Taylor, in discussing Fred, apparently supposed no physiological or other change, there was no reason to attribute a change in *vision* to him. But even if there were, Taylor's argument for the possibility of differences between us *now* is invalid. He argues that if the change occurred in Fred, we should know that Fred's vision differed from ours before or after the change, but not which. He concludes that now, before any change, Fred's vision might conceivably differ from ours: 'the proposition that everyone's colour experience is the same is falsifiable and hence not a necessary truth'. But, if the change occurred, we could choose *arbitrarily* to say his vision was like ours before and unlike after, or *vice versa*, since, *ex hypothesi*, there is no appeal to physiological or other matters. If we said that before the change his vision was *unlike* ours, we would be adopting a *convention*. It does not follow therefore that now, no change having occurred and without adopting this convention, it is possible that Fred's vision and mine may differ, unknowably. To suggest that, because Fred might wake up changed tomorrow and we might attribute the change to his vision, it is equally possible that his vision is now either like mine, or different, implies that nothing now determines which, and that we are free to choose now to say that his vision differs from mine, i.e., to adopt this convention even before a change occurs. But this would be to adopt a rule which we do *not* have in our present language. The fact that a change might occur, therefore, does not reveal a *contingent* possibility that we are different now.

IV

Where P may be attributed truly to things, it is often held, no doubt rightly, that there must be some measure of agreement in application, and some principles and procedures which would settle the correctness of attribution. I have suggested the conditions that do this for colours. I consider 'simple' qualities, like colours, because the conditions that settle a thing's colour cannot be short-circuited. Properties like 'square' are entailed by the presence of other ascertainable properties; but 'simple' properties make direct reference to people and their agreement in discrimination, and the language of attribution is tied directly to this. So with the simple qualities of other senses. I chose properties of this kind, I confess, because my eye is ultimately on other sorts of properties or alleged properties important in aesthetics (e.g. graceful) and exemplified also by certain so-called tertiary or Gestalt qualities (e.g. kind-looking). For when we attribute these 'properties' too, the correctness of attribution is not entailed by the object's possessing certain other properties (contrast 'balanced', e.g., with 'symmetrical'). I attempt no discussion of these matters here since, whatever the similarities, the differences between colours and these aesthetic or Gestalt properties are so enormous. But it is to approach that discussion that I add this last section; for, with descriptions in aesthetics, sceptics often deny objectivity by alleging that no decision procedures exist, and by citing the existence of widespread disagreement.

If the conditions I offered ultimately settle the colours of things (and what matters, if these are not fully sufficient, is that something similar but more careful would suffice), then what I might call an 'ultimate proof' (to distinguish it from asking a man *already* tested for colour vision) would consist in mustering facts so as to show, in a given case, that the conditions are met. To see if the conditions for X being green are met, one could assemble people, test them to see who is now making maximum distinctions, see if they group X with emeralds or grass, and whether they say that grass is green and that it looks as green things always have, etc. Of course, I need not ordinarily do all this to be justified in asserting or believing that X, before me now, is green; the point is that, if X did pass these tests, it would be. We raise questions of ultimate proof to meet sceptics, or to explain the foundations of language. But though complex, this 'proof' is *relatively* simple. The questions I raise now are these: if objectivity, i.e., truth and falsity of attribution, require decision principles and a measure of agreement, do they require *simple* and *easily applied* principles and a *wide* or *easily achieved* agreement? In my remaining comments I indicate how straightforward things are, contingently, with colours, and how much more awkward they could be.

First, many things never change colour. We could imagine them doing so; but I ignore this as irrelevant to my purpose. Secondly, most people have full colour vision and there are fairly few types of colour-blindness. Moreover, the colour-blind remain so; the condition is incurable. It is easy to imagine things otherwise. People with full colour vision might be a minority. The majority might be wholly colour-blind, or partially so in more ways than now. Colour-blindness in a person might fluctuate, regularly (say, after food) or irregularly (by diet or 'for unknown reasons'). A person's *type* of defectiveness might vary thus. The fully colour-sighted might not be so at all times. No one might have full colour-vision in all parts of the spectrum. Of course, with too many of these changes, we might have developed no language of colour attribution: 'things might be coloured without our knowing it'. But much change is envisageable; and so long as some *noticed*, if patchy, regularities in making agreed distinctions emerged, colour attribution like ours would be possible. And if the distinctions that some people made some of the time were of practical or other importance, as is so with colours, the likelihood is that our colour

language would appear (the often reliable few being used as guides, camou-
flage experts, etc.), even though the majority might manage poorly to employ
it, and know this. Colour attribution would, as now, be linked to those making
maximum regular discriminations, though to a perhaps shifting minority
with subgroups operating at different parts of the spectrum. However, there
would now be extensive 'disagreement'; and though the decision principles
would be unchanged, providing a proof would be much more complex and
awkward than now. It would be much harder, when challenged, to establish
beyond reasonable doubt that the conditions were met; to establish that X is
green might require much waiting, cross-checking, hearing others' opinions
of how X and other things look, to be sure we had caught ourselves at a
moment of maximum discrimination. Consequently, when alone, I might be
far less justified in pronouncing with confidence than now. To teach and learn
the language would be correspondingly difficult, though perhaps a vital necessity; for some it might be impossible.

    Next, I want to indicate how the accepted language of attribution, and
hence the acknowledged properties of things, might be linked to less than
maximum discrimination, and how a grosser and widely accepted attribution
of properties might exist alongside a finer, élite attribution of properties
under constant sceptical challenge. These situations are more easily illustrated
from taste and smell than from colours, because they can occur only where
finer discrimination has little practical utility and the majority are consequently not forced to recognize their limited capacities. Suppose, for
instances, that a few isolated people in fact regularly made more detailed
discriminations than anyone else, without the sameness of their discriminations being noticed (imagine one fully colour-sighted person in each genera-
tion, and all others variously colour-blind); if, as with taste (but not vision),
this ability had little utility, no one might credit or bother to test their separate claims to discriminate more finely. There could then be the (unrealized)
possibility of a language in which things *generally* agreed to taste alike *really*
(i.e. to the few) taste different; but in the *existing* language, these things might
be said to taste alike, and indeed be accepted (in learning and teaching) as
paradigm-cases of identical flavour. The existing language would be tied to
people with less than maximum discrimination. Again, if the minority regularly making the same finer discriminations (but in unimportant matters)
were large enough, and had noticed and were sure that they did, the majority
might still not credit them with this ability.[9] As before, therefore, the accepted

    [9] I leave many issues undiscussed: whether, if the matter were important enough for the
majority to bother, they could dispel their scepticism about others' abilities by careful testing (I think here of the layman's scepticism about whether experts can really distinguish,
not just claret from burgundy, but one château or vintage from another, and of a similar
scepticism in aesthetic matters); whether, if the majority were interested enough to bother,

language of the majority might be linked to their rough discriminations, finer discriminations not being widely accepted as genuine; but now the minority might operate among themselves with a language of their own, decisions about both people's abilities and the truly attributable properties of things being linked to *their* discrimination, and the language not being generally or widely accepted. The result would be a hierarchy of languages and discrimination, the more precise one being regarded as probably bogus by most people. With this situation sceptical challenges could be more widespread, and proofs that satisfied more difficult to provide.

Finally, one more imaginary change with colours or tastes which seems conceivable and would leave a language of correct and incorrect attribution intact. Everyone, say, until puberty, is partially colour-blind (or able to make only certain taste discriminations), but they make the same discriminations. About this time a change, somewhat like Fred's, regularly occurs to a minority; they say they see the same range of colours, but things look systematically different to them. They agree about this and make as many distinctions among things as before. But now, in addition, some who have changed gain a fuller range of colour-vision, i.e. they are aware of more colours and make more distinctions between things than they did previously. (A similar pattern could be imagined for tastes; we may either ignore physiological matters or assume appropriate changes there.) The resulting situation could be that the colours of things are decided by the post-puberty agreement of those with (changed and) most-detailed discrimination. If the changes were moderately regular, the pre-change period could be a perfectly good time for teaching and learning *some colours*,[10] and we might be glad to see children making the expected limited distinctions (rather than proving *completely* colour-blind), even though we might have to tolerate either teaching them that things are not really the colours they look, or allowing them to say, for the time being, that things we call green are red. Difficulties more insuperable than this are not beyond our wit to cope with.

This example suggests a possibility, while retaining colours or tastes as objective attributions, of seeing a partial analogy to one sort of change and

they themselves could discriminate equally finely; the contingent obstacles often preventing extensive checking into the genuineness of these abilities (wines are consumed in tasting, there may be too little to submit it to great numbers of people—it is more like judging the ephemeral performance of a dancer than the qualities of a painting). It would not be surprising, where only a minority regularly agree on finer discriminations, where checking the genuineness of their agreement is bothersome, and the majority are uninterested, to find widespread uncertainty, scepticism, or accusations of snobbish and spurious superiority. (Note that my concern is with discriminations of properties, i.e., similarities and differences, not with whether minute differences of flavour are liked, preferred, or valued.)

[10] That we could learn and teach colours, without attributing them to things, is implicit in my earlier hypotheses. I do not think it need present difficulties, *vide* Elizabeth H. Wolgast: 'Qualities and Illusions', *Mind*, 71 (1962).

disagreement encountered in aesthetics. The reversal of previous judgements about things grouped as similar exhibits some likeness to the reversals or changes of aesthetic judgements (cf. also 'funny') that come about as people mature (mature judgements of what is P not necessarily coinciding with immature judgements, P having nevertheless been initially learned from examples later rejected or downgraded); though only some people mature. It shows too that 'mature' could be determined partly, as it is here wholly, not by questions of value, but by the making of more detailed agreed distinctions (though I do not suggest that the *sources* of the reversals—here wholly a matter of the senses and, we may suppose, physiological—constitute an analogue for aesthetics).

I have indicated various ways in which imaginable contingent changes could give rise to extensive 'disagreements', difficulties and complexities in stating and applying decision procedures, and, consequently, apparent grounds for scepticism, *even* with matters as objective as colours or tastes. I do not claim these as exact parallels of what happens in aesthetics; they could not be, since I have discussed only simple *sense*-properties. My implicit suggestion has been that, if partial parallels of phenomena that may occur, for other reasons, in aesthetics and elsewhere can occur in this realm without ruling out truth and falsity of attribution, the occurrence of similar phenomena in other realms may not by itself exclude objectivity there. But I have not attempted to argue that here, only to make elbow-room for another discussion.

6

Objectivity and Aesthetics

In this paper I am concerned with aesthetic descriptions. I have in mind assertions and disagreements about whether, for instance, an art work (or where appropriate, a person or thing) is graceful or dainty, moving or plaintive, balanced or lacking in unity. I deliberately ignore, by a partly artificial distinction, questions about evaluation, though many assertions of the sorts I discuss are relevant to whether a work has merits or defects.

Since aesthetic descriptions are of many types, the very general suggestions I make, even if on the right track, will, inevitably, fit some less well than others. But I shall not worry if details in what follows fail to fit this term or that, since I discuss no term in detail. That would require long and piecemeal investigations. But I hope elements of my account fit all of them to some extent. A bold sketch of a large terrain may best reveal the general lie of the land. Indeed, my remarks are intended to apply widely outside aesthetics, to many phenomena sometimes labelled tertiary or Gestalt properties, and much else.

Even within aesthetics the area is larger than my examples suggest. It embraces not only statements employing single terms like 'graceful' or 'moving', but also those lengthier remarks of critics which provide more complex and specific descriptions of the same general sort. I include, moreover, those remarks, metaphorical in character, which we might describe as *apt* rather than *true*, for these often say, only more strikingly, what could be said in less colourful language.[1] The transition from true to apt description is a gradual one. (These many sorts of remarks can be illustrated from many contexts besides art criticism, e.g. from writers on wines.)

The objectivity under consideration is that of these many sorts of remarks. Is it *true*, a *fact*, that some works *are* graceful, others moving or balanced; that someone denying it could be mistaken, blind to their character, that one man's assertion might contradict another's? Are there correct and incorrect aesthetic descriptions? Or, where a description is metaphorical and aptness rather than truth is in question, might the work be such that a remark *really is* apt or fitting?

[From *Proceedings of the Aristotelian Society*, Supplementary Vol. 42 (1968). Presented as the first paper in a symposium at the Joint Session of the Aristotelian Society and Mind Association in 1968; the other symposiast being Michael Tanner.]

[1] For a fuller range of examples, see 'Aesthetic Concepts' [Ch. 1, this vol.]

I prefer these ways of putting the question of objectivity to certain others. Sometimes, for instance, it is asked whether the terms used connote 'properties' or 'objective characteristics' that are 'in', 'inherent in', or 'intrinsic to' the object; sometimes it is said that we *mean* to attribute an objective characteristic and it is asked whether there *could be* such characteristics. One reason often given for answering these questions negatively and denying that there are aesthetic properties (in addition to genuine, i.e. physical, properties) is that they would saddle us with intuitionism and a special quasi-sense as an 'extra source of knowledge'.[2] But it is less because of these disputes for and against intuitionism (surely by now has-beens) than for other reasons that I initially avoid stating the objectivity issue in these *property* and *inherence* locutions. First (a minor point), while we might replace the question 'Is she graceful?' by talk of properties, we might feel less happy, with metaphorical remarks, saying that a work has the *property* of gemlike fire or marmoreal hardness (though we might say it has properties that make these descriptions apt). Secondly, the philosophical uses of 'property', 'inherence', etc. are varied and often obscure. Sometimes, for instance, colours and tastes are held not to be 'properties in' objects as sizes or shapes are. Doubtless there are interesting differences to support this use of terminology—say, that colours and tastes are organism-related in ways that bona-fide properties are not. But I ignore this since, if such differences are admitted, they are not germane to the typical disputes in aesthetics. Often the boundaries are drawn elsewhere, presumably because of *other* alleged differences. Many philosophers, when discussing aesthetics (or ethics), speak of colours as properties, while denying that there are aesthetic properties with anything like the same status; their opponents would be content to establish that aesthetic 'properties' approached whatever degree of objectivity colours have.

The dispute therefore resolves itself into the questions I have mentioned, whether things can *be*, say, graceful, given that things *can* be, say, red. For if so, people making aesthetic remarks can be right or mistaken, and the remarks themselves, like remarks about colour, true or false. It is objectivity in this respect that the sceptic in aesthetics often denies (though he may think he is denying an aesthetic *sense*, or *intuition*, and that this is something additional). What is required first, therefore, as I see it, is an understanding of what is involved in a thing *being*, for instance, red,[3] since it is apparently being claimed that, with aesthetic terms, matters are in some vital respect *not like that*. We need to examine, in a general way, the characteristic features of aesthetic terms, comparing them constantly with colour words to bring out

[2] See, e.g. Margolis, 'Sibley on Aesthetic Perception', *Journal of Aesthetics and Art Criticism*, 25 (1966–7), 155 ff., and, for a similar view in ethics, J. Harrison, 'Moral Scepticism', *Proceedings of the Aristotelian Society*, Supplementary Vol. 41 (1967), 201–9.
[3] See 'Colours', [Ch. 5, this vol.] Sections I, II, and IV.

similarities and differences. This is what, very sketchily, I attempt. For if people deny an objectivity, a possibility of truth and error, to aesthetic descriptions which they allow to colour judgements, it is worth trying to see whether the differences warrant drawing such a sharp and crucial line. (If more is meant, by allowing that colours are properties while denying that there are aesthetic properties, than that colour judgements, but not aesthetic descriptions, are capable of truth and error, etc., we might legitimately request more information about the use being made of 'property', and wonder about its relevance to the traditional 'objectivity' dispute I have indicated. Meanwhile, with this said, I shall hereafter, for brevity, allow myself a (perhaps) loose use of the term 'property' to indicate those aspects of objectivity that interest me.)

II

I said that one reason for denying objectivity to aesthetic descriptive remarks has been the supposed need of a special quasi-sense or intuition to explain how we come by the knowledge they express. I prefer to put the matter another way, one which has frequently been implied or stated: that, with objective matters, there must be proofs, decision procedures, ways of establishing truth and falsity. Where proof is impossible, there is no objectivity. And since proof is a way of settling who is right and who wrong, there is the related supposition that, where unresolved disputes are endemic and widespread (as they are said to be in the aesthetic realm), matters are not objective. It is further said that, not only does extensive unresolved dispute indicate that decision procedures (and therefore objectivity) are lacking, but the very possibility of objectivity *requires* (what it is said we lack) a kind of widespread agreement.[4]

No doubt some test or decision procedure is requisite for objectivity. But, first, need it be possible *in fact*, frequently and on a large scale, to employ the tests fully and successfully? Need they be tests that would settle, even in principle, *all* individual cases beyond doubt, or even a *high* rather than *some* proportion of cases? The existence of a procedure might suffice for objectivity even

---

[4] 'General agreement is not a test of truth; but is a necessary condition of the use of objective language . . . . We could not treat roundness as an objective property, we could not talk about things *being* round or say that statements about roundness were objectively true or false unless two conditions were fulfilled (*a*) we must agree about the tests . . . . (*b*) the tests used must be such as to give a *high degree of agreement* in their application *over a wide field*' (P. H. Nowell-Smith, *Ethics*, Harmondsworth: Penguin Books, 1954, 55, my italics).

though (*a*) it was complex and hard to apply, (*b*) it was seldom pursued and applied, and (*c*) it would settle only *some* proportion of cases conclusively. Then disagreements might conceivably abound, some genuinely irresolvable, many others *in fact* often unresolved; but a realm of objectivity might be made possible by some *limited* (not widespread) actual agreement including some settled and virtually indisputable cases, together with a perhaps elaborate and hard to describe procedure that offers the possibility, by envisageable ways, of attaining wider agreement. Secondly, are we sure that sceptics do not vastly exaggerate the amount of unresolved disagreement about aesthetic descriptions that exists, perhaps by looking too narrowly or being blind to the obvious? (I shall not argue this matter of fact here.)

We need also be sure that those who say there are no proofs, procedures, or tests have not been looking for the wrong kind, appropriate, say, to concepts of other sorts which aesthetic concepts *could* not closely resemble. Indeed, the sceptic whose first move, when there are disputes, is to demand proofs in aesthetics, is likely to accept other matters as objective enough without making any such demand there. Nor is it prima-facie obvious in detail what a conclusive proof, even in some of these other areas, would come to: what would be involved in a *proof* that something is red, say, or that two brothers have a facial resemblance, or that a face is smiling? Still less have sceptics formulated what proofs in aesthetics would have to be like, before hastening to deny their possibility.

III

Suppose we assume, for trial purposes, that aesthetic terms do connote properties; it is obvious at once that these will differ markedly in kind from colours. They will be dependent or emergent in a way colours are not. That is, whereas there is nothing about the way a thing looks that makes it look blue, there are all sorts of visible features that make a thing look, or are responsible for its looking graceful (though their presence does not *entail* what they are responsible for); and any change in them may result in its being no longer graceful. So with the features that make a poem moving or a tune plaintive; and in non-aesthetic matters there is the same sort of situation, for instance, with the features that make a remark funny, are responsible for a facial resemblance or expression, and so on. The inevitable consequence is that unless one is in some degree aware of these responsible features, one will not perceive the resultant quality. Hence, often, the need of perusal, or prolonged attention, of *trying*, if one is to see aesthetic qualities (and resemblances, jokes, and so on). Hence also the kind of talking, pointing, and otherwise directing attention that may help someone to see them. There is no (or very little) counterpart to this with colours; when we look, we 'just see them', or not.

But though this immense dissimilarity separates most aesthetic qualities from colours, there is also a notable similarity. With colours, the ultimate kind of proof or decision procedure, the only kind there *could* be ultimately, consists in a certain kind of appeal to agreement in reaction or discrimination. The ultimate proof that something *is* of a given colour is tied to an overlap of agreement in sorting, distinguishing, and much else which links people present and past; and where different sets of people agree amongst themselves thus (e.g. groups of similarly colour-blind people), it is reference to the set with the most detailed discrimination that we treat as conclusive.

When I say the only ultimate test or proof, I mean that, since colours are simple properties in the sense that no other visible feature makes something the colour it is, one cannot appeal to other features of an object in virtue of possessing which, by some rule of meaning, it can be said to be red or blue, as one can with such properties as triangular, etc. With colours there is no such intermediate appeal; only directly an appeal to agreement. But *if* there are aesthetic properties—the supposition under investigation—they will, despite dissimilarities, be like colours in this respect. For though, unlike colours, they will be dependent on other properties of things, they cannot, since they are not entailed by the properties responsible for them, be ascribed by virtue of the presence of other properties and some rule of meaning. Hence a proof will again make no intermediate appeal to other properties of the thing, but directly to agreement. (This does not deny what I said above, that one may have to attend carefully to the properties responsible for the aesthetic property; but *when* one has, 'either one just sees or one doesn't'—one reason doubtless why aesthetic and other emergent properties have often been likened to 'simple' perceptual properties.) Thus, if the sceptic demands a proof that something is graceful, requiring us to cite truths about its properties from which this follows, we must concede that proofs are impossible; *but so they are with colours*, and many other prima-facie objective matters which he does not challenge. What then do I mean by ultimate proof? People often say that the only ultimate way to find out the colour of something is to look and see, perhaps adding, for caution, that the light must be good and the viewer not colour-blind. But this ignores what lies behind the interdependent notions of colour-blindness, good light, and of *being* a certain colour. All these notions depend, as I have said, upon there being agreement in discrimination of a certain sort. But this agreement is not easy to describe. Not *any* agreement will do; the fact that some of us, here and now, make identical discriminations need not settle the colours of things. We could all be temporarily colour-blind. By ultimate proof I refer to that complex set of conditions which specify those agreements in discrimination which ramify beyond the present moment and which settle that a thing is really red, or blue, *and* that people are not colour-blind. These are not conditions we are ready to state explicitly, or which we deliberately attempt to check on exhaustively to decide what colour a thing is; they are implied in our practice.

With aesthetic terms, *if* they connote properties, there should presumably be, for reasons given, similar possibilities of ultimate proof making reference to agreement. Again, one might say, the only way to find out whether something is graceful (or moving, or funny) is to look and see in suitable conditions. Only this time there is not just the matter of good eyesight and lighting; there is the noticing and attending to the features responsible for aesthetic qualities, already mentioned, and much else (see below). Because of the many things that may be done to focus our attention, or left undone, we may sometimes give up without agreement reached. But again, as with colours, even if after doing various appropriate things, we *do* here and now agree, we could conceivably still be mistaken. It would not be just *any* agreement that would settle cases beyond possibility of doubt and so, as the sceptic demands, *guarantee* a judgement correct. We should expect the conditions that specify *which* agreements in discrimination are significant to comprise a more complex set than those for colours. Without such conditions there would be no ultimate proofs, and, what is the same, no such thing as *being* graceful; for they are conditions a thing must satisfy to *be* graceful (or whatever), conditions that give sense to this language of attention. But if we cannot readily state the conditions implied in our practice even for the objective attribution of colours, our inability to state explicitly the (no doubt more fluid and complex) conditions for a conclusive proof, when challenged in aesthetics, need not, any more than the fact that disagreements are more common, oblige us, of itself and without more cogent arguments, to abandon the supposition that aesthetic descriptions are objective matters.

IV

I want now to look further at the possible sources of disagreement over aesthetic descriptions. The sceptic who emphasizes that disputes in aesthetics are rife and that widespread agreement is necessary for objectivity doubtless starts from an ideal where there is maximum actual agreement, as with colours. But, if there *were* aesthetic properties, they would *not* be like colours. We should, of necessity, have to expect additional sources of disagreement. We could not expect anything like the ideal of maximum agreement, but rather perhaps the minimum consistent with their being properties. And how little is *too* little the sceptic does not specify.

One built-in source of disagreement has been mentioned already: aesthetic properties being emergent, the features responsible for them must be noticed in interrelation. If people are unwilling or unable to attend appropriately, disagreement will result, even though, with attention and help, agreement would often occur. These failures may be of many familiar sorts, akin to missing the face in a puzzle picture, missing colour harmonies because focusing on linear composition, seeing a cornice instead of a staircase, etc.

But there are other sources of disagreement. Even with colours, where little or nothing corresponds to responsible details that have to be noticed, agreement comes about only if the viewer is in such and such a condition (not suffering from jaundice, not recently dazzled, etc.). With colour vision, however, we are, as a contingent fact, reasonably fortunate. We need do little to put ourselves in condition to distinguish colours, beyond such things as avoiding being dazzled. (We are unfortunate, too, in that colour-blindness is incurable.) Consequently, differences in discrimination and resulting disagreements are few. But one can imagine things contingently more bothersome. We might have been fluctuatingly and variously colour-blind, with only part-time full colour vision, say, after meals, or until middle age (rather as ability to hear high frequencies deteriorates with age). No doubt these imagined differences would be attributed to the viewer's *physical* condition, though without our necessarily knowing their physiological causes. But my point is that the *sheer amount* of disagreement in discrimination, unsettleable in the sense that one could not get people to see differently, might be much enlarged without threatening the objectivity of colours. The difference with aesthetic properties would be that a *similar* enlarged possibility of disagreement in discrimination would have a largely different *source*, in mental and experiential, rather than physical, variations in the condition of observers. What these differences in experience and knowledge are we cannot always precisely say (any more than we need know that physiological differences result in colour-blindness), except that many 'emergent properties' clearly depend for their recognition on obviously related knowledge and experience, emotional, linguistic, etc. As jokes and humour depend on all sorts of knowledge of human nature and customs, so does the realization that passages in *Lear* or *Othello* are particularly moving. One *could* not expect this recognition from a child or a person lacking certain broadly specifiable experience and development. It is odd therefore that this relevance of one's mental condition should often be cited as a main reason why they cannot be objective matters.

Some people, I am saying, when they develop certain everyday capacities and acquire a diversity of not uncommon experience and knowledge, exhibit a tendency to make similar discriminations. Others with apparently similar knowledge and experience—as well as those lacking it—simply do not. The persisting tendency to agreement (though it may be approximate, more like a concentrated scatter than convergence on a point) is analogous to that which allows us to form the concept of *colours* as properties, and may similarly make it possible to speak of things *being* graceful, moving, etc. If there *were* properties discriminable only by people in certain mental conditions, and if there were variations in mental endowment, knowledge, and experience, it would be unreasonable *not* to expect a good deal of disagreement in discriminations.

Numerous other factors, only some of which I can mention, help explain and mitigate the alleged seriousness of widespread disagreements. So far I have talked as if throughout the *whole* community a measure of honest and independently attained agreement in discrimination emerges, modified certainly by much actual failure to agree, though not more than might be expected for explicable reasons—lack of interest, cursory or ill-directed attention, inadequate experience or knowledge of the language, etc. I also indicated ways by which disagreements are often removed, by awakening interest, redirecting attention, allowing time and opportunity to acquire knowledge and experience of diverse kinds. As a matter of common experience all these things happen; a critic's remarks may enable us suddenly to see, people gradually come to agree there is more in something than they *could* have seen as children or adolescents. It is not myth or invention that agreement often comes about in these ways. And when our best efforts fail there is no certainty that the next critic's remark or the next year's experience will not bring about the change; so at no point can we say that *everything* has been done. But it would be unduly optimistic to suppose that, because other moves can always be tried, we may not have to rule some people out as apparently incurably insensitive, just as we pronounce some colour-blind. We may know why some of them, insensitive or inexperienced in other matters, do not see what we see. What we do not know is whether, by continuing efforts, we might elicit a large measure of agreement in the *majority* of people, or whether many simply lack the latent capacities. Educators in art appreciation assume the former; history may suggest the latter. Though we need not quickly be pushed by apparent inability to discriminate to this last resort of alleging blind spots, we nevertheless sometimes seem justified in doing so (when, for instance, the aesthetic quality is logically connected with some sense or sensitiveness in other matters which independently we know the person to lack).

Here another imaginary colour-vision example becomes relevant. As things are, the fully colour-sighted are a vast majority. But the facts could be different; they might be a small minority, the rest shading off in various degrees and sorts of colour-blindness towards totally achromatic vision. There would then be patchy areas of agreement, separate groups and subgroups, but one small nucleus regularly, at their best, making more detailed agreed discriminations than any other. The partly colour-blind majority might even find a more extensive agreement among themselves, though a less finely discriminated one; but none of this need cast doubts on the objectivity of colours. This pattern, with a minority 'élite', ill-defined at the edges but fairly constant over generations and marked out by their *performance*, is more like the situation in aesthetic matters. (In some ways the situation is more hopeful than it would be with colours. There, the variations would be physical, and largely beyond our control; here we cannot be sure that further efforts, knowledge, and experience will not bring more people into closer convergence on finer discriminations.) We may therefore regard much existing difference in discrimination as irrelevant. It is not the majority being colour-sighted that permits a property language for colours, but the existence of a nucleus (large *or* small) making regular, detailed, and closely identical distinctions. And as the 'opinions' of the colour-blind can be ignored, so, in aesthetics, we can concentrate on the perceptive 'élite' group, even if it is a minority; for if we are dealing with properties, we shall be no more interested in the 'opinions' and 'disagreements' of people who cannot or can only fitfully recognize them than in those of people who evince no interest at all in aesthetic matters. What concerns us is the state of affairs, including occasional disagreements, *within* the nucleus who largely agree. For it is here—roughly speaking, amongst professional and lay critics through the ages (by virtue of those broad agreement we classify them as critics)—that genuine disagreements without significant parallel in the realm of colours may occur (though, of course, no *sharp* line divides the nucleus from the rest; the fully colour-sighted, too, shade into the mildly colour-defective).

I have indicated briefly some of the sources of aesthetic disagreement. With colours there are not these sources, or the consequent disagreements; but in aesthetics, it would be odd *not* to expect extensive disagreements ranging round a nucleus of approximate consensus. And if this consensus were somewhat limited, spotty, and fragmentary, not virtually unanimous as with colours, the question remains *how much* one need demand before being able to speak of properties. I suggested, moreover, but did not argue, that the history of criticism exhibits in fact, over a long period, a very notable and stable consensus. Given the opportunities for disagreement, one could even imagine there being much less. It is thus far from clear that the existence of unresolved disagreement, often regarded as a conclusive argument against objectivism, is conclusive at all.

V

I mentioned earlier the view that we might think aesthetic terms 'connoted properties', yet be totally mistaken. I now raise what seems to me a related but preferable question—about how we operate, or attempt to operate, with aesthetic terms.

The occurrence of even considerable disagreement need not show that we are employing words, for instance, as mere personal reaction terms, any more than unanimous application of a word to the same objects need show that we are employing it as a property term. If to say that something was 'nice' were simply to indicate that one liked it, everyone could still like—find 'nice'—the very same things. For us to be using a word as a property term, it is required that, to be using it correctly, people *must* (not merely *may*) in certain circumstances apply it to more or less the same cases. Where a person does not apply it as others do, there must be some range of explanations available (the light was poor, he was inattentive, untrained—or, ultimately, lacks even the latent ability). A personal response concept, as I have pretended 'nice' might be, makes no such logical demand. Everyone might, or might not, like strawberries.

Thus two questions are separable: (1) whether we attempt to use a concept as a property concept, making, as part of its logic, these demands for agreement in application and for explanations where agreement is lacking; (2) whether, when we do, we find enough in the nature of things that fits with and permits this attempted use. But this needs a further qualification. If we invented property concepts *ad libitum* and tried to use them, in one sense the facts could not prevent us since we could, when no significant agreement occurred, allege explanations of the usual types, poor conditions, blind spots, total insensitivity in others, etc. But in another sense these concepts do not fit the facts and will not work; not only are the agreements so few, but the explanations are empty. We cannot begin to say how altering conditions or training oneself might help, and nothing we do is seen to get us anywhere. A property concept must be one we can work with if it is to gain and retain currency; and this means some agreement and some non-empty explanations. The questions therefore are (1), whether we use or attempt to use aesthetic concepts with elements of an objective logic, requiring some agreement and explanation of disagreement and (2), whether we have reasonable success in using them thus, actually finding some agreement and some workable explanations of disagreement.

It seems to me that the answer to both questions, however qualified, is affirmative. We do demand a measure of agreement on cases before we allow that someone can use these terms, and we do demand explanations of disagreements. Moreover, we find what we demand: a measure of agreement sufficient for us to continue to use the terms thus, and a range of explanations—I have mentioned only some—that in many cases (we would not expect *all*) are *seen* to work. We often know on evidence we cannot ignore what we and our friends are insensitive to, where we make finer discriminations than they, that we discern things now that we could not see when we were younger; we allow we may be wrong, we try again, and we seek help, often successfully, from critics and friends.

I said we manage with reasonable success to treat aesthetic concepts as objective. But two objections will be made. First, some people, perhaps a majority, do *not* manage to any extent. This I have already admitted. They do not, even with effort, notice similarities and differences they find others agreeing on. They may then abandon further interest; or perhaps attempt to simulate discrimination. They may deny that others do independently find themselves agreeing, and reject the whole thing as snobbish perpetuation of the bogus by means of dishonesty. Those, by contrast, who find themselves agreeing certainly have not attempted any such fake. What impresses *them*, at least in their developing years is that, having themselves noticed the grace of X, or found Y moving, they often find others noticing precisely the same things; they then learn that a string of critics through the ages have done so too. But whereas the colour-blind, even if a majority, could hardly challenge the colour-sighted, here, because of the complexities and disagreements already discussed and a lack of practical urgency,[5] there is elbow room for the sceptical to ignore the significant agreements often lasting over centuries and across cultures, and to cite the disagreements amongst critics (without asking how or why *critics* were chosen)—disagreements which, I have argued, we could hardly expect to be without. This leads to the second objection—about disagreements *within* the nucleus of generally agreeing critics. My argument has been partly hypothetical. I asked what situation we should expect if there were aesthetic properties. The answer, I have suggested, is 'Much like the situation we now have with existing aesthetic concepts'. Some people, even if a minority, *do* manage to use aesthetic terms as objective and with at least as much success as we might expect. If this is *admitted*, these concepts must be reasonably enough accommodated to the way things are, and it is not obvious why we should be dislodged from thinking if we wish—as in our non-theoretical moments we largely do—that we are dealing with objective characteristics. To admit that we use concepts as if objective with reasonable success, and yet suggest that it is *only* a matter of as-if and that there are really no such properties is, I think, to invite a request for illumination of the intended contrast and of its relevance to traditional debates. By contrast, to deny that, at least for some people, the attempt to use aesthetic concepts as if objective works with reasonable success is to disagree about the *facts*—a dispute to be cured only by surveying a wide enough scene in an unblinkered and undoctrinaire-sceptical way. The objection that might be made to this argument is that there *are* enough disagreements, even among the alleged élite, that *cannot* be explained merely by inattention, inexperience, etc., and where adjudication of right and wrong is wholly impossible; and that this suffices to scotch any claim to objectivity. I postpone considering this till Section VIII.

VI

Different objections to the notion of aesthetic properties spring from the view that, since the alleged recognition of them is relative to our physical and

---

[5] See 'Colours', [Ch. 5, this vol.], section IV.

mental condition (they are recognized only by beings of a certain sort in certain states), they cannot really be *properties in* objects. There are perhaps three distinguishable arguments here. (1) We cannot speak of properties when awareness of the alleged properties is relative to some type of organism. This seems irrelevant; colours are in the same position. (2) We cannot speak of properties when awareness of the alleged properties is relative not just to a certain physical condition, but to a certain mental condition, the result of experience, etc. But I see little reason why this, either, should exclude objectivity; it certainly applies to much outside the aesthetic that we regard as objective, recognition of faces as smiling, that sentences have meaning, and so on. Indeed, it would be absurd to require, for a thing to be *really* ϕ, that ϕ must be discernible by beings lacking the obviously relevant knowledge and experience. (3) Perhaps the real objection is that, since people differ and change, the choice of *which* group of people is held to discern the properties of things must be arbitrary. Now the principle we adopt with other matters, e.g. colours, is not arbitrary. The 'is' of attribution is tied, for obvious reasons, to the group (not necessarily a majority) able to agree regularly on the maximum of discriminations. And though the boundaries are not clear-cut, we do this with aesthetic terms too. Some people—I called them the 'nucleus' or 'élite'—tend, at least when they take time and trouble and have age and experience, to agree on many more detailed discriminations, similarities, and differences than others ever do. Just as we do not select the colour-sighted by physiological examination, so we do not select critics by 'ideal spectator' criteria; we select both by performance.

This leads me, however, to further characteristics of aesthetic concepts. Since discrimination often depends on experience, knowledge, and practised attention, the group to which the 'is' of attribution is linked is inevitably not homogeneous. There will be a nucleus, and a large and variable penumbra consisting of groups exhibiting partial and merging areas of agreement corresponding to what we ordinarily call areas of limited sensibility and levels of sophistication. These, of types too numerous to more than mention here, will account for the occurrence of various kinds of lesser disagreements. There is the sophistication that consists in making finer distinctions and employing a more precise vocabulary. Where the many lump certain things together under a common and generic term ('lovely' or 'pretty'), the few may agree in differentiating them more specifically as, say, beautiful, dainty, elegant, graceful, or charming (cf. the division of red into vermilion, crimson, carmine). Then there are hierarchies deriving from wider experience. What one at first thinks the epitome of some quality may be relegated to inferior status as one meets other examples (as if one first met with no bright hues, but only faded colours). Sometimes one *could* not recognize the finer cases until one can discern the more obvious, broader-brush examples. Then disagreements may show as differences less about degree than about related kinds: what we first think moving or tragic we later think merely sentimental or pathetic. Sometimes, with growing awareness of subtleties and nuances of style and language, reversals occur; what originally seemed monotonous (say, Bach) becomes subtly varied, moving, and exciting, while what was powerfully moving (say, Bruckner or Tchaikovsky) becomes naïve or blatant.

Given experience of our own development, we might (if it did not sound condescending) liken these differences between penumbra and nucleus to those between children and adults. Children may laugh heartily at, or be moved strongly by, things we regard as only mildly amusing or moving. But we welcome their reactions; they are on the track that may lead to fuller discrimination, and at least have 'agreed' with us in distinguishing the (for us only mildly) funny or moving from things they and we agree are neither. Indeed, this might be all in the circumstances we could (even logically) expect. So with the arts: within the penumbra, people of variously developed sensitivity tend to converge on a broad target of agreement, without making the more detailed or sophisticated distinctions that tend to mark out a central nucleus.

To which group then is the 'is' of attribution linked? With colours it is the group agreeing on most distinctions. Roughly the same might be said here. This does not mean that we cannot say e.g. 'funny for children', 'exciting for schoolgirls' etc., much as we speak of problems difficult for four-year-olds. Nor that we could not understand the use of 'is' by people who still find moving what we have come to divide into the deeply moving and the merely touching. If everyone was red-green colour-blind till 20, we might teach 'red' to cover our red *and* green; and *we* could recognize that in a community that died before 20 there would be sound justification for their property use of 'is'. But, when pressed, we would say that some things they call red (deeply moving) are *really* green (merely touching). The 'is' of attribution is thus linked to nucleus and penumbra alike, but in particular to the nucleus. Aesthetic concepts, if property-concepts, might be called minimally nucleate in character since the nucleus is small relative to the penumbra, and cannot be sharply divided from it. The notion is not difficult; most concepts share this structure, but less markedly. Even in vision and hearing some people have greater visual or auditory acuity and can distinguish minute differences of colour or pitch; we could, if strict, say the colours and notes they distinguish are different, though for some purposes we follow the ordinary man in saying they are the same. It is an illusion to suppose there is always a crisp 'Yes' or 'No' to questions of colour, or to the question which is the reference-group for the 'is' of colour attribution. A judgement broadly agreed within the penumbra may sometimes be more secure than the more specific judgement of the nucleus or élite, as a judgement that something is red may be more secure than that it is crimson or vermilion. Where there are frequent shifts and divisions of *specific* opinion about a work by critics, but within a widely held but more generic opinion, we may hesitate, or prefer the less discriminating group as the secure reference-group. Whether we accept the detailed agreements of a small nucleus or the broader ones of the penumbra in particular cases (or refuse to prefer either) depends how the minority claim is upheld by related considerations, and sometimes there is not enough to decide. Where we cannot exactly pinpoint a reference-group we correspondingly cannot sharply adjudicate the judgements of nucleus or penumbra as right or wrong, though we can still reject outsiders' judgements (as we can clearly say a face is not scowling, while disputing whether it is smiling, smirking, or leering).

VII

I return now to what earlier I called 'ultimate proofs'. If aesthetic concepts are as I have pictured them, a proof that X is ϕ will consist in a convergence of judgements in this direction. But this may require time—to study the object, to acquire varied knowledge and experience, etc.; time also over generations, so that detailed agreement emerges from the temporary variations we call fashions, fads, etc.

If, with aesthetic concepts, the situation is thus, there are inevitable consequences. In order (not to *be* ϕ, nor even to be *thought* rightly and with good reason to be ϕ, but) to be known beyond all doubt to be ϕ, a thing would need to exist unchanged over a long period and be regularly scrutinized with care by many people. Thus a work produced last week *could* not yet have met the decision procedure conditions, nor, if two or three generations are required for fashions and counter-fashions to neutralize each other, could works produced in, say, the last thirty years. We might insist that a new work *is* ϕ, and be right; but we could not, if challenged, give a conclusive proof. With a work thirty years old we could do only somewhat better, though—as critics often say—it might well look to be emerging as a prime example of ϕ. If any cases are utterly beyond question (if there are any 'paradigms', in one use of that term), they will be, in art, predominantly the older works, whether masterpieces (passages in *Oedipus* or *Lear* that have consistently been found moving, etc.), or minor pieces that have emerged as 'paradigms' of lesser qualities (Herrick or the *Georgics*). Outside art, the 'paradigms' will be natural kinds consistently celebrated for various properties (say, gazelles, deer, horses for grace), for we know they have not changed physically and we have recorded judgements over very long periods. By contrast, since many things we judge aesthetically are quite ephemeral, many disputes inevitably go unsettled; even where there may be widespread agreement (as over a dancer's performance on a particular evening), the judges (who may be right) are without a logically powerful riposte if a sceptic demands proof. (So, too, in a much modified way,

I might be quite sure (and right) in saying a coloured flash is green; but I *could* be wrong, a possibility that diminishes as more people saw it, and one that has long since evaporated with, say, emeralds.)

Are any aesthetic judgments about natural kinds and older art-works *logically* beyond question as is, say, the colour of emeralds (*if* it is)? This *presupposes* an affirmative answer to the question whether anything could really be φ, i.e. whether there is an intelligible, if non-explicit, set of conditions that give sense to the 'is' of attribution and that, if met, would settle certain cases. It is to ask instead whether anything is in fact known conclusively to have met these conditions; nor need there be a sharp line between having met and not having met them. As agreement on a given case, amongst those who make the widest range of detailed agreeing discriminations, collects over a longer period, it approaches more closely to absurdity to question the case. Enough is enough, though no *sharp* line divides what is questionable from what is not. Put otherwise, possibility of error with a case that has elicited long-lasting convergence decreases as possible *explanations* of error become more obviously absurd; e.g. we could not sensibly reject a centuries-spanning consensus about *Oedipus* as being the result of personal bias, enthusiasm for a novel style, or passing fashions or fads. I do not mean that, in *other* cases, there is always some reason for doubt; only that the long-attested cases may virtually exclude the *theoretical sceptic's* doubt as absurd. Many other points might be added. For example, there are certain asymmetries: it is harder to justify denying widely acknowledged qualities than to be right in claiming to discover qualities everyone has so far missed. Again, assurance might be strengthened by taking groups rather than single works as paradigms: it may be absurd to deny that the *group* A, B, C, and D contains paradigms of grace, even though considerations might just conceivably be brought to make us question one of them.

VIII

The forgoing remarks about proof, if correct, indicate that some aesthetic judgements may be characterized as right, wrong, true, false, undeniable, or by similar strong vocabulary. But my remarks about nucleate concepts indicate that this realm may not be rigidly objective; with some judgements (perhaps a sizeable number), we cannot demand or justify a clear 'Yes', 'No', 'True' or 'False'. This is because, even as time goes by, the judgements of the nucleus, who agree largely in some detail on other cases, may be split on certain cases, some agreeing amongst themselves, others agreeing with the less specific or sophisticated judgements of the penumbra. But the fact that there is insufficient reason to endorse one judgement as right against the other (since *ex hypothesi* no recourse to anything else could show this) by no means plunges us into subjectivity. The judgement that the poem is cold does not become a permissible candidate because there is dispute whether it is really moving or only mildly touching. If the proportion of cases in which there is no sharp right and wrong about such judgements as these is large in relation to cases which, whether in fact settled or not, might have a clear answer, this is only an enlargement of a kind of in-principle-undecidable area which already charac-terizes other objective concepts. It does not and could not erase all right—wrong distinctions in the area since these indeterminable cases exist only in relation to the others; only, that is, because the principles that *do* settle cases are not in fact met by *these*, or are half met and half not. Indeed, I can now mention some more extreme situations; when the penumbra agree in saying something *general*, like 'pretty', the nucleus of people whose specific judge-ments agree elsewhere may here form two nuclei, dividing equally over whether, say, 'elegant' or 'dainty' is the right *specific* word. Even more extremely, a few cases may occur where those who usually constitute nucleus and penumbra *together* split fifty–fifty, falling into two camps, even over a very long period. These are the notorious cases (perhaps Liszt or Wagner) where no consensus settles down either way. Here we may offer explanations (e.g. by appeal to types of people, the cool and the emotional, the moral liberal and the moral puritan), understand the differences, and see both sides, or we may find the explanations running dry. In either case we may just leave the differ-ences standing; either judgement is acceptable. Indeed, for some ranges of judgements we prefer terms like 'reasonable', 'admissible', 'understandable', or 'eccentric' to 'right' and 'wrong'. Here the rigid objectivist, fearful or giving too much away, might insist that one party *must* be mistaken; but, equally, we might allow that not all disputes are settleable as between certain alternatives. Whether or not we should insist that they are might be a matter for *decision*, though it might be an empty one ('*Something* must be preventing the other group from seeing its *true* character'). I suggest it would be a mistake to think that, in order to preserve objectivity *in general* in aesthetics, we need take the heroic line. Other objective matters exhibit undecidable areas; this may differ from those only in degree. In any case, at first-order level so to speak, it will still be the *critic's* duty firmly to give his own honest and careful opinion, for only thus can a genuine consensus emerge or fail to.

There is much in this ocean I have not touched: all the surface disagree-ments resulting from temporary fashions, the short-lived culture of the eye which makes wide lapels or long skirts look right one month and wrong the next, enthusiasms or satiations with new or old styles, etc. These are phenom-ena wherein no claims to objectivity might stand, as the sceptic who exploits them well knows. But there seem to me to be ground swells and prevailing currents as well as surface disturbances, and it is to those I have tried to attend.

I am far from thinking I have made a case for aesthetic properties, even in the weak sense that some aesthetic characterizations are true or false, apt or inappropriate, etc. I have simply suggested considerations that need exploring or disposing of before that case, which would refute some forms of scepticism, is abandoned. In giving aesthetic 'properties' a trial run, I have examined no aesthetic terms themselves. I tried a more schematic approach. Starting from certain paradigms of properties (if that is what colours are) and retaining certain similarities, I added differences of kind and degree which would result in concepts less rigid than colours (surely, even among properties, very rigid indeed) and closely akin to existing aesthetic concepts. I then asked why concepts like these should *not* be said to concern objective matters. As I warned at the start, I imagine that the abstract account given will not fit all aesthetic terms equally well. Probably a much weaker case must be made for some (like 'moving' or 'nostalgic') than for others (like 'graceful' or 'balanced'); but all may have some of these features. Nor do I attach importance to using the philosopher's term 'property', which (like 'in' and 'not in') suggests a sharp distinction, a picture of things with properties stuck on them or not. If we can sketch a continuum of cases, with 'properties' merging into 'non-properties', it will matter little whether the jargon of 'properties' is enlarged to include aesthetic properties too, in order to indicate important similarities, or whether the line is drawn to include, say, at most, colours. If I am right that in actual practice we do manage to give aesthetic terms a partial but not unsuccessful run as property terms, we will not need to abandon all claims to objectivity. If, on the other hand, a fuller development of the arguments I have offered for assimilating aesthetic terms to property words can be shown to fail, that too would be something. Moreover, the inquiry could have wider implications since, in ethics as well as aesthetics, some illumination about the notions, *descriptive* and *property*, which so many things are said *not* to be, would be welcome.

7

Particularity, Art, and Evaluation

It has often been thought that aesthetic judgement, assessment, and evaluation differ in some fundamental way from moral and other sorts of judgement, assessment, and evaluation. The long tradition to this effect has been revived in recent years, when a number of philosophers have attempted to describe and account for the difference.

Amongst the differences people have claimed to discern there seems to be, as Strawson says in an article not long ago,[1] 'a feature of aesthetic judgment, repeatedly but obscurely stressed by writers on the subject, which might contain the possibility of a general distinction', and one moreover that is 'a formal, or logical, distinction'. This has been variously described: for instance, that to moral and other assessments, general rules and principles are essential, but to aesthetic assessments irrelevant; that for many things, but not in aesthetic matters, there are general criteria of merit; and hence that, in supporting other assessments, but not aesthetic ones, reasons can be given which mention or employ these criteria. Strawson is half-inclined to scepticism over the matter, but also half-inclined to suppose there may be a genuine distinction to be made. I am somewhat less inclined to be sceptical, and I shall try in a way somewhat different from Strawson's to see what the difference might be if there is one.

As it stands, the claim about aesthetics is of course, as Strawson acknowledges, false. We have such general aesthetic merit-terms as 'handsome', 'elegant', 'graceful', and a host of others which function as criteria. (We use these both to support verdicts about works of art being good or fine, and also to support claims of aesthetic merit in people and natural phenomena where the general judgements of commendation supported by them may employ terms like 'splendid', 'marvellous', 'wonderful', etc. rather than, as often with art, 'good' or 'fine'.) Strawson however attempts a more careful statement. Although we may, he admits, support aesthetic verdicts by appeal to such general considerations, such general words as I have instanced are, he says, 'not non-evaluative'. He agrees with Hampshire that it is meaningless or empty to express moral approval without having reasons of a certain sort, and

[From *Proceedings of the Aristotelian Society*, Supplementary Vol. 48 (1974).]
[1] 'Aesthetic Appraisal', *Oxford Review*, 1966; reprinted in P. F. Strawson, *Freedom and Resentment, and Other Essays*, London: Methuen, 1974.

adds that 'giving the reasons would involve mentioning, in terms *not them-selves evaluative*, generally applicable criteria of excellence in men or rightness in acts' (my italics); but, he says, 'judgment in aesthetic matters is not thus wedded to non-evaluative descriptions of general features of the thing judged'. The situation is rather that if we examine those supporting *descriptive* remarks that we may make, we find them to be not general, but mentions of 'particular features . . . of the object praised and their relations to each other in the object'; so he sets himself to explain 'the putative tautology' that there are 'no general descriptive criteria of excellence in the aesthetic sphere' as, by contrast, there are 'not only in the sphere of moral behaviour but, it seems, in every other sphere in which we make assessments at all'.

Assuming there may be some logical distinction, a contrast of particularity and generality, between aesthetic and other assessment, the writers I have in mind share a central strand of thought in their attempts to explain such a distinction. Most of those who stress the 'non-conceptual character of aesthetic appreciation' link it logically with 'the individuality of the work of art'; that is, they think it is connected with and explained by a certain feature, 'uniqueness', 'particularity', 'individuality', or 'non-repeatability' inherent in the concept of a work of art. Strawson also, whose account is a more sophisticated version of a not dissimilar position, also holds 'there is point in trying to clarify the notion of aesthetic appraisal *via* the notion of the work of art' and says that 'the concepts "work of art" and "aesthetic assessment" are logically coupled and move together, in the sense that it would be self-contradictory to speak of judging something *as a work of art*, but not from the aesthetic point of view'.

The doctrine I wish to question in this paper is the view, adumbrated by these writers, that any peculiarities there may be in aesthetic assessment are connected with logical features of the concept 'work of art'. I want to argue that the nature of aesthetic appraisal is precisely *not* to be clarified via the concept of a work of art, and that those many writers who have supposed this possible have been confusing two different issues. The adumbrated doctrine is, it seems, one that relies on the criterion of identity of a work of art, works of art being types, not particulars. According to this doctrine, with which I do not wish to quarrel, there cannot be two numerically different art-works which have identical properties or features, or at least, not identical qualities and features relevant to their aesthetic appraisal. Consequently, it is supposed, there cannot be, in Miss Macdonald's words, two works which 'though numerically different, may be qualitatively exactly similar'.[2] Miss Macdonald adds that this fact 'follows from the way in which we use the term "work of art" '. From this it is supposed somehow to follow that two different works could not share or exhibit the same qualities or merits, and that general criteria in aesthetics are therefore out of place.

[2] Margaret Macdonald, 'What Are the Distinctive Features of Arguments Used in Criticism of the Arts?', *Proceedings of the Aristotelian Society*, Supplementary Vol. 23 (1949).

I am inclined to think these arguments largely misconceived because they consider aesthetic evaluation only with works of art in mind, which proves to be a red herring. I suggest instead that, even though there may be philosophically interesting features of the concept 'work of art', any such peculiarities as lack of generality and a non-conceptual character which may characterize aesthetic assessment characterize the latter *independently*. They are typically present in aesthetic assessment as such *whatever* is being judged aesthetically, they do not result from the concept of a work of art, and they would remain in aesthetic judgement and assessment even if we did not have, as we conceivably might not, either any art-works or even the concept 'work of art'. To assess something as a work of art but not from the aesthetic point of view may be, as Strawson says, self-contradictory, but to assess something aesthetically but not as a work of art (as indeed Strawson certainly allows) is not.

I shall therefore suggest that if there are significant differences between aesthetic and other sorts of assessment, they result from certain features of aesthetic judgement as such, not from the concept of art. I shall aim partially to describe what these features might be, and how and why they come to be so. (However I shall not maintain that these features, which may characterize aesthetic assessment, are present in all aesthetic judgements, but only that they are present typically or in most cases of aesthetic judgement.)

Strawson's argument for the main issue involves certain claims about which I want to raise some questions. It is clear from his manner of describing the putative difference between aesthetic and other assessments that he thinks it intimately connected with an evaluative character possessed by aesthetic criteria. As I said, he does not claim that there are no general terms used in supporting aesthetic verdicts; but his claim is that all such general terms are evaluative, not descriptive. He says, e.g. 'there are no aesthetic merit-conferring *properties*, with non-evaluative names', there is an 'impossibility of general descriptive criteria of aesthetic excellence', and 'either [the] names of shareable properties are themselves evaluative, or, if not, then in applying them we leave our listeners in the dark as to what evaluations to make of the individual works to which they are applied'. He certainly takes it however that works may 'share these qualities', viz. 'characteristics whose names are not non-evaluative'. I want to question whether this is really the distinction between aesthetic and other sorts of assessment.

It seems to me that on this matter Strawson's view is unclear or false, at least as regards many aesthetic criteria. There seems, for example, no good reason to say that such criteria of merit as 'unified', 'balanced', 'evocative', 'moving', 'expressive', and 'dynamic' are not descriptive, or are somehow intrinsically evaluative rather than descriptive, or are names of qualities which have no non-evaluative names, whatever exactly that means. But to say what I have just said also raises questions as to the clarity of this evaluative-descriptive distinction of which Strawson avails himself throughout. For I find myself beset by a more radical difficulty than this first easy answer may imply. Despite, or perhaps because of, the sheer amount of writing, especially in ethics, in recent years, I find the notion 'evaluative' (and its correlate, 'descriptive') surrounded by murk and ambiguity, and I am not therefore sure how 'evaluative' should be taken in the present context. For example, should terms be called 'evaluative' when they are simply descriptive but happen to name qualities *valued* in a certain sphere? I will therefore attempt a brief and certainly inadequate conspectus of some of the things that might be meant by 'an evaluative term or expression' by sketching broadly some of the distinguishable things people might have in mind in calling a term evaluative (and hence not descriptive, or not simply or solely descriptive).

First, there may be terms the correct application of which to a thing indicates that the thing has some value without it thereby also being asserted that the thing has some particular or specified quality. It will no doubt be 'contextually implied' thereby that the thing has some qualities in virtue of which it is valued or disvalued but no indication is given of what these qualities may be. Perhaps, if we have such a kind of word in English (besides 'good', 'bad', 'mediocre', etc.), 'nice', 'nasty', 'obnoxious', 'valuable', 'effective', ineffectual', and 'worthless' might be examples.

Such terms as I have offered I will call *intrinsically* or *solely evaluative*: that is, with explainable exceptions in special contexts, they will be evaluative (pro or con) whatever the subject-matter they are applied to, and may be applied to any subject to which their application makes sense. The main point for our present purpose is that, though the thing in question merits these predicates, if it does, in virtue of some or other of its properties, applying the terms to it is not attributing any particular property and, when applied, gives little or no indication of what these properties might be: presumably therefore they may be called 'evaluative' but not 'descriptive' by anyone employing this dichotomy. (I shall ignore the much-discussed question whether the evaluative or non-descriptive element is commendatory, expressive, etc., and I shall assume that judgements applying these predicates are genuine judgements that can be true or false.)

Secondly, I turn to what might be regarded as the extreme opposite of such expressions. A term may simply name a property, but a property which, *vis-à-vis* some sort of things, happens to constitute a merit in those things. 'Sharp' names such a property for razors, 'selective' for wireless sets, 'spherical' for tennis balls, and so on. I see no reason in this fact to suppose that such adjectives should be called 'evaluative' or 'not non-evaluative' rather than simply 'descriptive'; it is not a rule of their use that to apply them to anything, even these things, is to indicate some merit in (or to commend or express approval of) that thing. And, indeed, as applied to some things, the term need indicate no merit at all. I shall therefore assume that these terms are descriptive; I shall call them *descriptive merit-terms*, and whatever quality they name (e.g. sharpness in a razor), a *merit-quality* (of razors) to make clear that they are straightforward property terms. In general one does not need to know, with such a term, 'P', though one often will, that the property counts as a merit in something in order to be able to ascertain that the thing may correctly be called 'P'. This, I believe, is the situation with regard to very many merit-terms in all spheres, including many of those in aesthetics, and is true of many terms that might mistakenly be thought to be of some other type.

I come now to a possible third category of terms, over instances of which there might be dispute. These are terms which are supposed to have both a descriptive and an evaluative component: that is, when they are applied to something, not only is a property being attributed to it but an indication is being given that the speaker has a favourable or unfavourable attitude to that property. If there are such terms in the language, it would be a rule of their use that they are so used; they would be both descriptive, as indicating that a thing had a quality, P, and evaluative, in indicating that the speaker values or disvalues the quality P. But they would not therefore have become what I called intrinsically or solely evaluative terms above, since their correct application to things still entails that the thing has the property P. I will therefore call them *evaluation-added* property terms. That we have such terms in the language I shall not seriously question. Examples might be 'tasty' and 'insipid'. Both would seldom be used without, in the one case, a positive evaluative, in the other, a pejorative force. But the former also clearly means, descriptively, 'having a good deal of flavour', and the latter means 'having little flavour'. Other examples might be 'fragrant', 'noisome', 'cacophonous', 'brash', 'rancid', and so on.

Some philosophers seem to have supposed that merit-terms used in connection with conduct are of this evaluation-added sort, words like 'courageous', 'honest', and 'considerate'. And if this is so, I see no reason why they should not have done the same with other merit-terms which apply to broad areas of human affairs in which we make evaluative judgements, for example, 'intelligent', 'perceptive', 'astute', and 'obtuse' with regard to mental endowment. About all these cases I am inclined to disagree. They seem to me all clear examples of descriptive terms which, it happens, are generally held to name properties which constitute merits or defects *vis-à-vis* certain spheres of assessment. In other words I see no better reason for denying that they are descriptive terms than I do in the case of 'sharp' or 'combustible'. One need not know initially that these qualities are held in esteem, though one doubtless usually will, in order to be able to attribute them correctly to things and people. However, for the sake of argument, I shall not deny that it may have come about in the language that some of these terms, correctly applicable only to things with a certain property, P, may have also come to obey a further rule, giving them a second, i.e. evaluation-added, use. If indeed it had become the case, as is sometimes suggested, that these terms have *only* the evaluation-added use, there would presumably be the possibility, if we were fastidious language users, of inventing a merely descriptive term, a name for the property P, and the words instanced above would then be the evaluation-added counterparts of 'P'. But I think no such heroic course is called for, first, because even if these terms do have an evaluation-added use, it seems to me to be secondary and that the terms 'honest', 'courageous', 'intelligent', etc. are available as plain *descriptive* terms, and secondly, because if their main use were evaluation-added, it would presumably always be possible to make clear by the context and appropriate disclaimers that only the descriptive element is intended.

If we now turn to the general aesthetic merit-terms that are widely used, into which of the three categories roughly sketched above, if any, do they fall? It might be held that some at least, the most general ones, 'beautiful', 'ugly', 'lovely', fall into the first, solely evaluative class and, attributing no property merely imply some of a range of properties. And I shall not dispute this here, though I am inclined not to think this is always so myself. Secondly, it seems to me that many of our terms fall fairly clearly into the descriptive category and could be applied by someone who did not value such qualities (though since they are widely valued, it would, as I said, be unlikely that a person using them would not either value these qualities himself or know that they were valued by others in a certain way). Such terms in aesthetics might include 'balanced', 'unified', 'evocative', 'vivid', 'funny', 'witty', 'dynamic', 'moving', and so. These are descriptive, and indicate qualities generally valued in art and aesthetic matters: that is, they are descriptive merit-terms *vis-à-vis* art (and some of them are descriptive merit-terms *vis-à-vis* things other than art too).

But there are many other terms used as criteria in aesthetic assessment, and we therefore have to consider these too. It is about these that it might be claimed that some evaluative element is typically present. Examples are 'elegant', 'graceful', 'handsome', 'pretty', 'ungainly', 'garish', 'hideous', and so on. But clearly, of the categories I have suggested, they seem not to be of the intrinsically or solely evaluative type since they indicate the presence of a particular property. But it does seem possible that people would normally learn to use these words and know how to apply them only by also learning that they have an evaluative component and that speakers use them evaluatively *vis-à-vis* aesthetic matters. I am therefore prepared to admit that they may be in their basic or original use evaluation-added quality words. They seem to me in this respect not unlike 'tasty' or 'brash', and, though evaluative, give a clear enough idea of the quality to be found in things to which they are correctly applied. But even if this is so, I see no reason to suppose that, once we have come to recognize the property, P, which people generally value or admire, we cannot continue to use most of the terms in question, 'graceful', 'handsome', etc., in a neutral and purely descriptive way. This can and, I believe, does happen with the majority of aesthetic merit-terms, with the result that we have purely descriptive uses of many of these terms. That is, it can happen that a person can recognize that something is handsome or graceful, and is willing to call it so, without thereby making any positive evaluation or commendation. Such purely descriptive uses seem to me common in describing the particular aesthetic quality an object or an art-work has (though it is still recognized by those hearing the description that the work has a property which counts as a merit or defect *vis-à-vis* aesthetic evaluation). I therefore see no overriding case for denying that we have a use for many or most aesthetic terms which is not only partially, but is wholly descriptive, and where, as with 'sharp' or 'honest', a quality is named which happens to be one widely recognized as being of value in a certain sphere.

If I have given a remotely acceptable sketch of different kinds of 'evaluative' terms, it seems to me that, even if in both ethics and aesthetics, terms used as criteria of merit are sometimes used in the evaluation-added way, there are many that are also commonly used in a purely descriptive way, to attribute qualities which happen to be, *vis-à-vis* ethics or aesthetics, widely regarded as names of merit-qualities. And if this is so, no sufficient logical difference to distinguish between aesthetic and other realms of appraisal and assessment has yet been delineated. If so, the distinctive feature, an alleged form of 'particularity', present in aesthetic assessment, if there is such, still needs further investigation. So I turn to this now.

Where 'P' is a merit-term, it is generally the case, and perhaps nearly always is in aesthetics, that if x is P (say, graceful), something else is also true of x, this something else being that in virtue of which X is P, or which is responsible for x being P. If a woman is graceful, it is *because of* some properties she has, such that, if these latter were changed in some ways, she could no longer truly be called graceful. But in a superficially similar way, if a man is courageous or honest, it is *because of* some facts about him or properties he has, such that, if these latter had been different in some way, he could not have been truly called courageous. Thus, x's merit *consists* in x's being P (graceful or courageous) and something else, Q, is, and ordinarily must be, *responsible for x's being* P, or having that merit. I shall call these respectively *merit-constituting* properties and *merit-responsible* properties. But if we ask about the nature of merit-responsible properties and the relationship indicated by the words 'because of' or 'responsible for' we often find, I believe (I hesitate to say always), significant differences between aesthetic instances and others. Perhaps it is in this area, rather than in a specially evaluative character in aesthetic criteria, that differences should be sought.

Now the stress that writers on aesthetics place upon particularity seems to be a stress upon the alleged fact that that because of which 'P' is applicable to x is x's possession of some particular feature Q which it and *only it* can have. Such 'features', 'respects', or 'parts' are not to be confused, according to

Strawson, with properties or qualities, which are shareable and hence general. Being individual they are not shareable, except in such ways as being for instance capable of being *incorporated in*, as a part of, another art-work. But it is here that there seems an unclarity.

A part of a work, it is true, is an individual, incapable of being shared, capable at best of being incorporated in another work. Parts are individual elements, not general features. But a part of a work has some characteristics or qualities, and these, being general and shareable, might be found also in, and so characterize, a part of another work, as for instance there are many parts with common qualities shared by Goya's *Maja Vestida* and *Maja Desnuda*. Indeed, if a part or feature of one work were identical with a part or feature of another work, being, say, of exactly the same colour, shapes, and arrangement, it would be because the parts or features shared identical qualities. This requires us to make a different distinction, not that between individual parts and properties, but between different types of properties and descriptions, namely, between particular properties and descriptions on the one hand and general or non-particular properties and descriptions on the other. And since there is clearly a possible ambiguity here about the word 'general', I shall use, instead of the terms 'particular' and 'general', the terms 'determinate' and 'determinable' in the sense in which, with respect to shape, 'square' is determinate and 'triangular' determinable. For whereas 'general' and 'particular' may be used to mean shareable and non-shareable respectively, in which case all properties, including determinate ones, are general, they may also be used to mean respectively 'determinable' and 'determinate', in which case only some properties would be general, though all are shareable. With this distinction, it may be said that, even if a part or feature of one work cannot be shared by another work, one work might have a part or feature qualitatively indistinguishable in all respects from part of another, both parts sharing the same determinate, not merely the same determinable properties.

I can now say what I want to, though what follows applies most directly to visual objects; slightly different but partially parallel things must be said about literature and music. When we apply a merit term, 'P', to a thing, *x*, we do so (as Strawson says) on account of some feature or part of *x*, and such parts or features are individuals and may be, as he says, unshareable. Nevertheless we do, of course, apply 'P' to *x* because of the properties of the parts or features, and these properties, even if determinate, could be shared by parts or features of other works.

We may now be able to describe what I think may be the situation with much if not all aesthetic assessment. First it seems that, typically, when 'P', an *aesthetic* merit-predicate or evaluation-added predicate applies to a thing, *x*, it is normally because *x* or a part or feature of *x* has some *determinate* property (or complex of properties); and it is because of the fact that *x* or a part of *x* has this determinate character, not some merely *determinable* character, that *x* is P and therefore valued. More accurately, a thing is P (and valued for being so) in virtue of some *determinate* property, Q, because of which it possesses the (determinable) merit-property, P. A thing is graceful in virtue of being curved in exactly the way it is, not just in virtue of being curved. A slightly different curve might not be graceful, and so on. There is, it seems typically, no *determinable* description, 'Q', such that, if the description applies to the thing or part of it, the thing can be said to be P, even though having the *determinate* quality Q_1 is the reason for, or responsible for its being P. This may be where and how 'particularity' comes in. A line is not graceful because it is curved, but because of its particular curve, etc. Indeed it is a commonplace in aesthetics that the slightest change, of a word in a poem, a colour or line in a painting, or a note in a musical composition may give an entirely different aesthetic character to the whole or part. To say that 'general', as opposed to 'particular', explanation of the applicability of merit-terms is not possible may therefore often be to say that mention of merely determinable characteristics is no good. In many other spheres, especially those, like morality, often contrasted with the aesthetic, such a situation does not perhaps ordinarily obtain.

If this account is in the main correct, if in the aesthetic sphere the possession by x of determinable characteristics is not what is responsible for x being P (though something is), *it follows at once* that a thing cannot be judged to be P, or to have merit, by 'general descriptive criteria' if this means criteria mentioning determinable properties which are responsible for merit-qualities. To be assured that a thing, y, has P, one has to be assured that it is *exactly* like x in respects relevant to P, and no criterion of the form 'If a thing has the *determinable*, Q, it will be P' can be used. Yet if, on the other hand, 'general descriptive criteria' must mean criteria mentioning *determinate* qualities that are responsible for merit-qualities, we are at a loss how to proceed. With respect to colours and shapes for instance, the language contains such a (possibility ineradicable) paucity of words naming determinate properties; we might be able, uncharacteristically, to give a fully determinate description, say, of a Mondrian (two vertical black bars on a white ground, etc.) but we presumably could not for a Turner or a Pollock. And when we come to poems or music it is hard to see what a description of their determinate properties would be at all. Indeed the notion of a fully determinate description of a poem or a piece of music is a somewhat dubious one, amounting perhaps as Strawson says to no more than saying 'It goes like this'—and then reproducing 'or quoting or playing it', which, as he says, is not a description. But there is not after all much difference here with lines and colours; for a graceful line, we might equally be reduced to saying 'it goes like this', and drawing it. So perhaps for present purposes we could allow as a determinate description of a line of poetry, anything which tied it down exactly; e.g. 'it contains the words "Of", "Man's", "first", "disobedience", in that order', etc.

It is here, perhaps, that considerations about particularity, in the sense of *determinateness* (which is what, by many of their remarks, writers on this topic seem obscurely to have in mind) will take us. It is this apparent fact, namely, that a thing which is P (say, graceful) because of a determinate property Q_1, might fail to be P if it had instead a different determinate property Q_2, even where Q_1 and Q_2 are determinates of the same determinable (say, curved), which, I believe, is part of what aestheticians may have sought to express when they have said, e.g. that each thing must be judged by its own standards, that they cannot be judged by general criteria, that there are no rules for judging aesthetic excellence, etc. And this, if true, is about the relation between merit-terms or criteria and the sort of properties in virtue of which they are applied, and would presumably be so whether the correct account of aesthetic merit-terms, like 'P', is that they are descriptive merit-terms, or that they are evaluation-added ones. (I want to suggest only that this is a typical, not an invariable feature of the relation between merit-responsible properties and merit-constituting properties in aesthetics. There may occasionally be cases of merit-responsible properties which are not determinate, in which case x is P simply because it has the determinable property Q. A possible example might be symmetrical (Q), which I take to be determinable, and in virtue of which a thing must be balanced (P). But if so, these are exceptional or peripheral cases, as is shown by the fact that a building or a picture might be balanced without being symmetrical, symmetricality being the limiting case into which balance shades off. We might call such terms as 'symmetrical', if there are a few such, terms for *determinable merit-responsible qualities*.) But, generally and typically, the qualities responsible for aesthetic merit-qualities are determinate. What of course may be the case is that, for instance, the applicability of the term P (graceful) may entail that the thing x has some determinable character (curving); but it does not entail that it has this or that determinate curve. Whether the determinate curve it has is one that makes it graceful is an open question to be decided by inspection.

It should be noticed that a general consequence of the foregoing would be that, if it were known that a thing, x, had a determinate characteristic, Q, and that Q was responsible for x having the aesthetic merit P, and if—as would be rare indeed—we had a name or description of the *determinate* characteristic Q, the general criterion, 'Any thing which has the *determinate* (merit-responsible) character Q will have the merit P' *would* be available for use. But, given the resources of language and the almost total absence of determinate descriptions, such a criterion would rarely, if ever, be achieved, and, even if it were, it would be of little value since it would be usable only with other things, y and z, which had precisely the same determinate characteristic, Q. For instance, if one knew that the particular curve of the glass of a goblet gave it a graceful outline, one could safely say of identically shaped goblets, but only of those (whether of glass or silver), without inspection, that they would be graceful too. (It is to be noted that this principle, that even a slight difference in the merit-responsible qualities or features of an object may result in a very different aesthetic quality, is in no way tied to the notion of art-works. It applies to natural objects like trees or face-profiles and so on. The fact therefore that, with art-works, the criterion of identity requires us to count two identical lines of poetry as one line (tokens of one type) has nothing to do with the matter of the absence of and virtual impossibility of stating determinate descriptive criteria of merit.)

I said that this may be where the question of particularity in aesthetics will take us in describing the typical character of aesthetic assessment. But there may be more that is characteristic of the aesthetic, and perhaps of equal importance, to describe. The all but abortive attempt to find general i.e. determinable merit-responsible qualities (as symmetrical was for balance) may bring us face to face with something equally fundamental about the conceptual character of aesthetic assessment. This is that the kind of responsibility relation that connects even determinate properties with the merit-predicate for whose correct application they are responsible is essentially non-conceptual and therefore different from the connection in many other spheres of assessment.

For instance, in many spheres, including ethics, there is often a connection of meaning perhaps approaching an entailment between some description of those features or properties (Q, R, etc.) responsible for the merit-term 'P' being applicable and the merit-term 'P' itself. This is why one can use the determinable descriptions 'Q', 'R', etc. to move with an assurance guaranteed conceptually from those descriptions to application of merit-terms and assertions of merit. Anyone who *understands the language involved* can see the relevance of the sort of description that appears in the citation, 'he held several men at bay despite realizing the great danger to himself', etc. to 'courageous', or of 'he always returns lost items, not his own, to their owner', etc. to 'honest', and will understand the connection. To fail to would be a failure of linguistic understanding. This may be typically the situation in ethics. But there are no or few such connections of meaning between descriptions, even wholly determinate ones (on the rare occasions they may be possible) of those properties responsible for the applicability of an *aesthetic* merit-term and that term itself. No such conceptual connection holds for instance between a description, even if determinate, given say in co-ordinates, of a particular curve and such a term as 'graceful', or between being the determinate British Standard Colour BSC 8-090 (Columbine) and being delicate, let alone between *determinable* descriptions, say, of poetry or music ('it is strophic, monosyllabic, deals with unrequited love', etc.) and such terms as 'moving' or 'elegant'. Indeed, although, as I said, the notion of a fully determinate description of a poem, and perhaps of a piece of music is a dubious one, if we attempted to describe determinately a line of poetry by citing the words that occur in it and their order, there would be no conceptual connection between the fact that the line went *like that* and its being, say, moving. Thus it seems to be that while in the aesthetic case, typically, a thing with such and such a determinate responsible property or character is, by having it, an instance of what is rightly described as 'graceful', 'moving', or 'elegant', in the moral case the *description* of the responsible property is a description of something which, *because it fits the description*, constitutes an instance of, say, courageousness. In the aesthetic case it is because of certain particular properties (Q) of x that x is P; in the moral case it is because a certain *description* of certain facts (Q) about X is appropriate that it follows (barring disclaimers in special contexts) that X is P. The one true application of 'P' is simply dependent on the fact that x is Q, the other on the fact that x is describable as 'Q' and upon the relation of the descriptions 'Q' to 'P'. This may be why it is said we have to read the poem, hear the music, or see the picture (not merely have it described in non-merit and even determinate descriptive terms if that were possible), and then *judge* or *decide* whether an aesthetic merit-term applies to it or not, whereas we can often apply moral merit-terms on the basis of a description containing no moral merit-terms. This, then, may be a main difference, whatever may account for it, between ethics and other matters on the one hand and aesthetics on the other.

It might be worth noting a further contrast between aesthetic and certain other assessments which may be made. I have suggested that in aesthetics there would typically be lacking any conceptual connection between the descriptions (if one were possible) of the (usually determinate) merit-responsible characteristics and the merit-term. The aesthetic case is distinctive in another way and must be distinguished from other non-aesthetic cases where there is equally no conceptual or meaning connection. This may be best exemplified by contrast of examples. It may be the case that being easily visible, at varying distances and in varying light, is a merit *vis-à-vis*, say, motorway-workers' clothes. It may also be a contingent fact established by experience (not a connection of meaning between 'plain colour' and 'easily visible') that clothes which are plain colours are more easily visible than clothes that are speckled or flecked. Because of this contingent fact, being of one plain colour (Q) is a property responsible for the applicability of the merit-predicate 'P' in question ('easily visible'); it may even come to be treated as a criterion of merit. In such a case, however, the two facts about the clothing can be established or ascertained separately and independently; one might notice that certain clothing was more easily visible in certain lights or at some distance and discover later, when it was brought nearer, that it was of one plain colour. It need not be the case in such instances that, in discovering that the material has the merit of being more easily seen than others, one can at the same time see or be able to tell that it is monochromatic. That is, one property of it, which is a merit-property, for which another property is responsible, might conceivably be discovered without, in those circumstances, it being the case that one could simultaneously discern the other which is responsible for it. But in an aesthetic case, if a man were not in a position to see or discern that a line had such and such a curve, or a poem contained such and such a concatenation of words, or that BSC 8-090 was of a certain shade, he could not conceivably tell that the line was, or pronounce it to be, graceful, or the poem moving, or the colour delicate. The two facts must be co-perceptual or co-discoverable. It is thus distinguishable from the visibility case. The perception of the merit, P, is not possible without the perception of *x* being Q. It is this particular way in which such aesthetic characteristics as being moving or being graceful are properties of a particular combination of words or of the particular curvature of a line that is distinctive. Just as a rich red is not just a rich colour and red, so too a line is not just curved in a certain way and graceful, nor are the words of a poem put together just so and also moving; the curvature is a graceful curvature, the combination of words a moving one. This is why one is able to decide the applicability of 'moving' or 'graceful' only in so far as one is at the same time able to discern the (responsible) properties which the lines or word-combination have; this is why they have to be co-discernible. One sees the grace in that particular curve, sees that that particular curve is a graceful one. And if one cannot clearly see or discern the determinate character or properties which are responsible for the merit-term 'P' being applicable, one cannot discern that 'P' applies. This is what, in aesthetics, tempts one, understandably but doubtless too inexactly, to think of these connections as perceptual matters. I return now briefly to the doctrine with which I began, that in the aesthetic sphere, unlike the moral, the reason there are no general descriptive criteria of merit results from the fact that, given the way we use the concept 'work of art', two or more works of art cannot be identical, identical ones being instances of one art-work type; and hence that there is no place for general, i.e., shareable criteria of merit. There are, I believe, many objections to this view. I shall consider however only one, and one that applies, I believe, even to Strawson's more sophisticated version of the doctrine. He rejects the simple view that the absence in aesthetics of general non-evaluative criteria (and he must mean what I call merit-*responsible* as opposed to what I call merit-*constituting* characteristics, for he thinks the latter *are* evaluative and shareable) rests upon the fact that art-works are individuated by types, for so are wireless-sets, postage stamps, and motor-cars. His supplementation of this view is that in so far as a work of art is being judged *aesthetically* (as works of art often, though not always, are), we are restricted to exactly that range of characteristics that make it the work it is and not another. He says that 'when we have a class of objects of which the name "works of art", marks them out as primarily to be assessed in this way' (i.e. aesthetically), 'then there cannot be numerically distinct members of the class . . . which yet share all the features relevant to this kind of assessment'. An art-work, considered as a type, is coextensive with the features relevant to its aesthetic appraisal. Everything that is relevant to its being this work, not another, is also relevant to its aesthetic character and value. Consequently, with works of art, all features relevant to their individuation as type-instances are also features relevant to their evaluation as works of art; whereas with cars or wireless-sets, merits might be identical but the objects be of different types. From this he concludes that one wireless-set (type), unlike an art-work (type), could be distinguished from another, yet both have, and so share, the same wireless merit-properties; and consequently that there logically is a place for general criteria of merit applicable to numerically different types of wireless-sets.

But if this were the explanation of the lack of general criteria in aesthetics, there would be the result, as Strawson seems to admit, that the same would be true of the *aesthetic* features of wireless-sets and other things which are *not* works of art. For if I understand him aright this would mean that whereas there logically *could not* be general non-evaluative aesthetic criteria of merit, shareable by more than one *work of art*, there *could* be such general aesthetic criteria available in judging things *other* than works of art. He says for example that 'as far as works of art are concerned, the idea of an aesthetic merit-conferring *property*' (presumably with a 'non-evaluative' name) is a mistake, but that 'the idea in question might have application in some cases of things other than works of art of which we may make aesthetic assessments'. For instance, two motor-car types might be 'identical in aesthetically relevant respects and yet be numerically two' and that 'here we might perhaps think of their *appearance* as a shared property'.

Thus it seems that he thinks that it would be *only* in relation to works of art that aesthetic descriptive criteria would be, for logical reasons, unavailable. With other things there might be such descriptive aesthetic criteria. Yet Strawson has admitted that what I called merit-*constituting* properties (though he thinks the names of these properties, like 'delicate', 'graceful', 'economical', etc. are evaluative) are shareable by works of art and therefore presumably also by other things (whereas I have argued that most such aesthetic merit-constituting properties have, as names, merit-terms which are simply descriptive). So there is no difference *here* between judging works of art and things which are not; which leaves us with the question whether, with things *other* than works of art, but not with works of art, there are general descriptive criteria of merit available in merit-*responsible* descriptive terms. And if what I argued earlier is right, it seems that the situation here is the same for other things as it is for art. We cannot, and largely because we lack the ability to provide determinate descriptions, use any criterion that would guarantee that, say, the lines of a car were graceful. The most that could happen would be, as in my example of the goblets, that we could know that an object that shared the identical (descriptive) merit-responsible property would also be graceful. But the property in question, even if we could describe it, say by co-ordinates, would still have to be determinate, and so not applicable to even slightly different objects. All we get is some such statement as 'Anything which is exactly like this in respects Q, R, etc. (a determinate description would follow here if one were possible) is graceful (or handsome, or balanced, or whatever)'. It would therefore be virtually useless as a criterion of merit, even if it were attainable. And it is this unattainability of adequate determinate descriptions in our language that I have been at pains to stress. The useless-ness in aesthetics of trying to give general criteria of merit in *determinable* merit-responsible terms or descriptions, and the virtual impossibility in our language of giving them in *determinate* merit-responsible terms or descrip-tions are the two main points I have wished to emphasize throughout. And this situation applies equally whether the criteria are to apply to works of art or to anything else. Thus, whatever 'particularity' and 'non-conceptual' char-acter there is in the relationship of merit-responsible characteristics to the applicability of aesthetic merit-terms—features which distinguish aesthetic from moral and other sorts of assessment—these continue to exist in aesthetic evaluations even when the evaluations are not of works of art. They are not linked essentially to, or dependent upon, the concept of a work of art, and could exist without the existence of this concept.

I summarize what I have said about the particularity and non-conceptual character of aesthetic assessment: (1) There are criteria of merit in aesthetics in the sense that, if certain terms ('merit-terms') are applicable to a thing, it has thereby some aesthetic merit. But these terms are not significantly more 'evaluative' or less 'descriptive' than merit-terms to be found in many other spheres. (2) But there are at best few criteria of merit in aesthetics if this means that there are *determinable* descriptions of properties responsible for a merit-term being applicable which can serve as criteria or justifications for the application of a merit-term, whereas this is often the case in ethics and other spheres. This results from the fact that the properties responsible for an aesthetic merit-term being applicable are normally determinate. (3) Even if we could achieve *determinate* descriptions of those properties which are responsible for an aesthetic merit-term being applicable—and usually we cannot—they would be virtually useless because usable only with determi-nately identical things; nor would they be, as descriptions of merit-responsi-ble features are in ethics, conceptually connected with the merit-terms in question. (4) Finally, I have suggested that, if there is a peculiarity, namely a certain sort of 'particularity' about aesthetic assessment, it concerns the nature of and relation between the neutrally descriptive properties of a thing and its possession of aesthetic merit-qualities, and does *not* therefore result, as many recent writers have thought, from the logical character of the concept 'work of art'. It is because writers on aesthetics have so constantly had their eyes on works of art, and have been bewitched by the criterion of identity for art-works being such that identical instances count as one work, that they have supposed this fact, which is in reality irrelevant, to be accountable for the 'particularity' present in aesthetic assessment. They are particularly prone to this because musical and literary creations form a large part of art and have no counterparts in nature. But if one thinks of natural objects (which are non-verbal and non-musical and do not therefore tempt us into this mistake), objects like faces, bodies, mountains, trees, swans, as well as visual artefacts like motor-cars, etc., one can see clearly that the features characteristic of aesthetic evaluation remain the same there, even though the criterion of identity of art-works is not involved.

8

General Criteria and Reasons in Aesthetics

It is a somewhat daunting task to attempt to discuss the work of Monroe Beardsley, especially his work on aesthetics. Over a long period he has been more than prolific; he has pursued many issues with a wholly admirable pertinacity, developing and modifying his views bit by bit and in detail, with great good sense and sensitivity, not only as he has come to think his own positions need amending, but also in the light of criticism directed at him by others. There is a vast amount of his work with which I agree, and I doubt that I can say much that he has not already himself thought of, even if he may have rejected it as unsatisfactory. Given the bulk, subtlety, and complexity of his writings, it is almost inevitable that at some point I shall misrepresent him or do him an injustice. It is likely that I may simply have overlooked or forgotten some important points he has made. I shall have to risk this and rely on his customary appreciation of those who tend to support views similar to his own from their own particular standpoint as well as his constant interest in and generosity towards those who either misunderstand him or attempt to oppose his views.

Throughout his writings Beardsley has steadily sought to uphold the view that in criticism there are and can be general reasons for aesthetic judgements. On this point I stand and have always stood on the same side as he does. Thus, basically, we face together those many writers over several decades—I dub them 'particularists'—who have argued that in criticism there are no such general reasons. The dispute arises because both we and those we oppose agree that reasons, to be reasons, must have a consistency about them; but our opponents allege that any 'reason' offered to support the judgement that one work has aesthetic merit may be offered to support the judgement that another work has an aesthetic defect. To debate this issue adequately would require several complex chapters; so in the space available I can indicate my defence of the 'generalist' position only in the sketchiest way and with the simplest of examples. I shall argue that through not making certain distinctions adequately, Beardsley adopts an extreme and heroic position that is unnecessary even to dispose of the most serious of the denials of consistency just mentioned. Later I shall argue that the particular kind of heroic attempt

[From *Essays on Aesthetics: Perspectives on the Work of Monroe C. Beardsley*, ed. John Fisher, Philadelphia: Temple University Press, 1983.]

he makes is inadequate to establish a deeper claim; that by means of it he can isolate ultimate criteria of aesthetic merit from ultimately negative aesthetic criteria. On the first question he attempts more than is necessary to defeat our common adversaries; and for the second question, the line of defence he adopts through the bulk of his work is unsatisfactory.

The line of defence that he employs for both questions consists in claiming that there are three primary or basic positive criteria—unity, complexity, and intensity of regional quality—that can never in any circumstances count otherwise than in a positive direction. These criteria he regards as ultimately 'safe'; all other (secondary) criteria are 'risky'.[1] To make any of the latter safe in a given case, they must be linked to one or more of the primary criteria. I shall argue that a sharp distinction is essential within the criteria that Beardsley allows to be risky, a distinction he at times hovers on the brink of making. To take some of his examples, the presence of puns (or four-letter words) in a work may be either a merit or a defect; equally, he allows, may the presence of dramatic intensity (or a touch of humour).[2] Each is a secondary criterion. To show that either is, in a particular work, a merit, he maintains, ultimately requires a linkage to the primary criteria. But this, I claim, overlooks a vital difference. '*X* contains many puns' (I use *x* throughout to mean an art-work, not any specific kind of work like a tragedy, a pastoral poem, a sonnet, a statute, or a fugue) attributes to *x* a property or feature that is in itself entirely *neutral*. To claim that the puns are a merit in *x*, I agree, demands a linking explanation—they are striking, vivid, evocative, and so on. To claim that they are a defect also demands some such explanation—they are distracting, insipid, etc. So '*x* contains many puns (metaphors, etc.)', *tout court*, carries no implication of aesthetic merit or defect but this is not so, I maintain, with '*x* has dramatic intensity'. The attribution to an art-work of dramatic intensity, *tout court*, like the attribution of grace or elegance, is the attribution to it of a property that inherently possesses aesthetic merit. I would say that there are a whole host of properties that inherently possess a positive aesthetic polarity when applied to works of art, not just those I have mentioned, which seem to me aesthetic *par excellence*, but many, like witty, balanced, and joyous, that have applications of another kind entirely outside the arts. Similarly there are a host of inherently negative properties, like garish, sentimental, bombastic, and ugly. If these properties are not themselves grounds of aesthetic value (positive or negative respectively) in the realm of the arts, I cannot conceivably see what could be.[3] They are like 'honest', 'conscientious', 'considerate', in

[1] Monroe C. Beardsley, 'The Discrimination of Aesthetic Enjoyment', *British Journal of Aesthetics*, 2 (1963), 297.

[2] Monroe C. Beardsley, 'On the Generality of Critical Reasons', *Journal of Philosophy*, 59 (1962), 484–5.

[3] Beardsley, of course, constantly admits that there is a very large variety of reasons (see e.g., *Aesthetics: Problems in the Philosophy of Criticism* (New York, 1958, 462, and else-

the realm of ethics. Whereas the neutral properties that can be offered in reasons for merit or demerit possess, without linking explanation, no inherent polarity whatever, these do inherently possess an aesthetic evaluative polarity. One cannot intelligibly say *tout court*, and with this Beardsley certainly agrees, 'This work is bad because it is graceful', or 'This work is good because it is garish'. I would want to say that all these, not Beardsley's three, are basic or primary aesthetic criteria, some of merit, some of demerit.

But now the question arises why Beardsley should suppose them inadequate as basic or primary general aesthetic criteria and why he should regard them as 'risky'. The reason is clear. He is only too aware, as are the particularists, that grace or elegance or dramatic intensity need not necessarily be a merit, may even be a defect, in a particular work. And for this too, most certainly, an explanation is needed in each particular case. But this time it is not an explanation of why an inherently neutral feature (the presence of puns or metaphors) is a reason for merit in a work; it is an entirely different kind of explanation: why a feature, inherently a merit when taken *tout court*, is, in the context of a particular work, a defect. Beardsley, I think, never adequately distinguishes the two cases. he regularly lumps them together. He therefore tries the same sort of explanation with the second group, linking them again to his one-way criteria. But though an explanation is needed, it does not have to be of this sort. Indeed, it is here that the second crucial distinction not explicitly emphasized by Beardsley must be made. To save what I have called general evaluative criteria from the attack of the particularists, Beardsley supposes it necessary to perform what I called the heroic task of finding certain criteria to fall back on: not merely ones that, applied to a work *tout court*, inherently count one way, but ones that always, in every work, can count only one way.

It is clear that, and why, Beardsley makes this move. If there are genuine reasons, there must be generality; if generality, consistency; and if consistency, the reasons given must always count one way only. As he says about butchers' knives, 'if a certain degree of sharpness is a merit . . . then to say that a knife has that degree of sharpness must *always* be a reason to support the conclusion that it is good, and it will apply to *all* knives of the relevant sort. . . . *It will, at least, never be a fault in a knife*' (my italics).[4] And so what I called his heroic task is to find primary positive criteria that are such that 'the addition of any one of them or an increase in it, without a decrease in any of the others, will always make the work a better one'.[5] But the distinction that must be made clearly here is that between overall judgements of things, like

where), but he thinks we can find room for them in his three main groups. He would probably reject my line of argument here as 'a simple appeal to paradigm cases' ('On the Generality of Critical Reasons', 478).

[4] 'On the Generality of Critical Reasons', 479.　　　　[5] ibid., 485.

butcher's knives, where the relevant criteria are *independent* of each other, and overall judgements of those many things, including art-works, where the relevant criteria are *interacting*.[6] In the former, once the thing is discovered to have certain merit-qualities and if it possesses enough, the judgement that the thing is good is merely summative; the inherent merit-qualities do not interact. If the blade is sharp, the knife well balanced, the handle convenient to hold, and so on, then in the absence of overriding or defeating negative qualities (for example, that it breaks after one day's use), it is a good one. But with very many things, though we can set out criteria of merit, these are not independent; they can interact within the whole in various ways. What are merit-features *tout court* or *in vacuo* for that *sort* of thing may not work satisfactorily together with other such *tout court* merit-features in a *particular* thing of that sort. It is the sort of object sometimes spoken of as an 'organic whole'. This is not a case of defeasibility, inherent positive features being overridden or defeated by inherent negative features. With defeasibility, inherently positive features never become negative in a particular instance: duress may defeat a contract, but offer and acceptance never count against a contract. But where there is possible interaction in a complex whole, as in art-works, what *in vacuo* is inherently an aesthetic merit may *itself*, in conjunction with other inherently positive features in that complex, become a *defect*.

For this an explanation will be necessary, but it can be a perfectly intelligible, though special, sort of explanation. It will be a *reversing* explanation, not the sort that showed why the occurrence of puns or metaphors (neutral in themselves) gave merit to a work. And such reversing explanations are common. Indeed, the sorts of cases needing detailed discussion are legion. Here I can take only one of the simplest, suggested by one of Beardsley's examples. When someone has decided that certain parts of a work are highly comic and other parts intensely tragic—both *tout court*, or inherent, or, in my usage, primary criteria of merit—he has to judge for himself whether the comic episodes detract from or enhance the tragic character, or vice versa. If he decides that the comic elements do detract from and dilute the tragic intensity, *and* that the tragic element is predominant, the comic elements, though of aesthetic worth in themselves, will be defects in that work precisely because they dilute the predominant tragic intensity.

I have argued elsewhere that there are no sure-fire rules by which, referring to the neutral and non-aesthetic qualities of things, one can infer that something is balanced, tragic, comic, joyous, and so on. One has to look and see. Here, equally, at a different level, I am saying that there are no sure-fire

---

[6] Beardsley hints at this, but little more, in *Aesthetics*, 465, where he says, 'It does not seem that the contribution of each feature of an aesthetic object can be considered in an atomistic fashion', and in several other places, including his remarks about secondary criteria in 'On the Generality of Critical Reasons', 485.

mechanical rules or procedures for deciding which qualities are actual defects in the work; one has to judge for oneself. But if the critic does decide that the comic elements are defects in this work, a perfectly general reason can be given. A work that might otherwise have excelled by its tragic intensity is marred by certain (inherently valuable) comic elements that dilute and weaken that (inherently valuable) tragic intensity; or vice versa. It is a matter for deciding, judging, that one dilutes, rather than contributes to, the other, for deciding which of the elements is on balance predominant, and hence deciding that a feature, in itself valuable, is the detracting feature, or defect, in the context of that work. This is a built-in and unavoidable phenomenon, not only in art-works, but wherever inherent merit-qualities may interact, and not one we need or should regret.

Beardsley comes closest to this position perhaps in his article 'On the Generality of Critical Reasons'. There he adequately refutes several of the more simple-minded arguments of the particularists. But I think it is clear that by ulti-mately striving for what I called the heroic solution, he falls back on his three primary criteria, and in doing so fails to convince where conviction is possible. It is precisely in dealing with the most crucial case, where an inherent merit-qual-ity constitutes a defect in a particular work, that he hovers on the brink of the right answer. He claims that 'the General Criterion Theory [by 'general' he means criteria that *always* count only one way] can easily take account of such varia-tions'.[7] Rightly he says, just as I do, that a general criterion theory 'does not mean that this desirable feature can be *combined* with all other desirable features', or that 'all plays that lack a high degree of [dramatic intensity] would necessarily become better by increasing it, for some plays might thereby lose some other quality that *especially* adorns them' (my italics).[8] But here his argument falters. In his Shakespeare examples (*Hamlet* and *Macbeth*), having agreed that humour is a merit in one context but a defect in another, he, in my view, wrongly concedes that a 'touch of humour is not a *general* merit' (my italics), because something else, namely, high dramatic tension, is.[9] But he should not have given way thus on the generality of the merit of humour, especially as in the next sentence he in effect concedes equally that high dramatic tension is not a general aesthetic merit either; for some plays that lack it would, if it were increased, 'thereby lose some other quality that especially adorns them'. So by parity of reasoning dramatic intensity is not a general criterion either.

My claim is that humour and dramatic intensity are *both* inherently general aesthetic merits, though either may be a defect, given an appropriate explana-tion, in the context of a given work. Instead, Beardsley falls back onto his three 'always positive' primary criteria, a position that I am arguing is unnecessary. (It is true that Beardsley then says that even secondary criteria are general 'in

---

[7] 'On the Generality of Critical Reasons', 485.
[8] ibid.   [9] ibid.

an important sense', which may seem to coincide with the view I am espousing.) But his secondary criteria, though general, are 'subordinate and conditional'. 'X is a *secondary (positive) criterion* . . . if there is a certain set of other properties such that, whenever they are present . . . the addition of *x* . . . will always produce an increase in one or more of the primary criteria.'[10] I would deny that any such 'set of other properties' can ever be specified.

Incidentally, if the particularist's fear is that the admission of general criteria of the sort I admit—grace, elegance, humour, subtle characterization, dramatic intensity, which I called basic aesthetic criteria—would make evaluative judgements a mere matter of mechanically testing a work against rules, or that it would preclude the possibility of these inherently valuable aesthetic qualities being defects in a particular work, my answer to him has already been given. In fact, my answer amounts to a direct denial of the claim of one particularist, Mary Mothersill, who says that 'there is no analogue in criticism to what in moral philosophy have been called "*prima facie* duties" '—or, we might add, virtues.[11] The general qualities that, when mentioned *tout court* or *in vacuo*, I have called inherent merit-qualities are, in the context of a particular work, prima-facie merits, but not necessarily *actual* merits.

The situation is analogous—I stress analogous, not identical—to that in ethics (and many other areas where criteria interact). If one accepts that promise keeping, truth telling, honesty, and so on are inherently moral virtues, it may nevertheless be necessary, even right in certain circumstances, *either* to lie or to break a promise.[12] Unless one accepts some fixed hierarchy of virtues or some plausible overriding principle like Utilitarianism, one is left to a non-rule-governed decision, weighing, for example, the seriousness or relative unimportance of the lie against that of the promise breaking, rather as one has to decide, in a hypothetical play containing both comic and tragic episodes, which are the defects and which therefore ought to have been expunged. (The disanalogy with ethics is that telling the truth may exclude keeping the promise, whereas the comic and tragic episodes are not mutually exclusive.) So I would call primary or basic those sorts of inherent aesthetic merit-qualities I have indicated, just as I would call the cited moral virtues or general duties primary or basic. And this is to use 'primary' and 'basic' in a way quite different from Beardsley's, for in the context of a particular work these qualities will be only prima-facie merits, not necessarily actual merits of that work—though they will be actual merits too if no appropriate reversing explanation is available.

I have said that Beardsley's heroic attempt to find (three) always-one-way

---

[10] ibid.

[11] Mary Mothersill, 'Critical Reasons', *Philosophical Quarterly* 11 (1961), 77.

[12] Again Beardsley comes very close to this position in what he says about ethics in 'On the Generality of Critical Reasons', 481.

basic criteria is not necessary to refute the particularist who raises the reversibility phenomenon. I can now say why. I take three different kinds of examples. If we can say that x is hilariously comic *tout court* (being made so by the puns, etc., in it), if we can say that x is exceedingly graceful *tout court*, or if we can say that x has a tragic intensity (enhanced by its comic episodes) *tout court*, we have thereby given fully adequate and sufficient reasons for attributing aesthetic merit to x. Yet all of these fully adequate reasons—being hilariously comic, being exceedingly graceful, and having tragic intensity— cite Beardsley's 'secondary' criteria, which could, in certain circumstances, count negatively. But not here. There is no necessity, when these reasons are given, to secure them yet further by linking them to permanently one-way positive criteria.

I turn now to my second claim: that Beardsley's appeal to his three basic criteria is inadequate for isolating ultimate criteria of aesthetic merit from ultimately negative aesthetic criteria. Again, to justify this claim fully would need lengthy argument. I can attempt only the briefest sketch. I shall have to concentrate on unity and intensity of regional quality, saying little about complexity. It is only fair to point out that Beardsley has always admitted the possibility that his three canons might not be adequate, and he has frequently attempted to rebut possible criticisms. He admits that it might be argued that 'some [human regional] qualities are cited as grounds for dispraise'; he regards the question whether '*all* Objective Reasons can be subsumed under these three Canons' as 'a very bold question'; but he is prepared 'even to go as far as to say' that they can, adding, 'This may be too sweeping a claim', but 'at any rate, it is stated explicitly enough so that it can be attacked or defended'.[13] It is certainly the case that through most of his work he has adhered to the claim and has not conceded any insuperable objections.

I shall consider unity first. Unity must be unity *of* something[14] and for some *purpose* or of some *kind*. Unity in itself is an empty concept. For, first, we cannot employ the criterion of unity except in a second-order way. We cannot just look for unity. If we have before us a simple poem exhibiting—to use one of Beardsley's examples—heroic strength', we find this latter quality exhibited in the work either intensely or confusedly. If the former, we can conclude that the basic elements (words, rhythms, etc.) possessed unity; if the latter, they did not. If we are considering the play containing both tragic and comic episodes, we decide whether the episodes enhance or dilute each other. If the former, the work is unified; if the latter, it is not. So the judgements that the work has one or more of the qualities that I have called inherently aesthetic qualities is logically prior to the judgement of unity. Secondly, unity, unlike grace or elegance, is not a criterion that is inherently aesthetic at all.

---

[13] *Aesthetics*, 464–70.
[14] This is implicit in various things Beardsley says, e.g., in *Aesthetics*, 198–200.

Almost anything may exhibit unity (organization, completeness, etc.): for example, a political rally. But even if we seek unity in what is in fact a work of art, that work may still exhibit a unity that is not an aesthetic or artistic unity. A very bad novel, its episodes thrown together haphazardly, could be unified in the sense that it preaches a single, coherent political doctrine throughout. It may have a unity, coherence, even a developing complexity of political view-point, but no artistic worth. But if we have to qualify unity by saying *artistic* or *aesthetic* unity, unity itself can hardly be an aesthetic criterion, and, *a fortiori*, it cannot be a primary aesthetic criterion. So as a basic one-way aesthetic criterion, unity cannot fill the bill. Somewhat similar comments can be made about complexity. We cannot necessarily decide independently that a work is complex or varied; this may also be second-order in the way unity is. And for complexity to be an *aesthetic* merit, the work must have a (reasonably unified) complexity that yields inherently valuable *aesthetic* properties. Like unity, complexity or variety can characterize political rallies and political points of view within an atrocious novel, as well as technical manuals, sporting activities, and so on.

If we now try to give appropriate content to unity, interpreting it, say, as unity of an intense regional quality or unity of a variety of such qualities, we come to difficulties over both intensity and regional qualities. 'Intense' is ambiguous. The most common understanding of this term would be 'extreme'. A work may have an intensity of sadness, calm, tragedy, gaiety ('intensely graceful' and 'intensely elegant' sound somewhat odd). But Beardsley cannot mean that regional qualities are, *ceteris paribus*, aesthetically better for always being intense in this sense. Some fine works are not intense in this way; they have a gentle humour, a hint of wistfulness, a faint suggestion of melancholy underlying a peaceful calm or quiet serenity. We value these regional qualities too and would not be without them. In the sense in which 'intense' means 'extreme', intensity is not necessarily what we seek in qualities of aesthetic value. So perhaps we must sometimes take 'intense' to mean something like 'pure', 'quintessential', 'epitomized', a clear expression of some regional quality. Intensity may mean simply that some regional quality has been securely grasped; characterlessness, insipidity, unclarity, and confusion have been avoided.[15] I shall say no more about this, but use 'intensity' here-after allowing it to take whichever sense is appropriate.

The far more serious question concerns regional qualities. Do we trans-form unity and complexity into clearly *aesthetic* qualities (and hence perhaps aesthetic merits) if we simply say unity (and complexity) of an intense regional quality? This question goes deeper than the one I began with, whether

---

[15] Beardsley seems to note this point briefly, e.g., in *Aesthetics*, where he says, 'The essential thing is that the work have some quality that stands out, instead of being vapid, char-acterless' (p. 298), and speaks of both 'higher intensity and greater purity' (p. 382).

the 'reversibility' of criteria emphasized by the particularists must always be met by a linkage to one or more of the three always-one-way primary positive criteria, of which intensity of regional quality is one. It calls in question the very claim that intensity of regional quality *is* a primary or always-one-way criterion of aesthetic value. And the reason it does that is that only some (intensive) regional qualities would seem to be aesthetic in character at all, and of those that are, only some are inherently positive, while others are inherently negative. In his various accounts and lists of regional qualities, Beardsley has given examples as different as triangularity, squareness, lyric grace, heroic strength, and dramatic intensity, as well as the qualities pompous, precious, subtle, garish; and I suppose we could add a few thousand more: mottled, pin-striped, leering, face-like, politically biased, ugly, sentimental, boring, and irritating (though I believe Beardsley would exclude the last three as 'affective', not 'objective'). All these, I think, could be (unlike perhaps insipid and characterless) more or less intense in one or another of the senses of 'intense' indicated. But I would suppose that triangular, mottled, pin-striped, face-like, and politically biased are aesthetically neutral; and that while some of the intensive regional qualities listed above are aesthetically positive, others, like ugly, garish, and sentimental are aesthetically negative. (Beardsley has been aware of these problems from the start;[16] at times he restricts positive regional qualities to 'human' regional qualities, but he admits even then problems that I touch on below.) It would seem clear therefore that intensity of regional quality is far from being a primary positive criterion; only those regional qualities that are not aesthetically neutral and not aesthetically negative are positive. But, put thus, this is vacuous, and we seem forced to limit ourselves to some selected list containing only the sort of examples I gave earlier as primary positive criteria in my sense.

If the position I have presented so sketchily is correct, *some* (even 'human') regional qualities possessing unity, complexity, and intensity are negative, capable of being 'independently cited as a ground' of *negative* evaluations. Unless Beardsley can meet these objections, he fails to reduce the 'very large variety' of positive reasons to his three primary criteria, a move that he regards as important—though I do not—to support a generalist position that in a broad way we equally accept. I believe that this kind of underpinning is not only inadequate but unnecessary. It is interesting to see how, characteristically, Beardsley has turned on several occasions in his more recent writings to these problems, which he recognized, as I have said, as early as the publication of *Aesthetics* in 1958. In all his relevant articles up till 1968, with one exception, he adheres regularly to the view that there are 'exactly three basic criteria' that always count positively, never negatively. But in the 1966 article[17] the difficulty reappears, at least for the reader, though Beardsley does not tackle it: proper-

---

[16] *Aesthetics*, 463–64.
[17] 'The Aesthetic Problem of Justification', *Journal of Aesthetic Education*, 1 (1966), 32, 39.

ties (likely unity and intensity) are 'instrumental'; they have the capacity to provide aesthetic enjoyment. But, the reader is forced to ask himself, 'What if some instances of unity and intensity have the capacity to provide aesthetic revulsion? In 1968 he returns again to face directly the question 'Why are some aesthetic qualities artistically objectionable?'[18] He himself speaks of, and so admits, 'defects due to negative regional qualities'. He still tries to cope with them by reference to his three criteria, but with some lack of confidence ('Some of the other negative qualities are difficult to accommodate to this scheme. . . . But I hope that even those can be dealt with by dint of more sensitive and precise analysis').

I believe his attempt fails, as it did earlier. If intensity of some regional quality is to be a merit, then certainly, as he says, it is easy to see why *privative* qualities (e.g., insipidity, which entails lack of intensity) would be defects. Perhaps we can also admit that the qualities he calls *disruptive* (e.g., franticness) are destructive of unity (and hence of a pervasive intensity of desirable regional quality). But those he calls *reductive*, that is, lacking in complexity (crudeness, pomposity), along with others he finds hard to accommodate (grossness, preciousness), to which I would add bombast, garishness, sentimentality, and ugliness, seem to me capable of intensity (i.e., not privative), and not necessarily disruptive of unity or for that matter exclusive of complexity (i.e., reductive). A novel might contain a complex variety of kinds of sentimentality, not internally discordant but uniting, and so 'enhancing' each other, to yield an overall and intense sentimentality. A vase might have a variety of ugly features—shape, decoration, colour combinations—a uniting or mutually reinforcing complex of ugly elements adding up to an intensity of ugliness. Such works, it seems to me, would have unity, complexity, and a resulting intense regional quality—but a wholly negative one. If Beardsley cannot evade such cases, his position becomes similar to mine: some intense unified and complex regional qualities are defects, basic and primary defects. In what seems to me a tell-tale remark, he seems almost to concede this: for he speaks of a good poem as one that 'generates a regional quality of aesthetic *interest*'[19] (my italics), where 'interest' strongly suggests 'value'. But within a few lines he is resorting again to his three basic criteria: 'the critic . . . must have the taste to tell how unified and complex a pattern is, how intensely it glows with regional qualities—unless the word 'glows' surreptitiously gives the game away.

The last relevant paper I know of fairly and squarely faces the difficulty.[20] He admits with his usual candour that he is left with a large problem, 'how to explain why certain qualities, but not others, *can* be cited in reasons support-

---

[18] 'Bad Poetry', published in *The Possibility of Criticism*, Detroit: Wayne State University Press, 1970, 98–100.

[19] ibid. 110. [20] 'What Is an Aesthetic Quality?' *Theoria* 39 (1973), 65, 69.

ing judgments of aesthetic value'. He refers us back to his previous attempt (just discussed) 'to come to grips with this problem', but admits characteristically that 'it is far from being solved'. I feel this to be an admission that appeal to his three canons never solves (I should say, cannot solve) this problem. The 'hint of a solution' he then offers is that certain value-grounding qualities, in particular 'human qualities' (he concedes a possible difficulty about some others), are properties 'naturally *interesting* to us . . . we can work up feelings about them. They touch us where we live.' These are, of course, the ones that are positive, but I find this no more than a hint; and here, so far as I know, the discussion of this particular problem ends to date. One might hope that Beardsley had at last abandoned as unnecessary and inadequate the Three Canons view; but as we shall see in a moment, they reappear in another context even more recently.

Perhaps, with his customary persistence and ingenuity, Beardsley will yet offer an acceptable account of why some aesthetic criteria are inherently positive and others negative. This, as he has always recognized, is an additional and difficult task. It is just as necessary for him to show *why* his basic criteria (which, I have argued, fail to do the trick of collecting all positive criteria under three heads) are aesthetically positive as it is for me to show why my suggested host of inherent merit and demerit qualities are respectively positive and negative aesthetically. No doubt he would regard it as an added difficulty for the position I have outlined 'that there seems no way of demonstrating that any particular list of qualities is an exhaustive inventory of those that are aesthetically valuable'.[21] I cannot attempt to offer any suggestion here. Nor is it my present task to discuss the persistent endeavours he has made to deal with this problem, starting in chapter 11 of *Aesthetics* and continuing through many more recent papers. Consistently he has adhered to the view that positive aesthetic qualities are instrumental, capacities that provide, in certain conditions, a certain state of mind, for which he has used, variously, the terms 'aesthetic experience', 'aesthetic enjoyment', 'aesthetic interest', 'aesthetic gratification', and so on. This state of mind he has in turn tried at various times to isolate and define by reference to *its* unity, completeness, complexity, intensity, and pleasure. To me it seems that these attempts result in difficulties, parallel to those I have discussed, breaking out again at a new level. Nevertheless, it strikes me as right that of the two available kinds of moves, he should at least attempt this one. The alternative, which Beardsley has several times rejected,[22] is to discriminate the state of mind—aesthetic enjoyment, or satisfaction—by reference to the set of aesthetic criteria we employ and the kind of properties we take aesthetic satisfaction in; instead, he

[21] *Aesthetics*, 509.

[22] 'The Discrimination of Aesthetic Enjoyment', 296, and 'Aesthetic Experience Regained', *Journal of Aesthetics and Art Criticism*, 28 (1969–70), 5.

wants to distinguish an aesthetic experience 'in terms of its own internal properties', not by reference to the properties of the object that are instrumental in giving rise to aesthetic experience. For the latter course would be analogous to a moral philosopher's accepting as not further explainable that honesty and considerateness are virtues and cruelty a vice without, as a philosopher should, continuing to seek an explanatory principle. To do otherwise is to do what Gilbert Ryle once said about 'family resemblance', to accept a position that should be adopted only as a last resort. It is odd therefore to find, though I must be misunderstanding him, that in one of his later papers he looks as if he is reversing his position and reviving his primary criteria: 'Gratification is aesthetic when it is obtained primarily from attention to the formal unity and/or regional qualities of a complex whole'.[23]

I fear that in the forgoing my admiration for Beardsley's work may have been obscured by the fact that I have been critical, not of his staunchly maintained position that there are general aesthetic criteria, for I share this view and regard myself as an ally, but of the detail by which he supports the position. I can only say that this is because I regard his work as so important that it merits careful critical scrutiny. My regret is that I must inevitably have done him far less than justice in so brief a paper.

I shall end with the more congenial task of trying to strengthen Beardsley's defence against a criticism that would, were it sound, endanger any general criterion theory, whether his or mine. Again my account must be schematic in the extreme. The objection is that made by Michael Scriven: that in aesthetic evaluation the independence requirement is 'difficult' to meet. This requirement 'demands that we be able to know the reason or reasons for a conclusion without first having to know the conclusion; otherwise we can never use the reasons as a means of getting to the conclusion'.[24] I shall ignore the word 'difficult' and the temporal suggestion of 'first'. The only claim of genuine interest would be the logical claim that in aesthetics we cannot meet the independence requirement since we cannot know the reason for an evaluation conclusion unless we already know this conclusion. I shall assume Scriven to be making this stronger claim because he also says that reasons must be 'such that we *can* know them without knowing the conclusion'. I think Beardsley also understands Scriven's claim in this strong sense, since he says that if Scriven were right, 'it would follow that critics *cannot* use reasons to arrive at their judgment'.[25] Beardsley's reply to Scriven is somewhat complex, and I find it hard to assess it; but at one point (p. 83) it takes the form of reiterating his own view that 'some reasons *must* be used by critics in arriving at' their judgements

[23] 'The Aesthetic Point of View' (1970), reprinted in *Philosophy Looks at the Arts*, ed. Joseph Margolis, rev. ed., Philadelphia, 1978, 12.

[24] Michael Scriven, *Primary Philosophy*, New York: McGraw-Hill, 1966, 57–9.

[25] *The Possibility of Criticism*, 77–85.

(which does not refute but simply denies Scriven's claim about aesthetic reasons) and that 'therefore there must be some basic features ... that are always merits or defects'—unity and intensity of regional quality again. I do not see this as an adequate reply to Scriven, nor do I see that Beardsley's appeal to his three basic criteria, already criticized, either helps or is needed, as he seems to suppose.

But I do think that Scriven's claim about aesthetic reasons is false, that nothing he says establishes it, and that it can indeed be refuted. We must, however, distinguish and set aside certain questions, important to discuss in their own right, but irrelevant to the central issue. We are not concerned, for instance, (1) with the ways in which, by various means, we can enable someone else to see for himself that a work is good; or (2) with the giving to someone of reasons that, if he accepts our statements as true, would require him to admit that a work must be good, though he cannot see that it is for himself; or (3) with the person who finds a work good and later looks for the reasons why it is, in order to justify his initial judgement. Our concern is with the critic who attends to the work for himself and in doing so finds in it qualities that serve as reasons for deciding or 'concluding' that it is good (or poor, flawed, indifferent, etc.).

I shall concede Scriven's claim at its strongest: that a reason must be logically prior to a conclusion. I shall argue that, even so, Scriven's scepticism about aesthetic reasons fails at least in some cases, and possibly in all, and fails because of an easily committed confusion. The possible cases to consider for a full refutation are legion. I can here consider only one sort of case, though I think the general principle could be invoked differently in other examples. The case I discuss is in one respect an extremely simple one, but in another respect one of the most troubling, since it is a case where a prima-facie merit is judged an actual defect. Scriven, I believe, is involved in an ambiguity involving two sorts of conclusions. For him, rightly, the ultimate conclusion is an evaluation that the work is good, perfect, flawed, and so on; that is, it is an overall judgement of *value*. But it is essential to distinguish this from an overall judgement of the *character* or *characteristics* of the work. (I deliberately use these terms rather than Beardsley's 'quality' to avoid any possible suggestion of evaluation.)

The crucial kind of case to consider (though there are many others of interest) is that of the critic who approaches an art-work looking for the character or characteristics it has (elegance, grace, garishness, etc.) but who also actively accepts for himself (not merely on someone else's word) that some of these characteristics are prima-facie aesthetic merits, others prima-facie aesthetic defects. In the work he approaches (call it x), he finds predominantly a build-up of characteristic P (say, tragic intensity); he also finds in it episodes with characteristic Q (hilarious comedy). In the case under consideration, he decides that these latter do not heighten, but dilute (render less intense), the predominant character *P*. He therefore judges these to be defects. Note, however, that he did not simply judge the episodes with characteristic *Q* to be detractions from the *value* of the work. This *in vacuo* would be impossible; there must be some reason why he judges them defects. What he judges is that they dilute or weaken the predominant (tragic) character *P*, a judgement of the *character* of the work. But he also himself accepts, *ex hypothesi* in our simplified case, that *P* is a characteristic of inherent aesthetic value. So his overall judgement of the value of *x*—that *x* is not perfect, but flawed—follows from his judgement that the predominant character *P* is weakened (in Beardsley's terminology, made less intense) by the presence in *x* of episodes with the character *Q*. But this latter was a judgement about the overall *character* of the work. It is from *this* that it follows that, since he regards *P* as a characteristic of aesthetic value, *x* is less valuable than it would have been without *Q* and that *Q* is therefore a defect in the work. But he could not have decided that *Q* was a defect in its overall value, and that *x* was flawed, *without* having decided that characteristic *Q* in this case weakened the predominant characteristic *P*. The overall judgement of (somewhat defective) value rested on his judgement that *characteristic P* was weakened by *Q*. This, together with his accepted premise that *P* is a characteristic of aesthetic merit, yields the value conclusion that *x* is of less aesthetic value than it would have been without *Q*. Schematically, then, his overall judgement of value—that *x* was flawed, and that *Q* was its defect—rested on his judgements (1) that *P* is the predominant characteristic of *x*; (2) that *P* is weakened, not intensified, by the presence of characteristic *Q*; (3) that *P* is inherently a prima-facie aesthetic merit; and (4) that though *Q* is also a prima-facie aesthetic merit, its presence dilutes the intensity of *P*. In short, an overall judgement of character is distinguishable from an overall judgement of value and logically precedes it.

Beardsley in fact put the position exactly enough, without the trimmings, when he said, 'A reason is some *descriptive* or interpretative proposition about the work. . . . Thus a reason always cites some *property* of the work, and we may say that this property is *then* employed as a *criterion of value* by the critic who presents that reason' (my italics).[26] This form of argument is in no way controverted by the fact that a person might, in temporal order, feel sure at the outset that *x* is flawed, without yet being able to say why. For when he does come to see why he initially thought it flawed, it will be because, in our simplified case, he realizes that *P*, the predominant characteristic, and one he accepts as aesthetically valuable, was rendered less intense by *Q*. Thus, though I have proved it for only certain sorts of cases, implicit or explicit acceptance of certain characteristics as being of aesthetic merit, and implicit or explicit recognition that *x* either intensely has, or in a diluted way has, some such

---

[26] 'On the Generality of Critical Reasons', 479.

predominant characteristic, function as the reason for, and have logical priority over, the overall conclusion as to the value of *x*. (This of course is only the simplest of cases; it has also to be distinguished from the sort of case already mentioned where hints of melancholy interposed within the gaiety, as in a Mozart movement, do not diminish or weaken the predominant gaiety, but unite to give the work a different and is itself valuable character, for example, the quintessence of a gaiety tinged with an underlying melancholy.)

One further point about Scriven's remarks. There is often a kind of absurdity involved in speaking, as he does, of reasons for a 'conclusion'. Ordinarily there need be no movement of inference to conclusion from reasons or premises. The critic does not normally say to himself, '*X* has strong and undiluted tragic intensity (or whatever); I regard this as aesthetic merit; so I must conclude that the work is good.' When you already accept that the characteristic *P* is one with inherent aesthetic merit, in seeing or deciding that *x* has *P* you are *ipso facto* seeing or deciding that *x* has some merit, just as the butcher, finding his knife sharp, has, in doing so, found it, at least in that respect, good. He does not argue by a process of inference from premise to conclusion, 'It is sharp; I accept sharpness as a merit; so I must admit that to that extent it is a good knife', even though an argument with premises and conclusion could always be constructed in this form. I cannot here deal with the many different and often highly complex examples that one can think of, but I am confident that an analogous answer can be made in most, if not all, cases to rebut Scriven's claim against the independence of reasons and evaluative 'conclusions' in aesthetic. Thus, I think Scriven's charge is the result of inadequate analysis, a failure to distinguish overall character from overall value. I hope therefore to have at least sketched a strategy that any upholder of general criteria, Beardsley included, can successfully develop against one objection that, if true, would be serious for us all.

In this short paper I have tried to outline, and defend against certain criticisms, a General Criterion theory, a kind of theory to which both Beardsley and I are adherents. Though this has involved considerable criticism of the substructure of Beardsley's views, I cannot end without emphasizing again my high admiration for his range, variety, ingenuity, fertility, and persistence in pursuing, with subtlety and determination, what seem to me the central questions of aesthetics. The corpus of his work, which I hope will be added to for a long while to come, will inevitably remain a storehouse of important ideas and arguments for anyone seriously interested in the subject.

9

Originality and Value

In recent times the high, even paramount, importance of originality in art has often been proclaimed. This importance has as often been questioned or denied. In what follows I assume 'originality' and 'novelty' to be used interchangeably. Similarly with 'worth', 'value', and 'merit'.

For Kant, 'fine art is . . . a product of genius', which has originality as 'its primary property'; but 'there may also be original nonsense'.[1] Originality is necessary, but only necessary, at least for great artistic worth. For Ruby Meager, originality is not necessary for good art though presumably relevant sometimes: 'the Assyrian and Egyptian Rooms of the British Museum would suggest that conformity rather than originality was *de rigueur* in art in those days. . . . In the whole history of aesthetic appreciation [originality] might appear as a local and temporary, rather than universal and essential, demand.'[2] For Beardsley, originality in a 'strict sense' (meaning that when an object was created 'it differed in some notable way from anything else that was known by its creator to exist at that time') is neither necessary nor relevant: 'originality has no bearing upon worth: [a work] might be original and fine, or original and terrible'.[3] In apparent sharp contrasts to these already differing views some artists and theorists have proclaimed, variously, that in art originality, far from being merely necessary for merit, is itself a merit, or the highest, or even the only significant merit. As Harold Osborne says in an interesting recent paper, 'In the more extremist sector of contemporary criticism novelty is put forward as a criterion and works . . . are ostensibly appraised in terms of their novelty', a position he firmly rejects: 'originality in the sense of novelty is not acceptable . . . as a standard of excellence. There can be originality which is sheer idiosyncrasy, novelty which verges upon idiocy'.[4] And we find

[From *British Journal of Aesthetics*, 25 (1985).]

[1] Kant, *Critique of Judgement*, part I, §46.

[2] R. Meager, 'The Uniqueness of a Work of Art', *Proceedings of the Aristotelian Society*, (1958–9), 49–50.

[3] M. C. Beardsley, *Aesthetics: Problems in the Philosophy of Criticism*, New York: Harcourt Brace, 1962, 460. All references to Beardsley are to this work.

[4] H. Osborne, 'The Concept of Creativity in Art', *British Journal of Aesthetics*, 19 (1979), 226–8. All references to Osborne are to this work.

Wollheim listing as qualities often considered 'the highest values of art: spontaneity, originality and full expressiveness'.[5]

How can reputable thinkers produce such diversity of apparently conflicting views? Either most must be wrong or we are facing a multiplicity of meanings and equivocations. I believe the latter to be true: interpreted appropriately, many, even if not all, of the views mentioned capture some truth. But showing this requires more distinctions than the disputants usually recognize. Evaluating art, in Osborne's words, 'involves a concept of excellence as well as one of novelty although the connection between the two has not been clearly worked out and has seldom been made explicit'. To part of this task this paper is addressed.

I examine therefore some of the meanings of 'original'. (Inevitably in an area where meanings merge my distinctions will be over-sharp.) Other meanings I ignore: e.g., when 'an original Rembrandt' means a genuine Rembrandt and when 'original' means 'first' or 'prototype' as in 'the original Model T Ford'. More important, I try to bypass certain much discussed issues that are easily entangled with my present topic: I am nowhere concerned with forgeries, nor, in so far as I can avoid them, with questions about copies as such and their value in relation to originals. I discuss originality, and any value it may have or result in, when being original involves, in various ways, being new and different, something a partial or inexact copy can certainly be even if a perfect copy cannot.

To begin, let us try: something is original if, when produced, it differs qualitatively from anything existing previously. For my purposes I shall restrict this immediately: to productions by animate beings (to exclude, e.g., differently shaped rocks thrown up by an eruption); also to things made with some degree of deliberate direction (to exclude, e.g., doodlings that differ from anything existing before). A more important restriction is that, to be original, a production must differ from anything previously existing in *relevant* ways; it might differ in some ways yet not count as original. Which differences are relevant will vary case by case. A dress or a car made exactly like another except, respectively, for size or colour will not count as original designs. A theory giving the same explanation of a phenomenon as an earlier but differently worded theory lacks the originality under consideration. Yet obviously, in other cases, size, colour, or wording might be relevant indeed.

Unquestionably 'original' is used in some such way (O_1), and wholly non-evaluatively. Phlogiston theory was original at some time. But a theory is evaluated according to some purpose; it can be original but worthless for that or any other purpose. Any of us could write an original poem, different from any existing poem in the respects we consider relevant, but in point of poetic value

[5] R. Wollheim, *Art and Its Objects* (Cambridge: Cambridge University Press, 2nd edn., 1980), §62.

worthless. Inventions of worthless ingenuity and originality abound; the Patent Office is full of them. 'It's certainly original, but utterly without value' need embody no absurdity.

We use 'original' in a second, still non-evaluative, way (O_2) thus: something is original if, though possibly qualitatively identical with another production even in relevant respects, it was the producer's own invention and produced in ignorance of the other. So something could be original (O_2) without being original (O_1). We can say, 'B's work is original, though identical with A's, because he produced it entirely off his own bat' as well as, 'B's production, though entirely his own work, is not original; A produced one exactly like it last year'. Clearly we do use O_2 as well as O_1 without always distinguishing them. In many spheres—with inventions, theories, etc.—we often concede that something was original, meaning *uncopied, unplagiarized, his own invention*, etc., without it being original, meaning *qualitatively different*. Questions about whether two relevantly identical inventions, say, should count as just one I shall side-step here. Questions, again, about whether in certain spheres, art being one, there could be two products identical in all relevant respects I shall ignore also as not germane to my present purpose; they turn, at least in part, on the boundaries set on what is regarded as relevant. But, even if the possibility is not ruled out in this way, it probably never happens that there are art-works that are original (O_2) without being also original (O_1). It perhaps happens with styles and genres: Picasso and Braque may have invented Cubism independently. But with individual art-works (provided criteria of identity are not drawn to include identity of authorship, time and place of production, etc.) the odds are probably large enough, since any art-work which is O_2 is virtually certain to be O_1, to justify me on this occasion in ignoring O_2.[6] So I shall merge O_2 into O_1 to mean *new, different, and uncopied, one's own work*, etc.

It seems evident then that 'original' whether O_1 or O_2, is used *non-evaluatively*: even two identical but independently produced works, if they occurred, could be aesthetically entirely worthless. But it seems equally obvious that we use 'original' in *evaluative* ways: often in calling a work original a speaker clearly means to attribute to it some, even considerable, merit (in our case,

---

[6] People have often wondered whether two poets, say, might independently produce identical poems. The odds against this must be considerable, but need not be as huge as often represented. Professor William Bennett at Yale recently tackled the familiar speculation about monkeys and Shakespeare: it would take a trillion monkeys 'on average, more than a trillion times as long as the universe has been in existence just to produce the sentence: *To be or not to be, that is the question*' (*The Daily Telegraph*, March 7, 1979). But it is not a question of random typewriter-tapping but of deliberate productions by language users. Odds against two contemporary English-speakers producing identical short epigrams in couplet form and containing only a few familiar words cannot be so enormous. Cf. e.g. Ruby Meager's remarks on 'Pippa Passes', 'Uniqueness', 57.

aesthetic or artistic).[7] If a critic I respect speaks of the originality of someone's latest poems I may justifiably anticipate finding them worth reading. If they prove worthless, though they are the poet's own work and different from any other poems, I may feel let down, so often is 'original' used to attribute value as well. When we say a man's originality flagged, that his later work lacks the originality of his earlier work, we do not mean that he kept writing identical poems or sonatas, nor yet that he produced strings of rather similar but very fine works; we usually mean that his later work was of lesser or indifferent quality. So 'original', used evaluatively (O_{le}), I shall take to mean *new, different, uncopied, one's own work*, etc. *and of some value*; using it this way one will not call a work original, however different it is, if it is without merit.[8]

The contrast sketched so far is sharp, exhaustive, and excludes degrees: anything original differs from other things in relevant respects, anything unoriginal is identical in relevant respects. But clearly there are common uses of 'original' and 'unoriginal' (whether evaluative or not) that are less strict, allowing degrees of, greater or less, originality. Works may be very or only somewhat original, rather unoriginal, fairly conservative or traditional, quite derivative, etc. Art-works called unoriginal in daily parlance generally do differ in relevant respects from other works and so would have been original in my first 'strict' sense. In *that* sense, most art-works are original, relevantly different, even inexact copies or imperfect plagiarisms. So the more common and important uses of 'original' and its negations remain for examination.

First, however, some comments on relevant differences; these, with art-works, are whatever gives a work a different aesthetic *character*. It might seem that we should speak rather of whatever makes a difference in aesthetic *value* for many of our questions concerning originality are about value or merit. But not without excluding a possible ambiguity first. Two Titian portraits of the same period, both fine works, similar in style and approach, are yet different; each has aesthetic value, but neither is a substitute for the other since each has a different aesthetic character, offers a different aesthetic experience, and therefore has a different *specific* value. Indeed, art-works differing in aesthetic character, if of value, *must* have different aesthetic values. But in another sense they could have the same, i.e., equal, value, neither being obviously more aesthetically valuable than the other. Giotto's *Death of St Francis* and Masaccio's *Adam and Eve Expelled from Paradise* clearly have *different* aesthetic

---

[7] I shall not distinguish 'aesthetic' and 'artistic'. I use 'aesthetic' throughout to encompass anything that could conceivably be characterized as aesthetic in an art-work. See 10 below.

[8] We would be taken aback, pace Kant, Beardsley, and Osborne, if critics often said 'This work is extremely original, but worthless nonsense, terrible, verging on idiocy'. Cf. F. E. Sparshott on 'original' and 'academic': 'These distinctions may be made in value-free terms . . . but in fact they are usually made for the purpose of grading rather than of neutral classification'. *The Structure of Aesthetics*, London: Routledge and Kegan Paul, 1963, 135.

values, but one might understandably hesitate to say that either had *greater* value than the other (though not to say that both had greater aesthetic value than any Whistler nocturne or Beerbohm cartoon). Similarly with Mozart's *Requiem* and the *Missa Solemnis* (*vis-à-vis*, say, 'Auld Lang Syne'). Despite some theorists' qualms, the same is true across different arts. We might hesitate over ranking works with specific values as different as those of Wolf's *Auch kleine Dinge* and Frith's *Derby Day*, but not question either's aesthetic superiority to Julia Moore's elegy on John Robinson. So two works may have roughly the same, i.e., equal, aesthetic value; but if they have different aesthetic characters, not inter-substitutable, each has a different specific value. The specific characters of works will differ in turn according to the different basic features that give them those characters. (This is typically so with artworks, but not with everything. Two different inventions, methods, say, of saving fuel, being equally effective, simple, safe, inexpensive and durable, have equal value but, having identical function, exhibit no contrast between equal value and different specific value. One could be substituted for the other without loss.)

I believe the terminology used will serve my present turn. The *basic features* which give a work its specific character include at least the selection and ordering of words in a poem, lines and colours in a painting, notes in a musical composition, etc. without excluding other possible factors over the inclusion of which theorists may dispute.[9] The *aesthetic character* of a work is the quality or assemblage of qualities in virtue of which it may be aesthetically praised or condemned—its grace, serenity, dynamism, gaiety, balance, unity, vividness, psychological perceptiveness, profundity, banality, sentimentality, etc.[10] By *specific aesthetic character* I mean that, e.g., Shylock's speeches are an expression of hatred distinctively different from that of Iago's speeches, the perfect balance of a particular Veronese canvas is not that of a Palladian building or even of another Veronese, the particular serenity of the close of the Goldberg Variations is not that either of a Claude sunset or of Beethoven's Op. III Adagio, and so on. So each work with a different specific aesthetic character is in some degree original and, if it has any aesthetic value at all, has a new, different, original *specific aesthetic value*. That is one link between originality and value.

I can now take up, but only schematically, some of the more common and less strict uses of 'original' and 'unoriginal'. Since in using either word we are

---

[9] Remembering that minute changes in basic features may enormously alter specific character while quite large changes may not.

[10] Obviously I intend no restriction to the 'merely' aesthetic, to 'surface qualities', etc. David Pole gave Leavis's view of art as 'valuable, and only valuable, because it deals significantly with human experience'. In 'Varieties of Aesthetic Experience', *Aesthetics, Form and Emotion*, ed. George Roberts, London: Duckworth, 1983, 6.

ordinarily dealing with matters of degree and by our various uses pick out positions further or less far along a continuum of difference, one way to understand the use on a given occasion is to consider what point or contrast is being made. I shall restrict myself to two sorts of contrast for the moment and number then as distinct uses. This makes matters look more tidy than they are, but the selections are not entirely arbitrary.

First, we may call a work original (O_3) when it differs *considerably*, but not *toto caelo*, from previous works. (The contrast is with works which differ, but not appreciably, from what has gone before; which have a close affinity or resemblance to previous work, no notable individuality, are stereotypes, predictable, routine, follow a formula, are all of a kind, mere modifications, even rehashes, etc.) We might use 'original' thus of any of Mozart's last three symphonies—they are distinctively different works—but withhold it perhaps from some dozens of Vivaldi or Telemann pieces.[11] Since a work may differ considerably from others yet be of either insignificant or high merit, we may use O_3 neutrally, implying only difference, or evaluatively (O_{3e}): in calling Mozart's last symphony original one would normally be attributing value as well as considerable difference. Thus a work that is O_{3e}, being considerably different in character, will have a new specific value; but how high or low this value is will be independent of its degree of difference. 'Unoriginal', the opposite of O_3, meaning *much like, lacking notable individuality*, etc., need not exclude value (though we have a pejorative use too); but any value it allows will be a specific value rather similar to that of some previous work. Thus each of the Titian portraits of a given period, like the later Mozart symphonies, is original both neutrally (O_3) and evaluatively (O_{3e}). Each offers something considerably different with a different specific value; and we would probably no more wish to substitute one for another than if, wanting the *Eroica*, we were offered the *Pastoral* instead. But with a dozen of the Vivaldi or Telemann pieces, though the aesthetic experiences they offer differ somewhat and may even have considerable aesthetic value, we might think, understandably, that they are similar enough in character and specific value and, wishing to enjoy the *kind* of experience they offer, be moderately indifferent about substitutions. If things, including art-works, are similar enough we may not unreasonably decide that any one will do.

Secondly, we might locate a stronger yet still familiar use of 'original' much further along the scale of difference. We use this to mark works that are extremely different, innovative, or revolutionary: Beethoven's late works, those of Giotto, Blake, Wagner, Cezanne, Joyce, Kandinsky, Schoenberg, Stockhausen. However different from one another the cited Mozart symphonies (or the Titian portrait) are, they inhabit, we say, the same world

---

[11] The reader is at liberty throughout to supply other examples at relevant points if mine do not appeal.

of experiences and employ nearly enough the same styles and techniques. This stronger use of 'original', meaning extremely innovatory or revolutionary, is not applicable to the last of Mozart's great symphonies or the last of the middle period Titians. But works which are not original in this extreme way will include those, and they may be very fine, that exhibit more moderate or gradual development, change, advance, as well as those deserving the sometimes pejorative adjectives, 'traditional', 'conservative', or 'academic'; but they no more need be routine or predictable or stereotypes or lacking individuality than the Mozarts or Titians are.

Clearly there is a familiar evaluative use of 'original' (O_{4e}) when it attributes both extreme difference in this way *and* value ('highly original but worthless' then rings oddly); but, in so far as this is understood merely as a conjunction, there is no reason so far to suppose that extremely innovative works that have aesthetic merit must have greater than slight merit, or that greater originality in this sense implies greater merit. But it is worth stressing that 'original', meaning extremely different and innovative, is also often used quite neutrally (O_4). Things original in this extreme way may have no value, or only the most trivial beyond the excitement of novelty for its own sake. Certainly there are reasons, emphasized by some, why any *activity* exhibiting novelty, experiment, change, seen as an indication of life, alertness, spontaneity as against the lifeless and unimaginative, may be valued and the more valued the greater it is. Activity may be valued independently of the value of its products, if any.[12] But theorists and critics who talk as if any *product*, any art-work, which is extremely original (O_4) must have aesthetic value, even high value, are surely failing to recognize that this neutral use occurs.

This aesthetically neutral 'original' is very commonly used for style, manner, technique, medium; Cubism, Abstract Expressionism, Pointillisme, the twelve-tone system exemplify large innovations, highly original. But there can be valuable and worthless work in any style or technique. In themselves, these were extremely original but aesthetically quite neutral: no one might— though fortunately some did—produce works of aesthetic value employing them. The value of such innovations is instrumental; it lies in what new aesthetic characters and values they render possible; but it is easily forgotten that some innovations in style, technique and medium, by the very limits they impose, open up and make possible little of aesthetic significance. Their importance is that, when they do yield works of value, the character of such works will be different, in look, sound, or whatever, and their specific value will be new and original, whether it is high or low. (Obviously, in calling innovatory styles, techniques, forms, etc. 'instrumental', 'means' to creation of

---

[12] Doctrines as popular with earlier writers (cf. Browning's 'I want to know a butcher paints, A baker rhymes for his pursuit') as with many modern educationists, artists, and art theorists.

aesthetic character and value, I am not asserting a merely external, but an indispensable and internal, connection. The aesthetic character of *Pierrot Lunaire*, whether one rates its value high or low, could not be achieved by the techniques of Scarlatti or Beethoven, the sting of Pope's couplets by blank verse, Rembrandt's exploration of character in mobiles, or Wagner's emotional world without chromaticism.) So the enthusiastic praise often lavished on works employing innovatory techniques, new stylistic tricks, novelties of form or medium is misplaced unless these bring, or have the potential to bring, some new aesthetic character of value. In this respect those who inveigh against the cult of the original are right; but equally, those are wrong who decry any extreme stylistic or technical innovation before assessing what is being done with it or what might be, what new worlds of aesthetic experience are opened up. Who could have foreseen the glories to be achieved, faced with the first stumbling efforts in sonnet form or the first essays in pictorial perspective?

Three additional comments. First, 'original' has other uses that cut across those so far mentioned and identifiable by the opposites with which they contrast. Within the *oeuvre* of *one* artist later works may be unoriginal (or original), technically, stylistically, or in aesthetic character, by being (or not being) self-repetitive, etc. Between *different* artists works of the later one may be unoriginal (or original), technically, stylistically, or in aesthetic character, by being (or not being) derivative, etc.[13] Secondly, nothing I have said denies that even very innovative works may be influenced by, based on, or variants of, previous works: variations on the Three Graces theme, the eclecticism of Stravinsky, the influence of African art on Picasso, and so on endlessly.[14] Thirdly, something that requires at least brief mention here. The meanings of 'original' I began with, (O_1), relevantly different from things previously existing, and (O_2), a creator's own invention, and all those mentioned since are relative simply to what has preceded. Such kinds of originality (and unoriginality) are unaffected by passage of time and later creations: once original, always original. We can say, timelessly, that Giotto's frescos or Schoenberg's Chamber Symphony exhibit great originality; they break with the past, constitute new beginnings. But we also sometimes use 'original' to mean 'nothing

[13] And uses across other bodies of work, cf. Alfred Lessing: 'by originality in art we can and often do mean the artistic novelty and achievement not of one particular work of art but of the totality of artistic productions of one man or even one school . . . the originality of Vermeer . . . or Impressionism . . . or even the Greeks'. In 'What is Wrong With a Forgery?', *Journal of Aesthetics and Art Criticism*, 23 (1964–5), 468.

[14] Cf. R. G. Collingwood: 'Individualism would have it that the work of a genuine artist is altogether "original", that is to say, purely his own work. . . . All artists have modelled their style upon that of others, used subjects that others have used, and treated them as others have treated them already. A work of art so constructed is a work of collaboration'. *The Principles of Art*, Oxford: Clarendon Press, 1938, 318.

relevantly similar *now* exists'. As soon as something does, a thing is original no longer. We may use it thus of forms, styles, and techniques: the symphony was original in the eighteenth century, Cubism in 1920; they no longer are. Also of the generic character of works: tragedy was original in the fifth century, Wagner investigated aspects of eroticism and Baudelaire aspects of evil not before attempted; many have done the same since, so explorations of these aspects of experience are no longer original. Perhaps we should eschew 'original' here and replace it by 'novel' or 'new'. But 'novel' more often hints at the trivial, the gimmicky, the mere thrill of the new, the quickly exhausted than 'original' does. Osborne suggested some such difference when, attacking the cult of originality, he spoke of 'originality in the sense of novelty'. Perhaps it is easier to think of novelty as not impervious to time and something that cannot last. Hence Osborne can add, 'A work of art which is novel today may well be old hat tomorrow'. But it is presumably things of small value, easily spawning imitations, that rapidly become, with their progeny, old hat and therefore negligible; their novelty value gone, their true worth is exposed. Moreover, this point about novelty is distinct from the issue raised by Osborne's next sentence, that a work's 'very excellence may contribute to the speed with which it becomes familiar'. These are interesting points, but quite unrelated: becoming *familiar* through excellence is worlds away from becoming *old hat* through loss of novelty. And, as Osborne indicates, neither is strictly relevant to what I have taken to be the central question. What Giotto or Michelangelo or Petrarch initiated and achieved may by now be utterly familiar, the aesthetic veins they explored exhausted, much that they introduced long since traditional, much imitated, and we may want no more of it. But they have not become old hat. Even if their achievements had been surpassed their work would remain original in a crucial sense and will never be otherwise. What may have rendered much recent art old hat is the facility with which certain methods, techniques, and styles have been re-used and the limited aesthetic character and value achievable by using them. Having once absorbed what they can offer, if we rate its value low there is little reward in returning to it or having more of it produced. But questions about temporary novelty or about familiarity do not bear on the central question: whether any originality that is time-impervious is relevant, and if so how, to the merit of *any* art-work, great or small, familiar or unfamiliar.

I have distinguished various uses of 'original', its conceptual associates and opposites. I have not multiplied them beyond necessity—indeed there are others—though I have admittedly drawn sharp lines where often there are only mergings. If we look closely enough at how we talk we find that something like these differing uses do occur and are needed for our various interests and purposes. With these distinctions made, and some misplaced enthusiasms about the value of originality questioned, some more central but not unfamiliar thoughts about its value must be faced.

The question whether originality in any sense is *necessary* for aesthetic value interests me here less than certain others. So I offer no arguments about it, only some remarks. It seems perverse often to deny that a work identical in relevant respects to one made before it can have the same aesthetic value.[15] When an artist designs a fine candlestick or chair, and he or his associates then produce a number of them, these may surely all be identical in character and value and the world richer by containing additional beautiful objects. Roman sculptors attempted exact copies of Greek masterpieces, making valuable aesthetic experiences available to more people. Writers, for similar reasons, strive to make good translations. We cannot blink the fact that much of our knowledge and appreciation of aesthetic excellence comes from photos, reproductions, or television. In certain traditions, without attempting exact copying, artists have produced successions of near-identical works, Buddhas, ikons, vases. A line, a texture, the size may differ slightly. But often the predominant aesthetic character, smiling serenity, sublime stillness, grace, or whatever, is all but identical. Originality, if it involves significant difference, is absent. In the neutral senses mentioned, originality is necessary (but not sufficient), as I have said, only for new or different specific values. Whole cultures seem to have been relatively indifferent to these; even we are happy sometimes to see the world more full of beautiful or moving, even if aesthetically indistinguishable, things. But many societies, including ours, seek variety, breadth of aesthetic experience, varied and new aesthetic values, works that reflect our changing times, varying perceptions, and contemporary insights. Hence part of the importance of and demand for originality.[16]

To deal with this I shall use the notion of *intrinsic value* in, I hope, a familiar enough way.[17] The intrinsic value of a work is its own aesthetic merit detached from whatever value it has as influence on later artists or trends, for

---

[15] Cf. Osborne: a critic would be 'arbitrary' and 'illogical' to hold that works possessing 'the other qualities of excellence but without novelty ... must fall short of excellence', 'Concept of Creativity', 227.

[16] Cf. Lessing: the question is 'why originality is such a significant aspect of art ... concern with originality is not a universal characteristic ... [it] is perhaps typical only of modern Western art ... if artists were concerned only with making beautiful pictures, poems, symphonies, etc., the possibilities for the creation of aesthetically pleasing works of art would soon be exhausted. We would (perhaps) have a number of lovely paintings, but we should soon grow tired of them for they would all be more or less alike. But artists ... seek to produce *original* works of beauty. And when they succeed ... we call their works great not only because they are beautiful but also because they have also unlocked ... unknown and unexplored realms of beauty'. 'What is Wrong?', 469–70.

[17] OED: 'Belonging to the thing itself'. Cf. C. S. Lewis: '[Wyatt's] real place in the evolution of English poetry (as distinct from his intrinsic value, his place of honour among English poets) is really an unfortunate one. His own lyric gift he did not bequeath to most of his successors'. *English Literature in the Sixteenth Century*, Oxford: Clarendon Press, 1954, 224.

historical explanation of subsequent developments, etc. It seems difficult to operate without allowing that any poem, say, has certain merits, is aesthetically fine, poor, or indifferent whether anyone ever reads it or not, for it is its merit that a careful reader attempts to recognize and assess. Equally, it seems hard to deny that aesthetic merit can be recognized and appreciated in a work without knowledge of or comparison with other works, and, *a fortiori*, independently of questions of originality since these require such knowledge and comparisons. Denying this would mean denying that countless thousands who knew nothing but the Bible, or *Paradise Lost*, or a print of a Raphael Madonna could have any authentic appreciation or genuine recognition of the power or beauty of those works—something I would not wish to question. (I am not saying of course that this could happen without background knowledge of the language, sights, and sounds in which any art-works are embedded.) But such recognition and appreciation achieved without knowledge of other works cannot but be, however partial and untutored, a recognition of intrinsic aesthetic value. Obviously without comparisons there can be no ranking of values and no adequate realization of how high the intrinsic aesthetic merit may be. *Gammer Gurton's Needle* must have seemed an unsurpassably comic artistic achievement until later comedies came along. But we can surely reject any extreme doctrine that to judge that a work has aesthetic merit we must look beyond it to other works. Indeed the need of comparisons to rank works reinforces rather than questions their possessions of intrinsic values. To rate, after careful attention, *The Confessio Amantis* aesthetically superior to *The Canterbury Tales* or *The Fleece* to *Paradise Lost* would reveal something amiss. But such comparative rankings would be impossible unless intrinsic values could be attributed. Some such notion of intrinsic value underlies much of what follows.

Returning to the demands for variety and originality that are often made, we can elucidate a kind of judgement that we make of art-works different both from judgements that a work has intrinsic value and and from comparative judgements that rank intrinsic values. These are judgements that *balance* the intrinsic worth of one work against that of another. Beardsley is alive to these judgements. Having said, firmly, 'We admire, and justly, the originality of Haydn and Beethoven and Stravinsky and Bartók, providing they wrote not only originally *but well*' (my italics), and added that from praise of a composer's originality 'nothing follows about the goodness of the work', so seemingly treating what I called judgements of intrinsic value as the only truly aesthetic judgements, he then allows that we make another kind of judgement, one that accounts for our admiration for originality. 'After certain sounds have come into the world—after eighty-three Haydn quartets . . .—for all their incredible variety within a certain range, we bow', he says, 'to the law of diminishing returns'. Admiration is due 'if another composer will enlarge the range of chamber music . . . with original innovations, rather than work within the same range'. But he apparently balks at regarding this as a genuinely aesthetic matter; rather, this admiration [for originality] is based on something like an *economic* ground, or on the *general welfare*' (my italics). The dispute may be only verbal; but I think these judgements can legitimately be regarded as aesthetic. I shall dub them *In-context Judgements*.

The issue is clear enough, though again I have to draw lines over-sharply. An extremely different new work of high merit has a new specific value. We may wish to balance this value against that of an earlier work. Suppose I think Bartók's third quartet and the 'Jupiter' equally great, of equal intrinsic value, but that the quartet speaks to our times and reveals a personality and aspects of twentieth-century consciousness worlds apart from anything in Mozart or elsewhere. I might in that context place greater value on the Bartók, i.e., regard its possible loss as greater than the loss, unhappy as that would be, of one Mozart symphony, even the 'Jupiter'. One might even argue that, since it illuminates our condition or enlarges our experience in ways no single Mozart work can, one *ought*, in some sense, to value it higher in context (which is not to say one would or should save it if that meant losing all Mozart). Such balancing is difficult enough. Balancing in-context values is yet more difficult if intrinsic values are judged to differ markedly, the modern work having modest intrinsic value but a character Mozart or Michelangelo could never have offered (say, at the reader's choice, Berio's *Sequenze* or various works of Pop art). Here, forced to lose one work entirely (and I mean a choice based on evaluation, not on mere liking or resulting from a surfeit of Mozart), many would choose to keep all of Mozart's last symphonies though the differences between them are not of the extreme sort, and would sacrifice instead any new work of modest intrinsic value however different and innovatory. Others, balancing values differently, conceding the lower intrinsic value of a new work, might yet value it more in context than any Mozart symphony because it contributes to contemporary life something that no existing or newly found Mozart symphony could. Issues like these about balancing values underlie Beardsley's remarks and can make some claims for the value of originality more intelligible.

How then should in-context judgements of value be described? Beardsley hesitated over regarding them as aesthetic judgements. Yet despite his remarks about 'an economic ground' and 'the general welfare' he concedes that the originality of a work, so long as the work is praiseworthy at all, is 'a contribution to our *aesthetic* resources' (my italics). I prefer to say that we simply have another kind of aesthetic judgement here. For nothing is involved, once personal likings and the work's value for future developments and historical understanding are ruled out, except aesthetic worth. We are weighing aesthetic worth in a context, it is true, and deciding whether X is more valuable than Y in context because of the *kind* of aesthetic worth it has; but it is still *aesthetic* values we are considering, the value of an addition that has a new, different, specific value. If represented as a matter of economy, marginal value, diminishing returns, the general welfare, it is the economy of aesthetic value, not of anything else, the value of the work to us, in our age, given the existing aesthetic legacy. The only aim is maximization of aesthetic values, the richness, variety, and range of our aesthetic life. To suppose that such judgements are not genuinely aesthetic but concern instead 'the general welfare' is to endorse the untenably narrow doctrine that denies that aesthetic judgements are thoroughly and inevitably permeated by our more general values and concern for human well-being.[18] There is no contradiction in judging X equal or superior in intrinsic aesthetic value to Y and also judging Y aesthetically more valuable in the circumstances. Both judgements of aesthetic value can stand together provided they are not confused or understood otherwise than intended.

We can perhaps try some tentative conclusions. 'Original' is used in various neutral ways to indicate only some difference from what has gone before; a work so described may have great or negligible aesthetic worth. If Kant, Beardsley, and Osborne had these uses in mind, they rightly rejected originality as a reason for aesthetic praise. To suppose that mere difference guarantees or constitutes aesthetic merit would be absurd[19] and also, *a fortiori*, that such originality is a high, the highest, or the only significant aesthetic value. 'Original' is also used evaluatively in ways that carry a clear attribution of merit. When used thus, on the interpretations I have given so far, it is true, but trivially, that originality guarantees merit; also true that an original work will have a new specific value. But nothing ensures that this intrinsic value is high rather than modest; that must be judged independently.[20] Certainly a more

[18] See 10 above.

[19] Cf. Collingwood: 'Originality in art, meaning lack of resemblance to anything that has been done before, is sometimes nowadays regarded as an artistic merit. This, of course, is absurd'. *Principles of Art* 43.

[20] Lessing proposes five meanings of originality. They do not closely coincide with my distinctions. Of his third meaning he says, 'By originality in art we may mean the kind of imaginative novelty of spontaneity which is a mark of *every* good work of art . . . e.g. this work of art is original because the artist has done something with the subject and its treatment which has never been done before', op. cit., p. 467 (my italics). This sounds like my evaluative use of O_3. But then it is doubtfully applicable to '*every* good work of art' because of what he himself says about other traditions, see n. 16 above. His fourth meaning is certainly important and one I do not discuss (though my remarks on p. 132f imply it): '*originality* is sometimes used to refer to the great artistic achievement of a specific work of art . . . whereas nearly all of Milton's works are good and original in the sense of (3) above, *Paradise Lost* has a particularly profound originality possessed only by really superlative works of art . . . the scope, profundity, daring, and novelty of the conception of the work [and] the excellence of its execution . . . [are] lacking in many—maybe the majority of— legitimate works of art', op. cit., pp. 467–8. He says this fourth meaning differs from his third only in degree. I said the same of my O_3 and O_4. But his is not even my evaluative O_4; mine stressed extreme differences in *character*, whether the merit was high or low; his

original work need not have a higher intrinsic value than a less innovatory, more traditional work.[21]

Some critics and theorists may seek to claim importance for originality, tying it more closely to value than I have so far. Indeed, besides those more extreme claims that are either absurd or hard to comprehend, others deserve considerable sympathy.

One at least understandable way of seeing any new value as the greatest value a work can have would result from an uncompromising commitment to in context evaluation. Earlier I shared Ruby Mager's doubt that to have aesthetic merit works must be original (in any, that is, of the neutral or evaluative ways discussed), a prima-facie dubious view in the absence of satisfactory, non-stipulative support. But one might argue that originality is necessary for creation of value in the following way. Any really different aesthetic value, however small, outweighs, in context, any aesthetic value, however great, that resembles too closely those existing already; only new sorts of values genuinely extend our aesthetic store, contribute a new dimension to our lives; therefore the most valuable work, that most worth producing at any time is any that will add any shred of significantly different aesthetic experience, any new intrinsic value however slight (rather as a collector may value the acquisition of a very different specimen above that of near-duplicates even of higher market value). Given an existing body of art, we can see how some might place a premium on originality. A new value outweighs an additional familiar value; by however little it enlarges, enlargement is all. This position is intelligible even if we do not endorse it, and may be that of some contemporary theorists whether or not they so state it. But its proponents may misunderstand or overstate it thus: among all works whatever, any with a new value, being the only sort that can enlarge our resources, merits the highest praise. This is to confuse intrinsic value with the value of additions. Perhaps few, if they thought clearly, would hold a doctrine with such paradoxical implications for long.

It may, however, be easily confused with a view that genuinely justifies enthusiasm for originality. The possibility always exists that a work with a new specific value may have high intrinsic and not just high-context worth. For such masterpieces originality is necessary, as Kant indeed said it was for genius. So we can encourage originality and experiments. The advice, Make It New, is not pointless and enthusiasm for originality need occasion neither

---

stresses extreme of merit ('really superlative works'), which *would* require differences of character but not necessarily innovatory abandonment of tradition. There are many dimensions along which differences may occur.

[21] Nicely pinpointed by Michael Scriven: 'in painting the aim of becoming a preeminent Pre-Raphaelite or a topical Turner obviously lacks appeal in the academic ateliers, and yet talent and even originality can as easily be demonstrated in that way as in the days when the Guardis and Canaletto put Venice on canvas'. *Primary Philosophy*, New York: McGraw-Hill, 1966, 83.

dispute nor hostility. The greatest artists as well as the failures have ventured among untrodden ways; we can be grateful for the dedication and courage of innovators. But they and their apologists alike should remember that more minnows are caught than whales, not proclaim every new minnow a whale, or deny that many whales have already been landed. Equally, less innovatory artists who shun the risk business or by choice tread a more conservative path should remember that fewer whales may remain to be caught in the old waters.

An unexceptionable interpretation can also be put on remarks like Wollheim's that place originality among the highest values of art. They can be taken as applying less to particular works than to art, the institution, or enterprise; for one reason why we value this most highly is that it has by its very nature the capacity to provide, along with the great aesthetic achievements that already exist, new and enriching objects and experiences of value.

Finally I may be accused of misrepresenting evaluative uses of 'original'. Many might agree that 'original' often indicates not merely difference but also that a work has value: i.e., is 'creative', exhibits a new personality, insight, outlook, aspect of experience, etc. But I have treated 'original', used evaluatively, as attributing, simply conjunctively, some difference from previous works and some independently assessable intrinsic merit. The objection might be that both difference from and similarity to previous works affect intrinsic merit, are partial determinants of value; intrinsic merit is not independent of such facts. This charge probably needs closer scrutiny than I can give it. So only some brief comments.

If a work is significantly different from others being, in its own way, say, powerful, moving, and profound, these are merits. But if it is seriously derivative, significantly similar to works known directly or indirectly to the artist, it may fail to count as powerful, moving, and profound but only as having merits, if any, of lesser degree; it is too nearly a rehash to equal the earlier work in merit. But this simply reasserts the view that a measure of originality, difference, is necessary for (high) merit, that lack of it reduces or wipes out merits the work would have had if original. Similarly with judgements. For judgements, if correct, reflect what is true of the work. If, having carefully assessed a work new to us, we judge it in its own particular way powerful, moving, profound, etc. (allowing even that to make this judgement at all we might require background knowledge of some previous works from which it is seen notably to diverge), that would seem a judgement of its intrinsic merit. If we later discover it to be highly derivative, closely similar to even *one* previous work, and retract our judgement, judge it no longer (so) powerful, moving, and profound, decide that its supposed merits were apparent only, we are again accepting the view that significant aesthetic merit requires a degree of originality. By contrast, after the same initial judgement of the high merits of the work, a discovery that there has *not* been, unknown to us, any prior closely similar work leaves that judgement untouched: its apparent merits as we assessed them are its real merits. Certainly, when the originality of a work whose originality we were not sure of before is confirmed, we may rightly view its achievement as remarkable. Our wonder, admiration for the artist, his artistry, his imaginative leap, even for the powers of the human spirit are elicited by his having achieved, with so little help from his predecessors, precisely those qualities and merits we, perhaps provisionally, first judged the work to have. Authoritative assessment of the merit of a work may perhaps be impossible without takings its originality or lack of it into account. But even if originality is necessary for merit, or lack of originality lowers the merit one would, assuming the work original, deem it to have, no argument so far shows, except in a Pickwickian sense, that originality adds to, increases, or positively enhances its merit. It does not suddenly become moving, powerful, profound by being proved significantly different from its predecessors. It merely has its apparent merits confirmed.

Beardsley, as I quoted him, said that originality in a 'strict sense' has no bearing on worth; for that sense, which is non-evaluative and concerns merely difference, his remark is unquestionable.[22] But one wonders why he singled it out when other senses, evaluative and equally familiar, commonly appear in criticism. Since the slide from one of these many uses to another frequently goes unnoticed, equivocations and disputes easily arise. It is often unclear, even in context, and, one suspects, in the critic's or theorist's own mind, which of several things he means by calling a work original, how it bears on value, and what various claims for the importance of originality amount to. Often the most vocal enthusiasts for originality seem muddled about which version, or how many, they are espousing, and fail to realize what may be obvious to others, that some innovations are capable of yielding only minimal values. Distinguishing different uses of 'original' helps reveal the ambiguities underlying some of the apparent disagreements and allows some divergent claims to be assessed. Much remains to be elucidated; but it is worth reminding those who notice only neutral uses that evaluative uses of 'original' exist and their shared core of meaning has often enough been identified. Hazlitt, described by Eliot as 'perhaps the most uninteresting mind of all our distinguished critics', bluntly, as often, hit the main nail on the head: 'He is a man of genius who finds out a new *ore*. Originality is . . . the discovery of new and *valuable* truth'. Baudelaire similarly, who stressed as emphatically as anyone the importance of originality in art, states the matter as it must be if the claim is to have any acceptability: originality is striving after 'novelty of beauty'.[23]

---

[22] An object is original in Beardsley's strict sense if it differs 'in some *notable* way from anything else *that was known by its creator to exist* at that time', *Aesthetics*, 460 (my italics); this is akin to my non-evaluative O_4 (or to a parallel derivative from O_2), not to *my* 'strict senses', O_1 and O_2.

[23] Italics in the quotations from Hazlitt and Baudelaire are mine.

10

Arts or the Aesthetic—Which Comes First?

The question I want to raise here is about the genesis of the concept of the aesthetic. Where does it originate? Do human beings derive the notion of aesthetic experience from the arts and the work of artists, or would aesthetic experience be possible, perhaps in relation to natural objects, even if there were no art? Which, in short, is the more fundamental notion, art or the aesthetic?

During the eighteenth century, many writers on aesthetics, Hutcheson, Hume, Burke, and Kant for example, concentrated quite as much on the beauty, ugliness, sublimity, and other aesthetic qualities of natural phenomena as on the arts. With Hegel this changed. Since his time, writers on aesthetics, though not without exceptions, have largely focused on the arts. The titles of many of the best-known works and collections indicate this: *Art & Experience, What is Art?, The Principles of Art, Art and its Objects, Languages of Art, Philosophy looks at the Arts*. Even works with the title *Aesthetics*, like Croce's or Beardley's, are predominantly concerned with the arts. Much recent discussion in aesthetics, indeed, has narrowed to disputing, in ever more detail, whether and why the productions of the present century, from *objets trouvés* and ready-mades to automatic writing and aleatory music, are or are not art.

It is true that, with the recent emphasis on environmental, ecological, and preservation issues, this tide may be turning and emphasis falling again on aesthetic aspects of natural phenomena. For many of the arguments of environmentalists are probably as much aesthetic as they are moral or practical in character.

But it is not these switches of emphasis and fashion that I aim to discuss. The crux of my question concerns not fashionable emphasis but logical priorities. Is the concept of the aesthetic logically prior to, or logically derivative from, the concept of art? More colloquially, could there be art if we possessed no notion of aesthetic experience, or does the very existence of art depend upon our having this notion?

In the introduction to his lectures on Fine Art, Hegel wrote, 'the beauty of art stands higher than Nature' and concentrated thereafter on an account of

[From an audiotape for Open University Course AA301, *Philosophy of the Arts*, 1992.]

the arts. Many others since have contended explicitly that the arts have a logical priority over the aesthetics of nature. One recent writer of importance[1] holds that 'once the aesthetic attitude has been established on the basis of objects produced under the concept of art, we can extend it beyond this base'. Another[2] writes, 'when we judge a person's or a flower's beauty we are judging them within certain artificial canons, canons that we develop from our acquaintance with the arts'.

A fact that helps lend colour to these contentions is the realization that the way we see nature is often influenced, if not determined, by the way artists have depicted it. We may see, it is said, landscapes through Constable's eyes, clouds and sun through Turner's, water or flowers or dancers through Monet's or Van Gogh's or Degas's.

But I believe the contention that art is the prior notion may have little to support it. To my knowledge no convincing argument has ever been offered to prove it. Indeed I want to suggest that no such argument could be given. I even think that the exact opposite is almost certainly true, that is, that the concept of art is logically secondary or dependent on the concept of the aesthetic. I shall offer an argument for that in a moment. But even without argument it might surely seem, if one reflects, inconceivable, or at least wholly unlikely, that there could be no aesthetic awareness of natural phenomena, of the beauty or ugliness of human faces and bodies, of animals, of sunrise and sunset, of clouds, the sea, meadows and mountains unless some art already existed, or some deliberate attempt to make articles of aesthetic interest had already occurred.

However, it is arguments rather than likelihoods that concern me here. Here is an argument. If one considers the concept of art, at least that concept which underlies the obvious or central or paradigm examples of art over many centuries, it seems impossible that art should not be thought of as the production of things, audible, visual, or linguistic, which are attempts to create, if not beauty, at least things of some aesthetic interest, and this no matter what additional purposes they might have been meant to serve. But if this apparently obvious supposition is correct, the argument seems simple. It is impossible to have the intention to do or produce X, whatever X is, without already possessing some notion of X. I cannot set myself to produce, say, a sandcastle without having some notion of what a sandcastle is. Of course, I might be messing about with sand, a spade, a bucket, and happen by chance to produce something like, apparently indistinguishable from, a sandcastle; but unless I possessed that concept I did not, and could not have, set out or

[1] Richard Wollheim, *Art and Its Objects*, 2nd edn., Cambridge: Cambridge University Press, 1980, 97.

[2] Anthony Savile, *The Test of Time: An Essay in Philosophical Aesthetics*, Oxford: Clarendon Press, 1982, p. xi.

intended to produce that particular result. It would be like Charles Lamb's story of the accidental discovery of the delights of roast pig. Similarly, someone, adult or child, even an orang-utan, even a machine randomly operating, might produce something that happened to be of aesthetic interest. But if art is something produced with the intention, or even merely the hope, that it will be aesthetically satisfying, then the concept of aesthetic experience, enjoyment, satisfaction, or whatever, must logically precede the concept of art. The argument rests, then, on the claim that any acceptable account of the concept of art, as that term has been used to cover the familiar so-called fine arts, sees art as aiming at some kind of aesthetic achievement. But if that is correct, it follows directly that some notion of the aesthetic must have an origin, an existence, independent of the arts, not vice versa, and aesthetic experience of non-artistic phenomena, whether artefacts or natural objects, is logically prior to interest in, or even the existence of, the arts.

This argument, notice first, is entirely about a logical priority between concepts; it is not an argument about priority in time. In a similar way, the notion of a straight line is logically prior to the notion of a triangle; i.e., there could not be triangles unless there were straight lines, though the converse is possible. But that of course does not prove that there were straight lines before there were triangles. Secondly, another thing this argument does not prove: it does not prove that people took an aesthetic interest in natural objects before they took an aesthetic interest in man-made artefacts. It is perfectly conceivable that the first time anyone experienced aesthetic delight it was delight at a humanly made artefact, not a natural object. But, if the argument is correct, such an artefact was not a work of art, any more than the outcome of my random activities on the seashore was a sandcastle. My pile of sand might be called a sandcastle by others; but only because they, unlike me, possess that concept. Thirdly, the argument does not deny that you or I might have acquired our notion of aesthetic experience from contact with works of art; only that whoever created those works must have had some prior notion of the aesthetic.

The argument just given employed, as a crucial premise, that nothing is art that is not made with at least some aesthetic intention. This account of the notion of art—as that notion occurs in connection with the fine arts, not with such skills as, say, the art of healing, the art of public speaking, or the art of plumbing—this account I believe unquestionably fits those long periods of history during which most of our indubitable and paradigmatic instances of the fine arts have been produced. But one can immediately foresee that objections to this premise might be made, based both upon recent developments in the arts and upon the earliest examples of art, say, cave paintings.

Take recent developments first. It may be said that this supposition about art fails to fit many of the developments of the twentieth century. There have been works which are chance or random happenings, aleatory music, automatic writing, *objets trouvés*, ready-mades, computer productions, works over which the artist exerted little control or direction, or where there was no intention of producing things of aesthetic interest. Many distinctions can be made of course. Sometimes artists have left things to chance but hoped for and selected and salvaged anything of aesthetic significance; but in so far as they select the 'worthwhile' results and reject the 'worthless', they are still, by this selection, often intending to present items, differently arrived at, of aesthetic interest. But in other cases there has been the deliberate intention or hope that what is produced or selected will be ugly, banal, pedestrian, without traditional aesthetic values, will even be devoid of aesthetic interest altogether. Such productions may be, and have been, described as art-works; indeed, whether they are accepted as art-works depends on some kind of decision (though questions about criteria of artistic success or excellence then obtrude). Perhaps these decisions have already been fairly generally taken by the art world, though they may still be disputed by the general public; perhaps again, the decisions will be reversed in fifty or a hundred years.

Some contemporary aestheticians have expended much energy discussing these interesting but—as I believe—peripheral questions, even to the exclusion of other matters of importance in aesthetics. But it is not my present concern to take sides on these topics, either over particular productions or the criteria employed.

The point at issue here is this. If there are those who, because of these works, deny that aesthetic intent is essential to art, there is a ready reply to hand, namely, that these developments are extensions of, and impossible without, the art against which they are reacting. Attempts to produce works that lack aesthetic interest are parasitic on the traditional concept. For it is as much a logical impossibility to intend something that lacks aesthetic interest without having a concept of the aesthetic, as to intend something that has aesthetic interest. Equally, the intention not to produce art, or to produce what is not art, requires a conception of art. So, it seems, whether we allow these modern works to be new forms of art or not, they all presuppose a familiar concept of art and therefore of the aesthetic. Without the latter concept they could not exist. In so far as they are parasitic on previous traditions, works, and concepts of art, they necessarily involve those concepts.

The position of early and prehistoric art-works is different in some ways, similar in others. In most cases we have little idea why they were produced, what their makers had in mind, what intentions they had, what purposes their productions were designed to serve. Speculation is that they may have been for magic, religious, or practical purposes; since they are often in dark and inaccessible places, like caves, it is possible they were not intended, so to speak, for exhibition, contemplation, or to provide aesthetic satisfaction. But we do not know. On the other hand, perhaps their makers did find aesthetic delight in them. Often, certainly, they have remarkable aesthetic qualities which *we* can appreciate, whether their makers did or not. For this reason, and perhaps because it seems unlikely that such works were made by people with no appreciation of, or intention to produce, these aesthetic features, we give them the benefit of the doubt and call them works of art. Thus, if their makers did have some concept of the aesthetic in making them, they may have been, even for them, works of art. If they had no such concept—and we are uncertain, since we do not know if they did any of the things we characteristically do with artworks—then they were perhaps either like doodles or my sandcastles above, things produced for no purpose, or else things produced with quite other intentions. In which case, whatever *we* say about them and however *we* treat them, they were not works of art; it is we who choose so to treat them. They are artefacts that happen to have aesthetic interest. But who cares, except perhaps anthropologists, whether they were the art of those early people or not? We treat them as art much as Duchamp and others in this century have treated non-art artefacts as art, as ready-mades.

This, incidentally, provokes a further thought. If we have, perhaps for centuries, treated what were in fact non-art artefacts of earlier times as artworks, then ready-mades or something very similar, far from being an innovation of this century, have been around for a very long time. What distinguishes them is that, with prehistoric objects, we treat artefacts as artworks without knowing for certain whether they were or not, whereas with modern ready-mades, something is deliberately treated as art though known not to have been produced as such.

I must stress however that my argument is not really about history or prehistory. At some period in time, presumably, notions of the aesthetic (however named or unnamed—appropriate behaviour and forms of appreciation would be enough) first occurred or developed; some animals from which we evolved presumably lacked these notions. But whether historically this happened before or after the epoch, say, of cave paintings, whatever was produced before this happened was not art in that familiar central sense that underlies the art of many centuries.

If the forgoing argument is sound, it follows that, far from the aesthetic being logically parasitic on art, the reverse is the case. But the argument rests on the premise I stated, that art, paradigmatically, is something produced with aesthetic intent. So what if that premise is rejected, and the concept of art is thought of as involving no aesthetic intention, a concept little different from that occurring in, say, the art of the wheelwright or the art of healing? That would still not serve to establish the position I questioned at the outset, that art has a logical priority over the aesthetic. To deny that I have given a conclusive proof of the one view provides no proof or evidence for the other view. We would simply be left with the notion of art-works as artefacts which by chance possess and are enjoyed for their aesthetic qualities, together with a merely factual, historical, but unsupported assertion—that aesthetic interest in artefacts preceded aesthetic interest in natural objects. But besides there being, as far as I know, no evidence for this latter, it seems, as I said earlier, extremely improbable: improbable when we consider the extent to which the basis and origin of aesthetic interests seem even now, as probably they always have been, deeply rooted in our responses to natural objects.

If we ask which objects human beings most widely respond to with either satisfaction at their beauty or revulsion at their ugliness, it is probably their own kind: human faces and bodies, male and female. We can think too of the simplest aesthetic responses—'How beautiful!' 'How pretty!' 'How lovely!' 'How ugly!'—that people have to flowers, animals, butterflies, birds, coloured stones, skies, sun, moon, stars, all things striking enough to attract attention, and evoke admiration and wonder. Almost certainly, also, such things are among those that children early respond to with pleasure, spontaneously or under our encouragement. Many of these responses can hardly be anything but primitive or simple instances of aesthetic interest. And, incidentally again, the delight that leads primitive people—and children and not so primitive people—to collect, and surround or adorn themselves with, coloured stones, feathers, etc., suggests that *objets trouvés* also have a long history before the twentieth century. None of this of course denies that, once art is in existence, some of a child's most primitive aesthetic responses might be elicited by art-works.

Once our attention has been redirected away from art and on to natural phenomena, it becomes easier to realize just how widespread are the aesthetic interests of ordinary people. A considerable part of most people's satisfaction, not only in natural phenomena but in many non-artistic human activities, both work and play, is in some measure fairly obviously aesthetic, whether people explicitly realize the fact or not. Consider how much satisfaction and fascination people find in plants and gardening—witness the proliferation of the nursery industry—in animals, whether pets, in zoos, or in the wild, in travel to places of notable natural beauty; and it is no surprise that there is such widespread interest in the photography and television that shows colour-ful tropical fish, birds, coral reefs, magnified studies of insects, crystals, and so on; the list is endless. Some of this interest is mere curiosity, or fascination with what is strange, some is scientific; but undoubtedly much of the wonder and admiration is aesthetic. So is, whether it is realized or not, much of the interest in popularly appreciated games and sports—football, cricket, tennis, ice skating, and so on—where economy, grace, and perfection of movement and action are admired. These and many others are activities to which consid-erable numbers of people respond with some measure of aesthetic pleasure—people who often have no significant acquaintance with or response to the arts. When such interests, quite outside the fine arts, play so extensive a role in most human cultures, interests which can hardly be anything but aesthetic, perhaps our investigations in aesthetics should focus at least as much on the nature and origins of these aesthetic satisfactions as on the more recherché questions about art. For, by comparison, interest in the arts—at least the highly developed arts that aestheticians largely focus on—is almost certainly a fairly restricted and minority interest.

11

Making Music Our Own

This paper is about interpretation of music in the broadest sense, about how and why it interests us. And since examination of practices should precede theorizing about any topic, I shall consider the role played by certain common descriptions of music. For this, I shall ignore the much discussed descriptions that employ the language of feelings and emotions, e.g., the familiar 'sad music', and the problems these supposedly raise. Musicians and critics draw equally upon all manner of other non-musical phenomena both mental and physical. If when writing on music they feel the need of so many kinds of descriptions in order to say what is important to them, to neglect so much of the language of criticism might be to risk impoverished theory. Besides omitting feeling and emotion vocabulary for the moment, I omit much else, e.g., 'aesthetic' terms like *beautiful* and *graceful*, the technical vocabulary of music, and so on.

The samples that follow are all drawn from writings by musicians and critics; they are all, I think, intelligible to anyone familiar with music, though what they say could not obviously be expressed as well, if at all, in other, particularly technical, language: 'It has querulous energy and lean writing', 'The work is coarse-grained', 'In his symphony he is, as always, a tough plain speaker', 'Shostakovich's Seventh Symphony has some of his loneliest music', 'Sibelius's Fourth Symphony is brooding, dark, spare and bleak', 'superfine richness, with deep-pile carpets of sustained wind sound', 'those imposing and sombre pyramids of sound of the old Italian and Dutch schools, and the finely chased salt cellars and silver candlesticks, so to speak, of venerable Sebastian Bach' (Hanslick), 'The playing is sensual yet refined, with the slight edginess of the strings preventing the textures becoming languorously sumptuous', 'Its playing of the wonderful water music prelude suggested that the Rhine must be a river of treacle—and rather lumpy treacle at that' (G. B. Shaw). Such descriptions are given both of works, and, as in the last two, of performances. In addition, I list some adjectives, extracted from typical descriptions, to exhibit their variety: from light—*sparkling, shimmering, bright, luminous, glowing*; from weight—*light, ponderous*; from movement—*sinuous, abrupt, soaring, turbulent, placid*; from sound and speech—*thundering, murmuring,*

[From *Interpretation in Music*, ed. Michael Krausz, Oxford: Clarendon Press, 1993.]

sobbing, conversing, arguing; from smell and taste—*bitter, sour, sweet*; from atmosphere—*sinister, threatening, spooky*; from feel, touch, and textures—*soft, supple, gritty, thick, melting, liquid, brittle, sinewy, icy, silky*; from physiognomy—*smiling, laughing*; from gait—*ambling, strutting, striding, plodding*; from character—*gentle, bombastic, aggressive, plaintive, tender, wistful, bold, good-humoured, solemn, animated*. The list could go on indefinitely. These sorts of examples are not more important than feeling and emotion descriptions, but, besides being neglected, they offer little temptation towards certain kinds of theories that beckon with the others: it is implausible to think that, where music is so described, a composer or listener was, or felt, icy, or brittle, or shimmering, or that music expresses grittiness or sinuousness.

One might propose that descriptions of all kinds, those I exemplified and those I omitted, help us 'interpret', 'understand', or grasp the 'meaning' of music. I shall not quibble with this though these locutions are not always the happiest. We may indeed come to understand how parts of a work connect or interact, or why a composer uses certain devices; we may not understand music from innovative composers or non-Western traditions; it feels alien and excludes us. But they are not always appropriate locutions with familiar music. For me, 'Do you understand the *Appassioniata*?', 'Have you grasped the meaning of Scarlatti K.115?', and 'What's your interpretation of Bach's Third Violin Partita?' are odd questions. But we can use other locutions. Descriptions may help us grasp, realize, pin down, the character and qualities of works, appreciate them for what they are. They may 'give a face' to music— or, less narrowly, a gait, sound, feel, or physical texture as well as a physiognomy. Similarly with people, animals, or scenery. We understand or interpret their gestures or facial expressions. But we recognize, grasp, or realize, not understand, that a figure, posture, or gait is solid, haughty, or shambling, that gestures are brusque or speeches florid. We see, not interpret, scenery as stark or smiling, streams as skipping or leaping. Chaplin's walk, a bloodhound's face, the Matterhorn, each has a distinctive character, not meaning; similarly with music which we characterize as jaunty or murmuring.

Describing music in such diverse extra-musical terms is a practice that almost everyone who discusses music falls into naturally. Such descriptions, if neither strictly true nor false, can be good or poor, apt or inappropriate. Bringing music under non-musical concepts often seems to help us, musicians included, to connect with it, articulate our experience of it, humanize it, make it our own. It is worth asking therefore what music and our experience of it must be like for such descriptions to perform these roles.

But despite the facts I have cited, there are familiar objections against the possibility of verbal descriptions playing so central a role. It is sometimes said, for example, that music is not really describable, that words cannot capture something so non-verbal and unique. Sometimes such objections seem to rest on misunderstandings about the nature of description. If the demand is for a description to provide a substitute for music, the demand is absurd; descriptions are never substitutes, or intended to be. Some suppose that *music*, which can only be *heard*, must be indescribable in words. Another absurdity: the *Mona Lisa*'s smile can only be seen, not heard or felt; that does not prevent its being described. Nor does the fact that music does not depict, portray, describe, or narrate prohibit description; nor do some paintings, or any natural objects. Again, no description, some assume, given the complexities of music, could be *adequate*. But this flirts with a spurious notion of adequacy that no description could meet, in two respects. (1) 'Exactness'. Performed music is determinate in every detail—timbres, pitches, duration, etc. But no description is exact in this way; any description will fit many similar but distinguishable things, whether music, paintings, or faces. (2) 'Completeness'. Any piece of music is complex, much is going on; to describe everything at once—rhythms, harmonies, melodies, whole movements—is impossible. But the same is true with pictures—their colours, brushwork, lines, subjects—or anything else, say, street riots or horse-races. Such 'exactness' and 'completeness' are unattainable limits, and not uniquely with music. For given purposes, descriptions, being always selective, can be exact or complete enough. Skimpy descriptions are still descriptions, and often adequate; calling the opening of the 'Moonlight' Sonata serene or the sea angry is to describe, and excludes contrary descriptions. Finally, perhaps the main objection: music should be described, if at all, in purely musical terms; extra-musical descriptions are improper.

Before I consider this, some further points about descriptions. Besides the question of *what* is described—rhythms, timbres, melodies, phrases, movements—there are *kinds* of descriptions. These range from literal and technical to those I shall loosely group as 'figurative'—various non-univocal uses, 'secondary senses', and obvious metaphors; certainly it is sometimes unclear whether some well-established descriptions should be regarded as 'figurative' or not. Figurative descriptions again are roughly separable into *levels*. There are (*a*) what I shall call 'scenarios', more or less extended pictures, programmes, or narratives: e.g., 'A Ländler danced by ogres', 'A conversation between a cheerful man and a melancholy man, who ... argue with each other, each trying to win the other over to his point of view; until at the end of the second movement ... the melancholy man at last gives in, taking over the main theme of the other ...', etc.; (*b*) descriptions in terms of substances and processes: *steely, silken, shimmering, murmuring*; (*c*) those in terms of qualities: *heavy, cold, grey, smooth*. These three types constitute different levels because, roughly, scenario descriptions imply substance/process descriptions, which in turn imply quality descriptions.

One kind of 'purist' objection to figurative description can be seen as insisting that genuine descriptions should be literal, in 'purely musical', not borrowed terms. But it is not obvious what counts as literal here: presumably most technical terms, both purely auditory and structural (*C major, six-eight time, pentatonic, sonata-form*); non-technical auditory terms (*loud, silent*); and some shared with non-auditory phenomena (*augmented, slow, repeat*). Many other pure or borrowed auditory terms (*ring, gallop, murmur*) would not generally figure in technical descriptions, and many are arguably figurative. Some musical terms are hardly technical for speakers of some languages (*pianissimo, martellato*), and many true technical terms are, however clumsily, dispensable by paraphrase. 'Literal' descriptions would therefore employ whichever of the above musico-auditory types could be regarded as non-figurative.

But now it must be asked what these literal descriptions can achieve. Certainly they can serve to analyse the construction of a work and explain by what devices its character is achieved. Attention to them can change our view of a work or reveal qualities we might otherwise have missed. But despite their importance, they fail to articulate what, following others, I have been calling the 'character' and 'qualities' of music, and do little to explain why music may engage us as appreciative listeners—which is why non-musicians and musicians alike employ figurative characterizations. Without such appreciation, they are little more than nuts-and-bolts descriptions. But music is only exceptionally composed to interest analysts. One might even risk putting it more forcibly. Consider a typical 'dry' description (totally 'dry' ones are rare):

It is based on three ideas: the tone-row, Ex. 1a; the Carinthian folktune, Ex. 5; and the Bach chorale, Ex. 8; the last comes into full prominence not until the finale. Yet looking at the tone-row more closely you will find that the chorale's opening motif, which consists of four notes in whole-tone progression, is already contained in the last four notes of the row ... As for the first nine notes of the row, they form an arpeggio—an unusual arrangement as most rows go.[1]

It seems possible that, suitably trained, someone who had never appreciated music could give a purely musico-auditory description of a performed piece, and even someone deaf from birth who had seen music only in score might learn, however profitlessly, to give such descriptions, just as someone ignorant of the aims of chess might learn to describe games in the approved manner. By contrast, listeners incapable of technical description who felt impelled to described music in the figurative ways illustrated might convince us of their genuine grasp and appreciation.

If literal musico-auditory vocabulary truly is ineffectual for describing much of what appeals to us in music, and if some hitherto non-existent language developed specifically for the purpose is, as many agree, necessarily unavailable, two alternatives remain. Either much that matters to us in music

[1] Mosco Carner, 'Alban Berg', in *The Concerto*, ed. Ralph Hill, Harmondsworth: Penguin Books, 1952, 371.

is genuinely indescribable; or we must, without qualms, employ the extra-musical language that comes so naturally, recognizing that to eschew it here would be as much a self-inflicted impoverishment as denying ourselves figurative language elsewhere, both within and outside the arts, where it occurs equally naturally, and unavoidably. Smiles are sweet, remarks sour, sleep is deep, scenery mournful, clouds race, streams leap. In the arts, colours glow, designs are exuberant, buildings severe or serene. It is less the literal comments, that there is a haywain on the right or a cathedral in the distance, but the others that are significant—Constable describing a picture as 'pearly, deep, and mellow', Roger Fry describing Matisse's line as 'rhythmic' and 'elastic'; Ruskinesque descriptions of paintings parallel 'scenario' descriptions of music. There is no more reason to cavil at extra-musical descriptions of music than at extra-visual descriptions of paintings; they are not resorted to because of the special nature of music. Figurative criticism is alive where, appreciatively, literal comment is inert.

If these considerations can allay some of the misgivings about extra-musical descriptions, though most of us who find music important often feel them, we can return to the question, given the pervasiveness of such descriptions, of the role they play. To recapitulate the facts. People conversant with music unreflectively describe it in figurative ways. It is widely accepted that such descriptions (*a*) can illuminate and aid appreciation (otherwise why programme notes or the comments of professional critics?); (*b*) can modify our grasp of music we previously supposed we appreciated; (*c*) can articulate explicitly, in ways listeners find apposite, those qualities they have experienced a piece as having. If these successes can often be achieved by bringing music under extra-musical rather than musico-auditory concepts, the question arises how and why such concepts can be aids to musical experience, and what light is thrown thereby on the understanding of music.

So far my remarks touch only cases where descriptions are actually offered or accepted. But much music is heard and appreciated without any verbal intervention. So even if extra-musical concepts are sometimes implicated in achieving or articulating understanding, usually words play no role. Could there be reason to think that, even when we listen wordlessly (and non-pictorially), when no one offers or seeks descriptions, we nevertheless make sense of music by, without realizing it, bring it under verbalizable concepts, and without thinking of the words that might verbalize them? Equally, failing to understand it and misunderstanding it would be either failing to bring it under such concepts or bringing it under inappropriate ones. That might explain why, when descriptions *are* offered, we can often say, and confidently, that they do, or do not, fit the music. This view, that grasping the character of a piece involves hearing it in such a way that some possible extra-musical description(s) would be appropriate to our experience, would stand sharply opposed to the belief that extra-musical description is always improper. Much that is centrally appealing about music would be, paradoxically, essentially extra-musical.

For any musical purist—including most of us sometimes—the supposition is one to invite ridicule. To entertain it opens one to the charge of musical unsophistication, not knowing how to listen. But were it true, anyone obviously devoted to music who refuses, unlike many musicians, to countenance extra-musical descriptions must presumably be subject to some purist dogma. The supposition I am considering, however, if defensible, would lessen the 'mystery' of musical understanding by questioning the supposed 'isolation' or 'purity' of music and the 'discontinuity' between it and the rest of experience. To attempt that might be worth some effort. So since my intention is not speculative theorizing, I shall enquire how the supposition might be rendered plausible, not as speculation, but as an implication of familiar facts and practices, and whether opposition to it might rest on beliefs either dogmatic or incoherent.

One clear implication of the supposition is that *all* music must be describable (within the limitations of description itself) in aptly figurative language. Consider the evidence for this. I have stressed that critics, programme writers, and analysts constantly employ 'quality', 'process', and 'scenario' descriptions, even, in off-guard moments, those ascetic analysts who on principle would eschew them. Conductors rehearsing orchestras often do likewise. Composers not only mark their work *légèrement, maestoso, martellato*, etc., but may offer scenario-like programmes or titles (*Poissons d'or, La Poule, Peasants Merrymaking* and *Storm*).[2] Composers' and critics' descriptions operate in contrary directions: roughly, composers' descriptions turn 'absolute' into 'programme' music, critics' descriptions do not. But they must still fit; Beethoven could not plausibly have described the opening of his sonata, dubbed 'Moonlight' by Rellstab, as furious, leaping, or strutting.

Obviously, the supposition that music is always describable does not imply that the listener could always provide a description, or even that anyone could in fact hit on a suitable one for a particular piece, though that is only a remote possibility; critics are seldom completely tongue-tied. Nor need description be easy; it demands a combination of appreciation, verbal expertise, and imagination. But these are not difficulties unique to music. Many people could not easily give more than scrappy descriptions of, say, a horse-race, a friend's face, or Chaplin's walk, particularly if figurative descriptions are called for as they often are for art-works. Fortunately, for most purpose, as I said, descriptions need not be highly detailed. As 'ragged' may suffice to describe an ice-hockey match, or 'angry' to describe a torrent, so 'fugal' may often suffice to describe a piece literally, and 'gently rocking' or 'gritty' to characterize it figuratively.

---

[2] The 'conversation' example of a scenario description quoted above was modelled on a programme C. P. E. Bach provided for one of his trios.

All these facts suggest that most music could be described figuratively. And if most can, why not all? I add two further considerations. Possibility of description entails possibility of mis-description. Most, I suspect, would find the description of the 'Moonlight' I gave wholly incongruous, not because such description is automatically disallowed but because it absurdly mis-characterizes the music. But anyone denying the legitimacy of figurative description must hold all such descriptions equally improper. To say the piece is, or is not, serene, would be as inadmissible as saying it is, or is not, furious or that the number *four* is, or is not, green. That would be an extreme departure from common practice. Secondly, there is a game few are genuinely unable to play. Given a piece of music we know, and offered some pair of contrary descriptions, most would agree that one fits better than the other. For the opening of Stravinsky's Symphony in Three Movements, most would favour spiky, spare, or athletic, rather than melting, languorous, or gentle. It is sometimes said that pre-Romantic music is not open to these figurative descriptions; that might be true with 'scenario' descriptions.[3] But I doubt that there is any music for which no one could find some suitable 'quality' descriptions; and anyone who can play the alternatives game at all is already allowing description. If anyone who patently appreciates music cannot play this game, which I doubt (Hanslick and Tovey certainly could have)—though some might refuse on principle—they are certainly uncommon. One would wonder whether they are equally baffled by figurative description elsewhere. Are they uncomprehending with 'heavy sleep', 'pearly pictures', etc., or does their inability occur only, and suspiciously, with music? Too many undeniable facts and practices make it difficult to understand how anyone could hold extra-musical description of music improper unless the conviction rests on some general theory about music.

Suppose now that all music is open to appropriate extra-musical description. What bearing has that on our understanding of it, given that we mostly listen wordlessly? What happens to the suggestion that some extra-musical descriptions or other would always fit our experience of music even though those words do not cross our minds, and that that is, at least in part, why music means something to us? Certainly, unless we are critics we rarely attempt to articulate in words the qualities we hear in a piece. The more common case is where someone else gives a description and we feel that it is exactly right, or hits off the music rather well, or must be rejected as unsuitable. When this happens, it is, I suggest, a criterion of our having previously heard it in such a way that we sincerely assent to the proffered description.

But here one may encounter the objection that, if one can sincerely say, 'That describes the way I heard it', one must previously have had those words (or equivalent pictures) in mind. Yet this is surely a version of the philosoph-

---

[3] But see note 2 above.

ical theory that thinking—and, I'll add, perceiving, recognizing, realizing, experiencing, and hearing—must occur in words, pictures, images, or other 'vehicles'; that to have heard something as silky or exuberant one must have entertained those words, though subvocally. Against this, we may retort that to think, and equally to realize, understand, or hear that something is ϕ, and to experience, see, or hear it as ϕ, need not involve the saying or thinking of any words.[4] This is linked also to another general philosophical question. Music, it is sometimes urged, is not properly describable in words because it should be heard, understood, appreciated 'in purely musical terms'. The genuine musician, unlike the unsophisticated or philistine amateur, enjoys a purely musical experience appreciating music 'in its own terms'. If verbal and other extra-musical notions obtrude, tacitly at the time or subsequently, there was not a pure, but a tainted, experience, merely literary, narrative, or pictorial. Hence, to be willing to give or assent to extra-musical descriptions raises doubts about, even impugns or discredits, one's musicality. The charge is familiar and has analogies elsewhere.[5]

But this purist charge, I suggest, rests on an incoherence, and, if so, it must fail. Recall Ryle's attack on 'the obsessive philosophical notion of "thinking *in*", such as thinking *in* words or pictures . . .'. In some cases, he says, it makes no sense to say that the thinker 'is thinking *in* . . . words or phrases—or anything else instead'.[6] To suppose so is to enter an infinite regress. Thinkers choose words to express what they are thinking or have thought. They sometimes have to think what words they want, but they do not do this in words either. I suggest that, just as we do not think in anything, we do not experience or listen in anything, either words, pictures, music, or musical terms. We do not grasp, realize, or perceive the character of music—or of faces, paintings, or scenery—in words or in anything else. If this is so, there are no terms in which we hear or understand music; our hearing, grasping, or understanding of it is therefore not in musical or extra-musical terms, for to say either is nonsense.[7] *A fortiori* we do not have to experience or grasp it in musical rather than figurative terms. *Having* grasped its character however, or while trying to, we may try to describe it in either terms. The argument for describing it only in musico-technical language—or for not describing it in words at all—was that

---

[4] Cf. Gilbert Ryle, *On Thinking*, ed. Konstantin Kolenda, Oxford: Blackwell, 1979: 'some thinking does, but most thinking does not, require the saying or sub-saying of anything' pp. 33–4.

[5] Cf. Clive Bell, *Art*, London: Chatto and Windus, 1947: 'to appreciate a work of art we need bring with us nothing from life, no knowledge of its ideas and affairs, no familiarity with its emotions' p. 25.

[6] Ryle, *On Thinking*, 41.

[7] If, however, experiencing music 'in purely musical terms' means no more than experiencing it as music, i.e., as an art, not as natural sounds, this no more prohibits description than experiencing paintings, not as natural objects, prohibits describing them.

we should experience and appreciate music only 'in its own (purely musical) terms', in a way so distinct from anything extra-musical that no language, unless technical, can properly fit that experience. But if it cannot be said that we experience it in *any* terms, there is no question of language, technical or extra-musical, fitting or failing to fit, or of one fitting better than the other. The argument evaporates.

Music is not special in this respect. When I notice the colour of something or see it as having a certain colour ('a purely visual experience'), I do not notice or experience it in colour, in visual terms, in colour words, or in anything. I may however seek words to describe it as experienced; and as I may describe music literally as loud or fugal, or figuratively as chattering, so I may describe the thing's colour as orange, or as warm and cheerful. Anything capable of description may be described either literally or figuratively; that it is heard, or music, no more prohibits this than that it is seen, or a painting. If this disposes of objections to the legitimacy of describing a 'purely musical experience', and if with music, paintings, and many other things, the figurative can capture what the literal cannot, figurative description, far from being disallowed, is justified.

If experiencing is not *in* anything, the earlier alleged difficulty, that you could not have grasped the character of music (or anything) without the words that might subsequently describe your experience of it occurring to you, evaporates too. Hearing, listening, looking, watching, or experiencing in any way, like most thinking, requires no saying or sub-saying of anything. The fact that music is complex, and that much that is going on is unmentioned in most descriptions we actually give, makes no difference. Grasping music more than superficially certainly means noticing a good deal of what goes on, not just, say, the melody. But we would hardly try to articulate or describe to ourselves everything we hear as it goes along. The same is true, however, in our dealings with other complex things. If we are attentive as we walk through a building or watch the passing countryside, we notice many things and their features: warmth or coolness of colours, calm or turmoil of rivers. If we watch a horse-race or survey a painting, we could, immediately after, describe much of what we had seen; but unless alerted to do so, we probably formulated few or no words at the time. We experience most things, in varying detail, without words, aloud or subvocal. Many, like music, are complex passing sequences. Commentators, travel-writers, or critics may attempt fuller descriptions and probably draw on figurative language. But mostly we don't; full descriptions would usually be difficult and to little purpose. Brief impressions usually suffice: here the water thunders, there the river is peaceful, the room has warm colours, the Mondrian is flat. Likewise with music; having taken in its character, we describe it, if at all, sketchily, say, as harsh, anguished, or exuberant. Were there need, and had we verbal skill, we might describe more than such salient characteristics. But description of music, in any complexity and detail one wishes, is not proved less possible or legitimate than description of anything else.

If experiencing needs no words, my emphasis throughout on possible *description* needs explaining. To perceive something as having this character rather than that is to acquire various abilities; to misperceive is to acquire liabilities. To perceive something correctly as red is to be equipped, say, to use it as a danger signal; someone who misperceives something as a shadow when it is a dog is liable to get bitten. Exercise of such abilities may be limited by lack of other abilities. One cannot use red to signal danger without knowing red is used for danger, or perceive the dog as a shadow without knowing what a shadow is. Nor could one perceive music as silken or aggressive if one lacked these notions. Grasping something as having a certain character is not ordinarily one-track. To have grasped the character of a piece of music might involve any of many abilities: to recognize it again, to recall in your head roughly how it went, to know if it is wrongly played next time (but not necessarily these; you might have poor musical memory); to whistle parts of it (but not if you cannot whistle); to know, when whistling it, when you have got it wrong, without necessarily being able to correct it; to realize what harmonies are lost in whistling; to know, when it is being played, that an oboe or a new motif will shortly enter. Grasp can be partial, e.g., ability to vamp a melody correctly but with wrong harmonies. With these may go ability to describe aptly, but not if, being too inarticulate, one cannot command appropriate words; and ability to assent to proffered descriptions, provided one's literacy extends to the words used. So to have taken the music in a certain way may include, but does not require, ability to give or assent to descriptions that would fit your experience of it. Lack of these verbal abilities need not count against one's understanding the music in the way they describe it. But if acquisition of abilities other than verbal might constitute understanding a piece, why the emphasis on possible descriptions, even ones the listener might be unable to give or assent to? Why, in effect, stress that, in the ways indicated and contrary to purism, extra-musical notions may play a significant part in understanding music?

The reason is that acquiring and exercising abilities like the others I mentioned would not guarantee that one had grasped the character of the music—any more than ability to describe it in technical terms would. Someone might be able to whistle a piece perfectly, remember exactly where the oboe enters, tell when one performance differs from another, even conceivably play or conduct in exact imitation of a recorded Schnabel or Toscanini performance; none of this need conclusively show such a person to be more than an ear-and-memory-perfect mimic. It need have no tendency to establish the mimic's understanding of what, following others, I have called the musical character or qualities that we draw on figurative language to describe. Without that person's offering or genuinely assenting to some such description we could remain sceptical of there being understanding rather than reproductive mimicking. Similarly, a skilful copyist could conceivably copy the lines and colours of a painting, an actor read poetry with stresses and intonations modelled on the author's, and have no grasp of the work; analogously, a draughtsman might copy an engineer's drawings understanding nothing of their function. It is true that other indications may be convincing. That people spend time listening may rightly convince us that they find it rewarding, but we take their interpretation of the music largely on trust. Gestures and other bodily movements in listeners or performers may count for something. Stresses, emphases, ways of playing, if someone is performing or conducting, not copying, may be decisive. But descriptions sincerely given or accepted would be among the primary, most conclusive, and most explicit indications of understanding the music's character.

One further note about figurative descriptions. Since they are apt rather than true, equally apt alternatives drawn from other pictures, narratives, or sense-modalities may always be possible. Except with programme music there is no *right* description. Offered several, one could sometimes say only, 'something of that sort will do'. An 'intermingling streams' instead of a 'conversation' description might have suited C. P. E. Bach's trio equally well. 'Aggressive, hard, and energetic' might suit the Stravinsky as well as 'spiky, spare, and athletic'. Nor need there be any general answer to why rival descriptions may be equally apt, any more than to why some music is describable as 'bright' rather than 'dark' or 'icy' rather than 'warm'. Possibility of alternatives does however encourage charges of 'subjectivity': true in that I may not employ the same descriptions as you; false in that 'sighing, sobbing, and liquid,' say, would incongrously mis-describe the Stravinsky. It is here too that the 'abstractness' of music and its *sui generis* character show, not in any supposed impropriety of extra-musical interpretation. Imposing one rather than an alternative description is somewhat like pinning a play down in a particular staging and performance. Hamlet's voice must have some timbre, his face some features, his stance and walk some peculiarities. But neither Gielgud's nor Olivier's are the *right* ones, for there are no right ones. Such matters are unspecific in the play or a silent reading of it. Yet Hamlet with no legs or a Donald Duck voice would be wrong if not absurd. Music is different again: whereas Hamlet must have a voice and legs, but not specifically Olivier's music is abstract, in this respect, as it were, specifying nothing.

A corollary to the fact that descriptions constrain experience of music, rather as performed plays inject specificities absent from silent readings, is that listeners, like readers, may want to avoid them. Descriptions, whether of music, buildings, or mountains can be hard to shake off and can come to dominate one's experience. Inability to read *Hamlet* without hearing or seeing Olivier may become as infuriating as inability to hear the 'Pastoral' without seeing the cavortings of Disney's *Fantasia*. Even without this, one may want to hear music—or see paintings or scenery—without the necessarily selective intrusion of any words. Listening, looking, and enjoying are compatible with desiring to avoid all attempts at verbal articulation.

This paper has been wholly about descriptions, particularly figurative ones, and their relevance to, in a certain sense, the understanding or interpretation of music. I have deliberately avoided mention of feelings and emotions, important as they are; but my discussion is intended to apply equally to them. I have said nothing about the 'meaning', the 'language', or the effects of music, or about listeners' responses (in so far as these differ from understanding its character). I have not questioned the importance of technical description and analysis in enhancing understanding, only its ability to do certain things. I have not denied that there are 'purely musical experiences'—something we do not get from worded song or opera—or 'purely musical qualities'— the warmth or chill of music is only audible; it is not the warmth or chill felt in bath-water or seen in smiles. I have said nothing about the question pursued by many theories: why or in virtue of what—resemblances, analogies, shared features—we supposedly can employ figurative language; I simply accept that we do. Nothing I have said implies that listening with understanding requires or ordinarily involves having words or pictures in mind; it can be, and usually is, wordless, as is looking at pictures. If it is an assumption that any connection between music and extra-musical phenomena must imply this, I have challenged it. I have questioned the coherence of certain 'purist' positions and of the notion of understanding or experiencing 'in purely musical terms'. I have explored the possibility that an important element in the proper interpretation of music is covertly extra-musical, and questioned the supposition that extra-musical phenomena are merely peripheral except to programme music. Obviously there is vastly more to say about music. Much of what I have said applies to extra-musical sounds and noises as well as to music. It largely ignores the part played in our interpretation of music by the fact that it is an art working within structures, conventions, and a history, familiarity with all of which affects crucially the characteristics we hear in it. But we do, after all, characterize natural and extra-musical sounds in similar ways, as mournful, sighing, chattering, cheerful, murmuring, harsh, sweet, and so on. This at least suggests some continuity between music and other sounds, and so questions the alleged hermetic and isolated nature of music.

12

Adjectives, Predicative and Attributive

Some years ago Professor Geach pointed to a distinction between what he called 'logically predicative' and 'logically attributive' adjectives.[1] His chief purpose was to consider the word 'good' and certain disputes in ethics; the distinction was therefore explained with extreme terseness and then applied to his main task. There is no doubt that Geach pointed towards something important, and though questions have been raised about it, the distinction was accepted by one of the persons against whom the ethical arguments were directed, Professor Hare, and is not infrequently employed in discussions.

Since I believe Geach conflated at least two distinctions, I think the matter remains opaque and the distinction should not be employed until clarified. I attempt this clarification here. Even if I at times misinterpret Geach—though I do not think so—the points I make may be worthwhile in their own right and relevant to topics Geach was not then primarily investigating, i.e. adjectives besides 'good' and in fields other than ethics. Certainly the manifold logical complexities of adjectives are worthy of general philosophical examination; so I avoid more than the merest mention of 'good', and say nothing about its use in ethics.

Geach begins by saying flatly that his distinction (predicative-attributive) is 'between two sorts of *adjectives*' (my italics). Shortly after he says, 'There are familiar examples of what I call attributive adjectives. "Big" and "small" are attributive'; again, 'the sort of adjective that the medievals called *alienans* is attributive' ('forged' and 'putative' are his examples). Later he speaks of 'ordinary predicative adjectives like "red" and "sweet" '. These remarks strongly suggest this interpretation. There are at least two sorts of adjectives: 'red' and 'sweet', say, are always predicative, 'big' and 'small', say, are always attributive. If with one noun the adjective 'A' is predicative, then with all other nouns 'A' is predicative; similarly, once attributive always attributive—or as he says elsewhere of 'good' and 'bad', they are 'always' are 'essentially' attributive: adjectives are predicative *simpliciter* or attributive *simpliciter*. I call this the

<hr />

[1] P. T. Geach, 'Good and Evil', *Analysis*, 17 (1956–7).

'*simpliciter* interpretation'. Incidentally, nothing I have said or quoted so far implies an exhaustive distinction; there might be other kinds of adjectives, a question I raise later. Other remarks by Geach, however, suggest a thesis very different from the *simpliciter* interpretation. In explaining when an adjective is predicative or attributive, Geach is careful to say that '*in a phrase* "an AB" "A" being an adjective and "B" being a noun "A" is a (logically) predicative adjective if . . .' and the condition follows; 'otherwise "A" is a (logically) attributive adjective' (my italics). And though he say that 'big' and 'small' are attributive, he follows this immediately with examples providing in each case some particular noun for 'B', e.g. '*x* is a big flea'; he does the same for his other examples, 'small', 'forged', and 'putative'. Again, though he does speak of 'ordinary predicative adjectives like "red" and "sweet" ', he is careful to say that 'in the phrase "a red book" "red" is a predicative adjective in my sense'. Just as tellingly, he says not simply that 'good' and 'bad' are attributive adjectives, but, as I quoted, that they are always attributive, and essentially attributive, which seems to imply the possibility that some adjectives which, with one noun, 'B' in the phrase 'an AB', are attributive, may, with another noun, 'C', in the phrase 'an AC', be predicative, being only sometimes, not essentially attributive. Otherwise why say 'always' and 'essentially'? Perhaps significantly, he nowhere says that 'red' and 'sweet'—his only examples of predicative adjectives—are always or essentially predicative. I call this the 'in a phrase' interpretation. But the fact that two interpretations suggest themselves indicates that there may be two different distinctions to be made, not just one: two sorts of adjectives and two sorts of uses of adjectives.

This opens up a new possibility. If we are concerned, as Geach said at the start, with *sorts of adjectives*, we cannot rule out *ab initio* that there may be not two, but at least three, sorts of adjectives: those essentially predicative, those essentially attributive, and those in one phrase predicative, in another attributive. If we want only two of something to be marked out by the predicative-attributive distinction, we shall be wise, so far, to speak only of two ways adjectives may be used in a phrase. Yet if we adopt the 'in a phrase' interpretation, which may allow some adjectives to function sometimes one way, sometimes the other, it is still clear that Geach insists that 'good' and 'bad', and seemingly also his other examples, 'big', 'small', 'putative', and 'forged', are always attributive. But to claim that these are essentially attributive, i.e. attributive with any noun, is equivalent to applying, at least to them, the *simpliciter* interpretation. How could one justify this claim? Geach applies various tests to them, but with only a few selected nouns, 'flea', 'elephant', 'banknote', 'father', 'food', 'car', etc. With these nouns, he claims, they pass tests for being attributive. But to justify a general claim, that they will be attributive with any noun, existing or yet to be invented, would require either testing them with every conceivable noun, an impossible task, or, what is obviously needed, some indication of a logical feature inherent in the adjectives themselves and so necessarily present whatever noun they are applied to. If there is such a feature, however, we are left to see it for ourselves; it is nowhere elucidated. Equally, if some adjectives are sometimes predicative, sometimes attributive, we must see why combination with one noun or on one occasion makes the use of the adjective predicative, and combination with another noun or on another occasion makes it attributive.

Now to Geach's explanation of his distinction. He says, 'in a phrase "an AB" ... "A" is a (logically) predicative adjective if the predication "is an AB" splits up logically into a pair of predications "is a B" and "is A"; otherwise "A" is a (logically) attributive adjective'. Since my task is to elucidate what is meant by (logically) 'predicative' and 'attributive' , much of what follows will deal with the crucial but unclear expression 'splits up logically'. But first a minor point. Taken *au pied de la lettre* here and throughout, Geach gives only a sufficient, not a necessary and sufficient, condition of an adjective being either predicative or attributive; since it makes no difference to my arguments, and probably was intended anyway, I shall take the conditions as necessary and sufficient.

To understand what 'logically predicative' and 'logically attributive' mean we need, but are never given, a definition or elucidation. All we are given is a test, whether certain predications split up or not. But since this too needs elucidation I turn to Geach's presentation. What we find are four distinguishable and superficially different tests, though we are never offered an explanation of why they work. The first two are tests for splitting up, itself the test for predicativeness and attributiveness, so they are tests for tests; the last two are not stated as tests for splitting up, but directly as tests for predicativeness or attributiveness. I give the tests names derived from Geach's words.

First, the 'Simple Argument' test for not splitting up: if, from 'x is an AB', and some added true premise 'B is a C', a false conclusion 'x is an AC' or 'an AB is an AC' is derivable, then 'is an AB' does not split up and 'A' is attributive. Example: 'x is a big flea' and 'a flea is an animal' give the false conclusions 'x is a big animal' and 'a big flea is a big animal'. Secondly, the '*Alienans*' test for not splitting up: if 'A' is an *alienans* adjective, 'x is an AB' does not split up into 'x is A' and 'x is a B', because, as one initially supposes, 'x is a B' will be false, or at least not follow. Example: 'x is a forged banknote' does not split up into 'x is forged' and 'x is a banknote'. Thirdly, the 'Unsafe Predication' test for attributiveness (splitting up is not mentioned here). Geach says, illustrating with the adjective 'bad', that 'bad' is 'something like' an *alienans* adjective; but though this test might also be confused with Test 1, it clearly has a different form, viz. if 'x is AB' and 'B is C' together do not yield 'x is C', 'A' is attributive. Example: 'x is bad food' and 'food (is something that) supports life' does not yield 'bad food supports life'. The fourth test for attributiveness (again splitting up is not mentioned, only combining this time) I call the 'Independent Ascertainment' test. Its form is: if it cannot be ascertained that x is A, independently of understanding some substantive, 'B', that x is (or is being considered as), 'A' is attributive. Example: it cannot be ascertained that x is good independently of understanding that x is being considered as a car, in order to ascertain that x is a good car.

I shall examine these tests in a moment. But first I want to mention one over-facile interpretation of 'doesn't split up' (and of 'doesn't combine'), strongly suggested no doubt by the *alienans* example, an interpretation placed upon it by one of Geach's critics, Alfred MacKay.[2] This is that 'failure to split up' means that 'x is an AB' does not entail both 'x is A' and 'x is a B' (and, in combining, 'x is A' and 'x is a B' do not together entail 'x is an AB'). This interpretation is fostered also by the fact that when 'A' is predicative the entailments would seem to hold, both in splitting and combining—something I reject later. But Geach never speaks of failure of entailment, even though in the *Alienans* test there is a failure; and though with the Unsafe Predication test he seems to hover on the brink of saying that if x is bad food, x is not food, he never in fact says it. And I think one reason Geach never elucidates 'not splitting up' (or 'not combining') in terms of entailment is that he partly sees that something stronger than failure of entailment is involved. What it is I try to say later; Geach never explicitly brings it out.

I now consider each test in turn to see what illumination they provide. Consider first the Simple Argument test. Geach's examples are the adjectives 'big' and 'small'. Points to note are: first, though the only nouns examined with 'big' and 'small' are 'flea' and 'elephant', the test is obviously being used in a general way, as I put it earlier, to prove something *simpliciter*, i.e. essential attributiveness; for he says, without qualification, ' "big" and "small" are attributive', though on the basis of only one test with each; secondly, this test does seem successfully to prove 'big' and 'small' essentially attributive; for it seems that, no matter what noun 'B' is, it will always be possible, with 'big' and 'small', to add a premise that will yield a false conclusion, unless thirdly, we think of some very odd noun-expressions indeed; e.g. 'x is a big occupant of space'. The only possible premises I can think of adding are 'occupants of space are temporally extended phenomena' or 'occupants of space are physical-property-bearing entities'. But even if 'x is a big temporally extended phenomenon' and 'x is a big physical-property-bearing entity' sound odd, they are not obviously false. However, happily we can ignore these cases, since, as we shall see, Test 4 takes care of them.

But even if Test 1 always works with 'big' and 'small', proving them essentially attributive, we do not yet know what 'attributive' means or why the test works. Nor has anything explicit been said about the meaning of 'logically splits up'. We are simply told that, by the test, 'x is a big flea' is proved not to split up, whereas 'x is a red book' does. If not splitting up means that something is wrong with the parts, nothing is wrong with the noun-elements of the

2   Alfred F. MacKay, 'Attributive-Predicative', *Analysis*, 30 (1969–70).

split, '*x* is a flea' and '*x* is an elephant'; they follow and are true. So something must be wrong, and this is what we would expect, with the adjectival element of the split, '*x* is big', that is not wrong with '*x* is red'. Certainly '*x* is red' is not only clear enough, but is entailed; so what is wrong with '*x* is big'? A clue is provided by what Geach says about the allegedly attributive 'good' and 'bad' later: 'even when "good" or "bad" stands by itself as a predicate' (and presumably we may add "big" and "small") '. . . some substantive has to be understood; there is no such thing as being just good or bad, there is only being a good or bad so-and-so' (p. 34). But this is only partly illuminating: equally there is no such thing as being just red or sweet, there is only being a red or sweet so-and-so. So here too, in one respect, some substantive has to be understood. The adjectives Geach calls attributive have sometimes been said to be 'substantive-hungry'; but so are all adjectives. So perhaps some are more substantive-hungry than others, or in a different way. The difference, I think, lies in the interpretation of 'has to be understood'. And what it is tempting to say is that '*x* is big', and, for Geach, '*x* is good', even for someone who understands these adjectives perfectly, are somehow incomplete without some substantive understood, hence not fully intelligible, and hence can have no truth-value assigned to them. Not so with '*x* is red'. Adjectives like 'big' are substantive-hungry in a stronger sense than 'red' is. I think this right as far as it goes, certainly with 'big' and 'small'; but it does not go deep enough since, as we shall see, incompleteness of intelligibility does not occur with all essential attributives. Before considering Geach's other tests, however, I make two further points, one slightly frivolous, the other of extreme importance. By Test 1, if '*x* is an AB' and 'B is a C' together render '*x* is an AC' false, 'A' is attributive. This seemed to be because, in some special way, attributive adjectives are substantive-hungry, hence in some sense 'is a AB' is unsplittable, and with some adjectives, e.g. 'big', this seemed to be because '*x* is A' *simpliciter* is incompletely intelligible in a way that renders attaching a truth-value to it impossible. But there is a quite different way in which statements of the form '*x* is an AB' are unsplittable, namely when 'AB' is a unitary expression because either technical or colloquial. Some, like 'that is a Portuguese man-of-war' war 'that is a white rhino' may be ambiguous (so is 'he is in a brown study'); others, like 'that fellow is a bad egg', are not. Yet the fact that by Test 1 they yield 'that is a Portuguese ship', 'that is a white animal', 'that fellow is a bad ovum', does not prove that 'Portuguese', 'white', 'bad', are attributive, let alone *alienans*. So though unsplittable, they are unsplittable in yet another sense, not one Geach is concerned with. Perhaps the test for these cases is to ask either whether the speaker was willing to say 'that is Portuguese' or 'that is white', or whether, without the adjective, '*x* is a B' ('that fellow is an egg') could conceivably be true, at least in any sense intended. So we get Rule 1: even before applying Geach's tests, make sure that 'AB' is not used in a colloquially or technically unsplittable sense.

But far more important is that even if 'x is big', said *simpliciter* (and Geach holds something like this for 'good' and 'bad'), is not fully intelligible, it is easy to fall into supposing that 'x is red' and 'x is sweet', said *simpliciter*, are. But they are not. Not, however, because they are incomplete and some substantive has to be understood, as with attributives, but because most adjectives have more than one meaning. This is so with most seemingly 'colour' adjectives, 'red' ('communist'), 'black' ('villainous'), 'yellow' ('cowardly'), 'green' ('inexperienced'), and 'blue', as in 'blue film' ('pornographic'), and 'blue mood' ('melancholy'); the same is true of 'sweet'. To understand 'x is red' or 'x is sweet', said *simpliciter*, we need to know the meaning or sense of the adjective. Of course, this may be given by the context or by the subject 'x'; in 'her dress is red', 'red' is obviously a colour adjective, but not always: 'this pamphlet is red' may require explicit explanation. Similarly with many attributive adjectives: 'big' in 'x is a big man' may mean 'large' or 'important'. Nor can we dismiss these uses as colloquial or metaphorical; some may have been metaphorical originally, but by now they are accepted literal meanings. The point becomes acute when an adjective like 'forged', which, in the sense of 'counterfeit', Geach says—I think wrongly—is attributive, is potentially ambiguous as between an attributive and a predicative meaning ('made in a forge'). This is crucial when one makes some general claim about an adjective, as Geach does for 'good' and 'bad', for I believe this consideration applies to them. Of course the various meanings of potentially ambiguous words may be quite unrelated, mere accidents of language; or contingently related as 'red' (colour and 'communist'); or related in meaning in varying degrees ranging from 'dry' (applied to wines, wit, and umbrellas), and 'sour' (applied to fruit and faces) to 'intelligent' (applied to men and actions) and 'healthy' (applied to people and diets).

All this is not only familiar but may seem irrelevant. Geach's point is about adjectives, not about people's understanding, and 'x is red' (colour) is complete enough for a truth-value to attach to it without a predicate noun, whereas 'x is big' (size) is not, whether a particular person understands their meanings or not; some adjectives function one way, some another. But it is far from irrelevant; if one adjective has more than one meaning (or, if you like, the same word stands for two different adjectives), it is vital to know which meaning is in question before pronouncing the adjective predicative or attributive. So Rule 2 is: pin down the intended meaning of the adjective before applying the test for attributiveness. 'X is black' does not necessarily carry its meaning on its face. Only when an adjective is known to have just one meaning, like 'beige', 'indigo', and 'aquamarine', can we confidently say whether a substantive need be understood, and that, e.g. 'x is beige' is complete and fully intelligible when said *simpliciter*.

My review of Geach's first test seemed perhaps to have gone part way towards illuminating the sense in which, if 'x is an AB' does not split up, 'A' is attributive. The adjectival part of the split, 'x is big', failed to be fully intelligible in the absence of a predicate noun. But a further point must be made. I took Geach's first test to be that, if by constructing a simple argument by adding a true premise about B you get a *false* conclusion, then 'A' is attributive. His two illustrations both produced false conclusions. But so interpreted, the test is too weak to prove the very cases, 'good' and 'bad', that Geach asserts to be attributive. Adding a premise to 'x is a good man' or 'x is a good solicitor' you can get, e.g., 'A good man (solicitor) is a good vertebrate, animal, mammal', etc. But these conclusions are not obviously *false*; rather they are odd, or their sense is unclear, and taken in some ways they may be even be true. Nor can I think of any premise which, when added, would yield a conclusion, like 'a big flea is a big animal', which has a clear sense and is plainly false. On the other hand, if we are content without falsity, and settle for oddity or unclarity, then with the fairly obviously predicative adjectives, 'communist' and 'aristocratic' (since they seem complete and intelligible enough standing alone in 'x is communist' and 'x is aristocratic'), from 'x is a communist agitator' or 'x is an aristocratic person' we can derive 'a communist agitator is a communist mammal' and 'an aristocratic person is an aristocratic vertebrate', which seem equally odd or unclear. So there is a dilemma, at least for Geach: settling for less than a false conclusion makes the test too wide and excludes, as attributive, adjectives which intuitively are clearly predicative; insisting on a false conclusion leaves (as I think it should) the essential attributiveness of 'good' and 'bad' unproved. So by considering Test 1, we may have partially clarified 'splitting up', but either the test does not reveal all attributive adjectives or, if attributive, 'good' has not yet been revealed as such.

I postpone consideration of Tests 2 and 3 until much later. Even Geach would not claim much importance for them since he thinks them capable of exposing only certain attributive adjectives. I shall argue later that they are worthless in relation to the questions at issue and appear at all only as a result of confusion. I turn directly, therefore, to Test 4, the Independent Ascertainment test, since it, I believe, brings matters most clearly into focus. Paradoxically it does not mention splitting up, only combining, and because it focuses on possibilities of ascertaining truth, it has, as MacKay notes, an epistemological flavour which he dismisses as 'so much irrelevant window dressing'; he represents it instead as being concerned simply with mutual entailment or its failure. I shall return to this later. The test is stated as a sufficient condition: if to ascertain that 'x is A' one must understand some substantive, 'B', to be in question, 'A' is attributive. It is of course the predicate noun, not the subject noun if any, which must be known: we need to know whether what is intended is that this shark is a small shark or a small fish. But the test is surely meant as a necessary condition also: if 'A' is attributive in 'x is AB', it is impossible to ascertain that x is A without understanding some noun, 'B', as being in question. Note that it is not that 'x is A' cannot be ascertained without ascertaining that 'x is a B'; that would rule out ascertaining that x is a forged banknote. Truly, as Geach says, two people could find out independently that 'x is red' and 'x is a car' and pool their knowledge. But though *someone* needs to know, e.g., that elephants are in question to ascertain if x is small, *I* may only succeed in finding out that x is small *if* an elephant (what I measured in the dark was in fact a rhino). But we still lack clarification of certain matters: (1) why it is necessary to understand which predicate noun is in question; (2) whether this test reveals as attributive the same examples as did the previous tests; (3) whether it can show, as Geach needs, that certain adjectives are *essentially* attributive. I shall deal first with essentially attributive adjectives, leaving till later the question of attributive *uses* of adjectives that are not essentially attributive.

If an adjective, 'A', is essentially attributive, and to ascertain that x is A some substantive must always be understood, 'x is A' is necessarily an ellipsis for 'x is an AB' where 'B' is *any* noun. Since this is so, no matter what noun 'B' is, being essentially attributive must be a feature inherent in the nature of the adjective itself, not something for which any particular noun is responsible. Leaving aside 'good' and 'bad', I think some of Geach's examples *are* essentially attributive: certainly 'big' and 'small' are ('forged' and 'putative' I will return to). But if there are, as I shall argue, attributive *uses* of adjectives that are not in themselves essentially attributive, Geach's test—that the truth of 'x is A' can *never* be established without understanding some substantive—will be a test of essential attributiveness, not of whether an adjective happens to be attributively used with a given noun, 'B'. But we still need urgently to see why an essentially attributive adjective always requires a noun to be understood, since it is essential attributiveness that Geach particularly needs to identify (for the claim that 'good' and 'bad' are essentially attributive). But Geach does not explain this.

However it is not too difficult to see why some adjectives are essentially attributive. We saw that though we may understand the meaning of 'big', 'small', and, we might add, 'fast', 'hot', etc. perfectly (as Geach maintains we understand 'good'), it does not follow that we fully understand 'x is big (fast, hot)' standing alone. We could say (as Geach does of 'good'), 'there is no such thing as just being big *simpliciter*' (as there may be just being red *simpliciter*). And the reason why some predicate noun must always be understood with these adjectives is that they logically demand some standards or criteria, set by the noun in question. This is clear because these are scalar terms. X may be big for a car, for a star, for an animal, for a molecule. But big stars are enormous, big molecules minuscule (the standard here being set, roughly, by the noun phrase 'everyday objects'—the same standard we are using when we see some object we do not recognize (say, a giant excavator) and say 'That's an enormous thing; whatever is it?'). Knowing what the noun is is a necessary but only a necessary condition; if I know that x is an elephant but lack knowledge of the normal, average, standard sizes of elephants, I cannot ascertain that x is a big elephant.

Knowing the standard sizes of what is being judged, without knowing elephants are in question, I could ascertain that x is a big one; someone, however, whoever supplied me with the standard, had to know that elephants were in question. So the matter is easily understood with 'big', 'fast', or 'hot'. Hot days, ovens, and stars are on a continuum of temperature and we need to know which section of it we are dealing with; it is the substantive which tells us. This explains our supposition that failure to split up means that 'x is big' is not fully intelligible. But are there other adjectives (including 'good'), not on a scale of this sort, which are also essentially attributive? I postpone this till later. Perhaps we have now elucidated what an essentially attributive adjective is: it is one that, by its inherent nature, demands that some criteria or standards be set, and set by some substantive. It is, in fact, a kind of adjective, not a kind of use. This is why there is no problem about my earlier odd example: 'big' demands a standard of size to be set, but the noun-phrase 'occupant of space' cannot supply one. I turn now to attributive *uses* of adjectives that are not *essentially* attributive, a possibility, as we saw, suggested by Geach's presentation but not explored by him. Such adjectives are capable of predicative or attributive use: they are logically ambifunctional. I shall call them 'Janus-adjectives', though this is strictly a misnomer since Janus could look both ways at once whereas these adjectives can look only one way at a time.

It is clear that many adjectives Geach calls predicative (his examples were 'sweet' and 'red') are often used attributively. 'x is sweet' cannot always be ascertained without a substantive, 'B', being understood *if* you intend to combine it with 'B' to assert 'x is a sweet B', even though the truth of 'x is sweet' *simpliciter* can be ascertained and it can be used predicatively. These adjectives are therefore a different *type of adjective* from essentially attributive ones. It is not difficult to find examples of Janus-adjectives because most common adjectives are ambifunctional. I distinguish two categories of cases. First, x may certainly be sweet (*simpliciter*); it is not tasteless, sour or bitter. Yet given that it is a Sauternes and that Sauternes vary in sweetness, it may not be a sweet Sauternes (or for a Sauternes or as Sauternes go). x may be definitely bitter; but if aloes differ in bitterness, it may not be a bitter aloe. Second category: x may be slightly sour *simpliciter*, certainly *not* sweet. Yet it may, though not sweet, be sweet as crab-apples or Seville oranges go, and so, slightly paradoxically, a sweet crab-apple or Seville oranges. So, category (1): x may be sweet, but not a sweet B; category (2) x may be not sweet, even slightly sour, and yet a sweet B. The use of adverbs is interesting here: 'x is not a particularly sweet Sauternes'; 'x is a comparatively sweet Seville orange'. These examples involve combining, not splitting. It may be more convincing with examples of category (2) to make my point with splitting. From 'x is a pale-skinned Zulu' it does not follow that x is pale-skinned *simpliciter*; nor from 'x is a dark-skinned Scandinavian', than *x* is dark-skinned *simpliciter*. So with multitudes of adjectives. *x*, owing to embarrassment, may have a red or even scarlet face, i.e. red as faces go. But the face may not be scarlet *simpliciter*: someone looking at it through a peep-hole, not knowing it is part of a face, and with colour-chart in hand, may say rightly that it is deep pink, or, even more exactly, the pink called Orchis (British Standard Colour 1–021). Only in an extremity of rage might it reach Dusky Pink (BSC 8–091). Again the role of adverbs is interesting: 'very dark-skinned for a Scandinavian, not for a Negro', 'particularly or unusually red for a face'. An objection might be made here, though I doubt if it is cogent. One might seek to dismiss examples in category (2) as being not genuinely attributive uses by saying we are speaking only figuratively, or in a *façon de parler*, or with colloquial hyperbole; we did not literally mean that the Scandinavian was dark-skinned, the blushing face red or scarlet. But not only would this require a more satisfactory distinction between literal and metaphorical, figurative, colloquial, or colourful uses than we have available; we can and do speak of a dark-skinned Scandinavian or a pale-skinned Zulu without meaning that the former is nearly black and the latter nearly white, a scarlet face without meaning it to be scarlet by a colour-chart, or Seville oranges as too sweet for our purpose without meaning they are sweet: a somewhat dry Sauternes need not be dry at all the way a Chablis is. And none of this, except possibly the scarlet face, strikes us as metaphorical or hyperbolic. But even were this objection cogent, it does not touch my category (1) examples, and these suffice to illustrate predicative and attributive uses of the same adjective. As I said, nearly all adjectives that are not essentially attributive can be used attributively. What is intelligent in a 3-year-old would not necessarily be intelligent in a Master of Balliol, nor need what is skilful for an apprentice be skilful for a craftsman. Often it is unclear, even in context, whether 'A' is being used predicatively or attributively in '*x* is an AB'. If I simply ask for something sweet to drink with dessert, I may be told, 'This should suit you, it is a sweet Sauternes' meaning merely 'sweet' and 'a Sauternes'. But I may not be getting a wine that is an unusually sweet Sauternes.

We saw that there are essentially attributive adjectives and why they are so. Their inherent nature required, to ascertain that '*x* is A', that standards be met, these being supplied by a predicate noun, explicit or understood. We have now seen that there are adjectives, not essentially attributive, including those Geach called predicative, which are capable of attributive use. There is indeed a surface similarity. When these adjectives are being used in such a way that, to combine with '*x* is a B', '*x* is A' cannot be ascertained without the noun 'B' being understood, they are being used attributively. Hence if we interpret Test 4 with an exact parallel of Geach's words, 'I can ascertain that a distant object is a fairly pale-coloured man because I can see it is pale in colour and a more knowledgeable friend who can't see it knows it is a man; there is no such possibility of ascertaining that a thing is a fairly pale Scandinavian by pooling independent information that it is fairly pale and is a Scandinavian', we see that Test 4 reveals both attributive uses of potentially predicative adjectives and, *a fortiori*, essentially attributive adjectives. But this helps to mask the fact that we have two quite different phenomena. With essentially attributive adjectives it was necessarily impossible, without a noun understood, ever to ascertain '*x* is A'; with these other adjectives it is always possible to ascertain '*x* is A' independently, but not always thereby possible, even having established that *x* is a B, to combine the two pieces of information to yield '*x* is an AB'. Only when interpreted in the strict manner I indicated does it isolate essentially attributive adjectives.

What then is the explanation why adjectives like 'red' and 'sweet', which, unlike essential attributives, do not inherently demand that some noun sets up standards, can sometimes be used attributively? (Incidentally, it should be clear that I am using 'standards' loosely to cover a variety of notions: normal, usual, expected, or average (size, colour, taste, etc.) for Bs (as in elephants, Scandinavians, Sauternes); meeting the criteria for being Bs (as in 'genuine banknotes'); meeting the requirements or function for which Bs are intended or designed (food, barometers), and so on. There are obviously various minutiae which it would be tedious to pursue here. When we are told '*x* is a big elephant' we need to know whether what is meant is that it is bigger than average for fully grown elephants, bigger than average for elephants including babies, whether we intend bulk, weight, or height, whether we mean, by 'average', median, mean, or mode, etc.) How then can potentially predicative adjectives be used attributively and so demand nouns to set standards? The answer is that, though nothing in the inherent nature of the *adjective* demands standards, certain *nouns* may set standards *vis-à-vis* a given adjective. Where there is a normal, expected, or average degree of sweetness for Seville oranges or Sauternes, or of skin-colour for Scandinavians, or colour for faces, it makes sense to say 'sweet for a Seville orange', 'dry for a Sauternes', 'dark for a Scandinavian', or 'red for a face'. An optimum, average, or normalcy of taste, colour, etc. for these nouns sets a standard in relation to appropriate adjectives. This is why, with Geach's red car, the case is so straightforward. No attributive use is possible, since nouns like 'car' and 'dress' carry no standards as regards optimal, normal, or expected colour. There is no such thing as being 'red for a car', or 'blue as dresses go'. Similarly the noun 'drink' probably does not, and the noun 'liquid' certainly does not, carry a standard for sweetness ('sweet for a liquid' makes no sense). This helps to explain a point I made in an article long ago [see this vol., p. 30], without quite knowing why it was right, that while 'That is a beautifully blue sky' makes sense, 'That is a beautifully blue dress' does not. One reason 'beige' is never used attributively is that it is hard to think of anything which sets a standard for colour by which beige would be either standard or non-standard. We shall see a stronger reason in a moment.

It is easy, incidentally, to make a mistake which would lead one to think certain adjectives essentially attributive when in fact they are predicative or at most Janus-type adjectives. Adjectives have limitations on their range of intelligible application, and this is true equally of predicatives and attributives. 'Red' is applicable only to things with spatial extension; 'big' is inapplicable to mathematical points. If you are sent to ascertain whether 'x is A', you must understand 'A', and understanding it necessarily involves having some grasp of its range of application. But though some adjectives have an extremely wide range, 'red' and 'big' both being applicable to anything with spatial extension, others have a much narrower range: 'intelligent' is applicable to people, actions, plans, not to inanimate objects; 'hendecasyllabic' only to words or sentences, 'anapaestic' only to verses or metrical feet; a few apply only and uniquely to one noun, like Aristotle's 'snub' for noses (though I suspect even this has had a use with pen-nibs). Consequently one might suppose that 'snub' is essentially attributive. The formula can sound the same for both, i.e., to ascertain that x is snub you must know what noun, namely, 'nose', is in question. But this is only a special case of the general principle that to understand an adjective well enough to ascertain whether 'x is A' you must understand its range of application. Asked to ascertain if x is snub you will know that if x is, x will necessarily be a nose, and that if it is not a nose it cannot be snub; equally, asked to ascertain either if x is big or x is red, you will know that, if it is either, it will necessarily have spatial extension, and if it lacks this it cannot be red or big. In this respect there is no difference between predicative and attributive adjectives. The point can perhaps best be put thus: it is of the nature of an attributive adjective, 'A', that you can fully understand 'A' and yet still need a noun to be specified before you can ascertain that x is A. But you cannot fully understand 'snub' without understanding some noun,[3] and once you do fully understand the adjective, no noun need be specified for you to ascertain that x is snub. Asked to find out if 'x is big', and fully understanding 'big', you must still ask, 'big what'?. Asked to find out if x is snub, and fully understanding 'snub', you do not have to ask 'snub what?' any more than you need to ask 'red what'?. The point that 'snub' is not essentially attributive but of the Janus-type can be reinforced by noting that 'snub' can be used attributively: what might be a snub nose for a Red Indian need not be a (particularly) snub nose for a Negro. And as Aristotle says, 'snub' merely means 'concave' as restricted to noses; and 'concave' is not essentially attributive. Finally, a different kind of confusion that can lead to supposing adjectives essentially attributive when they are not. If you understand the adjective 'courageous' fully, and are sent to ascertain whether x was courageous, you do not need a predicate noun specified. Of course, unlike the case of the red car, on encountering x

---

[3] Aristotle speaks, in connection with 'snub', of 'terms that are predicated of the terms through which they are defined', *De Sophisticis Elenchis*, 18lb.

one will unavoidably discover that *x* was, say, an action, not a man; and to the latter but not to the former 'courageous' may apply in a dispositional sense. But this no more makes 'courageous' essentially attributive than it would make 'sweet' essentially attributive if, asked to find out if *x* is sweet, and not being a cannibal, you discover that *x* turns out to be a girl.

I indicated at the outset that we should not rule out the possibility of a third kind of adjective, the essentially predicative adjective. One may wonder, after all I have said, whether there are any. I suggest that there are. There is a way we sometimes use adjectives in what I shall call an 'absolute, extreme, *ne plus ultra*, or epitome' sense. We sometimes use 'A', that is, having in mind the highest conceivable degree of A: if say we cannot conceive of anything being sweeter than sugar or honey, are convinced that nothing could conceivably be more graceful than Pavlova or a gazelle, and, rightly or wrongly, that no one could surpass Aristotle, Aquinas, Kant, or Einstein in intelligence, we may be using adjectives to indicate some quality (to our mind and perhaps rightly) in its highest possible or extreme degree. That we are using an adjective in this way may be clear from the context or other things we say (e.g. we say grudgingly that Bacon and Mill were pretty intelligent, even that our reigning ballerina is very graceful, but clearly without intending to commit ourselves further); or we may make it explicit by saying e.g. that *x* is the epitome, *ne plus ultra* of sweetness, grace, intelligence, or that it is sweet, etc., in the highest possible degree, unsurpassably, and so on. We actually have a few epitome adjectives in use: 'omniscient' and 'omnipotent' are obvious examples. And we could easily coin others: 'all-good' is sometimes used of God, and we could invent 'ultimograceful', etc. if we felt the need. If we are using an adjective this way, a sweet B, *whatever* B is, will be sweet; and if someone tells me, 'This is a sweet wine', I might reply mischievously 'If you think that's sweet, compare it with sugar or honey'. Other examples of adjectives used in an essentially predicative way occur when they are clearly being used to indicate a paradigm or central or prime example, e.g. of red. This differs from the epitome use, since paradigm examples or red form a range from vermilion to crimson. That we do sometimes clearly intend a paradigm use accounts in part for possible objections to my earlier 'red face' example. We do use adjectives in paradigm senses sometimes, but I am disinclined to say that, even when speaking literally, we always do, which is why I was unwilling to dismiss the face 'scarlet with embarrassment' as hyperbolic or a mere *façon de parler*. But the general point should be clear and I would not cavil over this example. A third way in which an adjective can be essentially predicative is by being what I call 'ultimately determinate'. 'Red', even when used paradigmatically, is not determinate, covering a range of indubitably red shades: two things, both paradigmatically red, need not be identical and indistinguishable in colour. But 'square' and 'spherical' are ultimately determinate with regard to shape; 'triangular' is not. Perhaps outside mathematics and logic we have few such adjectives in our language. But we do have some, invented for the rare occasions we need them. 'Greenstone' (British Standard Colour No. 5–059) and 'Shadow Blue' (BSC No. 7–077) are determinate colours; we could easily invent 'centidecibelic' as a determinate of loudness, and so on. But some quite familiar adjectives as well as these artificial ones are determinate too: I suggest 'beige', 'indigo', and 'aquamarine'. So is the epitome adjective 'omnipotent' (though it cannot have two identical instances). So probably are some based on the flavour of particular substances e.g. 'aniseed-flavoured' or 'liquorice-flavoured'. With determinates, it makes no sense to say, e.g., 'particularly shadow blue', 'very beige', or 'somewhat centidecibelic', or to say '*x* is beige for a such and such', or 'greenstone as Bs go' (as it does to say, 'very red for a Cox's pippin'). There is no such thing as being more or less omnipotent or centidecibelic, no range or shades of beige or greenstone as there are ranges and shades of red. Nor do I concede an objection that might be raised about whether some of my examples, like 'aniseed-flavoured', are essentially determinate. Two liquids with a clear aniseed flavour might indeed be distinguishable, one tasting strongly, the other faintly, of aniseed. But this is a distinction of strength, not flavour, as it would be when a manufactured substitute flavour tasted very like, but not exactly like, aniseed. My examples are identical and determinate in flavour, though not in strength or intensity. Of course, we do use some of my examples as determinables, 'square' to mean 'squarish', and then *x* can be more square than *y*; but in their epitome or paradigm use these are determinate. Thus many paradigm adjectives, but not all, are determinate, and so are many epitome adjectives, but not all; two ballerinas might be unsurpassably graceful, but in their different ways. But all determinate, paradigm, and epitome adjectives are essentially predicative.

I hope I have shown that some adjectives are essentially predicative by their very nature. The same words which are usable as Janus-adjectives, like 'sweet' and 'graceful', are sometimes used in an *essentially* predicative way; but strictly they then have a different sense for which the different adjectives 'ultimosweet' and 'ultimograceful' could be coined. Unlike essentially attributive adjectives, those that are essentially predicative demand no standard-setting substantive. Unlike Janus-adjectives, they are inherently such that no noun *could* set up standards *vis-à-vis* them, and consequently they are incapable of an attributive *use*. Notice, however, that this must be a matter of necessity. There may be existing adjectives for which, contingently, no existing noun happens to set standards. But a newly coined noun might set up standards for them. One might also wonder whether the speed of light sets an epitome for 'fast' and absolute zero an epitome for 'cold'. To me these sound merely contingent, not points that it is inconceivable to suppose surpassed; but philosophers of science might have reasons to argue otherwise. But with essentially predicative adjectives, no nouns could conceivably set standards. 'Particularly shadow blue', or 'omnipotent for a such and such', or 'very beige as so-and-so's go' make no sense (unless you happen to think 'beige' is determinable and covers a range, but without any existing noun setting a standard for it), nor does 'somewhat paradigmatically red for this or that'. One might of course say 'unsurpassably graceful or the epitome of grace for an elephant', but that would not be to use 'graceful' in the epitome sense I intended, namely, 'graceful to a degree that could not conceivably be surpassed in anything'. We could, I suppose, invent 'ultimoelephantograceful', but this just shows why we do not invent all the adjectives we could.

If what I have said is right, the predicative-attributive distinction uncovers two distinguishable phenomena: sorts of *adjectives* and sorts of *uses* of adjectives. It marks out *three* sorts of *adjectives*: essentially predictive, essentially attributive, and those Janus-adjectives which are not essentially either. It marks out *two* sorts of adjective *uses*: predicative and attributive. Obviously, essentially predicative and essentially attributive adjectives can have respectively only a predicative and only an attributive use. The third, most common, kind of adjective can have both uses. To talk of predicative and attributive adjectives in the same breath as predicative and attributive uses is to risk serious confusion. It might be thought that I should allow a third, essentially predicative use since I have said that existing adjectives like 'red', 'sweet', and 'graceful' may be used sometimes in an essentially predicative way. But this would only be playing with words—something I would not dream of doing, so I prefer to resist the suggestion. When these adjectives are obviously being so used, it is rather that, though the *words* are the same, they are used in a different sense, and are thus different, though related, adjectives for which we could, if we wished, coin terms, 'paradigm-red', 'optimosweet', and 'ultimo-graceful'.

I postponed considering Tests 2 and 3 for, though they raise interesting points, there is little to be learned from them about the central issues. The *Alienans* test, like Test 1, actually gives examples of failure to split up, and as I said earlier, tempts one to suppose that such failure is simply failure of an entailment. Entailment-failure occurs, of necessity, due to the nature of an *alienans* adjective; but it is the *substantive* predication 'is a B' which fails this time. When Tests 1 and 4 were used as tests for essential attributiveness, it appeared that failure to split (or combine) had to do with some incompleteness in the *adjective* predication. While it was plausible to say that '*x* is big', standing alone, is not fully intelligible and hence that its truth cannot be ascertained, and while with some *quasi-alienans* adjectives an adjectival predication results that is somehow deviant ('*x* is putative' from '*x* is the putative father'), some genuinely *alienans* adjectives, it seems to me, give rise to nothing deviant or incomplete: '*x* is forged', derived from '*x* is a forged banknote' is truly entailed and as fully intelligible as '*x* is red' without any substantive being understood: it means something like '*x* was produced as a copy of something by someone with intent to deceive'. Moreover, I could ascertain that '*x* is forged' by seeing someone copy something and being assured by him that his intent was to deceive or defraud, without knowing what a banknote is, or what one looks like. Of course we would not know it is a forged banknote, but equally we did not know that the red thing was a red car. So some *alienans* adjectives are not essentially attributive according to the understanding of this we have achieved so far. Indeed, even some adjectives that can sometimes be *alienans* and sometimes not (a forged banknote is not a banknote, and a *trompe-l'œil* cornice is not a cornice, but a forged or *trompe-l'œil* painting is a painting) are essentially predicative and cannot even be used attributively. No noun is needed to ascertain 'x is forged' and different standards are not set by different nouns; 'forged for a banknote' or 'forged as paintings go' makes no sense. Oddly, 'genuine', in 'genuine banknote', though not *alienans*, is essentially attributive; to ascertain 'x is genuine' we must ask, 'genuine what?'. It cannot be used predicatively. But 'former' in 'former warlord' is both *alienans* and essentially attributive. So the *Alienans* test is in itself not only merely, as Geach thought, a partial test infallibly revealing some attributive adjectives; if not all *alienans* adjectives are attributive, as Geach supposed, it is no test at all.

This we might have suspected all along. Failure of the noun-predication occurs with *alienans* adjectives, but not with 'good', dubiously with 'bad', and never with 'big' or 'small'. But if *alienans* adjectives are attributive in the same respect as other attributive adjectives, there must be some feature they share with all other attributive adjectives which makes them attributive; otherwise there are two wholly different ways, or senses, in which adjectives can be attributive. So either the *Alienans* test must be rejected as irrelevant, which is my view, or we have not yet uncovered a unitary principle which makes all Geach's alleged examples attributive. And it would be reasonable to suppose that it is the adjective-predication which holds the clues. Incidentally, a question I raised earlier, whether there are essentially attributive adjectives which are not scalar, has been answered: 'genuine' and 'former' are examples. I also promised a comment on quasi-*alienans* adjectives like 'putative' and 'alleged'. Although 'x is putative' and 'x is alleged' may be thought deviant, or incomplete, the test that seems the significant one does now show them to be attributive. One does *not* have to understand some noun in order to ascertain that x is alleged or putative. If I hear people say 'We allege George to be . . .', or 'We believe George to be . . .', and what follows is drowned in hubbub, I *have* ascertained that George is an alleged or putative something. Of course, I don't know what; but nor do I know what if, after looking at x, my non-colour-blind associate says 'x is a red . . .' and the rest is drowned in hubbub. In fact, like 'forged', 'putative' is essentially predicative. Contrast this with 'x is a former . . .' where hubbub follows; to have ascertained that 'x is a former something', *someone* must have had a substantive in mind. Certainly, 'x is an alleged murderer' does not split up into 'x is alleged' (presumably deviant) and 'x is a murderer' on one understanding of splitting up; but this may only show that the loose expression 'does not split up' was too unclear to pin down the interesting notions of attributiveness. A noun needs to be understood for *some* purpose here, but not for it to be ascertained that *x* is an alleged something or other.

The third, Unsafe Predication, test, illustrated by Geach with 'bad', which is, he says, 'something like' an *alienans* adjective, contains no example of splitting up at all. Indeed there is something odd about saying that 'bad' is 'something like' an *alienans* adjective. If 'A' is *alienans*, '*x* is an AB' does not entail '*x* is a B'; if not, it does. What third possibility is there that would make 'bad' something like an *alienans* adjective? His example '*x* is bad food' together with a premise normally understood as predicable of food, namely, 'food supports life', does not, he says, permit the conclusion 'bad food supports life'. But if 'bad' were *alienans*, bad food would not be food, and Geach never goes so far as to assert this. Indeed, a bad egg is certainly an egg and a bad tomato a tomato.

Perhaps the partial similarity to *alienans* adjectives is that we are often left in a dilemma whether to call a bad B a B or not. But in any case, like the *alienans* test, this test is only partial; Geach admits that it will not uncover all attributives, since it will not apply to 'good'. As with Tests 1 and 4, it looks as if the trouble, if any, with '*x* is bad' may be that it is sometimes incomplete; but the cases that turn up the dilemmas with Test 3, '*x* is half-eaten, fossilized, male or dead', all seem completely intelligible without a substantive, unlike '*x* is big', and as do other dilemma-producing cases: '*x* is filleted, squashed, mutilated, or spoiled'. But Test 3, which yields these dilemmas, is as useless to prove essential attributiveness as the *Alienans* test: 'male' seems to be clearly predicative; so are 'fossilized', 'dead', and 'filleted'. Anyone who doubts these is falling into the confusion I discussed with 'snub' earlier; to understand 'fossilized' and 'dead' you must know they are applicable only to sometime living organisms, and 'filleted' only to normally bony creatures. 'Filleted' does not mean 'boneless', or a jellyfish would be filleted. You do not need a predicate noun, 'fish', 'lion', or 'herring'. But to ascertain '*x* is squashed, mutilated, or spoiled', you must know the standards set by some predicate noun, respectively e.g., a normal mouse, body, or food; these adjectives are essentially attributive. But as with most distinctions we can drift off into shady areas. To ascertain that an object found on the ground, say a banana, is half-eaten you need to know what constitutes a whole banana, or know what a whole object of that sort is like. But if you merely see someone eat half an unknown object, you have ascertained that it is half-eaten without any substantive being understood, apart from the noun-expression, 'object he was originally holding'. But I suppose even this is enough to make 'half-eaten' essentially attributive, for ascertaining that *x* is half-eaten demands that some standard be set, even by some such vague noun-phrase. So the fundamental test of essential attributiveness is not that '*x* is A' is incompletely intelligible when standing alone, but that some noun must be understood to set standards if '*x* is A' is to be ascertainable.

What can be said of Geach's four tests? Remember that his main target was *essentially* attributive adjectives, in order to claim that 'good' and 'bad' are always attributive. The Simple Argument test, we saw, must be used strictly, to produce a false, not merely an odd, conclusion, or else it pronounces some obvious predicatives to be attributive ('aristocratic'). Even used strictly, it is inadequate to uncover all attributive *uses* ('a sweet Sauternes is a sweet wine' is not false). 'A' *is* proved essentially attributive if a false conclusion can be obtained with every noun it can be applied to. But I doubt whether it is adequate to reveal all essentially attributive adjectives as being such, e.g. 'genuine'; and 'a squashed mouse is a squashed vertebrate' is not false. Nor does it prove 'good' or 'bad' to be essentially attributive.

The *Alienans* test was admittedly only partial, not applying to 'good', 'big', or 'fast'. It does not even prove genuine *alienans* or *quasi-alienans* adjectives to be essentially attributive unless the failure of the noun-predication entailment is relevant, a point I take up in a moment.

The Unsafe Predication test was also conceded to be partial. It also failed to distinguish predicative from attributive adjectives, since puzzles and dilemmas could be produced with both kinds of adjectives, as well as with 'bad'.

The Independent Ascertainment test, framed in terms of combining, not splitting up, threw the clearest light on inability to split up and hence on attributiveness. It suggested strongly that inability to split up might be a matter of standard-setting by the predicate noun. Often when one *could* ascertain that x is A independently, one could not safely combine it with the truth of 'x is a B' to form 'x is an AB' because 'B' sets a standard *vis-à-vis* 'A'; when this is so, the test infallibly shows that 'A' is being attributively used. But it was not the case that, when 'A' is attributively used in 'x is an AB', the predication 'x is A' must be false; simply that if 'A' is used attributively, the adjective predication, 'x is A', is not entailed. The test is also infallible if it is interpreted as meaning that, if the truth of 'x is A' can never be ascertained unless some predicate substantive is understood, 'A' is essentially attributive. But if the test is interpreted as Geach intends it, that if you cannot independently establish 'x is A' and 'x is B' and then safely combine them to yield 'x is an AB', 'A' is attributive, then 'forged' and 'putative' become attributive, whereas I have argued that they are essentially predicative. What has gone wrong?

I have purloined Geach's terms to make a variety of distinctions among adjectives and their uses. My distinctions are all the result, I confess, of pondering things he said. But since some of my conclusions are so different (e.g. *alienans* adjectives are not all attributive), it may be wondered whether I have departed entirely from his distinction and substituted a quite different one of my own. My contention, however, is that the complexities and confusions I have tried to unravel are really ushered in by the fact that both in his original formulation for being predicative or attributive and in his subsequent tests he used the phrase 'splits up' extremely loosely and conflated two distinct issues, *kinds* and *uses* of adjectives. When he said 'in a phrase "an AB" . . . "A" is (logically) predicative if the predication "is an AB" splits up logically into a pair of predications "is a B" and "is A" ', it is easy to suppose entailment is involved. It is, and indeed, it is mutual entailment that is involved when 'A' is merely *used* predicatively, and often when 'A' is essentially predicative. Consequently it is easy to suppose, as MacKay does, that failure to split up, which makes 'A' (logically) attributive, means failure of entailment, and to fall into the trap of thinking that any failure of entailment proves an adjective attributive. According to my analysis, 'does not split up', as Geach used it, is a composite covering two different notions: (1) failure of entailment of '*x* is A' by '*x* is an AB', where, 'A' being a Janus-adjective, '*x* is A' *can* have an independently ascertained truth-value, but is being used attributively (mutual entailment fails also); (2) failure of '*x* is A' to have a truth-value unless 'B' is understood, 'A' being then essentially attributive; but then Geach includes also (3) failure of entailment of '*x* is a B'. This opens the floodgates; *alienans* adjectives all become essentially attributive, though, if I am right, 'former' is, but 'forged' and 'putative' are not. We see the same in reverse if we consider the 'pooling' or combining exploited in Test 4. In combining, Geach took as one example a case where you can always ascertain independently '*x* is A' and '*x* is a B' ('*x* is (a) red (something)') and '*x* is a car' (we saw that 'car' never sets a standard for colour); this is a case where 'A' cannot help being predicatively used. His other example, 'good car', was one where '*x* is A' cannot be ascertained independently and where 'A' is therefore *essentially attributive*. He did not explicitly consider two other possible cases. You can independently ascertain '*x* is (a) sweet (something)' and '*x* is a Sauternes', but if you cannot safely combine them, all that is shown is that 'A' is attributively used. But there is also the other case where again '*x* is A' and '*x* is B' can be ascertained independently, but cannot be safely combined, i.e. '*x* is (a) putative (something)' and '*x* is a father'; for Geach this inability to combine makes 'A' essentially attributive, whereas I have argued that 'putative' is *essentially predicative*. So his test gives the results it does by being extremely broad: it is that when you cannot ascertain both elements independently *and* then safely combine them, 'A' is attributive; and when you cannot split up, achieving true and independently ascertainable elements, 'A' is attributive. But such a wide test does not *isolate* essentially attributive adjectives, since by it, when you cannot safely combine two independently established components ('*x* is sweet' and '*x* is a Sauternes'), it also catches attributive *uses* of his admittedly predicative adjectives too.

Of course, nothing can prevent Geach using 'splits up' and 'does not split up' in this very broad umbrella way, and indeed it will make all *alienans* adjectives attributive by stipulation. But I do not see what is gained; it is using a sledgehammer which obliterates interesting distinctions, potentially important for other purposes, instead of a scalpel which reveals them. Moreover it is an unnecessary sledgehammer for, far from singling out Geach's prime target, *essentially* attributive adjectives, it obscures it. A separate test for these in terms of splitting up and combining in no way involves entailment, and that is why I have concentrated on the adjectival predication throughout. It would suffice to say an adjective, 'A', is essentially attributive if 'x is A' can never be ascertained without understanding some noun, 'B'.

It remains to ask whether the epistemological flavour of the most helpful test, Test 4, is really only 'window-dressing', and why the issue with attributive adjectives is not simply, as MacKay claims, one of failure of mutual entailment. This helps show why the umbrella expression, 'logically splits up', was unsatisfactory. With predicative *uses* there is mutual entailment; with attributive *uses* there is a failure of mutual entailment. But with essentially attributive adjectives, though it may seem to be simply an entailment failure in that 'x is a big star' does not entail 'x is big', the reason 'x is big' fails to follow from 'x is a big star' is not that it may be either true or false, but that, standing alone, it lacks a truth-value. I assume that entailment concerns a relationship between propositions. The question of entailment arises when, if 'p' and 'q' are both true, 'r' must be true if they entail it, but may be false if they do not. Taking it in the other direction, the question of entailment or its failure can only arise if we start with complete propositions or propositional functions capable of having a truth-value when values are applied for their variables. But if 'x is big', like 'x is utterly' or 'x is redder', is incapable in isolation of having any truth-value assigned to it, the question whether, in conjunction with a genuine proposition, it entails or fails to entail anything simply cannot arise. So if identification of essentially attributive adjectives is the target, it is not just a question of failure of entailment, and to introduce cases where entailments fail was irrelevant. But can the matter be put in a less epistemological-sounding way than in terms of ascertaining? I think so. An adjective, 'A', is essentially predicative if no predicate noun can ever affect the truth of 'x is A'. An adjective, 'A', is ambifunctional or Janus-type if 'x is A' can have a truth-value independently of any predicate noun and if a predicate noun can sometimes set standards which determine whether 'x is A' and 'x is a B' together mutually entail 'x is an AB'. An adjective, 'A', is essentially attributive if some predicate noun has to be understood for 'x is A' to have a truth-value. From this, the 'epistemological' results, about possibility or impossibility of *ascertaining* truth, follow.

I said earlier that there were three kinds of adjectives and two kinds of uses. That is one way of illuminating these questions. But another way of putting it may provide supplementary illumination. We could say instead that there are two kinds of adjectives: those essentially attributive, which always demand a predicate noun understood if a truth-value is to be attached to the adjective-predication ('big', 'former', 'genuine'), and those that make no such demand (Janus-adjectives, 'red' and 'sweet', and essentially predicative adjectives, 'omnipotent', 'greenstone', 'forged', and 'putative'); we could simply call all these predicative. We could then say that in a predication of the form '*x* is an AB', and according to which adjective 'A' is, there are three ways in which different adjectives may operate: (1) some always have an essentially predicative use, viz. '*x* is A and *x* is B' mutually entails '*x* is an AB'; 'omnipotent', 'greenstone', and 'forged' (when not *alienans*) always do. (2) Some adjectives always have an essentially attributive use, viz. '*x* is A and *x* is a B' and '*x* is an AB' are not mutually entailing; some *alienans* adjectives ('forged' when *alienans*) and *quasi-alienans* adjectives ('putative') always do. Most adjectives (Janus-adjectives) may have either of these two uses. (3) Some adjectives have a third use, viz. when the question of entailment or its failure between '*x* is A and *x* is a B' and '*x* is an AB' cannot arise; all essentially attributive adjectives ('big', 'genuine', and always-*alienans* adjectives like 'former') always have this use. This would show clearly that being an essentially attributive adjective has nothing to do with entailment, and that introducing questions of entailment into a test to identify them is irrelevant. Thus again we differentiate types of adjectives and their possible uses, the topic of this paper and, I believe, of Geach's. But one must not be confused by the fact that, when an adjective is *attributively used* in my new sense *and* when an adjective is in itself essentially attributive and so is used in the *third* way, to ascertain that '*x* is an AB' (a forged banknote or a sweet Sauternes, *or* a big elephant) one must know the predicate noun involved. For one *can* independently ascertain that *x* is forged or sweet without the noun, but never that *x* is big. Once the nature of and test for essentially attributive adjectives are clear, but only then, can one ask whether 'good' and 'bad' are always essentially attributive adjectives. Here at least I agree with MacKay. Geach did not prove his claim, and cannot, because, contrary to Geach and following the dictionary and common usage, 'good' and 'bad' have more than one meaning, are not essentially attributive or even always attributively used, and so the claim is false. But that is a topic for another paper.

I hope this paper is an interesting paper even as far as it goes. Unfortunately it has not yet gone quite far enough. Though I rejected Geach's umbrella test for essentially attributive adjectives, I played along with supposing that a *noun* must be understood to ascertain the truth of '*x* is A' when 'A' is essentially attributive. But what needs to be understood is not necessarily a noun. Geach misled himself and others by the way he set the question up at the outset: 'in a phrase "AB" . . . "B" being a noun'. Of course, to ascertain that *x* is a big *elephant*, a good *car*, a red *car*, a putative *father*, a forged or genuine *banknote*, a former *warlord*, one must have those nouns in mind. With 'big elephant', 'good car', and 'red car', someone has to ascertain that *x* is an elephant or a car; with 'putative father' and 'forged banknote', you do not have to ascertain that *x* is a father or a banknote, but you do have to hear the speaker say 'I believe *x* to be the *father*', and you have to know it was a *banknote* that was being copied. But this is irrelevant to determining the type of adjective. When 'A' is an essentially attributive *adjective* you have to understand *something*, when 'A' is not you do not. But it need not be a noun. What you must have in mind is some class of things, without necessarily knowing the noun by which they are called. You may recognize elephants, monoliths, excavators, and, provided you know their average size, without knowing what they are or what they are called, you can ascertain it is a big one of those things. So with attributive *uses*: if you can recognize Sauternes, so long as you know their standards for sweetness you can say that *x* is a sweet one of those things, without knowing their name at all. Equally with predicative adjectives: you can ascertain that *x* is red without knowing it is a car, or that *x* is forged by ascertaining that it is copied from something with intent to defraud, but without having any idea what the thing is that is being copied. But with predicative adjectives no standards have to be set by the class of things for which you know no name. 'Alleged' and 'putative' remain predicative; the truth of '*x* is an alleged something' is ascertained simply by hearing someone say, 'I allege him to be . . .' followed by hubbub. 'Former' remains attributive: even if you hear someone say, '*x* is a former . . .' followed by hubbub, someone originally has to know what sort of thing was in mind to ascertain the truth of '*x* is a former something'. So I retract nothing of what I have said, except to remove the need of a noun and replace it by a class of things for which you may know no noun, for which there may in fact be no noun but for which a noun-phrase could always be invented ('items of junk in my attic'), but for which you must know the standards (e.g. average size). To *ascertain* that *x* is big, you must have a class of things in mind, not necessarily a noun. But the point can be put in a less epistemological-sounding way: for '*x* is big' to have truth-value, some class of things, not necessarily with any existing noun applying to them, must set a standard. I believe Geach obscured this by originally setting the problem up in the form ' "*x* is an AB" where "B" is a noun'.

13

Aesthetic Judgements:
Pebbles, Faces, and Fields of Litter

In 1956 in two brief pages in *Analysis*, Professor Geach introduced a contrast between logically predicative and logically attributive adjectives. (Following him, for brevity I shall omit the word 'logically'.) Since then some such distinction has been variously discussed by many philosophers, and occasionally even applied, within ethics and aesthetics. Geach certainly pointed towards something important—different relationships between adjectives and the nouns they grammatically qualify. But the topic is, as Geach would agree, far more complex than his original article indicated. Strictly, lengthy exploration of these complexities should precede this paper. Since I cannot do that, my aim is to make some suggestions, doubtless needing many qualifications, and then try applying them within aesthetics.

Geach put his distinction thus: where 'A' is an adjective and 'B' a noun, 'if the predication "is an AB" splits up logically into a pair of predications "is a B" and "is A", "A" is a predicative adjective' (example, 'is a red car'); if the predication does not so split up, 'A' is an attributive adjective (example, 'is a big flea'). I shall not dally over the meaning of 'splits up logically', but say loosely that if 'A' is predicative, the relation of 'A' and 'B' is something like mere conjunction, whereas if 'A' is attributive, the relation of 'A' and 'B' involves some more complex interaction.

Geach's formulation ignores problems. '*X* is a nuclear scientist', or 'an utter fool' do not split up; and '*x* is a beautiful dancer', 'a weak king', 'a red lamp', 'a French teacher', being potentially ambiguous, do not split up on one of their possible interpretations. Yet the thrust of Geach's article is surely not aimed at examples like these. So I shall ignore them too.

Perhaps to get at the questions that centrally interested him, and centrally interest me, we can restrict our dealings to cases where adjectives are used to ascribe some characteristic directly to a thing of the kind B. We are applying

[This paper is printed in a version that was prepared for oral delivery. A reader may be perplexed to learn at one point (p. 181) that he is being shown some pictures and that the speaker is deliberately not saying of what. The content of the pictures is revealed later (p. 184). It is clear what point F. N. S. wished to make with his experiment, though without the pictures it cannot be demonstrated.]

'red' to the car, the lamp (not the light it emits), 'large' to the flea, 'French' to the teacher (not to what he teaches), etc. If we can thus set aside cases where the adjective ascribes a characteristic to something of kind other than B, we can begin to ask why 'is a red car' splits up and 'is a large flea' does not, why 'large' interacts with 'flea' as 'red' does not with 'car'.

A significant clue to one form of interaction occurs when Geach speaks, not about 'splitting up', but about combining. 'I could ascertain that a distant object is a red car because I can see it is red and a keener-sighted but colour-blind friend can see it is a car'; this shows that 'red' in 'red car' is predicative. 'There is no such possibility of ascertaining that a thing is a good car (or a big flea) by pooling independent information that it is good (big) and that it is a car (flea)'. When this is so, the adjective ('good', 'big') is attributive. The point Geach treats as crucial here is that to ascertain that an attributive adjective applies to x, 'some substantive has to be understood'; equally, if some substantive has to be understood, the adjective is attributive. But why? One answer seems obvious. Some substantive is needed to provide what, with deliberate looseness—since I want to cover a variety of cases—I shall call 'standards' relevant to the adjective in question. We cannot ascertain that x is big without some noun, say, 'mouse', in mind; or that x is good without, say, 'car', in mind.

But perhaps we need a complexity not explicit in Geach's brief treatment. He says his distinction is 'between two sorts of adjectives', and gives as 'familiar examples' of attributive adjectives, 'big' and 'small'. Later he speaks of 'ordinary predicative adjectives like "red" and "sweet" '. These remarks suggest two sorts of adjectives, 'red' and 'sweet' being always predicative, 'big' and 'small' always attributive, or, as he says of 'good' and 'bad', 'essentially' attributive. But other remarks he makes permit, perhaps encourage, a different interpretation. Though he calls 'red' and 'sweet' 'ordinary predicative adjectives', he also says that 'in the phrase "a red book" "red" is a predicative adjective', and that certain adjectives (for him, 'good' and 'bad') are *always* and *essentially* attributive. This seems to allow that some adjectives might be in *one* phrase used predicatively and in *another* attributively, being only sometimes, not essentially, attributive. Otherwise why call some 'essentially' attributive?

If two interpretations suggest themselves, *two* distinctions are needed: sorts of *adjectives* and sorts of *uses* of adjectives. In an adjective-noun phrase, certain adjectives—I suspect most—are sometimes used predicatively, sometimes attributively. This gives us two uses of adjectives, predicative and attributive uses, and three sorts of adjectives: essentially predicative, usable only predicatively; essentially attributive, usable only attributively; and ambifunctional, capable of either use.

I propose first a difference between a predicative and an attributive *use* of an adjective. If, to ascertain that 'x is A', for example when aiming to establish that x is an AB, we need not understand that the noun in question is 'B', the adjective 'A' is being used predicatively. When the adjective 'A' is being used attributively, we need to understand that 'B' is the noun in question before we can ascertain that '*x* is A' (in the course of establishing that '*x* is an AB'). But before saying more about *uses*, I turn to *kinds* of adjectives. If, with a given adjective 'A', some noun must *always* be understood in ascertaining that *x* is A, 'A' is an essentially attributive adjective. And since this is necessary with that adjective no matter what noun is in question, being essentially attributive must be a feature of the adjective itself, not a feature for which any particular noun is responsible. Geach's examples, 'big' and 'small', like 'hot', 'cold', etc., are essentially attributive; they all demand a standard, and the standard is set via the noun understood on that occasion (big flea, hot oven, etc.). There are also essentially predicative adjectives. An adjective 'A' is essentially predicative if it can *always* be ascertained whether *x* is A independently of any noun understood. Two sorts of essentially predicative adjectives that we have are those I might call 'epitome' adjectives (e.g. 'omnipotent' and 'omniscient') and those I might call 'ultimately determinate in some respect' (e.g. as 'square' is in respect of shape, but 'triangular' not). Other determinate adjectives, I suggest, include e.g. 'beige', and 'aquamarine'; and we do or could invent others when needed. 'Greenstone' (British Standard Colour No. 5-059) and 'Shadow Blue' (BSC No. 7-077) are determinate colours; we could invent 'centidecibelic' as a determinate of loudness, etc. Like 'omniscient', these do not allow degrees: we cannot say 'very beige', 'particularly shadow blue', 'somewhat centidecibelic', or 'greenstone as such-and-such's go'. So, essentially attributive adjectives inherently demand a standard-setting substantive; essentially predicative adjectives inherently disallow standard-setting by any substantive.

But many adjectives, including Geach's 'ordinary predicative adjective "sweet" ', are ambifunctional. We have a predicative use of 'sweet', paralleling the red car example, if someone, not knowing what he is tasting, ascertains that it is sweet, someone else, without tasting, ascertains it is a pear, and they pool their knowledge: *x* is a sweet pear. But it is not always possible in this way to ascertain that something is sweet independently of knowing what it is. Ambifunctional adjectives thus differ from essentially attributive ones. With the latter no truth-value could be ascertained, e.g. for '*x* is big', unless a noun was understood. With ambifunctional adjectives, a truth-value can be ascertained for, e.g. '*x* is sweet', without any noun understood. What is sometimes impossible is to add '*x* is a B', and, by 'pooling information', arrive at '*x* is a sweet B', *in the sense one intends*. 'Sweet' is then being used attributively. *x* may certainly be sweet, not tasteless, sour, or bitter. Yet given it is also a Sauternes and that, though all Sauternes are on the sweet side, they vary in sweetness, it may not be a sweet Sauternes (i.e. for a Sauternes, or as Sauternes go). Consider also, not combining, but splitting. We use '*x* is a pale-skinned Negro' merely predicatively—he is both pale-skinned and a Negro—but more often would intend it attributively; then it no more follows that he is pale-skinned *simpliciter* than it will follow from '*x* is a dark-skinned Scandinavian' that *x* is dark-skinned *simpliciter*. We may speak of a dark-skinned Scandinavian or a pale-skinned Negro without meaning that the former is nearly black or the latter nearly white. We mean dark-skinned as Scandinavians go or pale-skinned for a Negro. Presumably too, a not especially red apple could be red for a Cox's Orange Pippin. And unless this is dismissed as hyperbolic, when we say that x, through embarrassment, has a red, even a scarlet face, we mean it is red for a face. It is unlikely to be red or scarlet *simpliciter*; seeing it through a peep-hole, not knowing it is a face, we would rightly say it is deep pink, or, colour-chart in hand, that it is Orchis Pink (BSC 1-021). Even in extremity of rage a face might only reach Dusky Pink (BSC 8-091), never scarlet. It can be unclear, out of context, how an ambifunctional adjective is being used. Asking casually for a sweet wine, I may be told, 'This should suit you, it is a sweet Sauternes', meaning merely 'sweet' and 'a Sauternes'. I may not be getting, what it could mean, a wine sweet even for a Sauternes. Unlike essentially attributive adjectives, which always demand some standard set by some noun, ambifunctional adjectives may be used predicatively; but they may also be used in such a way that a noun sets standards for them, being then used attributively. Even so, for a given ambifunctional adjective, only certain nouns can set a standard. We can say 'sweet even for a Sauternes', or 'dark as Scandinavians go', because these nouns set some standard, average, or normalcy, of taste or colour for these adjectives. But other nouns supply no standards for the very same adjectives. This is why the red car example was so straightforward. No attributive use was possible; nouns like 'car' and 'dress' carry no standards as regards average, normal, or expected colour. 'Very red for a car', 'blue as dresses go', even 'brightly coloured for a dress' make no more sense than 'sweet for a liquid, or as liquids go'. Switch to a different noun, and we can make sense of 'brightly coloured for funeral wear' or 'sweet for a Chablis', etc. This point, that some nouns supply no standards *vis-à-vis* certain ambifunctional adjectives, which then must be used predicatively with those nouns, is important later.

I now try to apply the foregoing to certain adjectives, like 'beautiful', 'pretty', 'lovely', 'graceful', 'elegant', which are commonly, though not invariably, used to make aesthetic judgements. There is a view of aesthetic judgements in vogue which is sometimes quite uncompromisingly stated. For instance, Roger Scruton has written[1] of

the mistaken idea that one can somehow judge the beauty of a thing *in abstracto*, without knowing what *kind* of thing it is; as though I could present you with an object that might be a stone, a sculpture, a box, a fruit or even an animal, and expect you to tell me whether it is beautiful before knowing what it is. In general we might say . . . that our sense of the beauty of an object is always dependent on a conception of that object.

---

[1] *The Aesthetics of Architecture*, London: Methuen, 1979, 9 f.

This could be taken as the claim that judgements of beauty are always logically attributive. But if so, the only argument Scruton offers in support does not establish this claim: it is that

> our sense of the beauty of a human figure is dependent on a conception of that figure. Features that we would regard as beautiful in a horse—developed haunches, a curved back, and so on—we would regard as ugly in a man, and this aesthetic judgement would be determined by our conception of what men are.

But this only sustains, though correctly, the conclusion that at least some aesthetic judgements, e.g. of men and horses, are attributive. Anthony Savile has asserted explicitly[2] that 'one matter taken for granted' by various authors 'is that "beautiful" is a predicative adjective. This', he says, 'is false'. He speaks of the 'attributive nature of the adjective' and extends this to the main elements of the aesthetic vocabulary. 'What we have to analyse', he says 'is not the predicate "is beautiful" but "is a beautiful F" '. But he too supports this quite general claim with just one or two examples. The opposite, less fashionable, extreme, that to judge a thing aesthetically one never need know what kind of thing it is—tantamount presumably to holding that a judgement that something is beautiful is always logically predicative—might be attributed, at least about art, to Croce, more generally, if debatably, as it is by Savile, to Kant. I question both extremes by suggesting that such typically aesthetic adjectives are ambifunctional, frequently used attributively, but often legitimately used predicatively. The extreme attributive view can, ambiguously, take two interpretations: that without knowing the kind of thing one is judging one cannot make an aesthetic judgement of it at all; less strongly, that one could and might, but it would always be inadequately grounded, needful of reconsideration in the light of what the object judged is, and then quite possibly incorrect or mistaken. My suggestion that some aesthetic judgements are legitimately predicative opposes both these interpretations.

Quite ordinary remarks suggest that aesthetic judgments that are predicative are common and perfectly acceptable: you say, 'That thing over there is very beautiful, what is it?' I might reply, 'It's a pebble', 'a piece of coral', 'an abstract sculpture'. I need not reply, 'How can you say it's beautiful without knowing what it is?' Nor need my telling you what it is demand withdrawal or reconsideration of your judgement. An objector might say that this proves nothing since similar things might be said using essentially attributive adjectives like 'enormous'. 'That enormous thing in the field, whatever is it?' But whatever it is, the questioner clearly had in mind some substantival expression like 'objects commonly found in fields' to set a standard for size. It would be absurd, by contrast, to suggest that the previous questioner had in mind a

---

[2] *The Test of Time: An Essay in Philosophical Aesthetics*, Oxford: Clarendon Press, 1982, 166 f.

standard of beauty set by some substantival expression like 'things found somewhere or other'. But more argument is needed. If aesthetic adjectives are ambifunctional, each must be applicable to some noun which does not necessarily set any standard for it, as when 'pale-skinned' and 'sweet' were used predicatively; even better if some nouns have no standards to set for them, as 'car' set no standard for 'red' or 'liquid' for sweetness.

Certainly some nouns assuredly do set, in my deliberately loose use, standards *vis-à-vis* aesthetic adjectives like 'beautiful', 'lovely', 'pretty', 'graceful'. There are (no doubt multiple, varying, and shifting) standards of beauty, etc. for faces, horses, women, cats. One could not judge x a beautiful face, horse, woman, or cat (all normally attributive judgements) without judging it beautiful as a face, horse, woman or cat, and without some standards of facial, equine, female, or feline beauty.

But consider two other groups of nouns with which we use aesthetic adjectives. First, an artist might draw some lines, curves, or non-representational shapes on paper, or combine some colours together in a varicoloured patch. Asked what they are he might say, 'Nothing in particular' or 'just lines, curves, shapes' or 'a varicoloured patch'. 'Lines', 'curves', 'shapes', 'coloured patch' may be the only nouns in question. Yet we might judge some of them, but not others, beautiful lines, graceful curves, lovely shapes, pretty patches of colours. I shall not argue that, with these nouns, these adjectives are used predicatively. But I incline to think so. Whereas 'x is beautiful by standards of facial or equine beauty' does not sound odd to me, 'x is beautiful by standards of linear beauty, or standards of beauty for shape or colour patches' does. I only insist that we can speak of a mere shape as a lovely shape, a line as a beautiful line, a curve as a graceful curve, etc. Nevertheless I suspect this refutes Scruton's claim that we cannot judge the beauty of a thing *in abstracto*, without knowing what *kind* of thing it is—for though we *do* know it is a line, curve, shape, or coloured patch, I do not think these count as the sorts of things he is calling 'kinds'.

But, secondly, there are surely other things—I mentioned some just now—to which aesthetic adjectives can be applied truly, and merely predicatively, i.e. without needing to know what they are or having any appropriate nouns in mind, because the nouns set no standards *vis-à-vis* those adjectives. I could, I think, show you things—I must be content here with photos—expecting you not to know what most of them are, and ask whether you do not think some of them very beautiful, rather lovely, or at least somewhat pretty—all aesthetic judgements—and expect an answer rather than an obdurate refusal to reply. (Nor would it matter if you thought them definitely not beautiful, or ugly, or garish, for these are aesthetic judgements too.) I shall not say what they are, deliberately, for reasons given later. I suggest for example that no standards of beauty are set by nouns like 'pebble', 'crystal', 'sea shell', 'coral', or even 'abstract painting or sculpture'. There are no standards of pebble or crystal beauty as

there are of equine, female, or facial beauty. Some pebbles, shells, and corals
are doubtless more beautiful in shape, line, or colour than others. But they
may come in just about any shapes or colours. A horse, to have equine beauty,
must be beautiful *qua* horse. Not just any beauty of line, shape, or coloration
will do. But any beauty of colour, line, and shape may suffice for a beautiful
pebble or crystal. A pebble lovely in line, shape, or colour, worth keeping
perhaps and putting on the mantelpiece, is a beautiful pebble, predicatively:
beautiful and a pebble. But though horses and faces are judged beautiful, etc.,
partly at least in terms of their lines, shapes, and colouring, it need not follow
that something which is in fact a horse or a face, however beautiful its lines,
shapes, or colouring considered apart from its being a horse or a face, will be
a beautiful horse or face even in point of line, shape, and colour. A beautiful
face is not just something beautiful and a face; the use is attributive.

Now a further complication. I am not denying that aesthetic adjectives may
be used attributively even with nouns like 'pebble' or 'crystal'. This possibility
arises whenever, as with either 'large' or 'sweet', the adjective admits of degrees,
as indeed 'beautiful', 'lovely', 'pretty', etc. do. Earlier, when an attributive use
was intended, but not immediately apparent, it was made clear by remarks like
'It's certainly sweet and a Sauternes, but it isn't especially sweet for a
Sauternes'. Rather similarly, you might say of my prized Brighton beach
pebble, 'It's certainly quite beautiful and a pebble; but pebbles can be far more
beautiful. Look at mine from Waikiki. Now that *is* a beautiful pebble.' So I do
not doubt that '*x* is a beautiful pebble' can be used in a merely comparative,
or as I shall say, a 'weak' attributive way, but 'beautiful pebble' is often used
predicatively. It would be fairly unusual if someone, when asked 'Isn't this a
beautiful pebble?' replied, 'I can't tell till I know a lot more about pebbles'.

My deliberately loose use of 'standards' is now apparent. There are many
more sources of attributiveness than I consider in this paper. The standards in
my last examples, with 'sweet' and 'beautiful', were comparative standards,
involving degrees on a scale, rather as 'large' and 'hot' did. They imply reference to the average, the normal, the usual, the common, etc., and generate
weak attributive judgements. They also generally imply the existence of
members of the class which are less sweet, beautiful, large or hot. No one
could ascertain that *x* is a beautiful pebble, understood in a comparative way,
i.e. as 'unusually beautiful', merely by ascertaining that x is a pebble and beautiful and combining these facts. This source of attributiveness, resting on
degrees, and comparison—for which obviously one needs knowledge—can of
course occur also in judgements of faces, horses, etc. ('I see how you could
very reasonably consider that a beautiful face. But now see this one: this is a
beautiful face *par excellence*.') But attributive judgements of this comparative
sort, when about faces or horses, are doubly attributive. They employ not only
standards involving comparisons of degree; they also employ standards of a
kind that I shall refer to as norms or ideals incorporating notions of appro-

priateness, etc. It is this second kind of standard, or norm or ideal, which, I suggested, is lacking with pebbles—that is the reason I said there are standards of facial and equine beauty but not of pebble beauty. 'That is a beautiful face' is (ordinarily) always attributive in this stronger way; 'that is a beautiful pebble' never is.

By standards incorporating notions of rightness or appropriateness I mean this. The grace of a line lies in, say, its particular flowing curvature, the beauty of a pebble in its line, shape, and colouring; there are no particular restrictions on how these should be except that they should be beautiful (smoothly curving, rounded, brightly and harmoniously coloured, etc.). But upon those lines, colours, and shapes, on which, together with the interrelation of these, and no doubt much else, facial, equine, or female beauty depends, there are clear, if somewhat loose and variable, restrictions. However beautifully luminous the crimson eyes, however delicately green the mottling of the cheeks, however richly brown and however graceful the outward curve of the teeth, they are not beautiful *eyes, cheeks,* or *teeth*. Even if rosebud lips, lustrous almond eyes, regular white teeth, peaches and cream complexion, are individually beautiful in terms of line, shape, colour for lips, eyes, teeth, and complexion, for a beautiful *face* those eyes must not be minute, askew, at the top of the forehead, those teeth not enormous, or those lips partly up one cheek. Picasso's distorted faces can be objects of considerable beauty; but no woman unfortunate enough to have such a face would have a beautiful face. Standards of facial, equine, or female beauty incorporate lines, shapes, colours and their ordering that, within limits, have to be right or appropriate for a face, horse, or woman. There was no parallel restriction for pebbles, etc. But if to judge something a beautiful face or horse requires some conception of what the lines, colours, shapes and interrelations of features, etc., appropriate to its beauty are, the judgement is attributive, not a mere conjunction of 'beautiful' and 'face'.

That completes my attack on the two extreme views. Some things can legitimately be judged beautiful, etc., the adjectives being used predicatively; one need not know what these things are, because the nouns (or concepts) in question set no restrictive standards *vis-à-vis* beauty or beauty-giving properties. Other nouns do set standards incorporating notions of appropriateness; with them aesthetic judgements are attributive.

I have mentioned pebbles and faces; now for the other ingredient in my title, fields of litter. Here is a quotation from Eric Newton which I came across years ago:

A meadow of lush grass generously interspersed with buttercups and ox-eye daisies usually strikes one as beautiful. But what if on entering the meadow one were to discover that the buttercups were empty Gold Flake packets and the daisies torn up scraps of paper? One would protest to oneself in vain that litter and wild flowers can be equally pleasing to the eye, but despite one's attempts to preserve one's aesthetic judgements intact, one's attitude to the meadow would alter and the alteration could only be expressed in terms of disappointment.[3]

Can we throw light on his hesitations, puzzlements, and conflicts? Clearly 'the alteration' in his 'attitude to the meadow', his vain protests to himself 'that litter and wild flowers can be equally pleasing to the eye', and his disappointment when he apparently fails to preserve his 'aesthetic judgements intact' are directly related to discovering that the object, the meadow with yellow and white things in it which initially 'struck him as beautiful', is not what he supposed. There are many questions here deserving consideration; I must make short work of them. People often say beauty can be found in the most unlikely things if one has eyes to see it. Often, they say, the artist sees, and helps us see, beauty we ordinarily miss, so broadening our potentialities for appreciation. Rembrandt's painted side of beef draws attention to its rich and varied coloration. Ruskin said somewhere that Turner could open our eyes to beauty, presumably of line, colour, iridescence, etc., in rotting vegetation, rubbish, garbage. Modern artists have forced us to notice beauties of coloration, texture, shape in rusting metal and battered tin cans by painting them, incorporating them in abstract sculptures or simply exhibiting them. Earlier I tried to elicit your agreement that some unidentified objects had at least some, and perhaps considerable, beauty. But it might be important that they remain unrecognized. Suppose, with a photo, or a moving film, or even the real thing—provided you do not know what it is—I can get you to see its beauty: the combination of rich browns, greys, and creamy ochre, the intricately elegant changing shapes, the iridescence. It is in fact scum on a polluted stream, or worse, a cesspool. Two pictures I showed earlier—you might have wondered if one was a sunspot or an abstract, the other clouds after sunset— were medical photos of lesions on a human body. I could have shown photos of gangrene or ulcers, and imagination can suggest far more distasteful possible examples.

Often then for people to see whatever beauty x has, it may be important precisely that they *not* know what x is. Knowing what it is may be just what prevents them from attending to its beauty. The aesthetic switch-off is familiar. People who find snakes or caterpillars repulsive may have no eyes to appreciate their colourings or markings; a moment before realizing what the coiled object was, they might have remarked on its beauty. We are all liable to aesthetic blindness with things we find distasteful, repulsive, or disgusting. Was this the source of Newton's discomfort? He did, after all, use the word 'litter' in referring to the scattered paper. But to switch off aesthetically is to fail to see or cease to see, sometimes understandably, the beauty things have. This is not obviously Newton's problem. He still seems to think that things

[3] *The Meaning of Beauty*, Harmondsworth: Penguin Books, 1962, 64.

unsavoury—and we might add, dirty or even disgusting—may nevertheless be 'pleasing to the eye' though he struggles in vain to find the genuine meadow and the littered field 'equally pleasing', puzzled presumably because in some sense they look identical, visually indistinguishable. At all events I shall reject—at least for the moment—what some might say, that scum, ulcers, rusty cans, litter, etc., including littered meadows, cannot be beautiful (or are mistakenly judged so only by those ignorant of what they are).

There are some puzzles here which are perhaps only marginally related to Newton's but which are of some interest. There are, I take it, no standards of grace, beauty, etc., of the 'strong' sort—norms or ideals—that there are for facial, female or equine beauty, for rotting vegetation, garbage, rusty cans, ulcers, scum, or litter any more than for pebbles, crystals, lines, colours, or shapes. So aesthetic judgements of such things must in this respect be predicative. If adjective 'A' truly applies to x and is used predicatively, and x is a B, then x is an AB. So if x is beautiful and a rusty can, ulcer, garbage, or scum, x is a beautiful rusty can, ulcer, garbage, or scum. Why then would it sound odd, why would we probably balk at saying 'That is beautiful garbage, very pretty scum, lovely litter' and so on? We don't balk at 'x is a beautiful pebble, a beautiful snake, or a beautiful shape'.

I think we can offer some reasons why it might be odd to say such things. It might be suggested that we avoid such remarks because they would be misleadingly ambiguous. Assertions like 'x is a beautiful B' are often 'fine specimen' assertions. The teaching doctor who says, 'That's a beautiful ulcer' is normally using this as we use 'a beautiful black eye'. These are also attributive, but they are not ordinarily aesthetic judgements at all. (A doctor would be unlikely to say, 'It's a pretty ulcer'.) So unless there are scum specialists, garbage fanciers, and rusty can experts, as there *are* ulcer experts—which seems dubious—there is no risk of ambiguity and this move can offer no reason for not saying, 'This is beautiful scum, a beautiful rusty can', etc.

A better clue may be that it sounds less odd if one names the object as sentence-subject rather than in predicate position. 'This scum, garbage, rusty can is (rather, really, quite) beautiful (if you bother to look)' sounds less odd than 'This is (rather, really, quite) beautiful scum, garbage, etc.' Here are two possibly contributory explanations. First, adding the predicate-noun often strongly suggests one or other of the attributive uses I have indicated. 'That's a beautiful face' clearly indicates that facial beauty is being asserted. Even 'These are beautiful pebbles', by drawing attention to what they are, may strongly hint at comparison with the usual run of pebbles. Secondly, where our interest is primarily aesthetic, unless the judgement must be attributive (e.g. we are judging facial beauty), or unless we deliberately intend an attributive judgement (implicit comparison with the common run of pebbles), we need, *ex hypothesi*, be concerned little, if at all, with what the object is. If our conversational interest were simply colour and I ask you particularly to notice the colour of *x*, you will probably just say '*x* is greenish'. Even if you know *x* is a pebble, toad, dress, or scum, you will probably not say 'It is a greenish pebble, toad, etc.'. Equally, if I am drawing your attention to the beauty of *x*, though you know it is a pebble or scum, you will probably say, if you agree, 'Yes, it is beautiful' without adding the predicate noun since, in context, what *x* is is irrelevant to our concern. We are no more considering its beauty as the beauty of a pebble or scum than we were considering colour as the colour of a pebble, toad, or dress. We need not say all that is true. But whereas to say, 'That is a beautiful pebble' may be merely irrelevant to our aesthetic interest, 'That is pretty scum' or 'beautiful garbage' may be positively distracting and self-defeating. Drawing attention to what *x* is, when it is something considered distasteful or disgusting may serve precisely to switch off the aesthetic attention we intended to enlist. But though irrelevant or, worse, self-defeating to our purpose to say '*x* is beautiful scum', this latter, if I am right, is predicative and (perhaps with a qualification later) possibly true.

But this reveals at least one respect in which the littered meadow example is unlike these other examples of distasteful or repulsive things. For though we have no ideals or norms of scum-beauty, etc., and possibly none of ophidian or serpentine beauty, any more than we have of pebble-beauty—there are no beautiful colourings or patternings so inappropriate *vis-à-vis* snakes as to put a snake possessing them out of contention for snake-beauty—we surely do have some standards of appropriateness, loose ideals, some concept of what might count as constituting meadow-beauty. 'Beautiful meadow', like 'beautiful face', is attributive. And if this notion includes or allows, roughly, such things as grass, wild flowers, and their colours and scents, it does not include discarded cigarette packets, paper, and their colours. So their presence and colouring is not a contribution to meadow-beauty. The flowery meadow, but not the littered meadow, falls within the loose confines of our concept of what a meadow and its beauty should or at best can be. So the littered meadow, however visually beautiful, cannot qualify as a beautiful meadow.

But what of this visual beauty which even Newton, though he cannot allow it to be *equally* pleasing to the eye, seems able to question only with some unease and lack of conviction? Here the thought may occur that, in all these cases alike, it is not the rusty can, the scum, the ulcer, or the littered meadow that is beautiful; rather it is their colouring, lines, shapes, texture, patterning, shimmer, sheen, surface, or their bubbles, ripples, or whatever that are beautiful. This proposal, that cans, garbage, scum, or litter, being the sort of things they are, are not, and perhaps cannot be, beautiful, etc.—that indeed it is only certain of their properties, primarily visual ones, not the things, that are beautiful—they are 'pleasing to the eye'—is one some people might find welcome. I am uncertain about this principle. Certainly we speak of the beautiful colour of a dress, not of a beautiful dress, if its lines are ugly, and vice versa. But contrariwise, if an otherwise beautiful rose lacks all fragrance, do we refuse to call it a beautiful rose? But in any event, even if some concern about its other properties inhibits our calling a rusty can, or ulcer, or garbage, or littered meadow, beautiful in an unqualified way, if we are willing to go as far as the qualified remark, 'It is visually beautiful—beautiful in respect of certain visual properties', or even only as far as saying that the properties, not the thing, are beautiful, then provided my earlier suggestions about lines, colours, pebbles, etc. are right, we still have a plethora of examples of what are, on my account, predicative aesthetic judgements.

Suppose anyway that I stick to the view that the littered meadow, looking in some sense exactly like a genuine flowered meadow, has some measure of visual beauty, indeed an equal beauty in respect of colour, line, patterning, or whatever. They could after all be of equal aesthetic interest to the colour photographer, even if not to the would-be rambler or picnicker. Recall that Gainsborough and many another painter, used vegetable leaves, weeds, twigs, stones, bits of glass, etc. arranged on a table in lieu of painting trees, rocks, and lakes out of doors. Still, Newton is clearly dubious about whether they can, once one knows the facts, be 'equally pleasing to the eye'. This is obviously a question about whether in some sense, to the man with knowledge, they do look the same; as he says 'one would protest in vain' that they do. And I see some good reason to allow this. Indeed we could ensure that aesthetic judgements are not being inhibited, or Newton's attempts to preserve his aesthetic judgements 'intact' jeopardized, by knowledge that he is looking at litter, or something else generally unpleasant, dirty, repugnant, disgusting, etc. After all, the next field over the hill might look just like another field of litter but turn out to be full of flowers, just as the froth on the supposed sewage might look just like, and turn out to be, bubbles on fermenting wine or a fresh bubblebath. And that would put everything right again.

So to make sure it is not merely the connection with litter, associations with dirt, etc. that jeopardize Newton's attempt to preserve his aesthetic judgements 'intact', let the meadow be found to be generously interspersed with perfect artificial buttercups and ox-eye daisies, plastic if you like, or exquisitely made in fine silks, etc. I suspect that, on discovering they were not real flowers, Newton's attitude to the meadow might still have altered, perhaps almost as much, and brought a not totally dissimilar disappointment. For though some of the visual beauty—in respect of colour, etc.—is unchanged, some other aspects or sources of beauty normally attributable by vision are inevitably precluded, and precisely ones that attributively constitute some of the beauty of a meadow-with-flowers, but not of a meadow-with-artificial-flowers. They might be said to be attributive in being appropriate to some norm or ideal of meadow-beauty. Not only could a face hardly be a beautiful face however beautifully yellow and green its colouring, or a meadow a beautiful meadow (in respect of colour) if its grass were, as a result of charring, greyish-brown, but some of the beauty normally attributable to a meadow on the basis of seeing it is, at a stroke, necessarily eliminated, if the flowers are artificial. The meadow may have some beauty, e.g. of colour; but it cannot be in certain other respects a beautiful meadow, attributively, for the same sort of reason that an otherwise beautiful face with one glass eye, however beautiful, does not have beautiful eyes, or with artificial make-up, however beautiful, does not have a beautiful complexion or colouring. It is not that all visual beauty is eliminated, but that the sources of some peculiarly meadow-beauty are removed. One can no longer rejoice, for instance, in the rich abundance, the freshness, the luxuriant budding, and natural freedom of its flowers. Moreover, there cannot be what Hepburn calls 'scope for imaginative play':[4] there can be no appreciation of the beauties of its shy or timid daisies, its bold and joyous buttercups flaunting their glory in the sun, no reflexions upon the fragility and brevity of their existence, they neither nestle, nod, curtsey, or recover, or take the winds with beauty, and so on. If judgements of beauty springing from these sources seem too far-ranging to fall within some narrowly circumscribed category of aesthetic judgements, appreciations, responses, and rejoicings, I do not know into what obvious broader category they fall. To outlaw them by some restrictive stipulation or decision would itself demand reasons and arguments.

With the kind of case just considered, where some discovery is made about the object being judged—e.g. that the flowers are artificial—a whole range of qualities which might have been sources of attributive beauty of the object are of necessity eliminated. So one might think that with such cases, prompted by my consideration of Newton's remarks, I have moved away from the realm of (alleged) attributivity indicated earlier. For here one *can* truly discover that some adjective applies, that the flowers are plastic or silk, that the meadow is paper-strewn, independently of knowing what noun (flowers, meadows, etc.) is involved. But Scruton's example equally seems to imply that one could discover e.g. that something had developed haunches and a curved back without knowing that it was to be judged aesthetically as a *man*. So here equally we do not know, till the noun is known, whether coloured plastic or silk flowers detract from or add to the beauty of the object. If it is a meadow, they eliminate certain dimensions of beauty; but plastic flowers might make a children's playground or a fairground, if not prettier, at least less drab; and silk flowers might add greatly to the beauty of a tapestry.

So we are really not far removed from Scruton's examples. To echo his words with a different example, features that we would regard as beautiful in an English elm—the majestic sturdiness, solidity, and strength, which is part

---

[4] R. W. Hepburn, 'Contemporary Aesthetics and the Neglect of Natural Beauty', in Hepburn, *Wonder*, Edinburgh University Press, 1984, 16. (Originally published in *British Analytical Philosophy*, ed. B. Williams and A. Montefiore, London and Edinburgh: Routledge and Kegan Paul, 1966.)

of what makes it a beautiful English elm—might be regarded (though still making it perhaps a beautiful *tree*) as defects *vis-à-vis* the American elm (which has a vase-shaped form, a spreading, forking, open habit); to be judged beautiful as an American elm, a tree needs these characteristics, sources of its own characteristic beauty, spreading elegance, graceful branching, lightness rather than solidity or sturdiness. (This is still 'strong' attributiveness, with respect to a norm or ideal of a species, not involving comparison within a species, as we might say, 'Now that's an (unusually) beautiful elm'.)

And to come closer to Savile's examples, where a thing, *x*, may legitimately be considered either as an A (and a beautiful one) or as a B (and a not particularly beautiful one)—his example is a portrait beautiful as an element of the room's furnishing, yet not a beautiful portrait[5]—a fully grown Lebanon cedar might be beautiful in its stateliness and majesty considered as a cedar, in its dignity as an ornament to the lawns of a mansion, but as an ornamental tree for a bijou house and garden it might be considered elephantine, grotesque, overblown, inordinately pretentious—anything but a beautiful ornament for such a garden.

But through all these types of attributive cases, I have suggested, even having cleared our minds of all such concepts as men, faces, meadows, fairgrounds, tapestries, English and American elms, cedars of Lebanon, and ornamental trees for small gardens, though we may in some instances have eliminated some sources and elements of beauty, we are left with objects, which, careless of what they are or are considered as, we may still find quite beautiful, and judge them, rightly, to be aesthetically rewarding in some ways, even if only perhaps in respect of colour, line, shape, fragrance, and so on. If so, though many aesthetic judgements may be attributive, and in a variety of ways, nevertheless, if the drift of my argument can be accepted, *contra* Savile, not all aesthetic judgements are attributive, and, *contra* Scruton, we *can* make at least some aesthetic judgements of things without knowing (in the sense he obviously intends) what kind of things they are, though not without knowing they are (being considered as) beautiful patternings, lines, shapes, or colouring.

---

[5] *The Test of Time*, 166.

14

Some Notes on Ugliness

I

Ugliness is a topic which is seldom discussed, unlike beauty, and on which most aestheticians have written little. Yet it seems to me one of considerable interest and complexity even if, like many others in aesthetics, the issues it raises cannot be made too precise. So these comments are made in hopes of initiating further investigations. Whatever I say therefore, even if said with apparent conviction, is in fact put forward in a tentative and experimental spirit.

I believe not only that it is a topic of considerable fascination and perplexity in its own right, but that it is bound up, as I think many issues in aesthetics are, with the complex, insufficiently investigated, but widely ramifying questions of what some logicians have come to call 'predicative' and 'attributive' adjectives. Clarification of this large topic, which certainly impinges on problems in many areas of philosophy, has, I believe, a vital role to play within aesthetic in general, and not least in this small corner that takes ugliness for its investigation. Not that there is, to my knowledge, one standard notion of what it is to be 'attributive' that is accepted by all theorists, or any generally accepted account of why various adjectives—or even which—deserve this label. I am not concerned however even to attempt to fit the cases I discuss into any coherent semantic theory. I hope rather to make some observations, right or wrong but worth considering, on certain points, availing myself of the labels 'predicative' and 'attributive' without, I trust, transgressing too seriously the not very clear ground rules for their use. And if good reasons exist for employing these labels in some other way, they can be dropped. At all events, some writers do operate with notions so labelled; and Anthony Savile, for one, must regard them as sufficiently clear to permit some very general claims about aesthetic adjectives. He says, of certain writers, including Kant, that they have taken for granted, falsely, 'that "beautiful" is a predicative adjective', he insists, by contrast, on the 'attributive nature of the adjective' and continues, 'What we have to analyse then is not the predicate "ζ is beautiful" but "ζ is a beautiful F" ' and, (restricting for his purposes his choice for F to 'work of art') says it is a matter of asking 'about the truth conditions of the judgement that x is a beautiful work of art'.[1] Moreover I suspect that he also holds that 'the main elements of the aesthetic vocabulary' (his words) are attributive, even though he rejects as untenable a view (which he attributes to Samuel Johnson) that the way to treat 'the truth conditions of attributives' (these 'main elements of the aesthetic vocabulary') is 'as covert assertions of straightforward comparison'.[2] I agree that not all attributives can be treated as tacit comparisons; but if I understand him aright, he most probably holds nevertheless that the main elements of the aesthetic vocabulary are 'attributive words' of some sort—and I suppose these would include e.g. 'graceful', 'pretty', 'lovely', 'elegant', and, surely, one would think, 'ugly'.

I mean in this paper to argue that 'ugly' is indeed attributive and not merely a tacit comparison (so, in this, writers of Savile's opinion will presumably not disagree with me), and also to begin exploring in what way and why it is (on which they might well disagree). But I set this investigation against a background view, which I shall not attempt to argue here, that 'beautiful' is not always attributive, a view I think not difficult to establish but wholly at odds with the one I have mentioned. If I am right it would result that the traditional 'opposites', 'beautiful' and 'ugly', are in certain logical respects asymmetrical.

But first, five points. 'Ugly' is used in many judgements that are obviously not, or at best only debatably, aesthetic judgements. In 'ugly deed', 'ugly wound', 'ugly mob', 'ugly disturbance', 'ugly weather', 'ugly customer' (a pleasingly ambiguous remark if made by a shopkeeper), the word is not obviously used aesthetically or as an aesthetic term, any more than 'beautiful' is in 'beautiful bruise', or 'beautiful black eye', or any more than 'good' and 'wicked' are used as moral terms in 'good footballer', 'good hiding', 'wicked weather', or 'wicked delivery' in cricket. Throughout, I consider 'ugly' (and 'beautiful') only as used in judgements that are indubitably aesthetic.

Secondly, I shall use 'ugly' (and 'beautiful') in a wholly familiar, even if vague, narrow sense. Both in common usage and by some aestheticians, these two words are sometimes used respectively as broad catch-all negatives and positives. Anything with positive aesthetic value is called beautiful; anything with negative aesthetic value is called ugly. I use each as just one term of aesthetic value or disvalue among many: other positives include 'pretty', 'lovely', 'shapely', 'graceful', 'elegant', 'majestic', other negatives, 'garish', 'gaudy', 'ill-proportioned', 'ungainly', etc.

Thirdly, I shall take it that, in aesthetic judgements, 'x' is beautiful', *tout court*, and 'x is ugly', *tout court*, imply respectively that x has positive, and that x has negative, aesthetic value. That is, I take 'x has positive aesthetic value because it is ugly', *tout court*, and 'x has negative aesthetic value because it's beautiful' *tout court*, as equally unacceptable.

---

[1] Antony Savile, *The Test of Time: An Essay in Philosophical Aesthetics*, Oxford: Clarendon Press, 1982, 166–7.　　　　　　　　　　　　　　　　[2] ibid. 36–7.

Fourthly, by 'negative' I *mean* negative. We make aesthetic judgements lying between '*x* is beautiful' and '*x* is ugly', using expressions like 'plain', 'aesthetically nondescript', 'ordinary', 'undistinguished', when we find nothing aesthetically positive to admire or aesthetically negative to deplore. To say someone has a plain face, neither beautiful nor ugly, is to say, so far, that it has neither aesthetic value nor disvalue; aesthetically it is neutral, neither here nor there, unremarkable (though judging it a plain face is still an aesthetic judgement, attributing, so to put it, neither positive nor negative but a zero degree of aesthetic value; such 'neutral' judgements of aesthetic value must not be confused with judgements neutral in the sense of not being aesthetic judgements at all. *X* is square, or red, or ripe, or fully-grown, or striped simply carry no implication whatever of aesthetic value of any degree, positive, negative, or zero). I shall therefore take the 'opposites' in the range 'beautiful' and 'ugly' as somewhat analogous to other adjective pairs of 'opposites' which increase in degree in opposite directions from a central zero point, as sweet and sour do from tastelessness, loving and hating from indifference, and so on. Not all pairs of adjective 'opposites' function thus: for 'shallow' and 'deep' there is no mid-point of zero shallowness or depth; nor is there a zero point for 'heavy' and 'light', etc. Other pairs of 'opposites' are different again: one of them itself marks the zero point, there being no other scale, no 'opposite', on the other side of zero: perhaps 'silent' and 'noisy', 'dry' and 'moist', 'honest' and 'dishonest' are varying examples of some such sort. I shall treat 'plain' as the zero point of aesthetic value, as tastelessness is of sweetness, with respectively 'ugly' and 'sour' beginning different ranges on the further side of the zero point.

Fifthly, I shall say nothing about art-works. I confine myself to natural objects and phenomena, faces, bodies, animals, birds, reptiles, insects, plants, clouds, the sky, stars, the sea, landscapes, mountains, rocks, stones, pebbles: apart, that is, from a few comments later about certain man-made objects.

II

It is generally supposed amongst those who discuss predicative and attributive adjectives that in a sentence of the form '*x* is an AN', a predicative adjective 'A' is joined to its noun 'N' merely conjunctively, as a conjunction of two independent predicates of the subject *x*, whereas an attributive adjective is attached to its noun 'N' by some more intimate connection, some so-called 'semantic attachment'.

It has also been common practice to classify certain adjectives as belonging to one or other of these two types (Geach wrote 'two sorts of adjectives'); 'red', 'square', 'four-legged', 'spherical', 'sweet' being often offered as predicative, 'large', 'hot', 'deep', as attributive, though not all writers would categorize these words the same way. I shall exclude from consideration here those like 'forged' and 'alleged' which in a sentence of the form (1) 'x is an AN', because of the adjective, fail to imply 'x is an N' and confine myself to cases where sentences like (1) do imply (2) 'x is an N.'. I do this because the adjectives 'beautiful' and 'ugly' are of this latter sort. (I also exclude for simplicity what have been called 'implicit attributive constructions' where the adjective is attached to some noun other than that explicitly occurring in 'x is an AN', and confine myself to 'explicit attributive constructions' where the adjective is attached to 'N'. (In 'She is a beautiful dancer', 'beautiful', if explicitly attached, would be to the person, the dancer; if implicitly, to her dancing.)

I propose first that, in dealing with what I shall call predicative and attributive sentences, we must recognize not two kinds of adjectives but two kinds of uses, a predicative and an attributive use of adjectives; and, correspondingly, three kinds of adjectives, those 'essentially' predicative, which can be used only predicatively, those 'essentially' attributive, capable only of attributive use, and those dual or ambifunctional adjectives that can be used, sometimes, even when explicitly attached to the very same noun, either predicatively or attributively. This is something I merely exemplify but do not expand here. The adjectives 'spherical' and 'large' are almost certainly, respectively, essentially predicative and essentially attributive. If 'x is a spherical N' is true, and being an N entails or is entailed by being an N1, then 'x is a spherical N1' will also be true no matter what noun 'N1' is, so long as 'x is an N1' is true. Contrariwise if 'x is a large N' is true, 'x is a large N1' need not be true (where 'N1' is any other noun such that 'x is an N1' is true).

But an adjective such as 'pale-skinned' may be used either predicatively or attributively: (3) 'x is (predicatively) a pale-skinned Negro' mutually implies (4) 'x is pale-skinned and a Negro'; but (5) 'x is (attributively) a pale-skinned Negro' does not imply (6) 'x is a Negro and also pale-skinned'. He may be coffee-coloured, which would be dark-skinned for a Swede or a Finn. 'Sweet' may similarly be used predicatively or attributively, though it differs from 'pale-skinned' in other respects. For instance, we may use 'sweet' in (7) 'This is (predicatively) a sweet Sauternes' and in (8) 'This is (attributively) a sweet Sauternes'; both imply (9) 'It is a Sauternes and also (in some degree) sweet (not tasteless or sour)', but (9) does not imply (8) 'This is (attributively) a sweet Sauternes', i.e. even for a Sauternes.

What I shall say here about the semantic attachment exhibited in the attributive uses I'm concerned with is that a necessary condition of being able to assign a truth value to 'x is (attributively) an AN' is that it be known what noun 'N' is (so that appropriate use can be made of this knowledge). In the case of essentially attributive adjectives, like 'large', 'x is large' is necessarily incomplete (unless elliptical) and no truth-value can be assigned until some noun is understood to complete its sense. Ambifunctional adjectives, like 'sweet' or 'pale-skinned', by contrast, are complete predicates and a truth-value can be assigned, e.g. to '*x* is sweet'; but when used attributively, i.e. to mean 'sweet for a such-and-such', they are being used so as to require some completion and again no truth-value can be assigned until some noun, 'N', with which they are being used attributively to form '*x* is an AN', is understood. The reason it must be understood which noun, 'N', is in question for assigning any truth-value at all to the sentence '*x* is an AN' when 'A' is an essential attributive, and for assigning the correct truth value to '*x* is an AN when 'A' is ambifunctional but used attributively, is that it is the noun that provides a 'standard' for the use of the adjective. (By the vague word 'standard' I mean deliberately to encompass a large and diverse group of phenomena, some of which I shall detail, though only certain of them are of present relevance.)

With many essential attributives, e.g. 'large', 'old', 'heavy', relation to the 'standard' set by the noun involves some kind of comparative, a large or heavy N, for instance, exceeding in size or weight, some average, or range, or majority, etc. of Ns, (there being many variants and possibilities here). With some ambifunctional adjectives used attributively (my 'pale-skinned' and 'sweet' examples) the situation is similarly comparative in a relatively obvious way. So I shall call all such uses 'comparative-attributive uses'. With attributive uses of other, usually ambifunctional, sorts of adjectives, while reference to a noun is necessary to provide a standard, the standard may be of a very different sort, and reference to it need involve no comparison with other members of some class of Ns. For example, '*x* is a sharp scalpel/razor' makes reference to some fixed, if vague, point on a continuous scale of sharpness (higher than the standard reference point for, say, sharp garden spades) and a sharp razor has at least this degree of sharpness. We might perhaps call these, and many similar examples, when attributive, 'point-related' rather than 'comparative-attributives'. The truth of such sentences as these is not, as with comparative-attributives, related comparatively to some average or normalcy or majority of Ns in respect of A. Their truth does not imply that any razors are not sharp.

I make these points because I believe that 'beautiful' is almost certainly ambifunctional, but that (aside from the fact that it can be used in a merely comparative-attributive way, e.g. 'beautiful as mothers-in-law go') its typical attributive use is 'standard-related' in a way different from those I have mentioned so far. And I need at least to sketch this if I am to contrast 'ugly' with it. Briefly, I shall say that, when attributive, beautiful is ordinarily ideal-related. That is, to judge that *x* is a beautiful face, beautiful woman, beautiful body, beautiful horse, beautiful cat (non-comparatively, since it is conceivable that all faces, women, bodies, horses, and cats might be beautiful ones), reference must be made via the noun to some ideal (or group of ideals, since several ideals, say, of facial beauty might coexist) of respectively facial, female, bodily, equine, and feline beauty. (This is not to say that such ideals might not change or vary with fashion and across cultures; only that for any person or group making such a judgement, reference to an ideal for the thing named by that noun is necessary: a beautiful face is never just beautiful and a face.) About 'beautiful' I can say no more here.

Now for 'ugly'. There is even prima-facie an asymmetry that cries out for explanation, namely that there are many sorts of things, examples of which we would on occasion call beautiful but, even if we used other aesthetic negatives about them, would rarely if ever call 'ugly'—clouds, sunsets, the sky, the sea, etc. I return to this.

I am going to suggest, but not argue here, that whereas 'beautiful' is sometimes attributive (in a way of its own, viz. ideal-related as in my examples above), I believe it to be also usable predicatively. That is, it is ambifunctional. It is possible to judge, rightly, that some things are beautiful without knowing what they are (there just are not any ideals of beauty specifically for them, say, pebbles or driftwood); indeed one may judge something beautiful, not knowing it is an N and, even though it may be far from a beautiful N. It may still be a thing of very considerable beauty. By contrast I tentatively suggest that 'ugly' is always attributive, and in a way that is not merely comparative (though it can be used additionally in a comparative way), and is not what I called 'point-related', and can hardly be called ideal-related either. (It would be odd indeed to say we have ideals of facial or female or equine ugliness.) We need some other notion, for which, not very felicitously (though with some historical backing) I shall call 'deformity-related' attributivity. I risk misinterpretation by this, but hope to clarify the notion in a moment. At all events it would follow that if ugliness always involves deformity in some sense (though the *converse* is not true), 'ugly' must be attributive by its relation to non-deformed instances of whatever N is under consideration. Hence, while various other aesthetically negative judgements might be made about something, if it is a kind of thing that cannot be said to have deformed instances, that thing and things of its sort cannot be judged ugly. 'Ugly' will be inapplicable to them, one necessary condition of its applicability being absent (though applicability will tail off into vagueness with certain sorts of things).

A very brief reference to certain eighteenth-century debates may be of interest here. The existence of some connection between ugliness and deformity is to be found there, and so is the dispute over what some now call predicatives and attributives, though the writers are also grinding other axes. Hutcheson and Hume rarely use the word 'ugly'. Hutcheson, when he does, seems to equate them: he says 'ugly or deformed'. Hume speaks ordinarily of Beauty and Deformity, leaving it unclear whether he sees a zero or mid-point (plainness) between beauty and ugliness (there being no such point presumably between the non-deformed and the deformed). However Hume should be understood here, it seems clear to me that Burke, in supposing he is attacking Hume, is plainly right on one major point. He speaks of 'a wrong idea of the relation which deformity bears to beauty, to which it has been considered as the opposite; on this principle it was concluded, that where the causes of

deformity were removed, beauty must naturally and necessarily be introduced'. Here he is clearly arguing for a neutral or zero mid-point and the non-
equatability of beauty with absence of deformity: a man may be lacking in all
deformity 'without having ... the least perceivable beauty' and beauty is 'a
positive and powerful quality', not mere absence of deformity.[3]

On the other hand Burke seems to come close to treating beauty (and
presumably ugliness, since he imagines it 'in all respects the opposite') as
always predicative, since his procedure is to reject 'form' or 'proportion' as
'causes of', relevant to, the beauty of things, on the grounds that swans and
peacocks, both beautiful birds, and other beautiful creatures, exhibit very
different shapes and proportions, and to attempt a list of qualities that, in any
object, constitute or confer beauty (smallness, smoothness, gradual variation
of curvature, delicacy, clearness of colour, etc.). Hume and others, by contrast,
had argued, it seems to me rightly, that different forms, proportions, and
shapes were relevant to the beauty of different human or animal species, in
effect stressing attributive uses of 'beauty', and so opening the gate also to a
connection between deformity and ugliness.

There is, then, I believe, a strong argument for regarding 'ugly' in its narrow
sense as frequently attributive, and if, as I am suggesting, 'deformity' or something akin, interpreted more broadly, is a necessary condition, it would be
always and essentially attributive. It need not of course be the case that all
deformities are ugly, only that all ugly things are deformed, and perhaps to be
describable as ugly the deformity has often to be fairly extreme. But this wider
notion of 'deformity' I am relying on, for which we have perhaps no one word,
must not be as primarily or closely connected with form, meaning shape, as,
for example, 'ill-shaped', or 'misshapen' are (or as Burke treated it as being). It
must be broad enough to include such abnormalities and distortions as are
covered by a whole variety of notions (all, I suggest, essentially attributive), like
distorted, defective, defiled, soiled, mutilated, discoloured, blotchy, withered,
scarred, disfigured, emaciated, swollen, bloated, begrimed, stunted, dwarfed,
wizened, decaying, mouldering, blighted, festering, and a host of others indica-
tive of abnormality or defect in shape, colour, size, health, growth, etc. Perhaps
the best umbrella term would be 'denatured'. If the foregoing is correct, if 'ugly'
functions as an essential attributive, it works in a particular way: it is not what
I earlier called 'point-related', or 'ideal-related', and not even merely a 'comparative' attributive, though it could additionally function so. It is, as I shall say,
'deformity-related'. A first but inexact shot at an account would be as follows.
'X is ugly' is incomplete, unless elliptical, and can have no truth-value without
some predicate noun, 'N', being understood to form the explicit attributive 'x is
an ugly N'. In such a sentence, 'ugly' implies the possession by x of some

---

[3] *A Philosophical Inquiry into the Origin of our Ideas of the Sublime and Beautiful*, part
III, sect. V, 1756.

quality or set of qualities, unspecified (which incidentally might themselves be aesthetically positive, neutral, or non-aesthetic, as well as aesthetic negatives) which would constitute or be regarded as a (probably fairly *extreme*) deformity in an N—enough to warrant the particular aesthetic negative 'ugly' (e.g. in a human face). Moreover, since this account implies that, though not all deformed Ns need be ugly Ns, all ugly Ns are deformed Ns, and that therefore only things capable of being deformed can be ugly, it receives some support from, and gives some explanation of, the fact mentioned earlier that, where, in the broad sense I have indicated, 'deformity' has no obvious application, we do not in fact generally use the word 'ugly' (in the narrow aesthetic sense under discussion). We may at times call the sky, sea, stars, nebulae, clouds, sunsets, crystals, rocks, pebbles, boulders, etc. beautiful. We may perhaps, on other occasions, have reason to apply some aesthetic negative or other to them (dowdy, dull, unremarkable, plain, very ordinary, gaudy); but it would be odd or at least unusual to say that any such things were ugly (and I am excluding of course 'ugly clouds', 'ugly weather', 'an ugly sea', when 'ugly' means primarily, e.g. menacing, dangerous, etc., and is not obviously used as an aesthetic term).

But this still leaves several types of cases which, it might be argued, are obvious exceptions and need discussion. The forgoing has dealt only with examples where a particular individual, *x*, is an ugly instance of a kind, N. Something need be said therefore about the sort of judgements, commonly expressed, that all members of some kind or species are ugly, e.g. toads, mastiffs, bulldogs, warthogs, hyenas, vultures, certain species of reptiles, or whatever (such judgements are sometimes extended to particular human groups, say pygmies, and even occasionally to some kinds of (drab, spiny, slimy, or oozy) plants).[4] The principle is in some ways not unlike general judgements about whole species made using other adjectives, e.g. that the great cats are svelte and graceful, crows and seals on terra firma are ungainly or awkward, their movements ugly, but, in air and water respectively, graceful or beautiful movers. One seemingly obvious, but I believe mistaken, way of interpreting the general judgements I am interested in is to take them as saying that toads, say, are ugly animals or creatures (or even perhaps things). This would be to treat the judgements as merely comparative-attributive *vis-à-vis* a wider class, as beavers are large rodents but smallish animals (and I think this method might be possible with e.g. 'graceful', or 'ungainly', which are very probably ambifunctional—clouds and sunsets incidentally could be neither). But this would run counter to the thesis that 'ugly' is essentially

---

[4] Toads in particular, and some other species, historically seem to come in frequently for a beating on the ugliness issue. They are mentioned, for example, by both Hume and Burke. Since I do not wish to express any special *parti pris*, the reader is invited, if my examples seem inappropriate, to supply his own.

attributive and 'deformity-related' at that. Clearly, normal toads, or warthogs, or whatever, cannot all be regarded either as deformed examples of their own kind, or even as deformed animals, or creatures, or organisms. What happens, I believe, clearly in some examples, more obscurely in others, is that we select forms, varying from case to case, of certain normal and familiar type of animals, faces, eyes, mouths, proportions, gait, etc.; then the whole of a species, taken against some such familiar, often broadly human norm, is seen or thought of as if deformed. If toads, say, are seen as having large bulging eyes (surely in some sense true), broad mouths (true in relation to head size), a subnormal and imbecilic facial look, and are therefore seen as ugly, we are probably judging as much in relation to human and more human-like species as we are when we speak of the ungainly walk of a gorilla or camel. (We commonly, if impolitely, reverse the procedure calling a human face ugly 'because of its little pig-eyes', a profile ugly 'because of its reptilian look', etc. The process is not altogether unlike that involved in calling a St Bernard's face mournful, or certain fishes lugubrious, or crocodiles grinning, or camels haughty, or moose supercilious.) It is as such more or less tacit comparisons become more difficult, to the point where any reasonably obvious possibility fades out—as it does, largely but not wholly, with plants, and creatures like ants that are too small to compare—that a use of 'ugly' also peters out (though note how we readily use it again as soon as we get microscope enlargements of their heads, eyes, mouths, etc.).

A second kind of case where 'ugly' may be used, but this time once again of individual items, follows (and fades out) according to a similar principle of comparison with an invoked or tacit deformity. This occurs when people say of a rock, pebble, cloud, etc. that it is ugly, but where it turns out that they, sometimes quite explicitly, sometimes barely consciously, mean that it looks (to them) like an ugly face, a dragon, a wizened old man, a crone, or whatever. Here again the relation to ugliness via deformity is involved. We are seeing the objects in terms of human beings or other familiar creatures that can be deformed and ugly. But there is a difference from the previous sort of cases. It is not strictly an ugly cloud, or ugly rock, etc.; it is a cloud or rock that looks like, or is seen as if it were, or is vaguely reminiscent of, an ugly face or body or animal, and 'ugly' perhaps is rather like a transferred epithet, as 'tasty' is in 'a tasty plate of stew'.

Thirdly, we call some things ugly when they strike us, not so much as deformed in any narrow sense, but in the widened sense I gave it, as spoiled, disfigured, defaced, discoloured, etc., whether by natural events or human agency. Fields, hillsides, landscapes may be made ugly by fire-charred areas, craters, quarries, mine-workings, slag-heaps, lava fields, when we regard these as blots, scars, sores, warts, bruises, wounds, or excrescences on the landscape, or in general, as defects of some sort. Again we are sometimes, as it were, transferring the epithet; it my be less the craters, quarries, dilapidated workings, slag-heaps that are themselves ugly than the fact that they deface the landscapes, much as warts or a scar on a face, or a lopped or broken limb of a tree, a stump, may have, from an aesthetic point of view, nothing particularly ugly about them—rather they are what make or help make the face or the tree ugly, being an excrescence upon, or deformity of, these. Even things that are so changeable or variable as to have no one single or obvious or standard form, colouring, proportions, etc. can be seen as denatured, diseased, polluted, as when the sea is churned into muddy or scummy waves, a lake or canal surface coated with oil or slime, and 'ugly', even if only peripherally, may find a use. So, similarly, with entirely man-made features, when we see factory areas, rubbish tips, villages or towns as blots, scabs, rashes, or creeping and spreading diseases, as we say, on the fair face of the land, nature denatured and made ugly by the works of man.

And this makes the transition to a fourth kind of case, only to be touched on here. There are many wholly man-made objects, buildings, villages, towns, furniture, etc., that have no natural or normal shape, proportions, colouring, etc., and cannot therefore in anything like a literal sense be deformed, distorted, disfigured, bloated, stunted, crippled, emaciated, or diseased. Yet these are all things instances of which we may commonly characterize as ugly. I shall merely advert here to the explanation that has often been given, that we find them ugly when we see them, buildings for example, in human or animal terms, as cramped, dwarfed, ill-featured, bloated; furniture for example, as distorted by excrescences or with deformed or emaciated limbs; suburbs as sprawling, spreading, uncoordinated, and disorganized. The process is analogous to our describing these same kinds of objects in human terms, as pompous, arrogant, majestic, bold, gracious, shy, modest, reserved, or demure.

Finally, on the supposition that 'ugly' is deformity-related, it may be asked how we can speak, as we sometimes certainly do, of colours, lines, shapes, and sounds, i.e. not things that may be or may be thought of as deformed, including for instance certain spoken languages, as ugly; for here, it would seem, normalities and deformities have no place. Is 'ugly' here being used purely predicatively? To this, several replies might be possible. One, which I am not especially inclined to give, is to concede that there are a few predicative uses of 'ugly', rather rare and restricted in scope, which may have crept in parasitically on the attributive uses, so giving an infrequent and partial parallel with 'beautiful'. It would not worry me unduly if there were these few non-attributive occurrences of 'ugly' so long as it is agreed that an asymmetry with 'beautiful' remains, in that predicative uses of 'beautiful' are legion while predicative uses of 'ugly' are exceptional. But I am more inclined to one or both of two other suggestions. (1) When colours and colour combinations, or lines, or shapes (think of Rorschach blots, split ink, stain marks) or even sounds are, considered in themselves, called 'ugly', it may be either that they are seen tacitly (like

Rorschach blots and clouds) as ugly faces, dragons, or whatever, or that they are seen as deformities and blemishes on other things. I am much disinclined to say that they are, considered in themselves, properly called ugly. (2) I don't doubt that if a child were asked to draw an ugly line or shape, or do an ugly piece or colouring, or make an ugly noise, he would understand, and probably produce a zigzag line, an angular scribble, a muddy and dirty-looking finger painting, a raucous shout, or a cacophonous pounding on, say, the piano. Nor have I any doubt that lines, shapes, colorations, and noises, considered by themselves (without tacit comparisons and interpretations) may be characterized by terms clearly used as aesthetic negatives, e.g. twisted, formless, graceless, clumsy, awkward, stark, jagged, harsh, clashing, gaudy, garish, strident, faded, muddy, jumbled, cacophonous, clattering, rough, jangling, and so on. But I am not sure I feel happy in these cases using the word 'ugly' without supposing that it has by this time drifted back to that broad, undistinguishing cover-all aesthetically negative sense that I mentioned at the outset. I can appreciate of course that these two moves may be seen as attempts to put my suggestions above about ugliness beyond reach of refutation. But that could be because, in an inevitably blurry subject such as this, what I have said is mainly correct. I leave you to ponder whether it, or any significant part of it, seems to be on an interesting, even possibly acceptable, tack.

Now having pointed the way, I am going to return and make various modifications, because my account is unsatisfactory as it stands, too strong. I used the notion of deformity, since the eighteenth-century writers, who are the main writers on the topic, saw ugliness as a matter of deformity. Indeed, they usually discuss not beauty and ugliness as opposites, but beauty and deformity. But matters are far more subtle. I indicated that I was wary of 'deformed', it being too closely connected with form or shape, and instead instanced a number of other, I think, attributive adjectives, all indicating some kind of departure from some standard or norm. I therefore suggested, as an umbrella term, the broader notion 'denatured'. Thus if being denatured is a necessary condition for ugliness, a thing could be denatured by being deformed, scarred, discoloured, dwarfed, wizened, soiled, etc. But 'deformed' and those other notions I included under 'denatured' are in various ways far too strong. Deformed, as well as being limited to form, is a medical or quasi-medical notion. But many non-deformed people are ugly at least in some degree, and without being denatured in any of the ways I listed, and some 'deformed' are beautiful—departures from the norm, but not *away* from beauty. Some lesser deformities may be seen as a source of beauty (beauty spots). To take some familiar classical examples, Socrates was said to be ugly, so was Cyrano de Bergerac. But the one's snub nose and the other's proboscis were presumably perfectly good specimens from a medical point of view. Nor were they necessarily deformed or denatured in the sense of grossly discoloured, dwarfed, wizened, bloated, blotched, bleared, etc. They are not presumably in the same ugliness league as Gargantua or Quasimodo or Dorian Gray or Dracula or Frankenstein. Indeed, among any group chosen at random, say the government or opposition front benches at any period of history, a fair number would count as somewhat ugly; certainly, to put it politely, not as beauties. Often it is a matter of some kind of exaggeration, too much or too little, minor blemishes and aberrations, lips too thick, nose too long, ears too big, colouring too flushed or mottled, eyes too big or too small, chin too big, and so on. All these may be physically and medically perfectly all right, i.e. not deformed or denatured. But these notions are still attributive, i.e. they are departures from something, from some norm or standard for this or that.

How then can we express the standard or norm from which ugly ones depart or fall away? (1) First, it is not a departure from medical normality. They may all be medically perfect. (2) Secondly, the notion of physical perfection sometimes includes aesthetic perfection or beauty; cf. the Attic notion of physical perfection is itself an ideal of beauty. Obviously and trivially it is a departure from this, from ideal beauty, but it must also be a departure from, in some sense, the quite ordinary or normal too.

(3) But this cannot be taken to mean departure from the ordinary in the sense of the aesthetically plain, plainness in an aesthetic sense, for that too would be vacuous; it is necessarily true that ugly has to be some departure from plain in this sense. Thus for a necessary condition of ugliness (in xs) we need some other than an aesthetic norm. So we still need to give a sense to the norm from which the ugly departs or falls away. There must in effect be some notion of the normal from which there can be mere exaggerations (too big, too small) as well as deformities and distortions.

For a beginning one might suggest that the departure is from what is factually the dominant or majority or most common run of appearances. This notion (however formed) of normal appearance could be interpreted in several different ways: (*a*) the majority of xs, e.g. the majority of people, might have aquiline noses, while only a few have snub, *retroussé*, or bulbous noses; or (*b*) the most frequent or common or largest concentration of xs—e.g. the majority of people might have either snub or aquiline or *retroussé* or bulbous noses, the minority have aquiline noses yet these might be the more common. (Blue eyes, green eyes, grey eyes, hazel eyes, brown eyes.) Since neither of these is an aesthetic standard, we can still significantly say e.g. that (factually) (*a*) the majority or (*b*) the most common are (aesthetically) plain. But I suspect we need to be able also to say such factual things as e.g. the majority of xs, or most usual, common, or frequent xs are rather ugly (or beautiful). So I suggest therefore that what people employ is some notional standard or norm of what an ordinary, normal, standard X (fact, body) is like, and beautiful and ugly are departures in opposite directions from this notional neutral, normal, or common run of xs; and ugly ones are those seen as departures from this notion of how an ordinary face of body should be. (Note: not only does this not adopt the aesthetic notion 'plain' as standard, it allows that the norm is not initially seen as plain; I suspect concepts of beautiful (and perhaps of ugly) are logically prior to that of plainness (one cannot imagine a group with the concept of aesthetically plain but no concepts of ugly or beautiful). The concept plain—as neither beautiful nor ugly—comes to be applied to the norm from which beautiful and ugly both diverge, departure in one direction to what is admired, the other way to what eighteenth-century writing called uneasiness; whereas the normal is what people are accustomed to, don't blink an eye at, have no aesthetic response to until they have begun to have either positive or negative responses.) No doubt, in fact, the norm (notionally adequate man/face/body) will usually coincide with the familiar, usual, majority, the common run, the commonest type of appearances. These will be, for different groups or tribes, their own most normal types (hairless bodies, hair only in certain places, blue eyes, dark skin, fair hair, or whatever. For those groups, other hair patterns, hair colour, etc., may disqualify both from beauty and plainness. Obviously the three notions of 'deformity' may coalesce— medical, unusual (away from ideal), deformed.

I can now replace the overstated conditions—deformed, denatured, etc.,—by something less extreme. Ugliness requires some departure by way of exaggeration, extravagance, or discolouring, being too this or too that, swollen, bulging, twisted, red eyes, knock knees, from a norm or notion of xs by something out of place, inappropriate in an x. For this the weaker term 'denormalized' might appropriately replace 'deformed' or 'denatured'. Thus I might say that a necessary condition of a x being an ugly x is that it is denormalized in some way (or some of a number of ways). With this modification a necessary condition that a thing is considered ugly is that it is seen or thought of, not as deformed, but as denormalized. But of course the norm, say for ordinary, non-ugly faces, eyes, or noses will usually be broad and capacious in many ways, allow of degrees. For instance, normal eyes might be grey, blue, green, brown, but not pink or yellow; noses lightly snub, aquiline, *retroussé* or bulbous so long as not too exaggerated, bodies tall or short so long as neither dwarf nor giant. Within wide ranges many might be normal enough.

The modification I have now made will not significantly alter the approach to or the principles involved in the sorts of cases I indicated earlier. Certain species: (normal) toads, warthogs, bulldogs etc. may still be seen as exaggerations, distortions of some norm (probably human) of what ordinary faces should be or would be expected to be. Clouds, rocks, pebbles, and other things with no obvious normal form may still be seen as like ugly faces, dragons, demons, etc. Fields, landscapes may be seen as spoiled, defaced, blighted by departures from the norm for a landscape (which of course can contain many varieties of normality; pre-Romantics saw mountains as hideous, ugly, departures from a very narrow norm of acceptable classical countryside); the same with towns and villages. Buildings and furniture may be seen as exaggerated, bloated, emaciated, cramped, largely by tacit reference to human beings, their limbs, etc. But generally it will explain why applicability of ugly seems to fade away with clouds, the sea, the sky, pebbles, etc.; less now because there is no place for deformed and non-deformed but still because we do not by and large approach them with, or think of them with some notion of, a norm, of how ordinarily they should be (though we can think of fog as mist degraded with dirt).

This completes my main supposition. The central cases, the predominant cases, of ugliness are attributive in a certain way, i.e. they indicate departures from some notional norm (and in the opposite direction from any ideal of beauty) of what a face, features, walk, gait, posture, body shape, even a stretch of countryside should be or is considered to be. They are not necessarily departures from what the majority of such things are like. In some cases, e.g. with humans, it is a departure from a norm for them (faces, bodies, movements, etc.); in other cases it is perhaps borrowed from them (toads, buildings, etc.). In other cases again, it is more vague, drawn for example from norms of animals in general; e.g. toads are ugly compared to some vague norm for animals in general; some having an ungainly walk as if awkward, hindered, lame (camels or bears compared with horses, seals on land with otters); some an ungainly posture as if humpbacked (hyenas compared with wolves); some an ungainly flight, and so on. I have in mind such things as the humpbacked hyena, the turkey's crop, the vulture's neck (featherless, diseased-looking, plucked bare—quite wrong for a bird's neck), the pink and sore-looking eyes of the bull terrier, the red, sore-looking rear end of the baboon; and e.g. the blackened crater landscape of volcanic landscapes. Where there is no notional norm and we do not borrow and apply one, the use of 'ugly' finds no place except in some attenuated use to mean merely, say, garish or muddy for colours, jagged or threatening for line and shapes, etc. Double attributiveness can also occur: *x*'s face might be ugly even for or among toads' faces (weak attributiveness) as well as ugly for a face (strong attributiveness using a norm of human faces, the kind of attributiveness I have aimed to stress). But in either case it might not be ugly, but indeed rather beautiful as an abstract pattern of colouring, if you could see it not as a face or out of context or upside down etc.

One thing I have not mentioned is dislike, revulsion, being repelled, disgust, etc. Some have wanted to say e.g. the ugly is what repels or arouses revulsion. I do not really doubt that there is some kind of connection between ugliness and revulsion, etc., just as I think there is some connection between beauty and pleasure, admiration, etc. But I think it certainly is not likely to be straightforward. But even if I conceded this, I could still maintain that my view of ugliness as being, in all significant and central cases, attributive in certain ways is plausible. For instance, even if a toad's face repels you or a blotched skin or a bloated body, it is because you see it as a face, a skin, or a body. If you saw them only as abstract colouring and patterns, far from being repulsive, they might be very pretty, even beautiful and attractive.

Before I end I will nevertheless hazard a few tentative remarks about distaste, revulsion, disgust, etc. But as I said, I do not think the connection is straightforward. In most cases we can make quite cool judgements as to this or that being ugly. We do not have to show or feel disgust, distaste, or repulsion; we do not utter 'ughs' or 'ohs', turn away or avert our eyes. Recall my remarks about parliamentary front benches—or any group of colleagues. Nor do I think we could be helped by the hypothesis that we have inhibited a tendency to revulsion. It might be said instead that many instances of ugliness are only rather or somewhat ugly—insufficient strongly to repel us; or again that many are too distant: that you might coolly judge someone ugly and not feel strong aversion unless he or she had to be embraced, had to come too close for comfort and equanimity. There may be something in these suggestions. But I suspect there are other factors that may be more important. I am prepared as I have indicated to think that those exaggerations, departures from some notional norm, that strike us as ugly are those that we tend to see as having something, some degree however slight, of the dirty, squalid, polluted, diseased, spoiled, degraded, coarse, base, subnormal, brutish or subhuman, even foul or evil, either physically or spiritually—as well as threatening, dangerous, or frightening as etymology suggests. All of these are conditions against which there might be natural responses of distress, aversion, revulsion—in Hume's mild term 'uneasiness'. So no doubt we would be, in however mild a degree, repelled or distressed by such conditions if they were real. But in so far as ugliness is a matter of appearances, as so often it is, and in so far as we see certain things and people as ugly because they are evil-looking, or diseased-looking or coarse-looking or brutish-looking, sloppy or otherwise imperfect, we have, unlike children, often come to distinguish how something looks from how it is. To that extent these are cool judgements of appearances, and nothing to be revolted by. Just as some breeds of dogs have sad faces and children may take them to be sad and respond with pity and a wish to comfort, it would be absurd for adults to feel pity. Perhaps—somewhat analogously—in so far as something looks diseased, blemished, but we know it is not, we judge it ugly, but coolly. There is no place either for revulsion or pity as there might be if it were a dog with a sore on its back. Equally, when as with pebbles, clouds, seas, landscapes where 'norms' and with them the notion of ugliness disappear, there is no clear purchase for brutish, diseased, or otherwise denatured, etc., and distaste and revulsion disappear too. It is perhaps noteworthy that where ugly is used of clouds, storms, etc., they look (and may be) threatening, fearful, and a source of disquiet.

Coda

A view that is propounded from time to time, for a variety of reasons, that might appear to be in conflict with my conjectures about ugly things, is that, really, nothing in nature is ugly. Without going as far as those who would claim that everything in nature is beautiful, I want to show how this view may be both true and consistent with what I have said about ugliness. The trick, I think, turns on such phrases as 'nothing considered *in itself*, or *for itself alone* is ugly'. I will illustrate three ways this can operate (there are others). Take toads again. If, as I put it earlier, we cease comparing toads with, say, human faces and forms, and consider them as toads, non-deformed creatures—a procedure I recommend to anyone willing to appreciate to the full the beauties of nature, including toads—we may cease to regard them as ugly; some, indeed, in terms of colour, line, shape, etc., like various other ferocious-looking or lugubrious-looking reptiles and fish, may be extraordinarily beautiful—though others are just plain and dull. This might be an interpretation of 'considering toads for themselves alone'. Secondly, we may do something similar with man-made blots on the land-scape; consider *them* themselves—not as blots on something else. Artists who depict industrial features can help us here, though as environmentalists we may not want to take this step. Thirdly, take a grossly distorted, discoloured, by any held standards, hideously ugly human face. Now consider it 'in itself', 'for itself alone', i.e. for its combination of colours, lines, shapes: not as a *face*. It might then be seen, in terms of colour, shape, lines, as extraordinarily beautiful—though again it might be just plain and dull. But if it is being considered, assessed aesthetically, simply as a coloured, shaped *object*, not as a face or in relation to anything else, it cannot be considered, either in a straightforward or roundabout way, as deformed or denatured. There may be ways faces have to be not to be deformed or dena-tured or exaggerated; there is no way objects have to be not to be deformed or denatured or exaggerated. That notion is empty. Hence, considered for itself alone, as an object, while it might or might not be beautiful, it cannot be ugly. To adapt a saying, 'Everything is what it is and doesn't have to be compared or contrasted with another thing'. Hutcheson comes close to this: 'there is no form which seems necessarily disagreeable of itself when we . . . compare it with nothing better of the kind' and we may feel 'a disgust where there is nothing disagreeable in the form itself . . . Thus swine, serpents of all kinds, and some insects [are] really beautiful enough'. If I am right, one can consistently maintain both that some faces are ugly faces, that many toads, etc., are ugly creatures, while maintaining that even the ugliest faces and toads, 'considered in themselves' are not, indeed cannot be, ugly, and may sometimes be beautiful.

But to say this, that objects, considered merely as things, may be beautiful but cannot be ugly, is to indicate once again the asymmetry between beauty and ugliness that I proposed earlier in saying that 'beautiful' can have a predicative, but 'ugly' only an attributive, use.

15

Tastes, Smells, and Aesthetics

I

The question I want to raise in this paper is whether tastes and smells can have aesthetic interest or value. Some thinkers have believed, even offered sketchy arguments to show, that they can, that some actually have, and even that they are primitive paradigms of things from which we may derive aesthetic delight. More frequently, through history, thinkers have supposed, or made some show of arguing, that tastes and smells cannot be of aesthetic interest, and that any delight we derive from them is merely 'sensuous', not aesthetic. Yet, examining their writings, one often feels that, whatever view one should take, many of their assertions and attempts at argument may be motivated by convictions and interests extraneous to the question; the conviction that tasting and smelling are 'lower' senses is usually not far away.

In considering the matter one is hampered by the fact that philosophers have largely ignored the senses other than vision, even though the various senses differ so markedly and therefore offer fascinating opportunities for investigation and contrast. One might reasonably suppose that, when aestheticians' discussions of the visual and auditory arts have so frequently needed to draw on, and to further for their purposes, analyses of ordinary visual and auditory perception, conclusions positive or negative about the aesthetics of taste and smell must be precarious unless underpinned by further philosophical examination of these senses.

There is an additional impediment to progress. Those who do discuss tastes and smells in relation to aesthetics often argue, and offer conclusions, about whether there could be *works of art* whose main features are tastes and smells. But, besides the fact that questions about whether *haute cuisine*, wine-making, or perfume-creation are fine arts are vague, ambiguous, or philosophically not very exciting, and that speculations about perfume symphonies and taste epics take us into realms of fantasy, even discussions of familiar things like particular wines, or meals, or perfumes *as art-works* introduce a high level of sophistication—since they involve the concept of art—while humbler philosophical spadework on the senses remains neglected, and what must surely be prior questions remain unfaced.

I will explain in a moment why I avoid considering here whether the objects of tasting and smelling can be works of art. But first I must clarify the use of 'object' in these contexts. (1) The objects which are my concern are particular or individual *tastes* or *smells*, or combinations or sequences of these. I am not discussing (2) those objects or stuffs or substances that have the tastes or smells, things as various as tobacco, pork pies, daffodils, wines, or bottled perfumes. In this use of 'object' there are objects without taste or smell. Tastes and smells can be as various as the things that have them, the taste of garlic, peaches, or coffee, the smell of hay, seaweed, or cow dung. Also, (3) since by tastes and smells I mean the internal objects, not the causes, of experiences, smells are not airborne collections of molecules that exhale from substances, occupy rooms, or drift across fields; nor are tastes saliva-borne substances that linger in the mouth, solutions that can lose or change their aroma or flavour. The taste of honey and the smell of garlic neither travel, linger, nor fade. These are objects in a wholly abstract sense.[1]

My reason for not considering whether tastes or smells can be works of art (in the technical sense in which some writers on aesthetics use this expression) is that the notion of art involves various controversial complexities, and adds difficulties it is needless to tangle with if they can be avoided, but which writers on these topics tend to plunge into too precipitately and prematurely. For first, it is generally accepted that works of art must be artefacts, or at least things artefactualized in greater or lesser degree by deliberate human intervention; it is often held also that they must be products of some specific or general intention, e.g. that they should be intended for aesthetic consideration or appraisal or satisfaction. But it would seem that, if aesthetic questions can be raised, they can be raised both about natural, i.e. non-artefactual, tastes and smells—eg. of newly mown grass, wild flowers and fruits, tree resin, volcanic spring water (though tastes or smells of deliberately developed and cultivated odoriferous plants, flowers, fruits, or vegetables might be considered artefacts or quasi-artefacts)—and about artefacts or byproducts of human activity produced with no thought for any aesthetic interest their taste or smell might possess—aviation fuel, methylated spirit, or Charles Lamb's roast pork (there is an obvious analogy here with many primarily utilitarian objects, from neolithic pots and tools to buildings, cars, or kitchen ware).

There is no reason therefore to confine attention to those pure artefacts that we devise wholly or largely for their taste or smell—wines, spirits, perfumes, Christmas puddings, etc.—and we can bypass all the familiar ques-

---

[1] Osborne confuses my first kind of (abstract) object and this third sense. He says, 'Strictly speaking only visual or tactile sensations have the quality of localization but we can speak of the localization of smells . . . in a secondary sense to indicate association with some spatially oriented object or region which is regarded as their source . . .' and 'although smells persist through time, they do not continue unchanged' (Harold Osborne, 'Odours and Appreciation', *The British Journal of Aesthetics*, 17 (1977), 43). All this is false about smells, tastes—and colours—in the sense relevant here.

tions about whether to admit quasi-artefacts and objects produced without aesthetic intention as art-works. To put it another way, if 'work of art' is primarily the concept of something put forward for appreciation, as perhaps it is, the concepts 'taste' and 'smell' are certainly not (though 'perfume', 'aroma', and 'flavour' may sometimes be); but there is no obvious reason why things may not be capable of appreciation even though not created or offered for appreciation. So I put aside as avoidable all questions about whether tastes, smells, and objects with, or of interest mainly because of, their taste or smell are, or might be, works of art in virtue of these qualities, so as to avoid the above kinds of disputes, whether substantial or terminological.

Some might raise, I suppose, an objection to my procedure, namely, those who view the concept of the aesthetic as logically dependent on and derivative from that of art, and see aesthetic appreciation of nature as parasitic upon the appreciation and value of art, aesthetic appreciation of it being dependent perhaps on treating or regarding nature as art—a view enjoying a considerable current vogue. For example, Antony Savile writes: 'beauty in art needs to be seen as conceptually prior to natural beauty'[2], and 'when we judge of a person's or a flower's beauty we are judging them within . . . canons that we develop from our acquaintance with the arts'.[3] But even if this position were defensible, which I doubt,[4] it need not invalidate my approach to tastes and smells; we could still allow that any aesthetic appreciation we may have for them is something that requires our prior possession of a concept of, and acquaintance with, art-works and other aesthetically significant artefacts. And, moreover, it would have to be shown already—and this is part of what is at issue—that artefacts like perfumes or wines logically cannot be created, or offered, and sometimes successfully, for aesthetic interest and satisfaction; for, unless this is shown, the creation of such artefacts as perfumes and wines might qualify as the arts in virtue of, and dependent on, which we may proceed to aesthetic appreciation of purely natural tastes and smells.

My inquiry, then, bypasses all questions about art. It will focus on whether particular tastes and smells can be objects of aesthetic interest, appreciation, satisfaction, and value, and consequently also on whether objects like flowers, fruits, wines or foods, which have tastes or smells, can be of aesthetic interest in virtue of their tastes and smells. For it seems plausible that, if either the main or

[2] Antony Savile, *The Test of Time: An Essay in Philosophical Aesthetics*, Oxford: Clarendon Press, 1982, p. xi.

[3] Ibid. 181.

[4] There are arguments enough running in the opposite direction. For Kant, the imitated birdsong is inferior to a real one; cf. also recent discussions of plastic trees. See also R. W. Hepburn's 'Contemporary Aesthetics and the Neglect of Natural Beauty', in B. Williams and A. Montefiore (eds.), *British Analytical Philosophy*, London: Routledge, 1966. By parity of reasoning, artificially produced chemical tastes and perfumes would not be comparable aesthetically with tastes of real fruit or scents of real flowers.

one significant interest and value that art-works aspire to is aesthetic (whether or not it is thought that other interests and values may be as important, or even that some things may excel as works of art without aesthetic interest or value), this must be because the elements of which they are constructed, in some cases combinations of colours and shapes, in others sounds, are capable of having, in however minimal or rudimentary a way, aesthetic interest and value. For the same reason, it seems that the question whether tastes and smells are possible objects for aesthetics should precede questions about whether they can be (the possibly principal) aesthetically valuable components of works of art.

This direction of approach, I said, seems plausible. But it may not be the only, or even the most sensible, approach. It would not be obviously absurd to hold, instead, that particular lines, shapes, colours have no aesthetic interest until incorporated into relatively complex combinations. But the claim would have to mean *no* interest; to allow even minimal interest would be capitulation. (Nor need even this severe view make art the first target to approach, if non-artefact complexes of line, colour, and shape, e.g. human faces and figures, animals, flowers, etc. are independently capable of providing aesthetic delight, or disappointment.)

A more serious objection to my inquiry is that it could hardly proceed without some concept of the aesthetic, some notion of what is and what is not an aesthetic matter or concern or interest. But this is not something I set out with; it is something I hope to illuminate. For while the primary but lesser topic of this paper is an investigation of the neglected aspects and features of tastes and smells, and with it the question, interesting in itself, whether they can be objects of aesthetic interest, the secondary but larger aim is precisely to try, via tastes and smells, to discover where people draw the boundaries of the aesthetic, what conditions they regard, or might stipulate or choose to regard, as relevant, necessary, or sufficient for anything to be a possible object of aesthetic interest or value. In that way I hope to throw light on the nature, character, essence, domain, boundaries, or limits of the aesthetic. The strategy should be obvious. If some thinkers hold that smells and tastes cannot have aesthetic qualities or be capable of aesthetic appreciation, but only of sensuous pleasure or distaste, we need to ask why and how they suppose they differ from colours, shapes, sounds, and words. If others hold that smells and tastes are admissible to aesthetics, even if only peripherally, we need to ask why they think this. But there is a limited number of explanations of such disagreement. If both sides have fully considered, understand, and agree what tastes and smells are like, they must differ in what they deem necessary, sufficient, or crucial for aesthetics, some finding that tastes and smells fail these demands, others that they meet them. Alternatively, they could differ about the nature of tastes and smells, while agreeing on the demands of the aesthetic. But if they differ about the nature of tastes and smells, one side or the other must be mistaken in ways we should be able to discover; in which case, either someone must change opinion about allowing or excluding them, or they do want, after all, to sustain differing criteria for admission or exclusion.

Hence, by examining tastes and smells, and displaying what features they have or lack, we may throw light on the larger questions whether there are different and conflicting, wider and narrower, conceptions of the domain of aesthetics, what they are, and why. For this purpose, I believe discussion of tastes and smells, about the admissibility of which aestheticians differ, should prove rewarding by throwing underlying differences about criteria of the aesthetic into high relief. But I return to this larger question only later, after a more detailed consideration of tastes and smells. I shall regard any illumination of varying concepts of the *aesthetic* as enough; I shall not attempt a similar examination of the *sensuous* for those who relegate our interest in tastes and smells to that domain.

I shall illustrate the sharp differences of opinion I have mentioned only briefly here. On the one hand, to instance only recent writers, Roger Scruton claims it to be a fact that 'not every "sense" lends itself to aesthetic pleasure'; but the claim seems to be buttressed by a combination of unsupported assertion and appeals to authority and tradition, rather than by any convincing argument: 'Now it is difficult to describe the difference here, between vision and hearing on the one hand, and taste, smell, and perhaps even touch, on the other. But *the fact in question is clear enough*, and has been noticed by philosophers from Aquinas to the present day.'[5] Again, 'it seems that only the senses of sound and sight *can* be involved in aesthetic appreciation . . . Hegel argued that the senses of taste and smell cannot embody sufficient of the intellect to be involved in the appreciation of art. In this he was repeating Aquinas who argued that . . . the perception of beauty, being contemplative, is only associated with the more cognitive senses, namely, sight and hearing'. In our aesthetic perception of anything 'we attach a concept . . .' and 'It is extremely interesting if the important part of aesthetic interest—the imaginative involvement that is its principal value—should be absent or attenuated in the case of taste and smell. But it is difficult to give a fully satisfying explanation of why this is so.'[6] (The references to Aquinas and Hegel are the only ones given; and, as I have said, the argument must claim absence, not mere attenuation of interest.) But I believe much more than is offered would be needed to explain why it is so; indeed, to me, *pace* Aquinas and Hegel, 'the fact in question' seems so far from clear as perhaps to be not a fact at all. Perhaps the differences are 'difficult to describe' because they do not exist, or at least are not differences such that 'there is no such thing' in the case of taste and smell as there is in that of vision and hearing.

[5] Roger Scruton, *The Aesthetics of Architecture*, London: Methuen, 1979, 113–14 (my italics).

[6] Roger Scruton, *Art and Imagination: A Study in the Philosophy of Mind*, London: Methuen, 1974, 156.

Harold Osborne, by contrast, asserts that 'There is no difference in principle between attending to the sensory nature of a smell and enjoying good tone in musical performance or colour in painting',[7] while another writer is prepared to say that 'Artistically, . . . gastronomy . . . requires intuition, imagination, enthusiasm, and an immense amount of organisational skill'.[8] Most striking perhaps is Urmson's remark, offering a clear, if simple, paradigm of the aesthetic: 'If we examine, then, some very simple cases of aesthetic evaluation . . . the grounds given are frequently the way the object appraised looks (shape and colour), the way it sounds, *smells, tastes*, or feels . . . if I value [a] rose aesthetically the most obvious relevant grounds will be the way it smells . . . these grounds seem to me really basic'.[9]

I believe a sufficiently close examination of taste and smell has hitherto been lacking and, though there has sometimes been a show of argument, most of the arguments deployed are too careless, or unclear, with too great a willingness to appeal to some authority, or alleged consensus, or supposed obvious fact. There has often also been a kind of puritanical or high-minded metaphysics or morality at work marking off the so-called higher interests and pleasures from the so-called lower and more animal ones which, as an initial *parti pris*, may have inhibited serious philosophical inquiry in these 'baser' matters. There is also probably a more respectable/justifiable reason for philosophical neglect. Even if tastes and smells are possible objects of aesthetic interest and delight, their importance is no doubt minor, even, some might think, necessarily trifling; and probably even someone who saw them as simple paradigms would be prepared to allow that, in aesthetic value, the finest perfume or wine is not to be compared with that of the greatest art. Urmson himself says, for example, 'it is tempting to consider the aesthetic as an isolated matter and within the field of aesthetics to concentrate unduly upon the most sublime and intense of our experiences',[10] rather as in ethics it is tempting to concentrate unduly upon the saintly and the fiendish. But that is no better reason for totally excluding taste and smell from aesthetics than for excluding, within literature, the probably slight aesthetic value of even the best of limericks.

The question I raise about tastes and smells is whether they are, as such, objects that, because of their very nature, are totally, irretrievably, excluded from the realm of aesthetics, and what arguments, if any, may be employed, *when we have examined* tastes and smells more thoroughly, so to exclude

[7] Osborne, 'Odours and Appreciation', 41.

[8] Peter Collins, *Changing Ideals in Modern Architecture 1750–1950*, London: Faber and Faber, 1965, 168.

[9] J. O. Urmson, 'What Makes a Situation Aesthetic?', *Proceedings of the Aristotelian Society*, Supplementary Vol. 31, 1957, 88. My italics.

[10] ibid. 76.

them. I shall try to question whether they do necessarily lack those features that would make eligible: whether they are ineligible in such a way that *no* aesthetic judgements or descriptions of them, positive, negative, or neutral are possible. More widely, I think it would be of interest to question whether there are any modes of our experience, pain and other bodily sensations included, from which an aesthetic interest is necessarily excluded.

II

I have said my concern is with tastes and smells themselves, in the abstract sense, not with substances or molecular clouds or solutions. But this needs some further explanation. Physiologically much of what we commonly call tasting counts as smelling. Physiologists define a sense by receptors; smell or odour or aroma is defined by the chemo-receptors in the upper nasal cavity and the olfactory nerve, taste or flavour by taste-buds in the mouth and tongue. Smells are determined by volatile components borne by air (for humans) to the nasal membranes, tastes by soluble components via saliva to the taste-buds. Taste, by these criteria, is a relatively minor sense for distinguishing solutions; smell is a dual sense for sniffing air and savouring by mouth and therefore much that goes in via mouth is perceived by nasal receptors i.e. much ordinarily thought of as taste is, physiologically, smell. The human nose is a much more sensitive detector than the tongue and by these criteria we can distinguish a relatively large number of scents and relatively few tastes.[11] However, in this paper I shall mean by 'taste' and 'smell' what we commonly mean: tastes are what we might be aware of via the mouth, and smells what we are aware of in using the nose even with the mouth shut. In this I follow J. J. Gibson, who defines taste and smell by function, smell by breathing and the nose, taste by eating, drinking and the mouth; thus taste covers both soluble and volatile components of food perceived together.[12]

It is true that human beings have limited sensitivity and powers of differentiation for smells compared with, say, dogs, who can pick out the specific odour of one person from a mixture of many more concentrated smells. Nevertheless, within the limits of human sensitivity, most people can discriminate and many can be trained to discriminate a very large number of subtly

[11] A standard experiment from Titchener's day shows that when the nose is held closed, the tastes of apple, onion and raw potato cannot be distinguished. See E. B. Titchener, *Experimental Psychology, A Manual of Laboratory Practice*, i, 67; ii, 105 f. London: Macmillan, 1906.

[12] J. J. Gibson, *The Senses Considered as Perceptual Systems*, London: Allen and Unwin, 1968; Ch. VIII 'Tasting and Smelling as Perceptual Systems'.

different tastes and smells, as do tea- and wine-tasters and perfumiers. One further note: many of the qualities perceived and discriminated via mouth and tongue are not for my purposes strictly tastes, though we ordinarily include them as part of the taste of something, and sometimes indeed there is no sharp demarcation. For instance, we perceive via mouth and tongue warmth and cold and also tactile and textural qualities, crumbly, chewy, crunchy, oily, sticky, hard, soft, thick, thin, more or less liquid or solid. Physiologists often speak of these as mechanical or haptic information. I exclude these qualities from consideration. I also exclude bodily sensations in the tongue, mouth, the nose, e.g. tingling from ginger or pepper, itching or tickling from snuff—and indeed the sensation of heat from strong peppermint (which is not temperature).

I next want to distinguish between particular or individual and generic tastes and smells. A generic taste or smell is a sort or classification, within which distinctions can be made, e.g. the taste of honey (not all honeys taste alike), the smell of new-mown hay, the taste of rum punch or red Bordeaux, even, more narrowly, the taste of Chateau La Tour. A particular taste or smell is e.g. the taste of *this* glass of wine, here, now, at a given temperature, the smell of *this* new-mown hay, here, now, and so on. (And *the* taste or smell *of* such things is how they taste to normal persons in normal circumstances, i.e. not while smoking or suffering from a cold, when they may taste different.) Anything with a particular taste has the very same taste as, and is indistinguishable from, any other thing with that particular taste; not so necessarily with two things with the same generic taste.[13] Nevertheless, for convenience and brevity, though I wish throughout to discuss particular tastes and smells, I shall speak loosely of the taste of watermelon or anchovies, the smell of tar, or pipe tobacco. I am not sure whether some nameable tastes are generic or particular, e.g. the taste of salt, smell of sulphuretted hydrogen, smell of Chanel No. 5, taste of Johnnie Walker Black Label; it depends whether all samples of e.g. salt (rock salt, sea salt) etc. have the very same taste or not. Manufacturers of brands of drinks and perfumes aim at precisely this.

Considering now only particular tastes and smells, I next make a distinction between single and mixed or combined tastes or smells. This, as we shall see, is not wholly straightforward, and as it is seldom attempted I confess I am not convinced I can get it right. But it is my first move in the attempt to investigate the complexities inherent in tastes and smells. For one of my aims throughout is to consider, and question, a familiar traditional view that tastes and smells (and sometimes elements in other sense modalities, like single

---

[13] By 'the very same taste' I am prepared to mean indistinguishable within limits of human (not canine) perceptivity—and of the humans we are at any point dealing with, allowing that some groups or tribes might have, or have developed, greater discriminatory (but not necessarily descriptive) powers than others.

notes) are simple, contain either no complexity, or too little, or inappropriate kinds of complexity to be possible objects of aesthetic interest at all. (I repeat: I am not concerned with claims that they may have only slight or minimal interest or value.)

By a single taste, and the same will go for smells (I deliberately avoid 'simple' here), I mean a taste that does not contain, is not composed of, or separable into, different tastes that could occur in isolation. An example might be the taste of refined white sugar or the taste of salt.

By a mixed taste, or a blend or combination or aggregation of tastes, I mean a taste which is the resultant of two or more different tastes that could occur in isolation. A straightforward example might be the taste of a solution—two coexistent tastes—of salt and chlorine in slightly chlorinated water.

I will ignore one dimension of complexity—weakness or strength in the sense of greater or lesser dilution. To strengthen or dilute a solution of salt and water, or of salt and chlorine in fixed proportions, does not add or remove an extra taste—assuming the water to be tasteless—and hence I shall treat the result as the *same* taste, but stronger or weaker; similarly with watered wine, diluted cigar smoke, a distant note on a clarinet (same pitch and timbre), ignoring volume. It must be noted however that greater or less strength or volume can sometimes make significant differences of various sorts—too much peppermint is hot, more pepper stings the tongue, and a note differently blown may have more harmonics and so have a different particular quality.

But there are further complexities and unclarities about the notion of a mixed taste. First, I called it the resultant of two or more different and separable component tastes. This need not mean that one can discern two or more tastes, let alone identify or name them; one might not realize that a taste was a combination of tastes that could exist separately. Often it is easy to tell, as with salt and chlorinated water; often one can have a good idea, as when one tries to distinguish the ingredient tastes, say, in punch: rum, lemon, sugar, cinnamon, etc. and when, mixing punch, one decides that the taste one wants requires a little more of this or that. But often it is virtually impossible, as with some subtly concocted liqueurs, to distinguish any or many of the combined tastes.

Secondly, note that I referred only to different component tastes, not substances. It is contingently possible that two or more (chemical) substances might have an identical taste (just as two or more substances might have an identical colour)—presumably the case with some 'artificial' flavours and sweeteners. (If tastes depend on molecular shapes, two substances might have similar enough molecular shapes to provide indistinguishable tastes.)

Thirdly, by speaking of the resultant taste of a mixture or blend as the outcome of separably existent *tastes* I do not mean a supervenient taste resulting from a chemical reaction between or compound of two or more substances.[14] In such cases any of the component substances might have no taste, or different tastes when separately existent which, *as tastes*, are not contributory to the resultant new taste (as compounds of chlorine and sodium, or sulphur and hydrogen—a quite different matter from weak flavours being wholly swamped or masked or ineffective in mixture).

Fourthly, about mixtures or blends (as contrasted with compounds) there are some puzzling questions one might raise. Sometimes two or more tastes, when combined, may produce a new taste which does not seem merely to combine side by side with the original tastes. Some combinations, e.g. wine and cheese, almonds and raisins, seem to me to produce such new 'supervenient' tastes. Yet in logic it would seem that a taste either must be the result of contributions of separate tastes where by varying the proportions of ingredient tastes, say, wine and cheese, one or the other would become discernibly predominant, as in mixing punch, or must be the outcome of a chemical reaction of substances. Which of these may be true in particular cases where there are some apparently quite new resultant tastes I do not know.

The fifth and most puzzling point. I offered the tastes of sugar and salt (sweetness and saltiness) as discernibly single tastes. Writers on tastes, interestingly, usually offer a short list of basic or primary or fundamental tastes; they usually include, along with sweet and salt, bitter, sour, and sometimes others, acid, fragrant etc. Similarly they offer short lists of basic smells. But it is not clear to me that bitter, sour, acid, etc., while descriptive of tastes, are themselves tastes. I am not sure that anything could taste simply and solely bitter or sour (as opposed to being the taste of sour milk or sour apple etc.), in the way that something can taste simply sweet or salt. Yet it is tempting to suppose that there must be some single tastes; that not every taste could be concocted by adjusting amounts of other tastes in combination (how conceivably could sweetness be produced by combining distinguishable ingredient flavours?). Moreover, it seems to me that there probably are many, not just a very few, single tastes. With my punch or mixed drinks examples, the resultant taste is clearly a combination of ingredient flavours in varying proportions, each contributing to the resultant. But there seem to be other tastes, whether of natural or of artificially synthesized substances (which may or may not duplicate and substitute for natural flavours) which it is hard to conceive of as composed or constructible additively from separately existing tastes. Consider the tastes of some of the following: ripe mangoes, fresh figs, lemon, canteloupe, raspberries, coconut, green olives, ripe persimmon, onion, caraway, parsnip, peppermint, aniseed, cinnamon, fresh salmon, pepper, mint

---

[14] 'The properties of a mixture are an aggregate of the properties of the constituents, whereas a compound has individual properties, often quite unlike those of the component elements' (*A Dictionary of Science,* ed. E. B. Uvarov and D. R. Chapman, 3rd edn. rev. Alan Isaacs, Harmondsworth, Penguin Books, 1964).

(and for smells, burning leaves, mould, lavender, heated vinegar, etc.). Are these mixtures of separate tastes, and if so of which? I cannot think of a plausible answer. To maintain that some at least of them are (or even must be) mixtures or blends one might take either of two routes. First, one might suppose them to be mixtures of so many ingredient flavours that, as with some liqueurs, we cannot in fact discern or guess the components—a failure of discrimination, and perhaps of experience and imagination—though theoretically the case might be provable if someone could mix substances with discernibly different flavours to give an identical resultant flavour within which one could now discern the distinct flavours. Secondly, it might be that we cannot discriminate separate elements in these tastes because, though mixtures, they are combinations of single tastes we never encounter in isolation in any substances we come across; perhaps a mixture of natural flavours no one has yet encountered, or artificial flavours not yet invented, would yield these familiar tastes. Both suggestions may have some plausibility. But with the second, it is difficult to imagine or conceive what these so far unexperienced single tastes might be—a consideration presumably not in itself conclusive; and with the first—though again this may not be conclusive—it does not seem possible, at least with some of the familiar tastes mentioned, e.g. mint or lemon, that they should be mixtures or blends of other tastes. Coconut may be somewhat sweet, and lemon sour or acid, but what other tastes combine with sweetness to give coconut, or with sourness or acidity to give lemon? How could one construct a blend of distinguishable tastes—I do not mean an artificial substance of identical flavour—to yield that of coconut, or lemon, or mint? Try to imagine a recipe: 'To make the flavour of onion (or pepper, or raspberries, or olives), add the following flavours (*not* substances) in the following proportions . . .'. So not only would it seem that some tastes are single, the way saltiness and sweetness are, but also, though it may be a failure of knowledge, experience, or imagination, that there must be quite a large number of single flavours which either are, or are needed to produce, the many familiar tastes I have mentioned. Neither the brevity nor the mixed bag of kinds of so-called basic flavours of the official lists seems to me adequate or acceptable. And all I have said applies equally, *pari passu*, with smells.[15]

I have proposed the distinction, Single and Mixed, with, as possible examples of single tastes, cinnamon, coconut, peppermint, lemon, etc. I have deliberately used 'single' (for unmixed) where traditionally 'simple' might have

---

[15] The flavour cube proposed by Henning, as reported by Gibson, *Senses Considered*, 149, may locate flavours along dimensions from sweet to sour, sour to spicy etc.—nor do I see that a multidimensional ordering of flavours is impossible—but this does not imply that a particular flavour, say marjoram, which might differ little from its next-door neighbours, is a combination of other flavours, i.e. it is not merely a slightly sourer version of its neighbour: it is a different flavour. The same is true with e.g. Henning's 'smell prism'.

been used. I am reserving 'simple' and 'complex' for descriptions and I propose to say that some tastes and smells are capable of more or less simple or complex descriptions (I do not speak of simple or complex tastes/smells).

Mixed tastes or smells would certainly seem capable of complex descriptions for at least the reason that they have potentially discernible and so nameable or describable ingredient flavours or odours ('a taste of rum or lemon with sweetening', or 'a mixed smell of burnt onion and hot vinegar', etc.). But it also seems to me, though without total assurance, that many and perhaps all single flavours (even the taste of sugar and salt) are capable of some degree of complex description, i.e. none is wholly or totally simple. It may be that tastes and smells lack dimensions in the way particular colours have hue, saturation, and intensity, but this does not mean they have no complexity that is discernible, any more than hues lack complex describability. Wholly simple qualities (as opposed to single qualities) are a figment. This is not to deny the matter may be one of degree; single tastes and smells (e.g. salt or chlorine) may be capable of relatively simple descriptions only—at least if language remains reasonably 'literal'. But if at least some tastes and smells I have mentioned are singles (lemon, coconut, thyme, etc.)—and I suggested there may well be a large number of singles though they may be tastes and smells of chemical substances met, if at all, in laboratory samples rather than common plants and substances—descriptions of them could be relatively complex, and perhaps very complex indeed; the taste of lemon is light, fresh, clean, sharp, biting, acidic, and fruity, but it has a sharpness and bite that ripe oranges do not have (let alone fresh milk).[16]

I now postpone fuller consideration of the description and characterization of tastes and smells till later. But in anticipation I should scotch certain objections that are regularly resurrected when description of sensory qualities (and various other things) is discussed. They emerge in the familiar cry that traditionally so-called simple qualities (which would include tastes and smells) cannot be either defined or described, or at least 'fully described'. And indeed it may be true that the range of literal descriptive vocabulary for tastes and smells in particular is restricted, even fairly meagre, though there is no very obvious border where the literal crosses over into the non-literal, after which restrictions disappear. But how, people ask, can the taste of coconut or caraway or aniseed be described? The task is not merely difficult through poverty of vocabulary, but impossible. But this lament is absurd in whichever of two ways it is taken. If the desire is for a complete description, a totally determinate verbal characterization so that, if any other smell or taste fits the description it will be a particular identical with the particular described, that

---

[16] Contrast Scruton, *Art and Imagination*, 156: 'We are able to discern an enormous number of features of an object on the basis of just one visual or auditory impression . . . to recognise the taste of something is to recognise only one feature of it'.

ideal is an *ignis fatuus*, not merely with tastes and smells, but with colours, sounds, timbres, and most shapes (though in each case we may be able to either name the particular, e.g. the colour British Standard Colour No. . . , the smell of sulphuretted hydrogen, the taste of citric acid, or refer to it as, e.g., the taste of this liquid (cf. the colour of this drop of blood etc.). Moreover, with almost everything else, particular faces, facial expressions, a person's mien, gait, smile, gesture, the distinctive Gestalt or silhouette or shape of particular persons or animals, clouds or trees, no description of any such thing will 'describe it completely' so that the description fits only others that are wholly indistinguishable from it. No heaping of adjectives, literal or other, can succeed. Have you ever tried to describe 'fully and exactly', using as wide a vocabulary as you like, a face, a facial expression, a simple drawing, a piece of music, a poem, or even a thistle or a gatepost? How far do Shakespeare, Dickens or the finest writers either try or succeed? Nor similarly will any verbal account, notational system, or music score exactly describe a particular musical performance. Once this impossible demand is exposed, we see the possibility that any taste or smell, even single ones, may be complex to the extent that, albeit with effort (for most of us are unpractised in attempting it), it can be correctly or aptly characterized though not 'completely' or 'uniquely' by an indefinitely extensive number of adjectival expressions, though not necessarily 'literal'.[17]

The other form of despairing cry is equally absurd. It is that no words, no description of tastes and smells can provide the experience of that taste or smell, can 'communicate' it, in Locke's words 'give . . . the taste', or, ambiguously, make you have 'any true idea of the relish' of it (where 'idea' means, not the concept, nor a definition, but an 'idea of sensation' i.e. an experience).[18]

It is not obvious that there is a difference, except perhaps of degree, between the possibility of verbal description of tastes and smells and most things visible, audible, or tangible. 'Communicating' pain or other bodily sensations, or electric shocks, or moods, etc., though alleged to be impossible, is no different.

[17] See J. Wesphal on the alleged impossibility of describing colours etc.: to the suggestion that a port-sipper cannot describe its taste, Wesphal says, 'Perhaps he hasn't given the matter much thought, he is not professional wine-taster . . .', etc. (Jonathan Westphal, 'The Complexity of Quality', *Philosophy*, 59 (1984), 459.

[18] 'For Words being Sounds, can produce in us no other simple *Ideas* than of those very Sounds . . . He that thinks otherwise, let him try if any Words can give him the taste of a Pineapple, and make him have any true *Idea* of the Relish of that celebrated delicious fruit' (J. Locke, *An Essay concerning Human Understanding*, ed. P. H. Nidditch, Oxford: Clarendon Press, 1975; book III, ch. IV, sect. 11). As Westphal, who cites this passage, says, 'Definitions [and, we may add, descriptions] do not give things, they are of things', ('complexity', 464). Hence the schoolboy clutching his chocolate bar and the port-sipper alike may be told 'Don't just talk about it —let's have a taste'.

For now I leave the matter there. It seems plausible that there are single smells and tastes as well as mixtures or blends, some, but perhaps not all, of which a person with requisite practice and knowledge can perceive and identify as mixtures; and that while of some single smells and tastes anything more than a fairly simple description may be difficult without faring beyond obviously literal uses of language, others will allow of quite complex descriptions.

III

I now turn to the facts and features of tastes and smells and to various claims and allegations adduced to cast doubt on their suitability as possible objects for aesthetics. First the allegation that they are 'lower' senses. Questions here are what precisely is meant by the claim, whether they *are* lower senses in ways sight and hearing are not, and whether, if it is true, it disqualifies them from aesthetics. I shall suggest ways this might be taken, though proponents seldom distinguish or set them out. 'Lower' seems to be understood as 'merely bodily', 'purely physical', or 'animal'. It cannot mean that smelling and tasting require bodily organs or that tastes and smells are closely associated with parts of bodies in ways colour, shape, and sound are not; the other senses have organs, and faces, bodies, eyes, skin, and mouths have colour, shape, and texture; and vocal cords make noises. The supposition that smells and tastes, but not colours or sounds, occur only in association with 'distasteful' parts or functions of the body, particularly those shared with animals, organs of feeding, digestion, elimination, and sex, functions of eating, drinking, sweating, defecating, urinating, and their products is absurd; such organs, functions, and products all have their colours, shapes, and sounds. It is not even that all bodily tastes and smells are distasteful, if we can talk of sweet breath and honeyed kisses. The best-seeming move fares no better, that certain specific tastes and smells occur only with bodily and animal functions, for the same is true of sights and sounds characteristic of vomiting, moaning, screaming, coughing, sneezing. Even if true this would be at most a contingent matter; the smell of sulphuretted hydrogen might have been found only in volcanic areas or in laboratories if we had no experience of rotten eggs. It is in any case not even true: diverse substances including some foods and plants actually have smells (and tastes?) similar to, even indistinguishable from, many body odours. But there are innumerable tastes and smells without any bodily or animal connections or associations.

A different argument sometimes offered proposes that in smelling and tasting our attention is primarily on the sensing organ or, secondly, on physical sensations in the organ. This has little force. When smelling or tasting something, one's attention is sometimes drawn to the nose or mouth or to bodily sensations in them, tingling or stinging from hot spices or acrid smoke; but we get dazzle, stinging, pain, and sensations of strain in the eyes and ears too. Usually we are not aware of such bodily sensations but of the tastes or smells themselves. We may when tasting hot spices or pepper, but not with tea or orange juice.

Another group of arguments connected with the view that taste and smell are lower senses is indicated in Scruton's words, '. . . in tasting, both the object and the desire for it are steadily consumed' whereas 'No such thing is true of aesthetic attention'.[19] Consider 'object' first. If this is taken to mean either the object with the taste or smell (the soup or the toilet water), or the taste or smell itself, considered scientifically, since some molecules stay in the mouth or nose after tasting or smelling, it is true. Not all the molecules are *in fact* returned to the soup plate or perfume bottle by any amount of spitting or blowing. Taken less strictly, soup, like wine can be spat out, *not* consumed by tasting; people who sniff a perfume are not 'consuming' it, i.e. using it up, as is the person who sprinkles it on his body. But these are contingent matters; touching things also 'consumes' them if that means that particles, though not taken into the body, are lost; similarly it is a contingent fact only that looking at or listening to things does not consume them. But all such arguments are irrelevant and misconceived. They confuse senses of 'object' I distinguished earlier. To talk in the relevant way about the taste of liquorice or the smell of apples is not to talk of something that can be consumed or used up. We consume stuffs, not tastes or smells, even if all the liquorice and all the apples are consumed. In the sense that interests us, smells and tastes, their character and quality (including any aesthetically appreciable quality), are no more consumed or destroyed than the colour scarlet is destroyed or consumed or fades when scarlet paint or pigment is used up or fades. To talk about the character of a taste or smell is no more talking about sticks of liquorice or bowls of apples than to talk about the character of a colour is talking about faces or plants or pigments.[20]

What of the claim that in tasting and smelling the *desire* for the object is consumed? Again, 'object' may be taken either way. It might mean that in tasting or smelling we soon want no more of the soup or the wine; we become satiated, full, have had enough of the *stuff* (though we might be far from tired of the taste or smell). Alternatively 'desire for the object is consumed' might mean that we tire of, have had enough of, the taste or smell itself, not the stuff, as a perfume-sniffer or tea-taster might become utterly tired of this taste or that smell (this may be what Scruton means by 'desire for the experience' being consumed). Both possibilities are different again from being tired of the

---

[19] *The Aesthetics of Architecture*, 114.
[20] Even if we *can* be thought of as consuming taste or smell, it is the character of the taste or smell as and while it exists that is of interest and perhaps to be aesthetically appreciated.

activity; one could get tired of *smelling* things or *tasting* things just as one gets tired of looking at or listening to things (another possible meaning of 'the experience of'). All these are irrelevant contingent points and they apply to all the senses and arts. Desires to look at various sights, including particular pictures, and to listen to various sounds, including pieces of music can wane and become satiated.[21]

Another general indictment of tastes and smells is that they 'do not sustain' aesthetic attention. This is multiply ambiguous. It can be interpreted to mean either (1) that they are contingently, or (2) that they are conceptually, unfitted to repay or reward aesthetic attention. Considerations of both sorts can be put forward to suggest that it is impossible for them to be 'contemplated' with the appropriate 'detachment' ('they do not lend themselves to detached contemplation').[22] The first is that they do not persist or last long enough (a different point from their being consumed). This argument is worthless for several reasons. They do quickly fade or change; but sounds also die away (some, like piano notes, cannot be indefinitely sustained), and so do many things that elicit aesthetic admiration. Sunsets fade, their colours and shapes change, firework displays are momentary, water colours fade, cave paintings deteriorate, an aesthetically striking pose changes if the model holding it tires. Works of art change, performances of music, dance, and mime are fleeting, some works are made to be self-destructive. One way to reply to this would be to develop Osborne's remark that 'length of time is not a criterion'.[23] We could say that it is the taste or smell *while and so long as it lasts unchanged* that is of interest, just as it may be a particular moment in a sunset or ballet performance that is of interest. Impermanence may prevent adequate intense attention to the 'object' before it ceases to exist, but this applies equally to many sights and sounds. It might be countered that we have no way of 'fixing' tastes and smells for prolonged study as we have photography and recordings for sights and sounds. Another group of arguments suggests that there cannot be adequate 'contemplation' because of physiological or psychological factors about us: that tastes and smells 'fade' until no longer perceived as the appropriate receptors become saturated and lose sensitivity (if true, a fact not dissimilar from what happens with vision where fading is overcome by rapid eye movements); or again, that even with tastes and smells that persist and to which we could pay attention, we cease to notice them because of sheer familiarity; but the same is true of sights and sounds, local traffic noise, ticking clocks, and our familiar surroundings, wallpaper, painting, even faces. But all these arguments

---

[21] Other ambiguities lurk here. To be tired of tasting and smelling might be to be tired of the 'activity', of doing something e.g. sniffing (cf. listening to or for, looking for or at), or tired of the 'passivity', of something inflicted (cf. hearing or seeing, having to hear or see).

[22] Beardsley, *Aesthetics: Problems in the Philosophy of Criticism*, New York: Harcourt Brace, 1958, 111.

[23] Osborne, 'Odours and Appreciation', 30.

are irrelevant. Even to reply that such difficulties may be overcome, and that we can return to savour tastes and smells, and take in what we would otherwise miss, if we can preserve them in stoppered bottles or by fixed brands, etc., just as we may with photos of changing skies, films, or recordings of performances, is to mistake the sense of tastes and smells that is of interest to us here; for in this sense they do not change, are not evanescent, and need no preserving.

A different group of arguments to deny the possibility of detached contemplation of tastes and smells, rests not on any kind of evanescence but on the claim that, as Beardsley puts it, 'The lower senses are utilitarian in function, and strongly connected with self-preservation so that they do not lend themselves to contemplation as colours and sounds do'.[24] Several interpretations of this suggest themselves, the simplest, that our interest is primarily in eating, drinking, getting on with satisfying hunger, slaking thirst, or whatever, and therefore not in smells and tastes themselves. Equally we might concentrate on concurrent activities, table conversation, and not notice the tastes and smells of food. We might even be totally unable to when getting some food down during a bombardment (cf. Ziff: 'Who could enjoy viewing Klee's *Twittering Machine* while being tortured?').[25] But none of this is always or necessarily true: often it is precisely our noticing the smell or taste that either persuades or dissuades us from eating or drinking, and sometimes actually eating or drinking may be the only way of fully relishing a taste or smell. Another interpretation, Beardsley's, is that these senses, being utilitarian and concerned with self-preservation—with practical knowledge acquisition—pass through to the object. Taste tells us that food is bad, or smell that the kitchen is on fire. But this need not be our only interest either, and anyway sound and vision are certainly practically important in similar ways.

Other arguments, if they can be called that, keep turning up that, oddly, run in the opposite direction, not that the 'lower senses' are too practical so that we pass through tastes and smells themselves to practical knowledge of things, but that they are not outgoing or 'cognitive' enough, too little involved with knowledge/intellect and understanding. A simple form of this argument is that they give us little information about the world, about things around us. Certainly taste, like touch, is not a distance sense, but smell is. But in fact both are vastly important as providers of information, as important as sight and touch and possibly more than sound; it is often knowledge of what is close, in contact, entering the body, that is vital. The rejoinder that for humans these senses are less discriminating than vision or hearing is open to question. They are less developed than in some animals, but so is our vision and hearing

---

[24] Beardsley, *Aesthetics*, 111.
[25] Paul Ziff, 'Anything Viewed', in E. Saarinen *et al.* (eds.), *Essays in Honour of Jaako Hintikka*, Dordrecht. Reidel, 1979, 133.

compared to that of some animals and birds. But cognitive power of these lower senses in humans should not be underrated. Our taste and smell are highly discriminating; we can distinguish a very large number of differences and the blind and deaf as well as specialists can develop discrimination to a high ability to learn about and recognize what is in our vicinity. All these involve mind, thought, understanding.[26]

But there is a more serious aspect than the utilitarian and practical arguments. Scruton's view echoed from Hegel and already quoted is that a cognitive element, the embodiment of 'sufficient of the intellect', is either inadequate or lacking for the purpose of aesthetic contemplation. He writes

> But not every 'sense' lends itself to aesthetic pleasure. The experience must be such that, in attending to it, one attends also to its object. In particular we should note how different in this respect are the eye and the ear from the other senses . . . . Visual experience is so essentially cognitive, so 'opened out', as it were on to the objective world, that our attention passes through and siezes its object to the exclusion of all impressions of sense.

By contrast, 'In tasting and smelling I contemplate not the object but the experience derived from it'.[27]

Superficially this sounds the exact opposite of Beardsley's objection that our attention with tasting and smelling 'passes through' to the object. But what Scruton means is hard to assess, being terminologically either careless or opaque. The unclarities lie in such expressions and contrasts as 'attending to the object' and 'attending to the experience' or 'attending to the experience derived from [the object]', and another pair of contrasting expressions he uses, 'savouring a visual impression' or 'savouring the sensation of red' and 'remaining incurious about its object' or 'remaining uninterested in the red thing one sees'. Now if these locutions are philosophers' terminology, and 'the experience [derived from the object]' and 'the sensation' referring, as I take them to, to the experienced taste, smell, or colour of an object and 'object' to that which has the taste, smell, or colour, I can see no significant difference between different senses. We can attend to and be interested in the colour or shape ('savour a visual impression') of a thing or equally to its taste or smell, as we do with peaches or perfumes. And we can do either without caring, or being interested in, what the thing is. 'What an unusual (lovely, awful) smell that thing has; I wonder what it is?' is no stranger than 'What a lovely blue, or unusual shape that thing is, but I don't know, or care, what it is'. But equally, as I've said, olfactory and gustatory senses can be 'cognitive' or 'opened out' to

---

[26] It is true that something different may be the case in lower animals (and also to some extent with us, especially as babies), where smell and taste may bypass the cortex and function simply as stimulus to response.

[27] This and all subsequent quotations in this paragraph are from Scruton, *The Aesthetics of Architecture*, 113–14.

the objective world, e.g. to find out if milk is sour, gas is leaking, fruit unripe, whether the 'object' is salt or sugar. If there is any argument of weight here, it eludes me.

There is one other aspect of the (usually fairly unspecific) claim that the senses under consideration are 'lower' because not 'cognitive' or 'intellectual' enough and are therefore inadmissible that I will mention here. This is (rather obscurely) that they cannot be endowed with meaning, used as a 'language' or means of communication to convey something that requires to be interpreted or understood. This is true in some respects. In a lesser and unimportant sense, that we cannot use tastes and smells as meaningful signs or signals, it is not true. We use them thus less frequently than visual and auditory ones (street-signs and air-raid sirens) because they are less static and more ephemeral (but so are smoke signals); but in some circumstances we can and do (smell is added to natural gas as a warning, just as colour is added to methylated spirits). The more relevant argument would be that tastes and smells cannot serve as a medium 'embodying meaning' in the way in which, in some sense, meaning or import may be inseparably embodied in concatenations of words, colours, or musical sounds; and if they cannot thus embody or express thought, emotion, or feeling, or function representationally there can be no question of understanding, interpretation, or criticism. Yet it is these possibilities, it is often held, that are essential to the aesthetic because essential to art, and are features which, however inaccurately, have led people to speak of music, painting, etc. as languages. To this there are several replies. First, one might question this currently fashionable and highly intellectualist view of art, a view according to which it is not sufficient to see art merely as the intentional outcome of an artist's activity, but to see appreciation as inseparable from understanding and interpretation. But must all aesthetic appreciation make this demand? Indeed, must all art, e.g. purely decorative friezes, non-representational mosaic floors, etc.? Secondly, even if requisite for all art, it is a demand with regard to aesthetic appreciation that would disqualify all natural phenomena from aesthetics. But, thirdly, it may be questioned whether tastes and smells are incapable of embodying 'meaning' or interpretable character, or whether it is simply that they cannot embrace sufficient of real human import—feeling, emotion, mood, or whatever—to qualify as aesthetic, whereas sounds and sights can. This question may receive its answer later, *ambulando*.

IV

I now turn to some rather different features of tastes and smells which are often held to debar them from aesthetics. Combinations of tastes or smells (and *a fortiori* single tastes or smells) are sometimes excluded on the ground that to be of aesthetic interest an object must exhibit patterning, structuring, or ordering of some kind, and that such forms of organization, possible with combinations of colours, or shapes, or sounds—or things seen or heard—are not possible with tastes and smells—or things tasted or smelled. Beardsley states it clearly: 'Some smells are certainly more pleasing than others. But there does not seem to be enough order within these sensory fields to construct aesthetic objects with balance, climax, development or pattern',[28] and again, musical tones are ordered, but whereas 'smells and tastes can of course be classified in certain ways . . . we cannot, at least not yet, arrange them in series and so cannot work out constructive principles to make larger works out of them'.[29] Of attempts to construct a 'scent-organ' he asks: 'How would you begin to look for systematic, repeatable, regular combinations that would be harmonious and enjoyable as complexes?', adding explicitly, 'This, and not the view that smell and taste are "lower senses" compared with sight and hearing seems to explain the absence of taste-symphonies and smell sonatas'.[30] It is noteworthy however, that whereas some writers allow that combinations of sights or sounds, even if unordered and unstructured in certain ways, might be of aesthetic interest (after all, sunsets, the ocean, cloud formations are complex but lack certain sorts of order and structure), and also allow that even single colours or sounds may be of minimal aesthetic interest, others who regard certain kinds of complexity of structure as essential anywhere (Beardsley is one) disallow any possibility of aesthetic interest to single qualities in any sense modality. Compare Beardsley's argument from 'lack of intrinsic order': 'Does a clear blue sky, a single note on a French horn, or a whiff of perfume constitute an aesthetic object? To say so would trivialize the concept'[31] (I don't know if 'trivialize' means he excludes them from the aesthetic, or thinks they can be of only trivial interest—limiting cases). Other writers are forthright. Sidney Zink, for example, contends that 'the perception of relations . . . is the essence of esthetic appreciation', and concludes that single colours, tastes, and smells are not possible objects of aesthetic appreciation.[32] Contrast Urmson's 'very simple cases of aesthetic evaluation': 'if I value the rose aesthetically the most obviously relevant grounds will be the way it looks, both in colour and shape, and the way it smells'.

Now unquestionably tastes and smells cannot exhibit some kinds of organization, structure, or ordering found most typically in certain art works. That shows at most that certain special kinds of structuring—and what kinds—are considered by some philosophers to be necessary in things of aesthetic interest.

---

[28] Beardsley, *Aesthetics*, 99.
[29] ibid. 98–9.
[30] ibid. 99.
[31] ibid. 89.
[32] Sidney Zink, 'Esthetic Appreciation and its Distinction from Sense Pleasure', *Journal of Philosophy*, 39, 1942, 705.

Without further arguments to clinch the necessity of such strict structuring, it shows little more than that; what other philosophers consider necessary or even sufficient in things of aesthetic interest might still be present in things with lesser structures, even perhaps in single tastes and smells—or for that matter, colours and sounds.

It could of course still be true that things exhibiting certain stricter kinds of ordering or structure, kinds impossible in concatenations of smells or tastes, or in single colours or sounds, might be of aesthetic interest in part because of these stricter orderings or structures. It might even be that such stricter structures are essential for an object to be of high aesthetic interest and value. Here I shall say only a little about kinds of order and structure. Clearly for some writers 'aesthetic objects' (as Beardsley calls them) must be bounded or framed if they are to have a suitable structure, and for some writers the object, whether requiring a boundary or not, must possess at least some heterogeneity, and, often, not merely heterogeneity, but some regularly ordered or patterned heterogeneity or design. Against this we can set the facts, first, that many natural phenomena widely regarded as having aesthetic interest, even splendour—sunrises, storms, expanses of sky and cloud, landscapes, mountain ranges—have no clear boundaries, or any obvious organization, order, structure, or pattern in their heterogeneity. Perhaps we 'find' or 'import' or impose or imagine order etc. in them, but if so why not with concatenations of tastes and smells? Secondly, we should remember that what constitutes a boundary is often largely a matter of convention or our own choice. Even paintings usually have a frame of chosen colour or material and further surrounding areas often deliberately chosen for colour and brightness.[33] A symphony is picked out as a bounded entity from surrounding sounds (the orchestra tuning); but a particular smell or taste can be too. A meal, considered as a combination and succession of tastes and smells, can have boundaries, limits, a beginning and end, and so some kind of self-contained totality. Thirdly, some works understandably called minimal but widely accepted as art, sometimes even as aesthetically significant art, exhibit a minimum of pattern, structure, or design, and sometimes little or no heterogeneity. Beardsley mentions Malevich's *White on White*,[34] 1918; Wollheim writes that one of Rothko's *Four Seasons* series is 'one of the sublimest creations of our time'.[35] Rothko later painted areas of almost uniform colour and Yves Klein produced wholly monochromatic canvases. Fourthly, Beardsley asks how

---

[33] 'A work of art is supposed to retain its identity from frame to frame wall to wall room to room: those who suffer from inept framers know how silly this view is. Seurat took care at times to prepare and paint his own frames. But he could do nothing about the walls floors company his works were forced to keep' (Ziff, 'Anything Viewed', 289).

[34] Beardsley, *Aesthetics*, 89.

[35] Richard Wollheim, *On Art and the Mind: Essays and Lectures*, London: Allen Lane, 1973, 128.

tastes and smells could be arranged so as to get 'systematic, repeatable, regular combinations'.[36] A rejoinder might be that repeatability and regular combinations are precisely what are aimed at—and who is to say they are not achieved?—by so-called classic dishes and menus. To quote one writer on architecture, 'The architectural theorists of the mid-eighteenth century tried to establish Classical recipes for good architecture in much the same say as the chefs of that period were trying to establish Classical recipes for haute cuisine'.[37] We can, intelligibly, say we want to have the same meal at so and so's restaurant as we enjoyed last year, or ask to have the same combination of dishes as last week. Nor, as far as systematic ordering is concerned, am I sure that any fundamental obstacle, as opposed to a great complexity of many dimensions, has ever been proved, against arranging tastes and smells analogously to the ordering of colours on a colour wheel.

Obviously there are differences between tastes and smells and objects of the other senses. Our senses of taste and smell may vary more from time to time and person to person; maybe they are less often in standard or optimum condition than our eyes and ears, whether because of hayfever, smoking, or things recently smelled or tasted. Perhaps these senses become saturated and we cease more quickly to notice or discriminate. For repeatability, it is more difficult to fix tastes, smells, or combinations of them: they are often fleeting (and not in the way musical notes may be). Whereas we can readily look again at a painting or listen again to a performance of a concerto, reproduction of tastes and smells for prolonged attention is not so readily possible; but skies too change, sunsets glow and fade, clouds shift. In some measure we can fix these by painting, or photography. Less easily with tastes and smells, but it is far from impossible: perfume, wine, spirit, and tobacco producers and blenders have ways of keeping their branded products constant over time. So, while admitting that some kinds of organization may be rarer or impossible with these two senses, it may in part be a matter more of degree than of kind; and if there are those who insist that aesthetics demands kinds of ordering and organization not attainable here, they must be prepared to exclude also some less complex art-works and many natural phenomena.

V

The last group of arguments was about combinations or aggregations of tastes or smells, not particular or individual ones. The remaining arguments apply equally to both. But I cannot proceed further without some comments on the

---

[36] Beardsley, Aesthetics, 99.
[37] Collins, Changing Ideals in Modern Architecture, 169.

notions of aesthetic interest, attention, and contemplation as I think they are generally employed and to which, at least here, I commit myself; for it is largely in relation to these that tastes and smells are often thought inadequate or wanting. In many theories that are in other respects very diverse there are two complementary halves. On one side is aesthetic interest, or attention, or appreciation—amplified variously as contemplation, expanded awareness or heightened awareness, imaginative perception, intuitive grasp, etc., often described as disinterested or detached. It is frequently held to involve an intellectual dimension, concepts, thought, understanding, imagination, and with this the possibility of correct and incorrect judgements and supporting reasoning; often it is held to involve liking, pleasure, satisfaction, thrills, or their opposites. On the other side, there is what contemplation, heightened awareness, imaginative perception, etc. are of, or what is liked or gives satisfaction, namely objects and their appearances, qualities, or characters. Putting the two halves together we get attention to the object, dwelling on, assessing its character 'for its own sake', out of interest in the character of the object alone or for any satisfaction therefrom and for no other reason.

But two versions of 'contemplation' or 'aesthetic attitude' need separate discussion, for some writers apparently stress one and some the other: David Pole, for instance, says 'An aesthetic response ... implies no more than a heightened present awareness of the qualities of an external or would-be external object; and any object may be looked at in this way'.[38] Osborne says similar things: 'We speak of appreciation or aesthetic activity when we clamp attention upon a part of a total experience ... and do this without ulterior motive for the sake of expanding our awareness of its qualitative nature and apprehending it more fully'.[39]

Other accounts, e.g. Urmson's, stress that some things have sensible qualities that 'affect us favourably' but with 'no ulterior grounds',[40] and the favourable effects are often spoken of as pleasure or satisfaction. I shall consider generically pure contemplation or heightened awareness versions first and various satisfaction versions later.

Various ways are pursued, sometimes with considerable detail and sophistication, to elucidate the none-too-self-explanatory notion of what attending to something for its own sake is or more often is not. There is a danger of course that, after emptying everything out that it is not, one may be left with aesthetic contemplation as mindless gawking, or, if expanded, intensified or heightened awareness of qualities is stressed, with concentratedly impressing on oneself, 'It's red with pink edges, it's red with pink edges' or whatever—a

---

[38] David Pole, 'What Makes a Situation Aesthetic?' *Proceedings of the Aristotelian Society*, Supplementary Vol. 31 (1957), 102.

[39] Osborne, 'Odours and Appreciation', 38.

[40] Urmson, 'What Makes a Situation Aesthetic?', 88.

vacuously unimpressive exercise (though even this would involve mind, thought, recognition, concepts). 'Aesthetic contemplation' of 'character' or 'quality', to be worth a bean, must be more than this. Hence arises a further appeal to other mental activities, understanding and imagination, awareness of more than meets the prosaic, pedestrian, and literal eye, or ear—or nose or palate. So I shall take it that a necessary element in any viable notion of aesthetic interest, contemplation, etc. will be some dwelling of thought on whatever is the object of attention, and that an explanation of why one is interested and in what, involves or consists in some kind of description of its qualities or character. Scruton writes:

> Thus we may define an interest in an object X for its own sake as a desire to go on hearing, looking at, or in some other way having experience of X, where there is no reason for this desire in terms of any other desire or appetite that the experience of X may fulfil, and where the desire arises out of, and is accompanied by, the thought of X . . . I shall respond to the question 'Why are you interested in X?'. . . with a description of X.[41]

Something like this is how we should understand, or expand positively, the often vague and only negatively delimited notions of 'savouring', 'contemplation', 'expanded consciousness' of things 'for themselves' or 'with no ulterior grounds'.

About tastes and smells therefore the two inseparable parts of the question, whether they can be 'contemplated', or an interest taken in them 'or themselves', for no other purpose 'beyond exploring the object itself' (Scruton's words) will merge into the question whether they can possibly be endowed with qualities and character of a sort which allows similar kinds of description, description perhaps involving 'imaginative perception', to those possible with sights and sounds.

To the first half, it seems unquestionable that the connoisseur, or anyone else interested in tastes or smells, whether of a wine, a perfume, a peach, a rose, a deodorant, a dungheap, can attempt to attend to precisely that smell or taste, and 'for its own sake', for what it is, with no ulterior grounds; obviously he may also be interested in whether he likes it or not, whether it 'affects him favourably', whether it is likely to please others, to be marketable, to combine agreeably with other tastes and smells, overcome or combat other odours, or even suit a certain style of dress, or personal image, or lifestyle.

It is to the second half of the question, whether tastes and smells have qualities or character capable of modes of perception and description that parallel those for colours, shapes and sounds, that I shall devote my attention since this is where their poverty or inadequacy, by contrast with colours, shapes, and sounds, is most likely to be alleged—for some it is equally the crux of the

---

[41] Scruton, *Art and Imagination*, 148.

matter also with single particular colours or sounds. Do they contain enough to interest us, to reward attention concentratedly given? Are they unsuited or resistant to the activities of mind, intellect, understanding, and imagination, requisite for aesthetic interest, attention, or 'contemplation'?

One would expect, presumably, if any tastes and smells do have qualities of suitable interest, some to be more pleasing than others, and also some to be more interestingly complex than others. I suggested earlier that the taste of refined white sugar or table salt might be less complex than that of a particular (yet possibly single) taste like ripe peaches or Cox's Orange Pippins or pineapple or mangoes, not to mention obvious mixtures like rum punch or sherry trifle. If the nub of the arguments against tastes and smells is their alleged lack of such qualities or characteristics as would make them adequate or appropriate objects for aesthetic attention and contemplation, given whatever intellectual or imaginative activities this involves (not merely, as in some arguments I have considered, a mere difficulty in subjecting them to aesthetic attention), I shall address myself to the hardest cases, single tastes and smells, rather than complexes or combinations (to what traditionally would have been called 'simple qualities' of taste and smell, since these would seem most to lack whatever richness of character aesthetic attention needs to fasten and feed on. If even these could be shown, even if minimally, able to sustain aesthetic attention, opposing arguments would have failed, a foot would be in the door; no case for combinations or organizations of tastes and smells would, *a fortiori*, be needed. Of course, failure to make a case for singles would leave the possibility of a case for combinations or structures still open. But I think there is much to be said even at the singles level and there are many objections worth examining.

My next investigation then is into whatever kinds—and the extent—of qualities and character tastes and smells possess. But this cannot be discussed without examining the ways of describing and pinpointing them available to us. For it is regularly supposed that our descriptive vocabulary for tastes and smells is far too spare, scrappy, undeveloped, and inadequate to capture even such meagre complexity of quality as they are thought to have. This I want to call in doubt. I want to offer reminders of the facts: that we can, if we wish, characterize even quite particular tastes and smells in very familiar as well as in striking and complex ways; that doing it unavoidably involves 'thought' about these 'objects' and usually also varied modes of imaginative activity and comparison; that to grasp and characterize them we can draw on a wide variety of concepts, as indeed we do for colours, shapes, or sounds, or, for that matter, highly ordered objects like human faces, bodies, and gestures (among natural objects) and art-works (among artefacts). Aestheticians who deny thought, concepts, intellectual activity, and imagination in our commerce with tastes and smells deny, for whatever reasons of their own, or overlook, something plainly true. This places on them the onus of convincing us that aesthetic interest or attention requires other and further involvements of intellect and imagination, beyond those that clearly are possible with tastes and smells.

Inseparable from this is one other important factor. Those who hold (I believe rightly) that aesthetic judgements are capable of a measure of 'objectivity', meaning thereby that notions of truth, correctness, aptness, or fitness may apply to them (truth where one feels like saying an aesthetic attribution is literal, shading into aptness or fitness where the matter is felt to be other than straightforwardly literal) could, I believe, claim that in these respects characterizations of tastes and smells are in much the same case as colours, shapes, sounds, and many other objects about which we make judgements. So again, the onus is on those who would exclude tastes and smells from aesthetics to show that greater 'objectivity' is possible with the senses of sight and hearing than here, and that this extra is a necessary condition for anything to be of aesthetic interest.

VI

I offer now a rough survey of the characteristics of tastes and smells and the possible variety of descriptions, though some, important for other purposes, I will no more than mention. I believe it is true however that there is a kind of complexity they lack; a particular note will have its pitch, volume, and timbre and another particular note will vary in one or more of these dimensions; a particular colour will have a hue, saturation, and brightness and another particular colour will vary in one or more of these dimensions. These are dimensions which are distinguishable but cannot exist independently. But a particular taste or smell will have a given flavour or odour (e.g. lemon or thyme) but will vary only in strength or intensity, so that in most cases a diluted version will be, for my purpose, the same flavour or odour. So the characteristics and descriptions that concern me are those of a flavour or odour independently of its strength or dilution.

I have said that, far from lacking variety of quality, there is an enormous range, and that our modes of comprehensible and appropriate description, far from being severely limited, are both wide and indefinitely enlargeable. As in any other realm, expansion and development are subject only to the interests and needs that prompt us to describe phenomena for ourselves and to each other. I can only suggest tentative categorizations. For as in all other realms, it is not profitable to attempt sharp demarcation lines between types of available descriptions or to set advance limits on kinds of expressions potentially and intelligibly usable. Between the literal and metaphorical there is not a line but a smudge; and we can draw upon concepts from indefinitely many other areas of experience, sometimes domesticating them in this terrain, to pinpoint our experiences of tastes and smells and bring them into clearer awareness.

However, since I want to focus on certain types of descriptions, I shall mention, only to leave aside, some categories of expressions that, though aptly used about tastes and smells, do not, as I shall say, *directly* characterize them. (Not all descriptions fall neatly into my categories and some may straddle more than one category.)

Descriptions I am leaving aside as not being direct include:

1. Those that indicate whether a person, or people generally, like some taste or smell: 'pleasant', 'unpleasant', 'nice', 'agreeable', 'horrible', 'awful', 'ghastly', 'intolerable', 'delectable' 'lovely', 'loathsome'.

2. Those that indicate effects on people (but this itself needs some care). There are adjectives that indicate straightforward causal and physical effects: e.g. 'stinging' and 'sickening smell', 'nauseous taste' may mean tastes or smellss that 'without thought', are liable to cause nausea (to be distinguished from causally emetic substances which make people sick but which may be tasteless or even pleasant-tasting). By contrast some of the same adjectives, including 'sickening' and 'nauseating', are used to indicate that a smell or taste tends to cause something because of some thought or association; 'offensive', 'disgusting', 'foul', 'exciting', 'mouth-watering' often function thus. (Note that some odours that are said to be sexual or appetite stimulants (musk or Bisto) may be of this sort, though some are claimed by physiologists to be of the direct stimulant sort already mentioned. Again, as with many adjectives, like 'exciting', 'moving', or 'thrilling', so 'sickening', 'disgusting', 'offensive' etc. may be used to indicate that a taste or smell is such that one should be sickened, disgusted, offended by it.

3. Adjectives that do not really describe a taste or smell but indicate something about a substance, e.g. 'it smells edible/drinkable', 'inflammable', 'poisonous', 'rotten'.

4. I leave aside what people often think the most notable feature of smells, and to a lesser extent tastes, that they can often be highly evocative, reminders that bring back a flood of memories of places, times, and events. Some evocations may be highly personal (Proust's madeleine, the smell of wet new leather evoking vividly for me childhood visits to an old bootmaker's workshop). Others, for obvious reasons, are as widely shared as many common experiences and associations: smell of fresh-cut grass widely, though obviously not necessarily, evocative of cricket pitches, tennis parties, picnics, or whatever. Smells and tastes are usually evocative of something other than a smell or taste, though presumably the smell of cigars could evoke for me a memory of the smell of brandy or my grandfather's leather chair. And of course, sights and sounds (e.g. of a steam locomotive) can be evocative in similar ways.

But none of the foregoing directly describes the taste or smell itself that happens to nauseate or excite or bring back memories. It is time to move in more closely on their direct characterizations.

5. We regularly describe by reference to substances, the smell or taste of roasting coffee, of tar, petrol, liquorice, aniseed, malt vinegar, newly cut hay, cinnamon, honey, lemon, etc. (or generally *X*-like, where *X* is some substance). With these go various broad adjectives, 'lemony', 'oaky' tastes, 'burning', 'cooking', 'singeing' smells, which can be expanded as 'a smell (as) of such and such burning', etc. But these are still not what I intend by 'direct' descriptions; they operate broadly as 'colour of blood', 'sound of a flute' operate for colours and sounds. That is, we could still ask someone to describe (directly) the taste of liquorice or cinnamon just as we could ask for a description of the colour of blood or the sound of a flute. It is only an evasion of this demand to try to target in exactly by saying 'the taste of this liquid now, or of Johnnie Walker Black Label'. This is only like pinpointing by saying e.g. 'the colour of this drop of blood or BSC 0006 (Salvia)'. We could, and as far as I know, may already, use British Standard Taste numbers as we have numbered food colours (E150), emulsifiers (E471), anti-caking agents (E341), and anti-oxidants (E320). All these manoeuvres classify, label, or name; they do not directly describe. 'Describe the taste of Johnnie Walker' is no more out of place than 'Describe the colour, Salvia' and so with this burning smell or this drop of blood. We might begin: 'It's slightly bitter, acrid, sour' or 'it's a dark rich intense red', saying what kind of red it is. It is these descriptions, and they can be quite complex, that I am trying to explore when I speak of 'direct' characterizations, and arrive therefore at my real target—'direct descriptions/characterizations/predicates of tastes and smells themselves'.

It is appropriate to begin with literal descriptives where by 'literal' I mean words whose primary use and meaning is with tastes or smells and which would have no use elsewhere if this primary sense did not exist. These would include 'tart', 'acrid', 'musty', 'fusty', 'bitter', 'fetid', 'frowsty', 'aromatic', 'rancid', 'fragrant', 'sweet', etc. This marks them off from those whose primary use occurs in some other connection, e.g. 'corrosive', 'burning', etc. Oddly, those specialist writers who offer lists of 'primary' odours, 'standard' tastes or basic qualities, not only offer very limited numbers, four, or seven, or whatever, and do not agree exactly even on these; they offer a very mixed bag in terms of the categorizations I have suggested. 'Corrosive' is often included with 'salty', 'acid', 'bitter', and 'sour' tastes. 'Primary odours' commonly given include 'fruity', 'musky', 'floral', 'spicy', 'ethereal', and 'putrid'.[42] Once lists are of this heterogeneous sort, not all direct in my sense, there seems no reason to exclude a host of others that seem pretty 'basic' yet fall into different categories amongst those I distinguished: 'tart', 'vapid', 'spicy', peppery', 'honeyed', 'brackish',

---

[42] Often the *number* of 'primaries' is determined by what is known about types and numbers of (physiological) receptor types or sites.

'sugary', 'saccharin', 'savoury', etc. (As earlier, I exclude from tastes and smells 'feels', like, 'velvety', 'oily', 'sticky', 'smooth', 'crisp', which are applicable to taste-less and smell-less substances; also 'strong', 'weak', 'insipid', 'mild', when they refer to degrees of dilution, rather than character (compare 'a mild tobacco'), and some other characteristics like 'lingering', 'persistent', 'evanescent', which do not apply to smells and tastes in my sense.)

It is obvious that attempts at what I call 'direct' descriptions soon move from the literal into the metaphorical. I use this to cover all uses of words whose primary sense occurs when used of other things. Without these latter we cannot get far. What I emphasize, however, is that this is equally true when we charac-terize almost anything, colours and sounds, music, paintings, scenery, buildings, and so on. It is just that with tastes and smells we move on rather quickly from a small literal base. I want to emphasize, moreover, that these moves away from the literal seem so obviously the right, apt, correct, or true way to characterize things, including tastes and smells, that many are hardly felt to be non-literal and perhaps should not be so regarded. Not only are they part and parcel of our way of characterizing tastes and smells; without them we would be seriously handicapped, and unable to characterize things as we in fact do and in ways which people can agree with, find apt, think right, or see the point of. Nor would it do to suggest as some do, e.g. Osborne, that we should invent, or could do better with, a larger array of literally applicable terms.[43] The quasi-metaphori-cal descriptions link us with what are felt to be acceptable analogues between tastes or smells and other matters, and strike us as apt, informative, and power-ful precisely because of these linkages. They do not necessarily strike us as star-tling extravagances. For this reason it is dubious, even if an enlarged literal vocabulary were possible (and this is dubious too), whether it would be helpful and certain that it could not be a substitute. To follow those purists who would debar anything non-literal in description and communication would leave us without much that we find illuminating to say about music, poetry, architec-ture, painting (think particularly of non-representational painting), and most other things, including people.[44] We need to borrow from the literal qualities of a vast range of disparate physical things, processes, substances, living and human characteristics, activities, and emotional, moral, and intellectual

---

[43] 'It is significant that the main European languages contain no names for the qualities of smells and we can refer to them only be metaphors, as is done in the perfumery trades or by mentioning their source—the fragrance of a rose, the smell of violets, etc. The latter way does not work for complex or blended odours. There is need of a scientific and recog-nized vocabulary for naming the qualities of smells, but this could only be constructed if it became possible to classify smells systematically' (H. Osborne, 'Odours and Appreciation', 43).

[44] Cf. Brian Stanley Johnson: 'The sound of rain / is like only / the sound of rain . . . in truth can be / like nothing but / the sound of rain' ('The Dishonesty of Metaphors', *Penguin Modern Poets 25*, Harmondsworth: Penguin Books, 1975, 148.)

domains to pinpoint or hit off how we see things. To renounce such resources of language is to all but silence ourselves on the qualities of our natural and artificial world.[45]

Clearly these are the ways people use the resources of imagination and language, when they bother to attempt to hit off the character of tastes and smells. There are of course no limits to the flights into those wildly exotic, exuberant, and flamboyant descriptions possible, and so often and easily ridiculed as pretentious, in the lucubrations of some who talk about food, wine, and perfumes. I shall comment on such extremes in a moment; but first there are other things to say. When in ordinary discourse people bother, as specialists on wine, tea, food, and perfumes have to, to describe tastes and smells fully or carefully, what they say can sound as normal and unpretentious, and as appropriate, vivid, and accurate, as does the language of poets, novelists, or critics describing nature or artefacts. To quote examples about wine from the less flamboyant, more moderate end of this spectrum, 'it has a lively, green, springlike taste', 'it is light and zippy', 'it is warm, elegant and flowery', 'it is dried out, stringy and lacking fruit', 'it is austere and firm', 'it is a big bold wine'; far from striking me as ridiculous or unintelligible they give me a far better idea of the wines, what to look for or expect, than telling me simply, say, that it is white, fruity, and sweet. It strikes me as precisely akin to what goes on in spheres that are not ridiculed, condemned, or ostracized. Scruton, for example, after ridiculing those who 'take the chatter of wine snobbery' with seriousness,[46] but who characterizes aesthetics in terms of 'imaginative perception', within a few pages happily (and probably rightly) characterizes a building (Borromini's Oratory) as giving expression to 'a remarkable combination of civilised self-confidence and spiritual humility', and speaks of finding a 'perfect marriage between the inventive and flexible interior, in which elegant variety is presented as at the same time a species of unassuming simplicity, and a quiet ponderous quality within'.[47] Is this the chatter of architecture snobbery? Is the pot calling the kettle black?

So it is worth listing various things that may obstruct realization of the close parallel with what goes on in describing people or art-works and make it easy to understand the accusations of preciosity and pretentiousness that in the end only prevent our examining the facts. People other than specialists do not engage in articulate description, whether of flower scents or food tastes,

---

[45] In saying that moves from the obviously literal towards the metaphorical are endemic, entrenched, and, unless we gag our descriptive powers, inevitable, I place no great theoretical weight on the terms 'literal' and 'metaphorical', and I have deliberately avoided mentioning Wittgenstein's notion of 'secondary sense', though some such thing is fundamentally involved. But this is because I do not wish to tangle here with theories of metaphor or with exegesis of Wittgenstein's remarks.

[46] Scruton, *The Aesthetics of Architecture*, 115.

[47] Scruton, *The Aesthetics of Architecture*, 120–1.

less because it cannot be done than because of such factors as the following. (1) People in fact often do not take much interest in tastes and smells—but they could. With good reason they will seldom take the time and trouble needed to savour them, as a wine-master or tea-taster does. There are more important things to occupy most people's time and energies. To do so requires hard work, intensity of attention, and the same care and exactness, as trying to describe in words a face or a place or a gesture, and any poet, novelist, or critic will know how difficult this is. (2) Even if we wanted to describe scents and tastes, most of us are poorly trained in discriminating and noticing, though it is pretty certain that almost anyone can be trained in these skills. But it requires time, opportunity, hard work, and intensity of attention, though no more than many people will devote, without feeling it silly or pretentious, in realms they do think important—scenery, people, painting, and literature— and it can probably be done in not too dissimilar ways with anything from pains (which might be of aesthetic interest) to plumbing. (3) Even then, if we can wordlessly discriminate carefully, most of us lack the verbal and literary dexterity to, as Ryle once put it, cap our experience with concepts, to hit the nail on the head. It requires a large active vocabulary subtly and imaginatively used to find the *mots justes*. But with other matters, including the arts, we can find it difficult to discriminate carefully what we see, feel, and hear, and most of us are inadequately articulate or imaginative to express ourselves; which is why we often feel that critics have put exactly right what we have noticed but could not express in words.

So, I suggest, the gradual transition into metaphor, from the dead, familiar, and customary, to those of the writer's own invention, the many varieties of concepts at work, exemplify nothing less than the working of comparative, contrastive, and creative imagination, and are in no way outrageous or unusual. Even the further slide from the apt yet unavoidably metaphorical into the extravagantly flamboyant is only one of degree. In any sphere this process can go too far and become ridiculous: Hardy's descriptions of rural persons and places were pushed over the top quite seriously by Mary Webb, and then pushed further into exuberant parody by Stella Gibbons. Consider, as parallel, the range of music description from the pedantically or pedestri- anly technical, through serious attempts at non-technical and often human characterization in the best critics to the familiar vapourings in some programme notes that take off like coloured balloons with only tenuous teth- erings to the music.

But even these extremes are worth analysis as well as laughter since the progress is along a gradual continuum from the spare and scarcely adequate, through subtle and imaginative characterization, and to what is too fanciful to give more than a vague and general wash of characterization. I suggest three points. (1) Examination will show some imaginative vapourings are just wrong; they do not fit even in a vague and general way or cannot without

effort and contortion be seen to fit. Just as it would be false to say that certain
tastes were salty, and right to say they are sweet, so it would be wrong to say
that certain wines are rich and heavy and right to call them thin and light;
equally it would be wrong to describe the average power station in terms
Scruton uses about the Oratory, as having an air of 'spiritual humility'. Both
literal and highly metaphorical characterizations can go off in mistaken directions where there is no discoverable 'fit'. (2) Descriptions that do go exuber-
antly over the top but in roughly the right direction and are not obviously
inappropriate, may be unsatisfactory in either direction (*a*) they get too
general and vague (e.g. 'a perfume of languorous, oriental quality'), (*b*) they
get too specific, often pictorially (e.g. 'this perfume is light, slick, and has the
inconsequentiality of barber-shop chatter'; compare: 'in this music, the theme
is a giant striding along clubbing down all opposition'). As Wittgenstein might
have said, 'This game can be played' and more or less sensibly and we all know
how. We may deplore these over-flowery descriptions when they are serious,
but it is when at their most pretentious that they are often funniest, 'wine-
speak' at its worst, e.g. from Dolomore: 'the 1982 and 1983 vintages in
Bordeaux are like two brothers. The first is extrovert, handsome, and charming, destined to be head of school . . . and for a brilliant career. The second is
reticent, attractive in character, promising at least a top second at university'.
But here and even in deliberate parody, the meaning need not be either over-
vague or over-specific; something obvious and intelligible was being said,
however absurdly. Here is Miles Kington in *The Times* making fun of wine-
speak : 'a smash and volley little red with nice footwork', 'too Hindemithian for
me', 'a lovely white Burgundy with a nice lived-in feeling', and 'it will never win
a race but it's a wonderful little jogger'. We know exactly the prosaic meaning
of this last one: 'not top class but a satisfying day-to-day tipple you won't get
tired of'. Here the metaphor performs no irreplaceable function; it is dispensable, unpackable, prosaically translated as Johnson's or Sitwell's description of
'The Rape of the Lock', or Ruskin's of a Turner is not.

So far I have considered aesthetic interest and 'contemplation' as active or
imaginative perception (as indeed I always have), and aesthetic appreciation
as the discriminating, noticing, dwelling on and describing a thing's qualities.[48]

But since one main area of traditional dispute has been about whether
anything is right or wrong (objective/subjective) in matters aesthetic (and I do
not intend to try a transcendental argument here), even if aesthetics is seen as
a matter of contemplation of 'qualities', some would still argue that our
perceptions, reactions, and descriptions can differ so much from person to
person, that proofs are impossible, and that unsettleable disagreements are

---

[48] I would allow this whether we speak of *qualities* (discriminatory powers) or *reactions*
(Wittgenstein's word), or some kinds of 'perceiving as'.

endemic. And those who maintain that in aesthetic matters judgements are justifiable by reasoning, as Scruton does, say this is precisely what is lacking with tastes and smells. All I will say here is that if there is any problem about justifiably acceptable descriptions of tastes and smells, it is not peculiar to them, but replicated with other senses and throughout the arts. We rightly say (but how would we prove?) that colours and sounds are warm, lugubrious, delicate, even that the Oratory is gallant and self-confident.

So if there is a problem, nothing so far shows that it is not a general one.

VII

But it is not enough to consider aesthetics only as the contemplation or characterization of the qualities of things. Throughout the centuries, particularly in the great writers of the eighteenth century, aesthetics and aesthetic judgements have centred crucially on pleasure, the agreeable, liking, enjoying, favourable reactions and their opposites. It is still central; Urmson for instance constantly mentions satisfaction, thrills, etc., with the salutory reminder that there can be aesthetic judgements of mere tolerance, as well as expressions of pleasure or displeasure. So this aspect of aesthetics cannot be ignored.

But here arguments turn slippery. They turn, usually, on two poles: first, that aesthetic judgement and appreciation essentially involve pleasure, satisfaction, etc., and secondly that they essentially claim a universal validity (the pleasure being personally disinterested), some adding that therefore they admit of support by reasoning. Hence a celebrated difficulty which for many becomes the central question of aesthetics. In Osborne's words 'Kant denies that sensuous pleasure is a basis for aesthetic judgment because sensuous pleasure varies from man to man whereas aesthetic judgments have a built in claim to universal validity'. Leaving aside what a 'sensuous pleasure' might turn out to be on analysis, the point is that likes and dislikes, things people find pleasing, vary from person to person, are in Beardsley's words possibly idiosyncratic; with no reason why they should not, they may legitimately differ. But objects of positive *aesthetic* judgement are ones in which all humans ought to find pleasure (if they perceive them aright?). In Kant's own words, 'As regards the agreeable everyone concedes that his judgment, which he bases on a private feeling . . . is restricted merely to himself personally. Thus he does not take it amiss if, when he says that Canary-wine is agreeable, another corrects the expression and reminds him that he ought to say: It is agreeable *to me*' and adds incidentally that this applies 'not only to the taste of the tongue, the palate, and the throat, but to what may with anyone be agreeable to eye or ear'. In contrast, 'when he calls it beautiful he demands the same delight from others . . . and then speaks of beauty as if it were a property of things'.[49]

Kant's reference to the eye or ear makes it plain that he thinks, and indeed it is obvious, that a similar situation may prevail anywhere else. A person's likes and dislikes of anything, including art works, may be purely idiosyncratic and 'restricted merely to himself personally' and there may be nothing right or wrong about the matter. The hope or claim is that in aesthetic matters, there are things that all people in some sense ought to like or find pleasing, but where there are differences someone is in the wrong. This is echoed in Scruton with additional emphasis on the possibility that by reasoning one should be able to show that a person ought to like what he does not or even to bring him by argument to like it. But with regard to tastes and smells such possibilities are emphatically denied by those like Scruton: 'You happen to like oysters, I happen to dislike them. You happen to like white wine, I prefer red . . . . It is felt that these are ultimate facts, beyond which one cannot go. And it is further held, on account of this, that here there can be little point in employing ideas of "right" or "wrong", of "good" taste and "bad" '; to which he adds, 'Of course there is discussion of wine . . . But even if one were to take the chatter of wine snobbery with . . . seriousness, this would still not suffice to turn *discussion* into *reasoning*'.[50]

Now I think it is a frequent assumption, though not always argued for, that whether something is (should be) an object of universal pleasure is the same question as whether it has aesthetic value, i.e. that saying *X* ought to be liked (disinterestedly by humans) is equivalent to saying it is of aesthetic value or ought to be valued. Most discussions jump this gap, if it *is* a gap, from universal disinterested pleasure to value. I want to bypass it here as perhaps a more general topic without special reference to aesthetics. For I suspect that if aesthetic judgement, appreciation, and the aesthetically admirable, or valuable, is essentially linked to pleasure or liking the connection is not simple, direct, or obvious; that it is not even necessarily linked with what some particular group—art lovers, initiates, connoisseurs—likes or takes pleasure in. It seems clear to me that anyone, or any group, may recognize, or judge, something to be of great or of minimal aesthetic interest, aesthetically admirable, awful, or insignificant, without necessarily liking, disliking, or being indifferent to it. We often recognize and agree that a painting, piece of music, or novel is a great work, of aesthetic value, yet dislike it, or is aesthetically a nonentity, yet like it. So I incline to think that if liking (which by the way is not preference, and not admiration—terms which writers interchange often with unprofessional insouciance) were fairly straightforwardly connected with

[49] I. Kant, *Critique of Judgement, Analytic of the Beautiful*, sect. 7, trans. J. C. Meredith, Oxford: Clarendon Press, 1952, 51–2.
[50] Scruton, *The Aesthetics of Architecture*, 115.

aesthetic judgement or appreciation, the claims to 'universality' or 'objectivity' in aesthetics might indeed have to be abandoned; I doubt if they can be saved by the sorts of ingenuities and conjuring tricks developed in the literature since Kant. If liking and pleasure play any straightforwardly important role, it may be simply that people often find they like many, but not all, of the things that are of aesthetic interest, and perhaps most important, that we probably would not originally begin to take a typically aesthetic interest in things if there were not some of them that we spontaneously liked and which readily gave us pleasure. But straightforward pleasure might only be an initial bait, the lure for the neophyte, leading some of us into a kind of valued interest that can then develop independently of obvious likings or pleasure.[51] I shall not therefore consider questions about whether it is right or wrong (whether one ought) to like X or Y, and what reasoning may be possible to support such claims. There may indeed also be interesting questions about how one can (justifiably) by reasoning (or talking) get someone (a) to like or take pleasure in something, (b) to agree that he ought, or ought not, to take pleasure in something, (c) to like what (he agrees) he ought to like. But to engage with these questions is already to venture further than the present argument requires. Whatever problems there are here seem to me not, or not obviously, central.

I shall assume that if aesthetics centrally concerns something other than discernment of qualities and their description, it is to do with *value* (= value of things when considered for themselves?). I shall therefore not discuss liking, pleasure, or delight further, but only what is aesthetically of value, desirable, or worthwhile. Whether value is connected at some deeper level with pleasure, I shall not consider. If Osborne can be seen as one who emphasizes, though not exclusively, discernment of qualities (his appeal to pleasure is not direct or superficial), Scruton can be seen as one who emphasizes value, though not exclusively, rather than pleasure. For after adumbrating some of the considerations I have indicated, he does not bother seriously to pursue them. He says he does not propose to study these features, while assuring us confidently, for reasons he does not provide, that 'were we to do so . . . the full complexity of the distinction between sensuous and aesthetic pleasure would become apparent', and that 'it would also become apparent that aesthetic experience (as has often been noticed) is the prerogative of the eye and ear'. He continues, 'The contrast between aesthetic and sensuous pleasure can be made, however, without going into those complexities. It suffices to study the notion of value'. He then attempts a contrast between value and 'mere desire',

---

[51] Perhaps this is what Scruton means: after saying 'Aesthetic experiences may be neither pleasant nor unpleasant' he goes on 'Unless a man sometimes *enjoys* aesthetic experience, he cannot, I think, ever be said to have it' (my italics). *Aesthetics of Architecture*, 112.

between, that is, 'desires which we are prone to justify and recommend to others' and 'desires we regard as personal idiosyncrasies'.[52]

There is however one directly relevant comment to make. Anyone who, as Scruton does at certain points, puts emphasis on pleasure in aesthetics is bound to make certain claims. He says, for instance, that 'aesthetic pleasure must be internally linked to aesthetic experience', that the relation of aesthetic experiences to pleasure 'is not merely a contingent one . . . [aesthetic pleasure] has an object, and not just a cause', and that 'the pleasure of aesthetic of experience is inseparable from the act of attention to its object; it is not the kind of pleasure characteristic of mere sensation, such as the pleasure of a hot bath or a good cigar'.[53] This is backed by pointing out that 'we can't get the pleasure we obtain from reading *Paradise Lost*' from tablets or anything else. But the same is true of his other examples; we cannot get the pleasure of a hot bath from a good cigar, or vice versa. The pleasure in the smell of a good cigar is internally linked to that smell; the pleasure in the taste of salmon cannot be got from sherry. If there is a difference here, the pleasure could be got from any other substance with a taste identical with that of sherry. Is this like getting the same pleasure from different copies (or recordings) of *Paradise Lost*? If we now take it that it is neither (imaginative) contemplation of quality, nor pleasure, that is central to aesthetics, but value, the problems will now become whether judgements of aesthetic value can be true, false, right, wrong, whether some things ought to be valued aesthetically, and since it is widely held that reasoning and justification must be possible with evaluation, whether such judgements are capable of support or defence by reasoning (whether this means the possibility of convincing by argument that things have value, or the possibility of reasoning people into approbation, into valuing things), whether some sort of claim to universality can be justified. So our questions, if they are to parallel other questions about aesthetic matters, will be 'Can tastes and smells ever be of aesthetic value?', 'Are some of higher value than others?', and 'Can such claims be supported by reasons?'. Scruton's verdict on all this is negative.[54]

These sound portentous questions. 'Value' and 'evaluation' in many philosophical contexts are very abstract and high-sounding notions. It is therefore not immediately obvious what it might mean to claim aesthetic value (value for themselves, without ulterior purpose) for tastes and smells. We should perhaps deflate the questions to humbler, more familiar and pedestrian, terminology if we are to understand and get to grips with what we are talking

[52] Scruton, *The Aesthetics of Architecture*, 114.

[53] Scruton, *The Aesthetics of Architecture*, 111–12.

[54] I continue to assume that aesthetic value will be value of experiences (or objects) 'in or for themselves', 'without ulterior purpose', not as means to other kinds of value or for purposes of social or moral life.

about. It is less daunting if we replace 'value', 'esteem', etc. by the still norma-tive notions, whether tastes and smells are things that matter to us or are worth bothering with, and some more than others, if we take the trouble to pay close attention to them and take an interest in our surroundings. Keep in mind too that few, certainly not I, are going to argue that any 'values' that tastes and smells might have are in the big league, more than something rela-tively trivial, a small corner in the multifarious affairs and interests of any rounded and normal life (and being nothing but a full-time wine-taster or tea-taster would be a life as little rounded and normal as being a philosopher investigating full-time only tastes and smells). If we put it thus, I am not convinced that there is any area of human experience where questions of value cannot arise, pains and other bodily sensations included. (Compare Osborne: 'The contrast between simple sensuous pleasure/displeasure and the satisfac-tion of expanded awareness extends over the whole range of sensation'.)[55]

But first another linguistic note. It has often been held that appreciation of tastes and smells is not aesthetic because we do not use 'beautiful' and 'ugly' of them. Aquinas says, 'We speak of visible things and beautiful sounds as beautiful. But we do not use "beauty" in regard to objects of other senses; for we do not speak of beautiful tastes or odours'.[56] Arguments based on this do not impress. They seem to assume that 'beautiful' and 'ugly' are the prime or only terms of aesthetic admiration or condemnation. But unless one stipu-lates this usage by fiat it is far from true. Not all aesthetically worthwhile things are beautiful, or all aesthetically unsatisfactory things ugly. Aestheticians, particularly recently, who have paid attention to how we actu-ally talk in life and in criticism of the arts, rather than to traditional simplis-tic categories, have emphasised the variety and amplitude of our aesthetic vocabulary. In fact it is not unusual to call some fragrances beautiful, but true that we seldom speak so of flavours, and that to call either tastes or smells ugly is distinctly unusual and awkward. We do, incidentally, use 'hideous' of both tastes and smells. But many would find it equally unnatural and awkward to use either 'beautiful' or 'ugly' in some clearly aesthetic contexts. I no more assess plays, whether tragedies, comedies, or farces, as beautiful or ugly, than I assess them as fragrant or luscious; I condemn them for banality, poor construction, sentimentality, etc. Even though I may call some colours beau-tiful, I am not sure I would speak of any single colour as ugly, though I might call some muddy or anaemic or garish. So I shall pursue this line no further.

Consider first then, head-on and quite generally, whether tastes and smells fall wholly outside the orbit of value. Is their existence in the world and our ability to be aware of them something to be glad about? Does it constitute—however rarely we might ask ourselves this—something we value, an addition,

[55] Osborne, 'Odours and Appreciation', 40.
[56] Thomas Aquinas, *Summa Theologiae*, Ia IIae, q. 27 a 1 ad 3.

a possible enrichment of life? Few surely would want to dissent, just as few would argue that it is better to be blind, or deaf, or to inhabit a world without colours or sounds. Ask anyone temporarily or permanently deprived of the senses of taste or smell—and I do not mean for their utility or survival value. He or she can no longer taste peaches or kippers, smell roasting coffee or roses. If anyone denies that this is a loss of something worth having—a clear value notion—I do not know how further to argue with him. We can and do say, using an 'ought', though not obviously a moral 'ought', 'You ought to be glad you can taste and smell', or 'you ought to explore any means of getting your lost abilities back, you'd be stupid not to, you're missing so much of the variety and richness life has to offer'. We surely understand such remarks; they are wholly intelligible, and most who are not convinced ascetics would regard them as good, convincing, or conclusive reasons. We could easily make them more flowery or pompous: 'You ought to be alive to the Reality all about you, to What There Is, to All Things Bright and Beautiful, the great arch of heaven and all things under it, to God's plenty, to everything life-enhancing and enriching; say Yes to life, etc.'—attitudes stretching from appreciativeness of one's luck to religious gratitude. For any one particular sense modality, the 'ought', as all 'oughts' in aesthetics, may be a weakish one; with regard to the whole lot, 'You ought not to go about with eyes, ears, and other senses closed to the world, to shut it out' can begin to sound much stronger—even to verge on the moral. And so also *within* aesthetics. 'You ought to try to open your ears to Beethoven or your eyes to Rembrandt' is stronger than 'You ought to open them to Satie or Dufy, or your taste and smell to Chateau Yquem and Chanel': which is understandable too—more of value is at stake, more is being missed. None of these 'oughts' is enforcable (which are?), or ones we feel strongly bound to get people to heed, though we might feel strongly obliged to try (why else are attempts at certain aspects of education thought valuable enough to be, until recently, made obligatory?).

But additionally, besides intelligible reasons for valuing our possession of sensory capacities, and why we should notice and rejoice in the sheer multiplicity and variety of the objects of the senses, there is some kind of 'ought' with regard to bothering to pay close attention to precise qualities and subtle differences, to noticing with exactness the characters of things, rather than existing in a bland half-noticing state. There is an interest, and it has an intellectual side, to categorizing, comparing, and carefully discriminating, and an additional and purely human one in trying to find words for what we discern and discriminate. All this, I suggest, is a minor aspect of a larger, intelligible, but unenforcable, 'ought' that ranges from noticing the subtleties of varying kinds of beauty and ugliness, grace and awkwardness, to the infinitely variable differences and complexities of people's faces, personalities, moods, wit, humour, and intellectual endowments. I feel no need to ask for further argument to show that I ought to try to see people I know, and myself, for what they are, rather than according to some crude and undiscriminating categorizations, and that it is worth doing. But if all this can be accepted as falling under the catch-all label, 'value' then we *are* operating in a region where notions like 'ought', and intelligible supporting reasons, have a place, not merely in one where purely individual preferences can claim exclusive sway.

But there is a more specific question that must be faced, perhaps the crucial one. What makes, why are, some tastes and smells more valuable, rewarding, worth bothering with, esteemed, when appropriately contemplated, than others, if indeed people do attach differing values to them? To quote Urmson again: we have to allow for 'finding something aesthetically tolerable or aesthetically dissatisfying, or even aesthetically hateful' as well as aesthetically thrilling or satisfying.[57] That is, we must allow, in aesthetics as elsewhere, for judgments of positive and negative value and for judgements of aesthetic indifference, in Urmson's phrase 'aesthetic judgements of toleration', and distinguish these from 'merely refraining from any aesthetic judgment at all'.[58] Indeed we must distinguish refraining from judging from claiming that certain things fall outside the domain of aesthetic judgement altogether, precisely the claim about tastes and smells that we are investigating. From what is impossible we cannot simply refrain.

However, when we come to investigate the principles by which people attach values, we find a criss-crossing of complexities that easily generate confusion and opposing theories that mirror those in other areas of evaluation. Though much is said about the ability of things to reward and satisfy, little enough is said in detail about how and why they might be valued.

One recognizable view (especially in aesthetics) is that, as between different qualities—in this case tastes and smells—there is no ranking or grading to be done. They are just different, each with its own value or interest. The parallel is found amongst various facial or character descriptions. As between *retroussé* and aquiline, ruddy and pale, hearty and gentle there is nothing to choose. So with tastes and smells; each is different, has its own particular, unique non-substitutable interest, to be valued for itself. There are no possible comparisons of relative values. There is just a gallery of different things, like a gallery of portraits. Different people may have their own likes and dislikes, and with some things, though not tastes and smells, and perhaps not physiognomies, other, e.g. moral, considerations might also enter; a character, unlike a face, might be interestingly complex but morally repugnant (or laudable). There are aspects of this position with which, as I shall indicate later, I have considerable sympathy. But it will not do on its own; there are further approaches to be considered.

The simplest principle by which people rank or grade values is to attribute

---

[57] Urmson, 'What Makes a Situation Aesthetic?', 75.
[58] ibid. 81.

positive values to what they like, find pleasing, negative values to what they dislike, find displeasing or offensive. It is suggested, but no more, by some of Urmson's remarks. He speaks of this 'affecting us favourably or unfavourably' and mainly uses 'satisfaction' but also 'disgust', 'delight', 'thrills', 'pleasing'. But others, including many major figures through history, treat pleasure/displeasure as central. But the view that being pleasing or likeable gives something a positive value and being displeasing or disagreeable a negative value seems too wide and simplistic. Those who try to escape from a totally simplistic account, as does Kant, reintroduce pleasure or enjoyment at some deeper or secondary level. Osborne indicates that he is in some way following Kant when he says 'The prototype of aesthetic judgement is not to be found in reports of our favourable or unfavourable reactions to the sensible qualities of things; it is to be found in the satisfaction which attends expanded awareness of the sensory content of experience'.[59]

A second principle, that aesthetic appreciation is appreciating or savouring the character of things, 'rolling them on the tongue', and that value resides in enhanced awareness of qualities—a view Osborne at moments expresses— immediately encounters the difficulty already mentioned, that since every quality has some contemplatable and potentially appreciable character, wherein its value, if any, resides, some principle is needed to provide difference of value. A common move at this juncture is to appeal to degrees of complexity. High value is attributed to the more complex, as being more rewarding, offering more to savour, as being fertile for potential imaginative exploration and description, having greater fecundity (to follow Bentham's use of the word). Low value is attributed to the simple, as offering less for contemplative imagination to feed or get a grip on, being of a too impoverished character to seize upon, grasp, or explore for imaginative description. Things complex are interesting, offering scope for careful sniffing, savouring, discriminating, imaginative effort in describing, pinning down, capping with apt concepts. Here we are not far from Croce and Collingwood: grasping an experience for what it is, and finding appropriate words to describe its character is not far from their notion of Expression. But this principle of value has its familiar attendant difficulties, and they appear in writers as different as Bosanquet and Beardsley. Since every object necessarily has some quality or character of its own, every one, even the simplest, has a potentially appreciable value. So nothing is merely 'tolerable' or indifferent and nothing of negative value—only of such low value as not to be worth bothering with. This again is too simplistic to account for the facts of our actual practice.

Easily confused with the distinction between complex and simple character is another: a strong, or marked, or aggressive character as against a mild, gentle, reticent, or discreet character (which again is not the distinction

---

[59] Osborne, 'Odour and Appreciation', 40.

between a strong and a weak or diluted version of the same taste or smell, e.g. watered milk). Ripe persimmons and refined cane sugar might illustrate, respectively, complex and simple. But strongly marked tastes or smells, say, ripe Stilton, and mild or discreet tastes and smells (mild tobaccos, some discreet perfumes) may both be quite complex and open to subtlety of characterization.

These last two distinctions, complexity/simplicity and marked/discreet character are independent of liking. Pleasant and unpleasant tastes and smells may be interestingly complex or not, and strongly characterized or not.

But it is unlikely, of course, that even those who bother to attend closely to smells and tastes, will stay to do so with what they find unpleasant. Few of us would deliberately 'savour' bad drains or rotten fish. But then, many people will not stay to investigate and discriminate closely the qualities of paintings or novels they find uncongenial or distressing. So, combining these distinctions, it is intelligible, if paradoxical-sounding, that some things can give more pleasure, that of discerning complexity and perhaps capturing it in words, than others that are less pleasant or agreeable. There are plenty of analogues: one person has an interestingly complex but not particularly likeable character, another is an uncomplicated but very likeable person. But I fear that the interest or value attached to tastes and smells does not turn simply on any of these dimensions, pleasant/unpleasant, complex/simple, strong/discreet. To do justice to the subtleties of evaluation one must see how the complex/simple and the strong/discreet dimensions can both be qualified either positively or negatively. They attract expansion by other adjectives or adverbs, and not only accuracy of description but, fairly obviously, attribution of value depends on such qualifications.

Here are some examples, some applicable only to tastes, others only to smells, all drawn from actual real life uses, though naturally they come from commentators on wines, foods, and drinks, rather than from sanitary inspectors, drain cleaners, or farmers. Novelists also often describe smells (think of Dickens) though seldom tastes. Consider first the contrast simple/complex. On the positive side simplicity may be a sweet simplicity, charming, gracious, innocent, pure, clean, clear, fresh, light, soft, gentle, summery, lean, austere; on the negative side, simplistic, bland, thin, meagre, spare, dried out, naïve, empty, pinched, puny, anodyne, stark, bare, diminutive, impoverished, dumb. Complexity, on the positive side, may be subtle, rich, interesting, intriguing, mature, well-balanced, round, having layers of flavour; on the negative side, confused, unclear, cloudy, murky, muddy, turgid, turbid, thick, unbalanced. Now consider the other contrast, strongly marked/discreet. The former can be, on the positive side, rich, big, bold, long, round, full, racy, beefy, meaty, majestic, fat, substantial, proud, positive, massive, ebullient; passing through the neutral to the negative, genial, masculine, macho, piquant, astringent, aggressive, assertive, rough, arrogant, bossy, brassy, brazen, brutal, biting, obstinate, and I have even found pert, boastful, and hoydenish. Now consider the discreet or less strongly marked character. On the positive side we find: delicate, light, subtle, small, slim, feminine, sensitive, reserved, modest, serene, gentle, caressing, demure, reticent, retiring, suggestive, diminutive, etc.; on the negative: bland, thin, vapid, timid, effeminate, feeble, puny, characterless, weak, flaccid.

There is of course no way of imprisoning these terms in rigid boxes. Our ways of using them are fluid, and exactly what we mean depends heavily on context and qualification. Besides charming simplicity there is merely empty simplicity; besides rich and subtle complexity, messily turbid complexity. 'Rough' might be expanded in context as 'honest, bold, clean, down-to-earth', or as 'crude, brutal'; 'dry' may mean 'dried up, thin', or merely 'astringent'. We also qualify adverbially: too positive, merely charming, over-rich, undersized.

These, I suggest, are the ways we at one and the same time describe and attribute value in all realms: descriptive/evaluative talk about tastes and smells functions no differently from elsewhere; we draw on characterizations appropriate to people and things, just as in reverse we draw on sweet, bitter, acid, and sour to describe people. We attribute value largely *by* describing in certain ways; and to the extent that this is so, questions about how we reason about and justify attributions of value are not separable from questions about justifying the application of descriptive adjectives. But, I argued, we can frequently agree, if we bother, on the aptness of descriptions, however far from literal they may be; so that only leaves us with such questions as 'Why do (should) you positively value cleanness, freshness, richness, delicacy, harmony, and set negative value on turgidity, lack of balance, puniness?' I am not sure how one answers, or whether one needs to answer, such questions. But if there are further problems about justification of values, they are no different in the case of tastes and smells from those elsewhere.[60]

Earlier I said that when questions of evaluation are raised, questions of relative values, greater and lesser, become unavoidable. I have now indicated how tastes and smells may have very different sorts and degrees of value attributed to them. I also said I had some sympathy with not attempting to rank or grade them in value. I will return to this.

But first I want to consider tastes and smells and what they contribute to our lives. For it is when we come to compare their value with other things that we value, that one who would exclude them from aesthetics might feel most confident. I take this in two parts. First, even if tastes and smells are of aesthetic interest, whatever value they may have, even at their highest, as in the

---

[60] Perhaps all this falls within Urmson's suggestion that many aesthetic criteria consist in 'looking to possess some quality which is non-aesthetically desirable' (Urmson, 'What Makes a Situation Aesthetic?', 89) if we widen it enough to allow e.g., harshness on occasion as well as delicacy.

finest fragrances and flavours, or the most desirable and intriguing combinations thereof ('perfume gardens', exquisite wines and cuisine), can hardly offer serious competition with many natural sights and sounds (though I am not sure about sounds here—running streams? thunder? bird song?) or with many products of the arts. For aesthetic importance there is presumably no case for setting a Chanel perfume against a Leonardo, or a Chateau-Lafite against the *Missa Solemnis,* or even perhaps against a reasonably good sonnet. But unwillingness to try to defend such comparisons is not enough to exclude tastes and smells, only enough to show that their value, if any, is relatively slight, even, if one cares to say so, trivial. But so is the aesthetic value, if any, of, say, single notes on clarinet or basset horn. What is sometimes called 'aesthetic surface' or the 'merely aesthetic' or even the 'merely beautiful', and might cover all such cases, is presumably the insistence that objects of aesthetic interest, at their highest, have essential links with vital human concerns. Perfumes and flavours, natural or artificial, are necessarily limited: unlike the major arts, they have no expressive connections with emotions, love or hate, grief, joy, terror, suffering, yearning, pity, or sorrow—or with plot or character development. But this need not put them out of court. The arts of the silversmith, the jeweller, the glassblower, the potter, of Fabergé, do not lend themselves to the great themes of human life either. To quote Urmson again

No doubt many of our most intense aesthetic satisfactions are derived from plays, poems, musical works, pictures and other works of art. But to me it seems obvious that we also derive aesthetic satisfaction from artefacts that are not primarily works of art, from scenery, from natural objects and even from formal logic; it is at least reasonable also to allow an aesthetic satisfaction to the connoisseur of wines and to the gourmet.[61]

(Compare also T. M. Greene: 'Perhaps the most essential characteristic of a major art is its potential expressiveness . . . the most expressive products of a minor art have a far thinner and less significant artistic content than that of equally distinguished products of a major art. Compare for example, the finest lace, or china, or silver, with the finest architectural, pictorial, or iterary productions . . . The one group shades imperceptibly into the other'.)[62]

Secondly, when it comes in certain situations to a choice between even high aesthetic values and values other than aesthetic, there is sometimes (some would say always) no question which should prevail (the old arguments against 'aestheticism', that any moral consideration outweighs any aesthetic value). Where urgent claims of humanity, social, moral, or religious claims are made on us, aestheticism could be a culpable luxury: aesthetic values compete in real contexts with values of other sorts. But crisis situations demand equally

---

[61] Urmson, 'What Makes a Situation Aesthetic?', 76.

[62] Theodore Meyer Greene, *The Arts and the Art of Criticism,* Princeton: Princeton University Press, 1947, 33–4.

that we set aside contemplation of a Michelangelo and of fine wines; there is no significant difference here. But we are not always in crisis situations, and unless we are extreme moralcoholics, a full life may not only allow, but require, appreciation of small-scale values in the interstices between more important activities. Nevertheless it is obvious enough why connoisseurships in odours and flavours, food and drink, may be held in low esteem. (Personally, I would not spend the time to become a wine buff, a gourmet, or a perfume connoisseur; but neither could I spend as much time on fine jewellery or carpets as I would on poetry or music; life offers too many major competitors. Indeed, I am not sure I would feel justified in spending much time philosophizing about tastes and smells unless I had more important game in my sights.) But to have minor, even minimal, aesthetic interest is not the same as being logically excluded.

To return now to the values and the relative values within the realm of tastes and smells. I have taken it that when philosophers talk abstractly about values they are talking about things that enrich (or in some cases even ennoble) life in any of many respects; that greater or lesser values are those that tend to enrich more or less; that by the rather grand talk about 'objectivity' or 'the claim to universality' they mean that such things would, whether people realize it or not, enrich life for anyone. It may be that there *are* things that would be worth having for all people indifferently in all circumstances whatever, and others it would be better not to have in any circumstances. But these are extreme claims. Most claims would be better understood as being true only *ceteris paribus*, i.e. subject to accompanying circumstances which, in the more grandiose claims, are conveniently taken for granted or forgotten. *King Lear* may be more valuable in many circumstances than *The Owl and the Pussycat*, but not necessarily if one has just seen it three times, or even at all to members of a primitive society, any more than either would have value for us after an accident rather than help from ambulancemen; or the taste of brackish water preferable to Chateau-Yquem to the parched survivor in the desert. Nor is it necessary that I have precisely the same hierarchy of values as you, or as myself at different times. Values may vary relative to different persons, and times as well as occasions. Here, as everywhere else, we encounter differing but comprehensible and acceptable value schemes according to people's characters and predilections. In tastes and smells some may prefer the broad, blunt, sturdy, plain, unfussy to the delicate, subtle, highly refined.

There are however cases of various sorts that put some tastes and smells beyond the pale for aesthetic evaluation. There are those that are physically unbearable so that one *cannot* in fact 'savour' or pay discriminating attention to the possible complexities of their character: smells that are *physically* nauseating, say, ammonia, or tastes like castor oil and some emetics, that make one retch; this is akin to trying to dwell contemplatively on the character of a painful and ear-splitting screech (including some fashionably amplified music) or on something so blindingly bright as to hurt the eyes. These are mere physical impossibilities. More interesting are those cases that have analogues elsewhere in aesthetics, where physically one could contemplate and anatomize the interesting complexity of a taste or smell, but does not, does not allow oneself, perhaps cannot because of some association or connection. These range from cases where one cannot bring oneself to because of randomly disagreeable associations—tastes may recall medicines and illnesses, smells of some disinfectants (otherwise not uninteresting or unpleasant) recall hospitals, Woodbines recall the trenches (as in the opposite direction one may dwell lovingly on the tang of Gauloises, recalling happy travel, or cigars, recalling childhood Christmases)—to the other end of the range, where one cannot, or indeed refuses to, attend to the complexity of taste or smell of something where the substance is offensive or disgusting— putrefaction or vomit or faeces. To dwell longer with interest or pleasure on these would, and no doubt ordinarily should, strike us, not so much as immoral, as at least degrading, brutish, and obscene. It is analogous to other cases where we feel aesthetic interest should be overridden, the compositional beauty and colour patterns of a road accident. But, as elsewhere, it is also possible to set aside aversions and qualms and consider the qualities them- selves when, for instance, it is known that the taste or smell does not emanate from a disgusting substance but from some similar-smelling but wholly arti- ficial and in no other respect disgusting concoction. Indeed, it is not only common knowledge that some foods smell like body smells, that some inno- cent substances taste like disgusting ones; it is slowly being established that in these cases there is often an identical or similar chemical substance present. These cases have some kinship with others that it would be inhuman to relish or admire aesthetically if they were not detached from realities, subtleties of suffering explored in fiction or drama, the colour-richness and composition of paintings of executions or martyrdoms. For that matter it is possible, and sometimes acceptable, to savour the smell, say, of something by detaching this interest sufficiently from the substance from which it emanates or any notion of its unpleasantness (the 'healthy sweet smell' of farm manure).

Apart from such considerations, there is little to outlaw tastes and smells beyond all aesthetic consideration; unlike most other things capable of aesthetic values, they seem incapable themselves of having moral value or being objects of moral interest, though they can have social, economic, and utility value. But though not to be preferred or condemned on moral grounds, they may figure, and some may be inadmissible or regrettable, in the realm of minor morality where morals merge into manners and politeness (avoidably breathing garlic over someone, and equally with sounds, though there is noth- ing *morally* wrong with the sound of belching in public).

I have now indicated how tastes and smells may be variously valued and for what qualities, and also ways in which certain of them might be excommunicated as irredeemably bad. But I also said earlier that I had some sympathy in general with not attempting any ranking or grading. Whether we describe tastes and smells either in their literal or primary terms—salty, sweet, sour, bitter—or by reference to substances—peppery, oaky, lemony, fruity, flowery, grassy—or by many of the evaluatively descriptive adjectives I discussed— soft, delicate, subtle, rich, aggressive, reticent—questions of relative values become insignificant. Few presumably would argue that the taste of sugar is more valuable than that of salt, or the smell of newly mown grass than that of roasting coffee, or that rich flavours are more valuable than delicate. But this is no different from evaluations in other areas. We do not feel obliged to argue the relative merits of colours, red, blue, bright, subdued; of facial features, aquiline, *retroussé*, pale, rosy; or of character, quiet, withdrawn, reserved, demure, ebullient, outgoing, etc., though personally we may like or prefer some to others. Even those whose tastes are for delicacy and subtlety may be glad of a blunt sturdiness on occasion, or find other qualities preferable for living with long term. Must it be argued among positives, that genial is better than witty, or among negatives, that surly is worse than brash? Apart from purely personal preferences, there is room for Botticelli, Rubens, and Degas, or for that matter Garbo, Marilyn Monroe, and Elizabeth Taylor. Much of the time, with tastes and smells, as with people, we move largely in the middle ground, are not constantly confronted by extremes, and need not seriously try to evaluate (*in abstracto*) one against another.

I might illustrate this analogy with the evaluation of human character by quoting one of Gilbert Ryle's finest and most sensitive pieces of writing. Jane Austen, he writes, was not of what he calls 'the Calvinist camp' but of 'the Aristotelian camp':

Almost never does she use either the bipolar ethical vocabulary or the corresponding bipolar psychological vocabulary of the Black-White ethic. The flat generic antithesis of Virtue and Vice, Reason and Passion, Thought and Desire, Soul and Body, Spirit and Flesh, Conscience and Inclination, Duty and Pleasure, etc. hardly occur in her novels. Instead we get an ample, variegated and many-dimensional vocabulary.[63]

He goes on,

Given the stilted bipolar vocabulary . . . it is easy and tempting to reserve the top drawer for the one and the bottom drawer for the other. But given the copious, specific and plastic vocabulary of Aristotle or Shaftesbury, it then becomes a hopeless as well as a repellent task to split it up into, say, fifteen top-drawer terms and seventeen bottom-drawer terms, into a platoon of sheep-terms for angelic and goat-terms for Satanic powers, impulses and propensities. To the employer of a hundred crayons the dichotomy 'Chalk or Charcoal' has no appeal. For example, John Knightley's

---

[63] Gilbert Ryle, 'Jane Austen and the Moralists', in Ryle, *Collected Papers*, i, London: Hutchinson, 1971, 289.

occasional testiness was obviously not a Virtue. But nor was it a Vice. At worst it was a slight weakness, and in his particular domestic situation it was even a venial and rather likeable condiment . . . . We would not wish to be surrounded by John Knightleys. But we would not wish to be without them altogether.[64]

Again, 'The questions Was Emma Good? Was she Bad? are equally unanswerable and equally uninteresting'.[65] Transfer this Aristotelianism in discerning evaluation to our present topic and it represents much of what I have been trying to say about evaluations of tastes and smells. But it remains, nevertheless, a matter of evaluations. The question that remains is whether they can be claimed for aesthetics, as aesthetic values. But if they are not aesthetics what are they? They do not seem to be moral, economic, political, matters of etiquette, fashion, or of the social graces. They seem to be more than matters of general liking or disliking; and they are assessments or evaluations of the qualities of objects (tastes and smells) 'for themselves', or 'with no ulterior purpose'. But it is not my intention to give an answer.

VIII

I said at the outset that disagreements over the admission or exclusion of tastes and smells from aesthetics might result from differing suppositions or convictions, traditionally accepted or inadequately articulated, about the nature of tastes and smells, what sort of objects they are. I have therefore tried to investigate their nature, a task seldom attempted and perhaps trivial-seeming. If my examination is reasonably accurate and acceptable, there can be only one reason for excluding them, namely, that they lack features found in objects generally admitted within aesthetics; and only one kind of reason why, after this investigation, some should accept and others reject them, namely, that philosophers draw boundaries of the aesthetic in different places. But to investigate this is to investigate the concept, or the differing concepts, of the aesthetic. So while the examination of tastes and smells may be in itself an insignificant matter, there can hardly be any enterprise in aesthetics more central, or more in need of clarification, than the concept, the boundaries, the criteria of the Aesthetic itself.

It is widely, and I think inevitably, considered that a necessary condition for aesthetics is that things should be contemplated for themselves, with no ulterior purpose. If my account of tastes and smells is correct, many reasons commonly given why they cannot be contemplated for themselves are worthless. That they are lower, more animal, cuts no ice; that they are too fleeting

---

[64] ibid. 289–90.   [65] ibid. 285.

and changeable is at best a contingent difficulty and at worst misconceived; that we must bypass them for practical purposes or cannot bypass them from experiences to objects (they are not 'opened out') is false. There is no logical impediment to contemplating them, and many specialists do. The claim that, if contemplated, they are inadequate as objects is false if this means that they are too simple to have describable qualities, or that our attention to them cannot be cognitive, involving concepts, thought, imaginative perception and description, or that descriptions of them cannot be right or wrong, apt or inappropriate, normative in the sense of demanding agreement (for Scruton a necessary condition of aesthetic judgement). Scruton's claim that we can attend to them but they *demand* no intellectual act does not mean they cannot get it—no objects *demand* it. There is no argument that shows they must be mere causes, not objects, of pleasure. Nothing prevents our characterizing them in evaluative ways as we do most other things; in doing so we supply intelligible reasons for valuing that are also normative, i.e. demand agreement as much and as little as anything else in aesthetics. We do not, unless we are crazy, and nor does Scruton, think we can provide proofs other than by getting others to experience them under the concepts we apply (what I once called 'perceptual proofs').

Are these parallels not enough? What further demands do tastes and smells fail to meet? If they must carry meaning, be 'cultural objects', demanding interpretation and understanding, they fail, but in company with all natural phenomena. If they must exhibit order, structure, heterogeneity, they can exhibit certain kinds, in common with some natural objects and art-works, but not other kinds found in other art-works. If they must be able to encompass some deeply human emotions, aspirations, and sublimities, they cannot; but nor do some kinds of art aspire to such heights and depths. If their greatest values are still only slight and trivial, it does not follow that they are never worth bothering with, or that they are not minimal *aesthetic* values on the lower end of a continuum. If it is alleged that they are off that continuum and onto another, say, the sensuous, we need reasons to suppose the aesthetic and the sensuous are separated by a line rather than merging along a further continuum. These are seldom offered; indeed writers arguing for total exclusion can vacillate over whether it is only attenuation. To espouse some of these many conditions will exclude or include certain objects from aesthetics. To espouse others will exclude or include different objects. Who is right? Whose conditions correctly mark out the aesthetic? This question I will not answer. There is no notion of the aesthetic; there are many criss-crossing ones, some very puritanical, some very catholic, some merely stipulative, some mere prejudice, some hand-me-downs, many for which intelligible reasons are available but with which one need not sympathize. So the question what *really* constitutes the domain of aesthetics has no answer, unless there is one laid up in heaven. I am not just suggesting that it has merely a vague boundary, or that it involves family resemblance. Reasons for including or excluding this or that run along very diverse dimensions and are diversely motivated. We can see why people might ask whether a hovercraft is a boat or a low-flying aircraft. The question does not have to be answered. We can see why people might ask if the hovercraft is a welcome advance on both or just a noisy nuisance. But the question 'Is it a boat or a noisy nuisance?' is a fish from another kettle.

16

Why the *Mona Lisa* May Not be a Painting

This paper is about the *Mona Lisa*. It is about Rembrandt's *Lucretia*, Botticelli's *Primavera*, and any other work of painting, drawing or carved sculpture—an important subgroup of traditional works of visual art. I assume an oil painting to be an object consisting of pigment on, say, canvas or wood, a watercolour to be dyes on, say, paper, a carved sculpture to be, say, a piece of stone. Paintings and sculptures are therefore physical objects. Hence if the *Mona Lisa* is a painting, it is a physical object. This, it is often said, is the common-sense or obvious view. It is also the professed view of many philosophers, who thereby endorse that same common-sense view.

We should, however, distinguish three matters. First, there may be the common-sense view about something, the view that might be offered without much reflection by non-philosophers and philosophers alike; secondly, a true account such as one might hope to reach by careful philosophical investigation; thirdly, the account, not necessarily correct, actually offered after reflection by this or that philosopher. Certainly the common-sense view even about common concepts is often naïve, superficial, and wide of the mark. Philosophers of a hard-headed persuasion often endorse the common-sense view of visual artworks. I believe that when they do, and do not merely assume its truth but argue for it, their arguments often beg the question. My inquiry therefore is this: given that oil paintings, carved stone sculptures, etc., are physical objects, is it a correct account of our existing notion of such works of visual art as the *Mona Lisa* or Michelangelo's *David* that in our practice *vis-à-vis* them we treat them, certainly, consistently, and unambiguously, as physical objects? If it is, unless we introduce conceptual change, which is not my intent, such works are respectively oil paintings and stone sculptures. But if philosophical investigation showed that, even in existing conceptual practice, we do not treat them certainly, consistently, and unambiguously as physical, objects, the answer to the question whether they are oil paintings and stone sculptures would not be unequivocal or clear-cut. They might both be and not be; for some purposes they might be, but not for other purposes. Were this so, while it would be wrong to assert that, according to common usage, they are not physical objects, it would be equally wrong to assert without qualification the common view, even though many philosophers endorse it, that they *are*.

Discussion about what kind of things the *Mona Lisa* and the *David* are is usually conducted alongside discussion about the kind of things pieces of music, poems, and plays are. Among recent philosophical writers there is a virtual consensus that these latter are of one general kind and the works of visual art under consideration are of another. Sometimes this difference is seen as one between performing and non-performing arts. Certainly in historically established practice there is no intervening performer or executant and no performer's interpretation with painting and sculpture. Consequently, for such works, it would seem, there is no accepted latitude for what counts as the same work as there is for works in the performing arts, where, for instance, some properties are determinate, say, note pitch and intervals in a piece of music, and others, say crescendos or accelerandos, are variable within vague permissible limits. Sometimes arts in this latter group are seen as defined by a notation, or a recipe or set of instructions, which allows variations in compliance; sometimes an account of them is given in terms of types, generic or abstract entities, and tokens of those types.

However, while theorists differ amongst themselves about those other arts, they are widely agreed about works like the *Mona Lisa* and the *David*. These are physical objects or, if not certainly such, not obviously anything else. Thus the *Lucretia* is 'the actual object made by Rembrandt' requiring 'physical identification' as 'the product of the artist's hand'.[1] Or again, that such works are physical objects is 'the common sense view which can be rejected only at the expense of conceptual innovation . . . It requires philosophical sophistication even to understand the suggestion that the *Mona Lisa* is not something that usually can be found hanging on a wall of the Louvre'.[2] Another writes that 'All paintings . . . are individuals'[3] and though he suspends judgement on what he calls 'the physical object hypothesis' he nevertheless rejects what he calls the likeliest alternatives to it.[4] Indeed, he thinks that 'the rejection of the [physical object] hypothesis has serious consequences for the philosophy of art' in those arts 'where there is such an object'.[5] This is the hypothesis, or, for many, the obvious truth I wish to examine.

I shall assume for the moment what is often supposed about the works of visual art under consideration—though I shall question it later—that they are, with regard to their visual properties at any one time, wholly determinate, i.e. that the marks on the canvas determinately fix the work's visual properties. I take this to underlie the belief that any change in or deviation from them is of aesthetic relevance, i.e., may, but need not, make some aesthetic difference.

---

[1] N. Goodman, *Languages of Art: An Approach to a Theory of Symbols*, Indianapolis and New York: The Bibbs-Merrill Company, Inc., 1968.

[2] J. O. Urmson, 'Literature', in *Aesthetics: A Critical Anthology*, 1st edn., ed. G. Dickie and R.J. Sclafani, New York: St Martin's Press, 1977, 334f.

[3] R. Wollheim, *Art and its Objects*, 2nd edn., Cambridge: Cambridge University Press, 1980, 167.

[4] ibid. 177 ff.   [5] ibid. 74.

Therefore in posing the question whether the *Mona Lisa* might, even as our concepts now are, be not a physical object but a generic or abstract entity of some sort, capable of multiple instantiations, I am supposing for the present that multiple instances, unlike those in the other arts, would all have to exhibit the same determinate (visual) properties. Manifestly then, since the question is whether such works of visual art may, even without conceptual innovation, be types or abstract entities, it would be begging the question to assume, or smuggle in by anything that entails it, that they are physical objects.

A type for a painting, I assume, would be that particular configuration, or display of visual properties—lines, colours, and shapes—that characterizes the front surface of the physical object in question, say, the one in the Louvre. (For a pencil drawing it would be nearly enough two-dimensional. For an oil painting it may be the configuration of a surface of coloured lumps and bumps, depending on varying thicknesses of paint, and so will be a three-dimensional figured surface, of which, so to speak, a coloured replica could be made from a cast. For carved sculpture, it will be the shapes, colours, and tactile properties exhibited by the outer shell of, say, a free-standing sculpture.) I shall call it a 'visual appearance', or, for short, an 'appearance', in the sense in which identical twins and their waxwork effigies may all share the same appearance. By calling a work an abstract entity I mean that such an appearance could occur in many instantiations at different times and places. This is the supposition I wish to consider.

Since on this supposition the *Mona Lisa* just is the appearance instantiated on the front of the object in the Louvre, some other properties of that object are not features of the work—the visual features of its sides and back, and its non-visual properties and relations e.g., its chemical composition, weight, age, place of manufacture, the fact that Leonardo applied its pigments, and the fact, if it is one, that the pigments have faded or darkened. Thus if new instantiations of the appearance of the front surface of the Louvre object were produced, some properties and relations of the new physical bearer might, and others must, differ from those of the Louvre object. The visual features of its back would probably be different; and even if it consisted of similar materials, not wood or plasterboard, and had been painted by Leonardo, its pigments would have been applied at a different time and in a place not occupied by the original bearer. Its history would necessarily be different.

On the hypothesis that other manifestations of the appearance of the Louvre *Mona Lisa* are possible and that the work itself is abstract, it is irrelevant what the physical nature of other bearers is and how the appearance is produced, by colour photography, printing, transparency, or whatever, so long as it is produced. It will be irrelevant whether the original instantiation was then achievable only with certain pigments and techniques, and whether or not to produce it then required long technical training and high skill; and equally with what materials and ease a reinstantiation might be achieved now.

What arguments, then, might be deployed to prove that the *Mona Lisa* must be the physical object in the Louvre, with its properties and history, rather than the type, the appearance exhibited by that object?

Least interesting is any argument from an alleged practical impossibility of reproducing further instantiations. Not only is it not obvious that adequate technology does not already exist, or could not, if desired, be produced; it is in any case beside the point. Doubts about the practical possibility of reinstantiating a type carry no weight in the argument whether the *Mona Lisa* is or is not a type. At most they could show that, if it is an abstract entity, there may in fact never be more than one exact instantiation.

Another group of arguments purports to show that the properties of any art-work are not determined solely by the properties appearing on its surface, the so-called 'presented' or 'exhibited' properties; the very properties attributable to the work may depend also in part on a host of non-exhibited facts and relations. A proper understanding and appreciation may require, besides close attention to the appearance, knowledge of the work's date and its place in a tradition, the materials used, and the artist's aims, and familiarity with works borrowed from, improved on or departed from, satirized or pastiched.

But these arguments concern only the background and tradition from which the original *Mona Lisa appearance* came; they show only that full appreciation of the *Mona Lisa or any reinstantiation of it* may require training and background knowledge. They require no reference to a physical object but only to the *appearance* whenever *it* is offered and whatever physical object now exhibits *it*. What is important is who produced it, at what date, in what tradition, etc. Nothing in the abstract hypothesis excludes the importance of all this. It can accommodate all views about such matters, and is neutral with regard to intentionalist, traditionalist, anti-presentationalist, and institutionalist arguments. None even remotely serves to establish the physical object hypothesis. Serious arguments must be quite different. We can similarly ignore aesthetic properties and other features that *are* exhibited. Appreciation might require us to see a certain shape as a face or a shadow, or to note a significant balance and tension between different colour areas or figures in a picture. But that would be equally true with either a later or the original instantiation. All that matters is that the facelike configuration or colour areas be there. If, as widely acknowledged, aesthetic and representational properties are supervenient upon colours, lines, shapes, etc., it is sufficient that *these* be present in anything purporting to be a new instantiation. So clearly, for present purposes, we need consider only literal visual non-aesthetic properties, i.e. colours, lines, and shapes. The same is true with the texture of a paint surface that indicates a painter's brushwork and manner of working; these may contribute importantly to the overall impression, but in a perfect replica they would equally be exhibited on it.

Since background, aesthetic, and textural questions can be dismissed as irrelevant to the abstract hypothesis, and only the literal visual features of the appearance of the original bearer matter, it is these that any other token must reinstantiate. But since the original objects, like that in the Louvre, exhibit wholly determinate properties, it would seem that any further token must possess the very same determinate visual properties. Here arise two familiar theoretical questions. First, it may be thought that reinstantiation of such a determinate set is logically impossible, or the suggestion meaningless. If only the original physical object could exhibit that determinate appearance, the appearance is necessarily tethered to that physical object and no further instantiations could be borne by other physical objects. Secondly, even if identical reinstantiations were possible, certification of them as identical would be impossible and anyway would require reference to the Louvre object. The problem this raises is not that the Louvre object is after all the *Mona Lisa*, for, barring a tacit *petitio*, all that can be claimed is that a new *visual appearance*, to count as a genuine instantiation, must be referred for certification to the *visual appearance* exhibited by the Louvre object; it is that, even were there a perfect reinstantiation, assurance of its perfect identity would be in principle beyond reach. Can these theoretical objections be side-stepped? I shall argue that they can. I shall try to show that visual identity, which for sake of argument I supposed necessary, can be replaced by visual indistinguishability. Later I will question the extent to which even this is necessary.

Consider the theoretical problems about identity and indistinguishability. At any given level of careful visual examination, A1 (the original appearance) may be indistinguishable from A2, A2 from A3, yet A3 distinguishable from A1. Again, A1 may be indistinguishable from A2 and from A3, but A2 and A3 distinguishable from each other. In either case A2 and A3 must both be different from A1, so must both be rejected an instantiations of A1. But consider a case where A1 is indistinguishable from both A2 and A3, and A2 and A3 are indistinguishable from each other. Here, within whatever limits we set for close examination (see below), while there is (and perhaps could be) no proof of visual identity of A1, A2, and A3, identity has been open to refutation (though not to confirmation) and has not been refuted. The examples have so far passed the test of indistinguishability (to the standards set). The test can be extended in a chain of further replications to any example, An. So long as An has been submitted to and not failed a chain of such tests, i.e. it remains itself indistinguishable either from A1 or from any other replication indistinguishable from A1, it is to count as an adequate replication of A1. We have a test procedure, whether or not it has been applied to a given contestant.

Now the second theoretical question: here I consider the possibility of attaining adequate similarity or indistinguishability between putative reinstantiations and the original.[6] To conduct 'chain' tests we can suppose, as

[6] The difficulties of replication of the appearances can be forced to absurdly extreme lengths, as by Nelson Goodman (in part I of his *Languages of Art*). The reply I suggest, equally theoretical, can match the absurdities step by step.

regards visual acuity and training, that we employ, square cm. by square cm., as large a panel as we like of optimally sighted persons, trained, experienced in, and employing any known method of visual scanning and comparison—superimposition of shapes, matching of colours, moulds for three-dimensional surfaces, and any technology, colour meters, magnifiers, etc.—specified at any level we wish beyond that possible to the naked eye. The examiners, remember, need have no interest in aesthetic considerations; nor need they know which is the original and which a later instantiation. Their interests need not be those of art historians, curators, or other art experts; unlike Goodman's examiners of possible fakes, their only task is to compare visual properties quite neutrally, however important their findings might be for other specialists. It must, of course, be allowed that at any threshold chosen, any expert team exercising the greatest care may overlook visual differences. Findings are always subject to the Odd Man Out or Emperor's New Clothes phenomenon, where someone, despite all expertise and precautions so far employed, claims a visually perceptible differences hitherto undetected. But at this point, since this is a theoretical argument, there are two theoretical possibilities. Either, once a difference is alleged, some of the examiners will come to see the previously unnoticed difference, or no one else can. The newcomer is then subject to familiar tests for his seemingly unique acuity: original and copy and exchanged in his absence, etc. If he passes such tests, we have the choice of admitting his visual superacuity or attributing his success to some other, non-visual, clue or ability. If he fails, we dismiss his claimed ability. This is the best we can do, and, I shall argue, it is more than enough. We can accept provisionally as a reinstantiation (and not merely provisionally) anything subject to tests as outlined that has not so far failed them.

I can now take stock of the role and importance of the physical object. First, the works of visual art under consideration appear originally in a physical instantiation, i.e. with a physical bearer. No such work could be reinstantiated without some kind of physical object (or process). Importantly, the visual properties of any physical object are determinate. Secondly, for the abstract hypothesis, accreditation for accuracy of further instantiations must be by reference to the original and authoritative appearance, and hence to the physical object, its bearer. This parallels, e.g., checking a printed score back to a composer's holograph. These, I believe, are the main substantial considerations that point to the physical object and the impossibility of dispensing with it. But, just as obviously, without some further premise they have no power to show that the work *is* the original physical object or inseparable from the object, and hence constitute no refutation of the abstract hypothesis.

It might seem that other facts do demand a physical object account, facts about what can be authoritatively discovered by reference to the original physical object, but not to copies. Investigations by microscope, fluoroscope, violet-ray, chemical analysis, or X-ray may be highly important to art historians and critics. They can be conducted only on physical objects. But a survey of their purposes shows they make no inroad against the abstract hypothesis. Investigations on two physical objects with indistinguishable appearances may be needed to establish their provenance: in general, authentication to place, date, and hand. But this establishes which of two instantiated *appearances* is the earlier and authoritative one and only determines the provenance, date, or authorship of the *appearance* to which later replications must conform. Secondly, X-ray examination can reveal underpainting, an artist's first thoughts, changes of mind, creative imagination at work—all matters important for appreciation. For this, again, appeal to the original physical object is essential (copies incidentally, could have such underpainting incorporated if that were not, for purposes other than forgery, an unnecessary absurdity). But, it is a purely contingent matter that earlier thoughts are hidden under paint; they might have been on a datable succession of different physical surfaces and compared in the way we learn of Beethoven's creative phases from sketches or erasures in the notebooks. In any case, if full appreciation of finished work requires access to earlier versions, and though authentication of these requires reference to their original bearers, it is the sequence of earlier and final *appearances* we need to get at by whatever means; it does not matter how. Once we have these we can appreciate reproductions in the light of that knowledge; often better indeed when we can set reproductions of underpaintings alongside final versions. Without that knowledge our ability to appreciate either the original final appearance or its reinstantiations may be equally limited. So again, only visual appearances matter. Thirdly, chemical and other specialist examination of pigments, varnishing, and the techniques employed can show how, and with what materials, the creator of the appearance achieved his effects. But, again, however important, what we learn is how an appearance—now replicated by quite other techniques and materials—was achieved at its first embodiment. Once we have elicited these facts from the original object, we can appreciate the skills, material difficulties overcome, technical brilliance, ingenuity, or innovation that went into the initial creation of that appearance while, in the light of this knowledge, looking at a modern replica, produced by different means and possibly without inventiveness.

One consequence of this is that materials and techniques are then to be seen as means, causally related to a work. The character of a work is not necessarily or internally related to precisely those materials, oil or charcoal, or those techniques, brush or palette knife, to—in a familiar sense—the medium. It is internally related to its medium in a quite other sense; its medium is visible shapes, lines, colours, contours, not words or sounds, and to precisely those shapes, lines, colours, or contours. (To compare the facial appearance of identical twins, or of their wax effigies, requires no investigation into, or similarity of, the causal characteristics of the bearers, even though there must be physical bearers.) This causal notion of medium and technique detracts in no way from a painter's genius with regard to such matters. It may still be a brilliant stroke, at that time, to conceive of such and such new effects and ways of causally achieving them. The bricoleur question remains: an artist can use only (and any) materials then at hand. (The same ambiguity of 'medium' occurs in other arts. Just as a work in oils is one with the look that oils, but not necessarily only oils, have, so a piano sonata is a sonata internally related to the sound made by, but not necessarily only by, a piano. The internal relation is to a kind of sound, not to whatever means of production there may be of that sound.) Fourthly, it is by processes such as cleaning, applicable only to physical objects, that the original or authentic visual properties of a work may be established. But this simply establishes the authentic appearance.

I have now eliminated, as irrelevant to my hypothesis, arguments based on the need to refer to non-exhibited properties, background history, or tradition, and proposed that only literal visual properties matter. I also indicated how visual indistinguishability might be achieved up to any chosen threshold. I now want to show how and why extreme demands concerning both identity and indistinguishability can be ignored as irrelevant to our actual practices *vis-à-vis* the arts.

First I distinguish visual features from visible features. Which visual features of an objects are visible is relative to factors that can be grouped as (1) the optical acuity of the viewer at the time, which might be supposed that of humans with normal or optimal vision; (2) magnification, to whatever power, by spectacles, magnifying glasses, microscopes, etc.; (3) distance; (4) angle of viewing; (5) lighting and other visibility conditions; (6) states of mind and body which affect vision—ageing, drugs, colour-blindness, etc. Because of all these factors, even if indistinguishability is substituted for identity, purists may cite the indefinitely numerous possible appearances of any object as insurmountable theoretical difficulties against deciding which appearance any copy must replicate. To meet this, I shall subsume group (6) factors under group (1), and take the other groups in reverse order.

Lighting and Angle

An artist might deliberately paint, say, under infra-red light, intending the work to be similarly viewed. But usually we have conclusive reason to believe that a work is created to be viewed within the range of normal daylight or, occasionally, in certain special locations/conditions (church alcoves, by candlelight, etc.). Again, we know most works are made to be viewed from a range of positions approximately in front of the work; only a few are painted to be viewed from odd angles (foreshortened figures to be seen from below) or from one very specific position (*trompe-l'œil*). We also know the position of the expected light source to be reasonably familiar not, e.g., raking light from some far off-centre source—though again an artist might choose so to paint, either providing instructions or relying on angled lighting, say, inside a building.

Distance and Magnification

Different works are intended to be seen at different distances, not usually precise but within vague known limits (painters themselves move forward and back to view their work). Most are not meant to be seen from several miles, or viewed from two inches under magnification, though there are such; even miniatures are not intended for the highest magnification now possible. It follows that, beyond certain roughly specifiable limits, limits that differ for ceiling paintings and miniatures, appearances resulting from unusual lighting, strange angles, or high magnification are irrelevant; they are neither intended nor obtainable in any reasonable viewing. But if detail not visible beyond vague but not indefinitely receding limits cannot be considered relevant in the original, such differences between original and copy are not relevant either. Moreover, this argument should carry particular weight with those theorists who stress the importance of background knowledge and tradition—often the same theorists who most strongly support the physicality thesis and the more extreme arguments against multiple instantiation. Such knowledge certainly includes traditional practices, intentions, and expectations within which artists and viewers have operated. We know that Leonardo and most other artists did not intend or expect their work to be viewed under infra-red light, raking illumination, or even the magnification attainable in their time. It is therefore a theorist's absurdity, given the known vagueness and limits of traditional and existing practice, to require an unattainable identity or greater detail and precision than tradition requires. If the foregoing arguments are correct, the only problem is how an *adequate* degree of similarity can be assured. For this, indistinguishability in normal circumstances is usually sufficient; but if indistinguishability beyond familiar limits were considered desirable as a safety device, reinstantiation could be provided, given sufficient care and existing technology, to any chosen limit of magnification, etc. Heroically impossible extremes are unnecessary.

I want now to draw attention to some uncertainties about the features and details that are constitutive of art-work, uncertainties that cast further doubt on the need to go to extremes to ensure an adequate degree of similarity. Anyone impressed by arguments that any replica is under constant threat from further potentially discoverable details of aesthetic relevance revealed by increasingly extreme stratagems must face some additional homely facts about artists and the theories under which they work. Some, we are told, sometimes work as close as possible to the margin of discrimination. This is surely true, and when true, important. But whose margins? Presumably either of their (expected) audience or their own. But these may differ. So ignore the audience for a moment and concentrate on the artist. The limits of *his* powers of discrimination will be determined by factors already discussed—by his eyesight and general optical acuity, by whether he works with or without spectacles or magnifying glasses, and of what power, whether he ranges while working between 20 ft. from the work and 2 cm., which angles he views from under which illumination, whether he is sleepy, astigmatic, or partially colourblind. Not least, upon his training, alertness, and sophistication in visual observation. Beyond these limits, whatever they are, he cannot work or be assumed to work. And now several points can be made.

First, at whatever point he works, at his own limits or not, there will be details of his work that escape his notice or that are irrelevant to him. This must be true of any artist at any time. But it can be given point in various ways.

1. *What the artist cannot see.* Since vision usually deteriorates with age, the artist's eyes will probably change with time. Suppose an ageing artist, his eyes less good than formerly and possibly without his realizing it, lays on a canvas what he thinks, and intends to be, a solid black brushstroke.

Suppose, though he cannot see them, it contains thin white streaks where underpaint shows through. We, even without a magnifying glass, can see this. He is working at his limits of discrimination; our limits go beyond his. Similar cases must surely be common, more common than an artist's partial colourblindness to which much attention has been directed.

2. *Not working at the margins.* Two cases: an artist may choose not to work at *his* margins (*a*) because if his work requires a broad method, he may know but not care about certain details, thinking, rightly, that they make so significant aesthetic difference even if they are seen by his audience—it is generally agreed that some quite large differences may make negligible aesthetic differences; (*b*) because it suffices to work only at the margins of his likely *audience* (i) if he thinks their vision inferior to his, (ii) if he thinks it pointless because they are unlikely to notice what is in fact visible to them, (iii) if he knows it is pointless because they will see the work only from a distance, say, a ceiling from ground level.

3. *What the artist does not notice.* It is not plausible to suppose that the artist, any more than the rest of us, however careful, will notice all the detail actually visible to him. Probably, though not necessarily, an artist will notice details that make a significant aesthetic difference or affect his aims. But potentially he is as imperfect an observer as anyone. Much detail visible to him may go unnoticed by him.

So, despite the dogmas that stress the importance of every minutest detail on grounds that it is constitutive of the work, it is hard to insist, though any detail might truly be vital, on the actual importance of all of it. Often, only that which is fairly readily visible to artists (or viewers), and which they care about, matters. The actual *un*importance of some detail is the general case. Indeed these reflections prompt questions about which visual properties are constitutive of a work. Case (2) leaves a work as consisting in part of details less determinate than those (necessarily determinate) that characterize the physical surface: some properties of the work are indeterminate within varying limited ranges around those on the canvas. Cases (1) and (3) however prompt deeper theoretical questions. Are the properties constitutive of the work those (*a*) the *artist* intended, or (*b*) could see, (*c*) had noticed (all possibly different); or those an optimally sighted and attentive *viewer* in conditions normal for the kind of work can see; or those again (necessarily determinate at any degree of magnification) that characterize the *canvas*? Perhaps the properties of the work should be thought of, at best, as lying or ranging varyingly between extremes set by these factors. Indeed the best conclusion about what the picture is may be, heretically, that minor changes in details will not matter provided that, after careful survey, the *general impression* of the character of the work remains the same—the very test by which we recognize a good replica and an original as indistinguishable. But without making a stipulation about such an obviously unclear matter the best practical solution is probably to require as close a replica of the canvas surface as would pass muster with a reasonably trained and optimally sighted viewer. It may not be what the artist intended or supposed the work to be but it is the safety first recipe in an area of unavoidable imprecision. If so, my supposition of a panel of judges outlined earlier may be seen as unnecessary absurdity generated only by the rigour of extremist theory. To insist on an unattainable identity or pursue indistinguishability to extreme limits is revealed as a theorist's extravagance. As I said earlier an appropriate degree of similarity is sufficient.

Since my aim is to avoid this stipulation, and simply elucidate the concept in use, and if the theorist's arguments just examined settle nothing, it is to our practices that we must appeal. It would be improper to assert that a work of visual art is abstract if in our practice and dealings with art we clearly treat it as physical, and vice versa. Here it is easy to suppose that practice, custom, and usage settle the matter and finally put paid to any abstraction hypothesis. I shall therefore argue that a large part of our practice is, and quite commonly through the history and tradition of Western art (to which we are constantly adjured to attend) has been, precisely not to treat visual works as physical objects. This has been so with members of the art world such as teachers, lecturers, and specialists in art appreciation as well as with audiences and connoisseurs, and even with those adjuncts to the world of aesthetics, the dealers, the chemists, the specialist sleuths, when they are engaged in appreciation and enjoyment rather than in identification, forgery detection, chemical analysis, or market valuing. In these latter tasks they have good reasons, already indicated, for referring back to and placing a premium on a particular physical object.

Before I cite what seem obvious facts about the widespread practices of artists, connoisseurs, and the artistic public (but not necessarily of museum curators or those in the art markets, who have their own problems) I shall mention some humbler examples that, being also primarily visual, differ in degree rather than kind. If the *Mona Lisa* is thought unrepeatable, William Morris designs or patterns on modern printed fabrics are considered both repeatable and reproducible.

What are the differences? Perhaps we do not demand of reinstantiations of these designs that they be as minutely faithful to the originals as with works we consider potentially far more important and subtle. Because of this, there may be less difficulty in reaching standards of approximation that satisfy. But beyond this there seem more similarities than differences. For example (*a*) a Morris pattern and many fabric designs would be no easier to encapsulate in notations than most paintings; some might be far more difficult than some Mondrians or Kleins; traditionally all are equally non-notational. (*b*) What is attributable to Morris on a fabric made yesterday is the design, not the physical substance. A Morris design on plastic or glass is no more a Morris fabric than a *Mona Lisa* reproduced by photography is a painting. But why should the Morris *design* not have the same status as the Leonardo *work*? (*c*) The colour chemistry of a reproduction Morris fabric may or may not be the same as in an original. A chemist might be needed to ascertain whether the fabric was nineteenth or twentieth century. (*d*) A Morris design on fabric, linoleum, glass, or plastic may have recognizably the same appearance, just as a reproduction of the *Mona Lisa* on glass, canvas, paper, or a screen may have recognizably the same appearance. We may identify either by looking. Yet despite minimal theoretical differences, heated debate is not generated here as it is over paintings.

Now for some facts about practices that receive scant mention by either common-sense or prescriptively inclined aestheticians, though they are well enough known.

At many periods in history it has been common practice in artists' workshops for students, fellow artists, and later artists to make copies of fine works: Roman copies of Greek art, Renaissance copies of Roman, multiple copies of Holbein and Lely portraits; prints made from paintings; sketches, watercolours, sepias, pencil copies made and brought back from the Grand Tour. In more recent times there is the proliferation of prints, black and white, coloured, photographic, art slides, fidelity to originals steadily improving. These are widespread and long-continuing practices spanning much of the known history of Western art; without them experts would less often need to decide whether works are originals or contemporary or later copies. Such extensive activity should not, if we are to theorize adequately, be brushed aside.

But a crucial question is: why all this time, money, and skill-consuming effort and activity? There are many reasons: developing and practising technical skills, training in careful observation, the multiplication of images, before photography, for political, party, or personal reasons—multiple portrait copies of Henry VIII or Louis XIV, dynastic portraits; for advertisement; duplication for utility, or to replace breakages, sets of identical chairs, plates, or glasses; or for aesthetic purposes—sets of candlesticks, identical statues, or other decoration needed for symmetry in furnishings or buildings. But not least, from earliest times, two other aims lie behind the practice of replication: the recording and preserving of things of aesthetic value, Greek, Roman, and Renaissance, many of which exist now only as copies but for which we are grateful; and the multiplication and dissemination of such works so that many people in different places can appreciate and enjoy them. They do not just fill gaps in art history but are sources of satisfaction themselves (cf. recordings of particular performances by Schnabel, Furtwängler, or Louis Armstrong). The fact that this has for long been a widespread, solidly entrenched, and, with modern technology, increasing and proliferating practice, with the attendant belief that works can be appreciated via copies, cannot be shrugged off, nor should it be ignored by aestheticians. Least of all is it to be condemned on a priori grounds or through prejudice, as not really constituting an aesthetic practice.

There is, indeed, a further aspect of these practices that serves to stress the aesthetic importance even of partial replications. Those who brought back pencil, sepia, or watercolour copies of Poussins, Claudes, or Berninis—and these importantly included painters like Turner and writers like Ruskin—might have thought they were just capturing such admirable but incomplete aspects as they could (cf. piano transcriptions of symphonies). But often they were providing selective versions that serve to enhance appreciation of particular aspects of the works from which they are abstracted. Partial tokens often have their own aesthetic importance. Black and white cannot show colour but can focus attention, without the distraction of colour, on gradations of light, tone, composition, and balance, the reason they can aid appreciation of many Italian masters, if not of Monet or Rothko. (The trick is also achievable by half closing the eyes—the most helpful thing to be learned from Clive Bell—to appreciate formal relationships and structure by ignoring representation, even colour symbolism.) It is the opposite kind of selective appreciation to that gained by close examination of facial expressions, small figures in Breughel or Canaletto, or the bravura of brushwork, something that cannot be done while appreciating overall composition from a distance. Art books which show details as well as whole works can make a positive contribution to aesthetic appreciation. Partial instantiation of complex works can have positive value for the aesthetic appreciation of complete instantiations.

So, I suggest, if practices count, and not just what we might say when offering a superficial opinion, these are facts of entrenched practice. It would be perverse to deny that, just as knowledge and appreciation of music have been vastly enlarged by recordings that preserve particular performances, so have knowledge and appreciation of vast ranges of art inaccessible to most of us except by copies, photography, colour slides, printing, and television. It would be hard to exaggerate the extent to which our knowledge and appreciation rest on familiarity with the lavishly illustrated art books from some of the specialist presses—just as those of connoisseurs in previous centuries were based on copies of sculptures and sketches of oil paintings and frescoes. And who is to say this is not really appreciation of the works themselves? Indeed, most of us who admire wide ranges of art have never seen many of the originals; we could not without visiting most of the collections of the world as well as distant sites from China to Peru. Are we not likely to achieve a better appreciation of the *Mona Lisa* or the Sistine ceiling by long study of good copies than in brief jostled moments in their actual presence? So much so that when we finally manage to look at the real things our response is just as likely to be the shock of recognition of something we know very well as the joy of finding it far finer than its reproductions. No theory should burke hard facts. Of course, there are reasons why even if your interest is aesthetic, not that of the art detective, you should seek out originals. Reproductions, however good, rarely replicate size; good reproductions can be rare because still costly; and the work you like most in an exhibition usually turns out to be unavailable even at postcard size. But these are reasons of fact, not theory.

What are the implications of the foregoing? (1) The aesthetic characteristics of, say, the *Mona Lisa* are characteristics of the *work*, whatever kind of thing, abstract or material, a work is. Though non-exhibited properties, history, tradition, and intentions may contribute to determine its aesthetic qualities, these depend also on its literal visual properties (or why suppose the smallest change in them may significantly affects its aesthetic character?) Aesthetic appreciation and judgement of a work require firsthand experience of it, where this excludes (say) *verbal* descriptions, but does not, without *petitio*, require the presence of the original object. Entrenched practices extending back over centuries suggest that people can find and point out, describe and criticize, similar properties in, and gain aesthetic satisfaction from, sketches, photographs, slides, and other reproductions. Their description, and discussion of a work's aesthetic character does not differ whether they are looking at replicas or originals. These practices and the pleasure they give presuppose transference of aesthetic values; to deny transference entirely would mean that looking at a copy of the *Mona Lisa* would be as pointless for appreciation of the *Mona Lisa* as looking at the *Primavera*, a Matisse, or a seaside postcard. Reinstantiations would be totally different works.

That seems absurd. Reinstantiations require no transfer of physical stuff— something that only occasionally occurs when, say, original pigments are transferred to new backing. All these facts would seem to allow, on pain of rejecting long traditions of practice and belief, that the *Mona Lisa* is capable of multiple instantiation. We somewhat similarly accept and rely on recordings of Schnabel performances, videos of opera, etc. (I have nowhere said that any *existing* copy shares identical relevant properties or equal aesthetic value; I have allowed an important role for approximate copies and copies of selected aspects.)

I have found no theoretical argument that establishes without a *petitio* the common belief that works like the *Mona Lisa* are single physical objects or that refutes the type-token hypothesis. (Arguments from technology are by general consent irrelevant either way.) All the most familiar theoretical arguments are compatible with the abstract or multiple object view, however initially counter-intuitive the latter. But for a variety of *historical* and *practical* reasons it is the original physical objects that seem of paramount significance—artists usually produce one copy, adequate reproduction has been and still is difficult and costly. And for certain unassailable *logical* reasons the image on the original physical bearer is rightly valued as the sole authoritative repository and exhibitor of the artist's finished conception, and rightly seen as the final appeal for all further instantiations. Often it contains authoritative information about earlier versions, changing intentions, etc., and only it can authoritatively yield information about the techniques, materials, underpreparation, and finishing stages by which, at its first embodiment, the image was created; chemical analysis of its materials can settle historical points like dating, and so on.

The physical object therefore, if not itself the work, has various unique relations to it. It is easy to see why, given all this, together with the fact that often it is, or has in the past been, *de facto* the only, or only remotely, complete and detailed instantiation, it should be uniquely valued. Add further the power, beauty, or majesty that gives many works their aesthetic value, and they become, historically, the unique repositories of such aesthetic marvels, objects for the possession and preservation of which much wealth will be offered and sacrifices made. Add to the market values achieved thus, an ever increasing rarity value, plus the pride and prestige, personal, political, or social, of possession and ownership of such symbols of wealth or discrimination and, not least, the awe, reverence, and mystique that collect as an aura round objects which are old, or made or touched by, or relics of, revered persons, and all the factors are present fully to explain the practices expressed in the familiar, supposedly obvious, and deeply entrenched beliefs that such works just are physical objects.

But despite the apparent obviousness of the physical object view being fully understandable, it in no way follows from the theoretical arguments that the abstract hypothesis, which lacks both vulgar and philosophical support, is false or that the work is a visual appearance indissolubly attached to the original physical object. And where theoretical argument is lacking, long-standing practice lends considerable support to the abstract hypothesis. Yet the two views are flatly incompatible.

We seem left with two options. Either, we might suppose, the concept we inherit of visual art-works like the *Mona Lisa* is a confused notion, which for easily understood historical and logical reasons, is internally inconsistent, an uneasy composite or hybrid of two conflicting notions. Employing it we ride two different horses, occasionally, though not constantly, being made to feel a latent discomfort. Nor need this be surprising; there is little reason to think that traditionally developed and bequeathed concepts must be perfect or coherent. It would not be the first such concept. Alternatively we could say we have inherited, whether we realize it or not, two distinct concepts, one lying behind the practices of, and employed by, specialists and non-specialists when functioning primarily as art lovers—non-owning connoisseurs, aesthetic critics, and appreciators; the other employed by those who want to, or must, bother about original objects—art historians, curators, conservators, dealers, auctioneers, art sleuths, scientists who need have no aesthetic interest, as well as snobs of ownership and suckers for mystique. Art historians especially, but others of us also, usually move between the two poles, depending on circumstances and the uppermost interest of the moment with little embarrassment, shifting from one concept to the other as need arises. But nothing prevents someone from being at once art lover, critic, dealer, proud owner, and reverer or relics. It may just be difficult to sort out which strand is dominant in someone, or oneself, at a given moment. But at moments also one aspect may seem utterly obvious, the other unthinkably absurd. Then those with one primary sets of interests will vehemently espouse the physical object view and regard as outrageous the views of others, equally vehement on their side, whose concern is primarily the love and enjoyment of the images artists have created. The recurring disputes are familiar: why shouldn't good copies be as aesthetically valuable though untouched by Leonardo's hand? How can a mere *copy* have the worth of the original? The analysis I have proposed seems to fit and explain these undoubted facts. If so, there is no right answer to the question whether the *Mona Lisa* is a painting (physical object.) That is why my title is not why the *Mona Lisa* is not a painting but why it *may* not be. Perhaps it both is and is not, can be and need not be.

It might be thought that since no argument or practice clinches the physical object view, I should favour the abstract hypothesis, seeing these works as akin to what poem and music are thought to be, but with the unavoidable requirement that each reinstantiation have a physical bearer. I would not find this antipathetic. But I have not argued this. If my analysis is correct, that, just as much as espousing the common-sense physical object thesis, would be a stipulation, a recommendation; either would be to embrace a conceptual innovation. But between the suppositions that we have either an internally

inconsistent concept or conjoined dual concepts there is no significant decision to be made. Either will equally explain the two-directional pull that most
of us feel if we are honest, from the man in the street to owners, investors,
curators, and dealers when not acting in their professional capacity. It surfaces
whenever someone dares to wonder secretly why, aside from market values
and as far as aesthetics and criticism go, a superlative copy might not be as
good as the original, why we should deny that we can gain as much appreciation of the work from reproductions by slides, photographs, or other teaching
devices—or, put technically, that aesthetic values are transferable. It is
suppressed a little shamefacedly when an air of artistic superiority, sophistication, and expertise is assumed towards such vulgar philistinism. As for the
argument that unsatisfactory concepts should, for convenience, be tidied up
by prescription, it is unlikely that any of the contradictory pulls would or
could be stilled by such stipulative fiat.

My conclusion is not innovatory but I hope revelatory (perhaps shock-
ingly). No matter what prescription is favoured, if any, and however appealing, it almost certainly is not, as most proponents of either side may suppose,
the elucidation of an existing concept and the dissipation of error; it is more
probably a lack of clear insight resulting more from wishful thinking than
argument or analysis.

BIBLIOGRAPHY OF THE
PUBLICATIONS OF FRANK SIBLEY

Articles

'A Theory of the Mind' (a critical review of Ryle's *Concept of Mind*), *Review of Metaphysics*, 4 (1950), 259–78.

'Seeking, Scrutinizing and Seeing', *Mind*, 64 (1955), 455–78.

'Aesthetic Concepts', *Philosophical Review*, 68 (1959), 421–50 (revised version in Joseph Margolis, ed., *Philosophy looks at the Arts*, 1st edn., New York: Scribner's, 1962, 63–88).

'Aesthetics and the Looks of Things', *Journal of Philosophy*, 66 (1959), 905–15.

'Is Art an Open Concept? An Unsettled Question', *Proceedings of the IVth International Congress of Aesthetics*, Athens: Édition du Comité Hellénique d'Organisation, 1960, 545–8.

'What is Aesthetics?' in *Planning for Urban Aesthetics: Proceedings of the Vth Annual Conference of the Organization of Cornell Planners*, Ithaca, NY: Cornell University, 1961, 1–6, 22–33.

'Aesthetic Concepts: A Rejoinder', *Philosophical Review*, 72 (1963), 79–83.

'About Taste', *British Journal of Aesthetics*, 6 (1966), 68–9.

'Aesthetic and Non-Aesthetic', *Philosophical Review*, 74 (1965), 135–59.

'Philosophy and the Arts', Inaugural Lecture, 23 Feb. 1966, *Inaugural Lectures 1965–1967*, Lancaster: University of Lancaster, 130–48.

'Colours', *Proceedings of the Aristotelian Society*, 68 (1967–8), 145–66.

'Objectivity and Aesthetics', *Proceedings of the Aristotelian Society*, Supplementary Vol. 42 (1968), 31–54.

'Ryle and Thinking', in *Ryle: A Collection of Essays*, Wood and Pitcher, eds., New York: Doubleday, 1970, 75–104.

'Analysing Seeing', in *Perception: A Philosophical Symposium*, London: Methuen, 1971, 81–132.

'Particularity, Art and Evaluation', *Proceedings of the Aristotelian Society*, Supplementary Vol. 48 (1974), 1–21.

'Some Notes on Originality', in J. Aler and M. Damnjanović, eds., *The Problem of Creativity in Aesthetics: A Selection from the Proceedings of the IXth International Congress of Aesthetics*, Dubrovnik, 1980, Belgrade: Serbian Society of Aesthetics, 1983, 211–13.

'A Role for Applied Philosophy', *Times Higher Education Supplement*, 1981.

'General Criteria and Reasons in Aesthetics', in John Fisher, ed., *Essays on Aesthetics: Perspectives on the Work of Monroe C. Beardsley*, Philadelphia: Temple University Press, 1983, 3–20.

'Originality and Value', *British Journal of Aesthetics*, 25 (1985), 169–84.

'Art or the Aesthetic—Which Comes First?', tape-recorded lecture for the Open University, Milton Keynes, 1992.
'Making Music Our Own', in Michael Krausz, ed., *The Interpretion of Music: Philosophical Essays*, Oxford: Clarendon Press, 1993, 165–76.

Edited Book

Perception: A Philosophical Symposium, London: Methuen, 1971.

Reviews

Philosophical Analysis: A Selection of Articles Published in Analysis *between 1933–40 and 1947–53*, Margaret MacDonald, ed., *Philosophical Review*, 65 (1956), 260–4.
Toward Reunion in Philosophy, Morton White, *Mind*, 67 (1958), 560–1.
The Psychology of Perception: A Philosophical Exploration of Gestalt Theory and Derivative Theories of Perception, David Hamlyn, *Philosophical Review*, 68 (1959), 263–5.
Aesthetics: Problems in the Philosophy of Criticism, Monroe Beardsley, *Philosophical. Review*, 70 (1961), 275–9.
Perception and the Physical World, D. M. Armstrong, *Philosophical Review*, 73 (1964), 404–8.
Attention, A. R. White, *Philosophy*, 41 (1966), 281–3.
The Concept of Criticism, Francis Sparshott, *Philosophical Books*, 9 (1968), 22–4.
Languages of Art, N. Goodman, *Philosophical Books*, 12 (1971), 9–12.
The Aesthetics of Architecture, Roger Scruton, *Mind*, 91 (1982), 143–7.
The Aesthetic Point of View, M. C. Beardsley, *Philosophical Books*, 25 (1984), 31–4.
The Forger's Art, Denis Dutton, ed., *Philosophical Books*, 26 (1985), 168–71.
The Imitation of Nature, John Hyman, *Philosophical Books*, 31 (1990), 250–2.

INDEX

adjectives, attributive and predicative
154–75, 176–9, 192–4
    Geach's tests for 156–7
    see also attributiveness; essentially
        attributive adjectives; essentially
        predicative adjectives
adjectives with attributive and predicative
    uses (ambifunctional or Janus
    adjectives) 155, 162–3, 178–9,
    193–4
    'beautiful' as one such 180–3; *see also*
        beauty, beautiful
aesthetic, concept of the:
    and the arts 135–41
    argument for the priority of, to art
        136–7
    boundaries of 210–11, 253–5
aesthetic character:
    as criterion of value 116–18
    dependence of, on salient non-aesthetic
        features of an object 36–7
    dependence of, on totality of an object's
        non-aesthetic features 35–6
    difference of, and originality 122–5
    distinct from aesthetic value 122–3
    explaining, the critical activity of
        37–8
    helping people to see, the critical
        activity of 18–19, 38–40, 78
    of an object, dependent on its specific
        (determinate) qualities 11–12,
        35–7, 95–7; *see also* determinate
        properties
    specific, and specific aesthetic value
        123
    see also aesthetic qualities
aesthetic concepts:
    application of, by rule 9–10
    contingent relationships of, with other
        concepts 48–9
    logical relationships of, with other
        concepts 47–8
    logically necessary conditions for
        47
    no positive conditions for 3–12,
        45–7

aesthetic contemplation (attention,
    interest) 229–30
    qualities fitted to stimulate, in sensory
        objects 22–3
aesthetic judgement(s):
    and aesthetic perception 34–5
    and justification, *see* reason-giving,
        general criteria of aesthetic value,
        proof
    merit ascribing 95–100
    overall, of aesthetic character 116–17
    overall, of aesthetic value (verdicts), *see*
        general criteria of aesthetic value
    quality-ascribing, their central place in
        aesthetics 34
    quality-ascribing v. purely evaluative
        (verdicts) 33–4
    of value in context 129–33
aesthetic qualities:
    and non-aesthetic, distinguished by
        examples 1–2, 33
    and non-aesthetic, relationships
        between 3, 6–7, 35–7, 95–7
    and taste or perceptiveness 1, 3
    see also aesthetic character; non-
        aesthetic qualities; discerning
        aesthetic qualities
aesthetics, philosophical importance of 53
agreement:
    and maximum discrimination 57–8,
        68–70, 82–4
    and objectivity of aesthetic judgement
        75–6, 82–4
    and objectivity of colour-attribution
        55–8, 75
    and the possibility of widespread error
        58–60
    sources of failure of, in aesthetic
        judgements 76–9
    and undecidable cases 85–6
    see also objectivity
ambifunctional adjectives, *see* adjectives
    with attributive and predicative uses
anti-art, works of 137–8
appearance(s):
    and aesthetic vision 24–8

appearance(s): (*cont.*)
  different senses of 'appearance' 25–7
  and reality 24–5, 28
  replication of, of a work of visual art
      259–61, 263–6
  suitable and unsuitable for aesthetic
      interest 27–32
  of a work of art, as an abstract entity
      258
Aquinas, Thomas, on tastes and smells,
      and beauty 243
Aristotle, on 'snub' 165
art:
  and aesthetic intention 137, 209
  innovative movements in 125–6
  originality as a merit in, *see* originality
  prior to aesthetic experience? 136–40,
      209–10
  works of, uniqueness of 11–12, 36
  see also works of art, visual
attributiveness, of adjectives:
  the *alienans* test for 154, 168–70
  the Independent Ascertainment test for
      160–7, 178
  and norms or ideals 182–3
  the Unsafe Predication test for 170
  unsplittability as a test for 157–60,
      177–8
  with standard setting nouns 164,
      177–9, 193–4

Baudelaire, C., on originality 134
Beardsley, Monroe C.:
  on general reasons in aesthetics,
      discussed 104–18
  on originality 119, 134
  on reason giving 43–4
  on the relationship of aesthetic and
      non-aesthetic qualities 46
  on taste and smell 222, 223, 226, 227–8
beauty, beautiful:
  attributive instances of 181
  and comparative standards 182
  and deceptive appearances 186–9
  and distasteful or disgusting objects
      183–6
  fine specimen uses of 185
  of lines, shapes, colours etc. 181
  as a particular aesthetic quality 243
  of pebbles etc. 181–2
  predicative instances of 181–2

  and standards of appropriateness 182–3
Bell, Clive, on aesthetic appreciation 149
      n. 5
Burke, Edmund, on beauty and deformity
      195–6

Carner, Mosco 145
Collingwood, R. G.:
  his (and Croce's) notion of Expression
      246
  on originality 126 n. 14, 131 n. 19
Collins, Peter, on gastronomy 212, 228
colour(s) 54–70
  and aesthetic qualities, compared
      66–70, 72–9
  agreement about and the possibility of
      error 58–60
  attributing, how it might be more
      difficult 67–70
  conditions for attribution of 55–8
  and the double reversal hypothesis 60–6
  language of, quasi-fictional account of
      its introduction 55–8
  and objectivity 54
  as objects of aesthetic admiration 30
  scepticism about 58–66
  systematic physical change of 62–3
  vision, physiological change in 61–2
complexity, as a basic aesthetic criterion
      111
conditions governing concepts 4–8, 45–8
  necessary and sufficient 4
  negative 5–6
  sets of, subject to defeating conditions
      7–8
  open sets of 4–5
criteria, *see* general criteria of aesthetic
      value
critical activities:
  explaining aesthetic qualities 37–8
  helping people to see aesthetic qualities
      18–19, 38–40, 78
  making overall judgements of aesthetic
      character and value 116–17
Croce, B., his (and Collingwood's) notion
      of Expression 246

defeasible concepts 7–8
description:
  aesthetic, sources of disagreement
      about 76–9

and evaluation: evaluating by
  describing 248
literal and metaphorical, *see* metaphor
of music, *see* music, describing
of simple properties, supposed
  impossibility of 218–20
of tastes and smells 232–9, 247–8
determinate property(ies):
  aesthetic merit qualities dependent on
    95–7
  connection of, with merit qualities,
    non-conceptual 98–9
  and dependent merit quality,
    co-discernible 99–100
  and determinable 95
  paucity of terms for 97–8
  unique combinations of 11–12
disagreement about aesthetic description
  76–9
discerning aesthetic features:
  dependent on perception of non-
    aesthetic features 15, 74, 100
  how critics can assist 17
  how different from ordinary perception
    14–15
  the natural capacity for and its
    development 20–3

emergence of aesthetic qualities 35, 37,
  74
essentially attributive adjectives 154–5,
  (defined) 161–2, 178
  'ugly' as one such 195; *see also* ugliness,
    ugly
essentially predicative adjectives 154–5,
  166–8, 178
evaluation, aesthetic:
  and the concept of a work of art
    89–90, 100–2
  and description 248
  and moral, compared 98–9
  particularity of explained 95–8
  Strawson's account of, discussed
    88–91, 100–2
  of tastes and smells 239–53
  see also evaluative terms; aesthetic
    judgement(s); general criteria of
    aesthetic value
evaluative terms 91–4
  descriptive merit terms 91–2
  evaluation added terms 92–4

in evaluation of human character
  92–3, 252–3
inherent merit terms 107–9
intrinsically or solely evaluative 91

Geach, P. T., on attributive and predicative
  adjectives 154–75 *passim*
general criteria of aesthetic value:
  basic 105–6
  Beardsley's three basic, discussed
    110–15
  independent v. interactive 106–8
  and inherent merit qualities 88, 107–9
  interactive and the exercise of critical
    judgement 106–9, 116–17
  and overall judgements of value
    (verdicts) 12 n., 33–4, 88
  and prima facie v. actual merits 109
  Scriven's scepticism about, refuted
    115–18
Gibson, J. J., on taste and smell 213 n. 12,
  217 n. 15
Goodman, N.:
  on paintings as physical objects 257
  on the replication of appearances
    260 n.
Greene, T. M., on major and minor arts
  249
Grice, H. P. 46 n.
  on scientific considerations about
    colour 64 n.

Hampshire, S., on the use of aesthetic
  discussion 15
Harrison, Bernard, on transpositions of
  colour vision 61
Harrison, J. 72 n. 2
Hart, H. L. A., on defeasible concepts
  8–9
Hazlitt, W., on originality 134
Hepburn, R. W., 188
  on natural beauty 209 n. 4
Holloway, John 15 n.
Hume, David, on beauty and deformity
  195
Hutcheson, Francis, on beauty and
  deformity 195

Intensity of regional qualities 111–13
Isenberg, Arnold, on aesthetic concepts
  5 n., 6 n.

Janus adjectives, *see* adjectives with
    attributive and predicative uses
Johnson, Brian Stanley 235 n. 44

Kant, I.:
    on beauty and the agreeable 239–40
    on natural beauty 209 n. 4
    on originality 119
Knight, Helen, on criteria 12 n.

Lessing, Alfred, on originality 126, 128 n.
    16, 131 n. 20
Lewis, C. S., on the notion of intrinsic
    value 128 n. 17
Locke, John, on words and simple ideas
    219 n. 18

Macdonald, Margaret:
    on aesthetic judgements 13
    on criteria of identity for works of art
    89
    on discerning aesthetic features 14–15
MacKay, Alfred F, on attributive-
    predicative 157
Margolis, J. 72 n. 2
Meager, Ruby, on originality 119
merit terms 91–4, 107–9
    applicability of, dependent on
    determinate qualities 95–7
metaphor, in aesthetic description 2,
    16–17, 20–3, 29, 144–6, 152,
    235–9
Mona Lisa, The, as example of a visual
    work of art 256–72
Mothersill, Mary, on aesthetic criteria 109
music, describing:
    alternative figurative ways of 152
    in extra-musical terms, functions of
    146
    and grasping the character of music
    146–7, 151–2
    in literal v. in figurative, extra-musical,
    terms 144–6
    and misdescribing 148
    supposed impossible 143–4
    and wordless hearing 148–50

nature, aesthetic appreciation of:
    and developing taste 22
    extensive role of, in human life 130,
    140–1

not parasitic on appreciation of art
    136–40, 209–10
Newton, Eric, on beauty and a deceptive
    meadow 183–4, 186–7
non-aesthetic qualities:
    aesthetic interest in, and our vital
    concerns 30–1
    characteristic associations of, with
    aesthetic 6–7
    discernible by normal senses and
    intelligence 1
    general and specific 11; *see also*
    determinate properties
    responsible for aesthetic character, *see*
    aesthetic character
    suitability for aesthetic admiration
    29–32
    see also aesthetic qualities
Nowell-Smith, P. H., on agreement and
    objectivity 73 n.

objectivity:
    of aesthetic concepts, defended 79–81
    of aesthetic description 71–87
    of colours and aesthetic qualities
    compared 66–70, 72–9
    and convergence of judgement 84
    and decision procedures, or proof (*q.v.*)
    53, 54, 67, 73–4
    its limits 85–7
    and the maximally discriminating
    group 57–8, 82–4
    as possibility of truth, correctness, or
    aptness 54, 71–2
    and properties 54, 58, 72, 79–82
    and sources of disagreement about
    aesthetic description 76–9
    and taste 52–3
    and ultimate proof 72–6, 84–5
    see also agreement
originality:
    evaluative and neutral uses 120–2,
    124–5
    and in-context-judgements 129–33
    and innovative movements in art
    125–6
    and intrinsic value 128–9, 133–4
    and novelty 126–7
    and (specific) aesthetic character
    122–3
    strict senses of 120–2

Osborne, Harold:
    on aesthetic attention 229, 243, 246
    on odours 208, 212, 222, 235
    on originality 119, 120, 128 n. 15

Particularism concerning reasons in
    aesthetics 88, 104
    supposed connection with the
      individuality of works of art 89,
      100–2
Passmore, J. A , on aesthetic judgements
    13, 15
perception:
    aesthetic, contrasted with sense
      perception 13–15
    required for aesthetic judgement 34–5
perceptiveness, *see* taste, aesthetic
perceptual proof 17–19, 38–9
    contrasted with giving reasons for a
      conclusion 39–40
physical object hypothesis about works of
    visual art 257
pleasure and aesthetic appreciation 239–42
Pole, David:
    on aesthetic response 229
    on Leavis on art 123 n.
practices:
    descriptive, of music 142–53
    prior to theory 142
    in relation to works of art 267–71
prehistoric artworks 138–9
proof:
    needed for objectivity? 53
    perceptual 17–19, 38–9
    ultimate, of quality attribution 67,
      73–6, 84–5
properties:
    aesthetic, emergence of 74
    determinable/determinate, contrasted
      with general/particular and
      shareable/non-shareable 95
    merit responsible and merit
      constituting 94
    and objectivity 52, 72, 81–2
    see also determinate properties

reason-giving:
    in explanation of why x is ϕ 44
    in justifying a truth claim 43–4, 50–1
reasons, general in aesthetics, *see* general
    criteria of aesthetic value

reference groups for property attribution
    57–8, 80–4
    minimally nucleate 83
Ryle, Gilbert:
    on the evaluation of human character
      252–3
    on thinking in words or pictures
      149

Savile, Anthony:
    on the attributiveness of beauty 180,
      189, 190–1
    on the conceptual priority of art to
      natural beauty 136, 209
scepticism:
    about the aesthetic significance of
      tastes and smells 220–7
    about colour 58–60
    about the describability:
      of music 143–4
      of simple qualities 218–20
      of tastes and smells 218–20
    about general aesthetic criteria
      115–18
    about the objectivity of aesthetic
      qualities 71–3, 80–2
Schwyzer, H. R. G., on reasons in criticism
    40
Scriven, M:
    on originality 132 n. 21
    his scepticism about aesthetic reasons
      115–18
Scruton, Roger:
    on aesthetic description 236
    on aesthetic interest 230
      and pleasure 240–2
    on beauty 179–80, 188–9
    on taste and smell v. sight and hearing
      211, 218, 221–2, 224–5, 240
sensible qualities, as objects of aesthetic
    interest 22–3, 29–32, 220–7
sensitivity, *see* taste, aesthetic
Sparshott, F. E., on originality 122 n.
Strawson, P. F., on aesthetic criteria 88–9,
    100–2

taste, aesthetic 1, 33, 52–3
    and disagreement in aesthetic
      discrimination 77–9
    and the discernment of aesthetic
      qualities 1, 29, 33

taste, aesthetic: (*cont.*)
  exercising, compared with using the
    senses 13–15, 29
  and likes and dislikes 52
  and objectivity 52–3
  and related terms: perceptiveness,
    sensitivity, discrimination 1, 33
  widely possessed, to different degrees
    3, 21
tastes and smells:
  and aesthetic pleasure 239–42
  the aesthetic value of 243–53
  and cognition 223–5
  description of 232–9, 247–8
  as internal objects of experience
    207–8
  objections to, as objects of aesthetic
    interest 220–7
  as objects of detached contemplation
    222–3
  as objects of supposed 'lower' senses
    220–2
  and order in aesthetic objects 225–8
  particular and generic 214
  single and mixed 214–18
  supposed impossibility of describing
    218–20
  as works of art, why not considered
    208–9
tasting and smelling:
  alleged to be 'lower' senses 220–2
  physiology of 213–14
Taylor, D. M, on changes in colour vision
  61–2, 66
Titchener, E. B., on taste and smell
  213 n. 11
toads, supposed ugliness of 197–8, 205
Tomas, Vincent, his view on aesthetic
  vision discussed 24–8
type/token distinction, applied to works of
  art 89, 100–1

ugliness, ugly:
  apparent non-attributive uses of
    197–200
  and beauty, assymetry between 195,
    206
  and deformity 195–7
  and dislike, revulsion, etc. 203–4
  Hutcheson, Hume, and Burke on
    195–6

  inapplicability of, to objects in
    themselves 205–6
  judgements of, always attributive 191
  non-aesthetic uses of 191
  as a particular aesthetic term of
    disvalue 191
  relative to some norm for things of a
    kind 195–7, 200–3
unity, as a basic aesthetic criterion 110–11
Urmson, J. O.
  on aesthetic criteria 248 n.
  on aesthetic pleasure 229, 239
  on the aesthetically tolerable 245
  on aesthetics and sensible qualities 24,
    29, 212, 226
  on the sources of aesthetic satisfaction
    249
  on works of visual art as physical
    objects 257

verdicts, *see* general criteria of aesthetic
  value
vision:
  aesthetic 24–8
  colour, physiological change in 61–2
  and hearing v. taste and smell, as
    aesthetic senses 220–8

Westphal, J., on describing sensible
  qualities 219 n. 17
Wisdom, John 15 n.
Wittgenstein, L. 238
Wolgast, Elizabeth H. 69 n.
Wollheim, R. 227
  on art and the aesthetic attitude 136
  on originality 120
  on the physical object hypothesis
    concerning works of visual art 257
works of art, visual:
  as abstract entities 258
  one concept of, or two? 271–2
  physical object hypothesis concerning
    256–7
  practices regarding, and the rival
    hypotheses 267–71
  replication of appearance of 259–61,
    263–6

Ziff, Paul 223
  on the boundaries of a work of art 227
Zink, Sidney, on aesthetics and sense
  qualities 226

DATE DUE
